# CROSS-CULTURAL MARKETING

*This book is dedicated to my wife*
*Isabella and my sons Jacopo and Giulio,*
*who share with me a strong curiosity*
*about the world.*

# CROSS-CULTURAL MARKETING

## EUROPEAN PERSPECTIVES

*EDITED BY*

TIZIANO VESCOVI

*Professor of Marketing, Department of Management,*
*Ca'Foscari University of Venice, Italy*

Cheltenham, UK • Northampton, MA, USA

Published by
Edward Elgar Publishing Limited
The Lypiatts
15 Lansdown Road
Cheltenham
Glos GL50 2JA
UK

Edward Elgar Publishing, Inc.
William Pratt House
9 Dewey Court
Northampton
Massachusetts 01060
USA

A catalogue record for this book
is available from the British Library

ISBN 978 1 80088 974 3 (cased)
ISBN 978 1 80088 975 0 (eBook)
ISBN 978 1 80088 976 7 (paperback)

Printed and bound in Great Britain by TJ Books Limited, Padstow, Cornwall

# CONTENTS IN BRIEF

## PART IV    CROSS-CULTURAL MARKETING CHALLENGES

# FULL CONTENTS

# CONTRIBUTORS

## EDITOR

**Tiziano Vescovi**, Professor of Marketing, Department of Management, Ca' Foscari University of Venice, Italy.

## CONTRIBUTORS

**Vera Costantini**, Associate Professor of Economic History of Mediterranean, Department of Asian Studies, Ca' Foscari University of Venice, Italy.

**Anilkumar Dave**, Head of Unit and Open Innovation Advisor to the President of the Italian Space Agency, Italy.

**Mitsuyo Itonaga-Delcourt**, International Research Center for Japanese Studies, Kyoto, Japan.

**Rosana Beatriz Fabbiani**, Independent Marketing Consultant, Buenos Aires, Venice and Argentina.

**Enav Friedmann**, Lecturer in Marketing, Ben Gurion University, Beer Sheva, Israel.

**Francesca Hansstein**, Lecturer in Marketing, Xi'an Jiaotong Liverpool University, Suzhou, China.

**Andreas Hinterhuber**, Associate Professor of Marketing, Department of Management, Ca' Foscari University of Venice, Italy.

**Anne-Flore Maman Larraufie** (PhD), SémioConsult, Paris, France.

**Idan Tschisik**, Ben Gurion University of the Negev, Israel.

**Beverly Wagner**, Professor of Marketing, University of Strathclyde, Glasgow, UK.

**Merav Weiss-Sidi**, PhD Candidate, Ben Gurion University, Beer Sheva, Israel.

**Juliette Wilson**, Reader in Marketing, University of Strathclyde, Glasgow, UK.

# PREFACE

The book deals with the analysis of cross-cultural marketing, and in particular the cultural comparison will be centred between East and West, according to a European perspective. Europe is the centre of intercultural confrontation and not the United States, a frequent feature in published books. For this reason, there is a group of co-authors (university teachers and managers), four from European countries (Italy, France, United Kingdom) plus China, India and Israel, and two of dual nationality (Franco-Japanese and Italian-Argentine). They will be involved in the drafting of case histories and several chapters. The world is therefore not seen by a single country, but by several European subcultures.

The point of view used in the book is mainly that of medium-sized multinational enterprises (MMNEs). There are a large number of MMNEs in the European economic reality and they are increasingly involved in international markets, even in those that are culturally very distant. These are markets that MMNEs have to face without having the huge resources of big multinational companies, which often instead represent the point of view used in international marketing textbooks. This is a real challenge for them.

The cross-cultural situation is constantly changing, but it does not follow a single direction. In reality it takes on new, sometimes unexpected forms, which arise from how different cultures intersect and evolve, influencing each other and not moving towards a single direction, that of a Western globalization, as was believed years ago. The ethnocentric vision of the American West, and in some cases of the European West as well, has vanished. The discovery and analysis of a reality in free movement is therefore the challenge launched by this book. Villages are global as well as local and it is becoming more and more complex to analyse their characteristics without risking falling into easy simplifications. Ethnocentrism is always lurking, even in newer and more modern forms.

The book is divided into four parts. At the end of each part, business cases and cross-cultural stories are included, as well as challenging questions for analysis and discussion. After defining the logical framework of the cross-cultural approach to business and international markets (Part I), the book develops in three successive parts, which address: (a) cross-cultural marketing strategies, considering new international challenges and opportunities (Part II); (b) the contents of cross-cultural marketing actions, affected by different cultural contexts (Part III); and (c) the challenges for the cross-cultural marketing approach in the near future (Part IV). The perspective of the analysis is that of European companies, partially influenced by European (national) subcultures, entering culturally different international markets.

The case histories will analyse cross-cultural issues concerning companies from different European countries, considering the cultural context of the home and destination countries. The approach is focused on the intercultural evolution taking place in a connected world that does not tend towards global homogeneity The book is aimed at business master's-level students and managers engaged in international marketing activities.

This book tries to offer a method to analyse the themes of cross-cultural marketing; obviously it does not aim to describe all its characteristics and evolutions. From the beginning it reveals that I maintain a European point of view, and this is obviously the point of view from which the world is observed. Other points of view certainly manage to see different things and offer insights that escape the lens of a European person, but they are equally interesting and important detectors of intercultural marketing relationships. Unfortunately, or fortunately, each one uses their own cultural filters to understand the world and this situation forces continuous and enriching exchanges with other cultures, which prevents their points of view from being perfectly reflected in their cultural mirror, giving the illusion that the world is homogeneous.

# ACKNOWLEDGEMENTS

This book would never have been born if I hadn't had the good fortune to meet so many people. First of all, I would like to thank the students who developed their theses on cross-cultural marketing topics with me. They gave me the opportunity to deepen many interesting and new cross-cultural aspects and from their work I have also drawn some cases contained in this book. More generally, I thank my international and Italian students in the master's courses in Cross-Cultural Marketing and International Marketing to China for all the things I have learned from them, through their fascinating stories about 30 different countries of the world. I cannot forget to thank my colleague in the Department of Management, Andrea Pontiggia, fellow scholar and travelling companion in many countries of the world, with whom I have discussed and exchanged opinions, suggestions and discoveries, and written books and articles on intercultural issues. My colleagues in the Department of Asian Studies of the Ca' Foscari University of Venice, and the many colleagues and managers I have met in the various countries where I had the opportunity to study, have also been a source of continual help, discovery and inspiration for me.

# PART I
# THE CROSS-CULTURAL APPROACH

# 1

# Cultures and markets

In this chapter the initial issues of the intercultural approach to markets will be discussed. The general concepts on which the following chapters of the book are based and the key concepts to follow will be explained. In particular, it will be explained why the guiding concept of the book is that of culture, what this concept includes and the complexity it contains, and what must be analysed and taken into consideration.

## 1.1    TOWARDS A NEW INTERNATIONALIZATION

The international market has constantly represented opportunities and challenges for companies motivated in their desire and often also in the need for expansion due to the insufficient size of the internal market. The company's internationalization process has thus been the subject of continuous and in-depth study since the Second World War, giving rise to numerous theories and tracing models that have tried to describe strategies and methods of expansion on foreign markets.

In the Uppsala model, for example, the internationalization process is described as the gradual and incremental acquisition, integration and use of knowledge about foreign markets. The contribution of Johanson and Wiedersheim-Paul (1975) describes internationalization as a slow and incremental process described by four distinct phases: (a) no regular export activity, but only random or temporary episodes; (b) export through agents; (c) the creation of a commercial branch abroad and, possibly, (d) the development of local production units. Johanson and Vahlne (1977) designed a model that describes internationalization as causal cycles, in which knowledge of foreign markets and market commitment decisions are influenced by the firm's current activities. In the Uppsala model, internationalization is modelled as a process of commitment of incremental resources, driven by growing knowledge and experience about the foreign market, but of a structural rather than a cultural nature (Johanson and Vahlne, 2009). The process starts from national markets, moves to culturally and/or geographically closer countries, and then moves to geographically and structurally more distant countries.

The OLI (Ownership, Location, Internationalization) model describes the best-known strategy of multinationals (Dunning, 1988). It explains how a multinational company can overcome competitive costs and disadvantages over domestic rivals in a host country by using a source of advantage that leverages internal assets in asset transfer and accessing to global value chains. Much of the logic of FDI (Foreign Direct Investments) is based on the paradigm according to which companies choose to engage in foreign direct investments, based on the belief that they can exploit the firm-specific competitive advantages of the company existing in the home country.

Traditionally, multinationals have played a crucial role in the transfer of technology and other forms of knowledge between countries, mainly from headquarters to foreign branches. The idea that a company can gain knowledge through its international operations is not new, but it has often been seen as a positive side-effect, rather than a key motivation for FDI. Corporate practice shows (Almeida, 1996) how companies can be increasingly motivated to expand internationally with the primary objective of acquiring valuable knowledge present abroad.

Exporting is a common way to grow international business. It is perceived as a fast and low-risk access system to foreign markets (Zucchella and Siano, 2014). In fact, it requires less use of resources than direct investments. While exporting reduces the organizational complexities created by establishing foreign branches and units, this strategy has obvious limitations. In a distant foreign market, the possibility of accessing information and knowledge is considerably reduced. Although export strategies provide faster access to the international market, they lack the ability to create a learning process, thereby reducing the potential for companies to go international. Knowledge of the foreign market and control of the company's presence on the market are very limited. In many cases, the export model also makes it difficult to adapt the offer of the company to the needs of emerging markets (Rugman and Verbeke, 2003).

The traditional theories on the internationalization of companies, however, have been developed with reference to a specific, albeit broad, socioeconomic framework that describes the world that emerged from the Second World War. The main characteristics of the markets therefore derived from an economic–political division which provided for a clear separation between two main realities, each one in turn segmented internally, to which was added a third, less marked one. Summarizing in an extreme way, one can distinguish on the one hand the North America–Western Europe quadrant and on the other the Soviet Union and related countries. The rest of the nations, not aligned with these two fields, referred to one or the other integrated economic system on the basis of influence, more or less heavily exercised, of political convenience and cultural affiliation.

The behaviour of companies, as socioeconomic organizations, could not ignore the geopolitical conditions in which these organizations were born and acted. Reading the genesis of the internationalization of companies according to this reality, we can understand how its history is that of the great American company that finds space in European markets and in those markets affected by the economic-political influence of the United States. It is the story of the great American enterprises, which begins in the 1950s, with a large home market as a starting point, the largest market, and which expands into smaller, culturally similar and politically conditioned markets.

The managerial theories, which in those years found their theoretical foundation, not only derive from this cultural approach, but developed in the USA. The theories of business internationalization are the result of a history developed in a specific economic environment: large companies in a large market that expand into smaller, politically conditioned and often culturally similar markets. Obviously, there are exceptions to this simplification, in countries that may be culturally very distant, but highly politically conditioned, like Japan, or not politically conditioned, like India. The reference models are based on the expansion of multinational companies, with a dominant internal market culture, marginally adapted to the destination countries.

At the beginning of the 1980s this approach adapted to a greater homogenization of traditional markets, guided by the drivers of technology and communication, giving life to what has been called the global approach (Levitt, 1983), large companies addressing their expansion towards markets smaller than their home market, and with almost nullified cultural differences. Medium-sized European companies, compared to the large companies involved in these choices, have followed similar approaches in search of an impossible set-up. The models, in fact, were born in an inverse world to theirs, a world of smaller companies with limited internal markets. Yet the managerial literature did not seem to address the problem, also because the initial hypotheses, based on big multinational companies, had not been denied, although evident application limits for SMEs were highlighted. Panacea theories were born (Cova et al., 2012) that tried to adapt by exception and specialization the general theories born in another era and in other conditions. This was like trying to add some partial adaptation explanation to the Ptolemaic theory to justify the apparently insufficient planetary rotation. It took a dramatic break in continuity, a catastrophe, as the physicists would say.

It is clear that managerial theories must be rethought in the face of a completely renewed global economic, social and cultural system. International European companies, especially medium-sized ones, have to face new large markets, still in the process of forming, with very distant consumer cultures, different social structures, which have a high rate of change compared to what they were used to finding in traditional markets. The three paradoxes to be resolved are those of: (a) small businesses in large markets; (b) sophisticated products in markets not educated to understand them; (c) strategies for replicating business models for markets that are culturally completely different from those of their origin. This book tries to address these three paradoxes.

One basic question in the relation between marketing and cultures is the standardization–adaptation debate, that is, the degree to which certain established marketing strategies and/or tactics would be applicable in different cultural contexts. The managerial discussion about the various degrees of optimal standardization versus adaptation may mask the standardized branding and marketing strategies, which may say more about marketers' persisting belief in simplifying and finding an easy way of reducing costs than verifying the required homogeneity of consumer preferences. Actually, the idea of globalization is a Western idea of globalization, let's say Western-American. It is quite paradoxical that the globalization theory has such a national root.

The question is: is globalization only a Western approach or we should expect also an Eastern globalization as the Far East countries will become more powerful economically? Actually, globalization cannot be considered a process of eternalization of each culture. More than global, it should appear colonial. Different cultural identities contribute to create a new concept of globalization, merging from multiculturalism. Nevertheless, cultures are open entities, so in continuous transformation.

The question is that there is always a dual approach in consumer choices: (a) the search for a global standard of quality and excellence combined with the desire to feel 'global'; (b) the search for a value of cultural and identity confirmation. From time to time one of the two prevails over the other, in some cases absolutely, in others less so.

## 1.2 WHAT IS CULTURE?

According to Guilford (1959), 'Culture is to a human community what personality is to an individual', and he defines personality as 'the interactive aggregate of personal characteristics that influence the individual's response to the environment'. This definition expresses the idea that culture could be defined as the interactive aggregate of common characteristics that influence a human group's response to its environment. In this sense, it is important to specify that culture is no king-sized personality, but that cultures are formed through the interactions of different personalities, both conflicting and complementary, that create a whole that is more than the sum of its parts. Kluckhohn (1951) defines culture as 'patterned ways of thinking, feeling and reacting, acquired and transmitted mainly by symbols, constituting the distinctive achievement of human groups, including their embodiments in artifacts; the essential core of culture consists of traditional ideas and especially their attached values'.

The word 'culture' comes from the Latin noun *cultura*, which derives from the verb *colere*, to cultivate the land. The abstract meaning of the word probably originated from the German word *Kultur*, used in the eighteenth century to refer to civilization. This later meaning eventually became dominant. The original concept was expanded at the end of the nineteenth century, encompassing not only personal study and experience, but also the configuration of learned behaviour and results of behaviour whose component elements are shared and transmitted by the members of a particular society. The anthropological meaning was introduced by Edward Burnett Tylor in 1871. He identified three main components: (a) what individuals think: religion, morality and law, that is, the sets of explicit norms and beliefs; (b) what they do: the customs and habits acquired by the human being by the fact of living within a given community. The culture includes ordinary actions that the individual performs in daily life, based on customary and traditional rules; (c) the artefacts they produce, that is, the objectified products of human work which include objects of worship and those of daily use.

Edward Hall (1981) defines culture as man's medium, because there is no one aspect of human life that is not touched or altered by culture. It affects personality, how people express themselves, the way of thinking, how they move, how they solve problems, how their cities and villages are planned and laid out, and how the economic system and the political system work.

Hofstede (2001) treats culture as 'the collective programming of the mind that distinguishes the members of one group or category of people from another'. Through this definition, the author reveals the greatest importance concealed in differences and on the base of his literature it is possible to de-structure culture into its core elements that are invisible until they become evident in the behaviour of people.

The manifestation of culture in order of depth levels is symbols, heroes, rituals and values. The first three layers are subsumed under the term of practices; as such, they are visible to an outside observer; their cultural meanings, however, are invisible and lie precisely and only in the ways in which these practices are interpreted by insiders. More specifically, symbols include words, gestures, pictures and objects that often carry complex meanings recognized as such only by those who share the culture. Heroes are people who possess characteristics that are highly prized in a culture and thus serve as models for behaviour. Rituals are collective activities that within a culture are considered to be socially essential, keeping the individual bound within the norms of the community. Values constitute the most intrinsic layer and the core element of culture which could be understood only through a deep comprehension of a culture's practices.

Kroeber and Parsons (1958) arrived at a cross-discipline definition of culture as 'transmitted and created content and patterns of values, ideas, and other symbolic-meaningful systems as factors in the shaping of human behaviour and the artifacts produced through behaviour'.

In line with this, people are dependent upon the control mechanism of culture for ordering their behaviour; therefore, they are conditioned by their sociocultural environment to act in a certain manner. Culture cannot be separated from the individual, or from the historical context. Shared beliefs, attitudes, norms, roles and values are all internalized in people at an unconscious level; they are speakers of a particular language who live during the same historical period in a specific geographic region. Language, time and place are all patterns in the background that help define culture. Moreover, cultural differences cannot be understood without the study of history.

Trompenaars and Woolliams (2003) describe culture as being composed of three layers. The first (outer) layer is formed by the visual reality of behaviours, clothes, food and language. This is the level of explicit culture. The middle layer concerns norms and values, that is, what is considered right and wrong (norms) or good and bad (values). Frequently values create norms, and when there is tension between them, society experiences conflict until the norms change. The third, inner layer concerns the implicit culture. It consists of basic assumptions, series of routines and methods to deal with the regular problems people face. Therefore, it is quite easy to identify explicit cultural differences while it is quite difficult to perceive implicit differences. This represents a real problem when a company experiences a different culture, because the managers, as individuals, use filter glasses: as the Talmud states, 'we do not see things as they are, we see things as we are'.

Culture is not a factor that can be introduced next to factors such as technology, socio/political, financial, and other elements of the transactional environment. Culture is the contextual environment.

Culture is shared by the members of a society and defines the membership of that society. Cultural preferences are shared in different societies even if they are not shared in the same way. Even if Italians and Chinese consider the family to be an important feature of their culture, it does not require both societies to consider family in the same way. It means that the definition of the same concept of value can also vary according to culture. Culture is learned through membership of a community. Parents, elders, teachers, friends, mates and colleagues teach a person about how to behave and what the values he or she should refer to should be. Religion can play a major role in defining the main values of a community too. Thus, values are acquired. Clearly culture influences the attitudes and behaviours of community members. What a person can consider innate beliefs and values, can be found in specific cultural training and socialization. Culture tells what acceptable and unacceptable behaviour is, therefore it heavily influences socialization processes and normative behaviour, and how we think those around us expect us to behave (Steers and Osland, 2020). In other words, culture makes the rules of the social game.

Its function therefore consists in practice in establishing patterns of behaviour and interaction with others and with the environment, which reduce the risks of relationships, making the world more predictable for people, thus favouring the survival and development of members of a community.

A set of shared cultural norms represents, for the members of the different communities, the sense of their common identity, as well as a way to relate to each other: for example, culture establishes rules and criteria regarding when, what and how to eat, how to welcome guests, how to relate to the hierarchy, how to identify social roles, and so on. It is therefore the cultural meanings that cause some activities to be considered normal and natural, while others are strange or wrong.

In summary, we can consider that culture is characterized in the following ways (Herbig, 2000):

- it is *functional*, as it indicates to each society the guidelines for the survival of the group;
- it is a *social phenomenon*, as it arises from the interaction between people;
- it is *prescriptive*, as it establishes which behaviours are acceptable and which are unacceptable;
- it is *acquired*, because it is not inherited genetically but is learned from the behaviour of other members of the community;
- it is *arbitrary*, as acceptable behaviour in one specific culture may be unacceptable in another;
- it brings *values*, as it defines what is good and what is bad and what is expected of people;
- it facilitates *communication*, both verbal and non-verbal;
- it is *versatile* and *dynamic*, as it adapts to new situations and new acquaintances;
- it is *durable*, as its roots persist over the centuries;
- it *satisfies the needs* of the members of a community, taking on new characteristics and eliminating those that are useless or obsolete, while maintaining the core values.

People and communities share characteristics and biological traits, leading to universal problems; these problems are addressed by choosing different solutions that reflect the different cultural values. Actually, there are a limited number of common human problems; while there is variability in solutions to all problems, all alternatives of all solutions are present in all societies at all times but are differently preferred (Kuckholn and Strodbeck, 1961).

The six major elements of culture, therefore the elements that reinforce the knowledge, beliefs and values that are useful to its continuation and duration, include (Usunier and Lee, 2013; Hall, 1981) language, institutions, time, space, material productions, and symbolic productions.

*Language* is the primary mechanism for sharing and transmitting information among members of a particular society. It is also clear that the language we learn in our community shapes and structures the way we think, our worldview, and our social behaviour. Eskimos have many words to express the concept of snow as the difference between the various types of snow profoundly affects their daily life, while other peoples have many expressions to identify different types of sea waves. A country's language expresses a culture's thought patterns, so you can identify what's important in a culture by analysing what's present in its language. In this sense, the dialects present in the different areas of the countries also highlight the existence of regional subcultures.

Considering communication, we should also include non-verbal communication. Non-verbal communication means any intentional or unintentional behaviour that goes beyond words and that can be interpreted by the recipient as a bearer of meaning. Non-verbal communication can include facial expressions, posture, gaze, gestures, movements, interpersonal distance, physical contact, and time management. Non-verbal messages can reinforce verbal messages or contradict them. Because they are instinctive, habitual and internalized, they almost always highlight the true meaning of communication. Different cultures develop differences in non-verbal communication, which are very important to know in order to be able to understand the messages. For example, silence during a discussion has very different meanings in Western cultures (embarrassment, opposition) compared to Eastern ones (reflection, respect). The same happens in looks. If in the West it is good to stare at the people you talk to, as a sign of sincerity, in some Eastern cultures this signals a lack of respect.

*Institutions* are the structures that define the cultural processes that link the individual to the group. Institutions include the family, political, administrative and religious organizations, the school system, and any kind of social organization that encourages an individual to comply with rules. Institutions organize individuals into groups. Culture uses institutions in order to organize people in a permanent and stable way, such as family lineage and gender, or in a temporary grouping, such as professions or common interests, clubs, and so on. There are some principles around which institutions are formed across cultures (Malinowski, 1944): (a) the principle of *reproduction*, integrating people around blood relationships; (b) the principle of *territoriality*, integrating people by neighbourhood and vicinity; the principle of *physiology*, integrating people around their gender, age, and physical traits; the principle of *spontaneous tendency to join together* around common goals; the principle of *occupational and professional* activities considering labour division and expertise (soldier, artists, farmers, etc.); the principle of *hierarchy*, integrating people around ranking and status; the principle of *totality*, integrating into a reasonably coherent role (political process as feudal, democratic, dictatorial, etc.).

The perception of *time* determines the importance that different cultures attribute to interpersonal relationships with respect to the efficiency of performance. Where time is considered the binding element, no great emphasis is placed on relationships, while, vice versa, where it is considered less binding, relationships take on a lot of value. Perception of time measures the degree of flexibility of a community as well as the value of rules. There are therefore cultures in which absolute respect for time represents a fundamental variable in the measurement of social relations (Germany, Japan, USA), providing for a precise beginning and end, with linear logic, and where instead time takes on a relative value with respect to other variables (South America, Latin countries, Arab countries), with an approximate beginning and end, according to a circular logic.

The *space* between people considered acceptable varies from culture to culture. While Americans, Chinese, Japanese and British people prefer to keep a physical distance of about one metre, limiting physical contact as much as possible, between South Americans, Italians, Spaniards and Arabs the distance is reduced, and physical contact is considered a positive element of a relationship. Physical contact becomes a form of communication. Even the succession of space can take on different meanings in different cultures, especially in connection with the direction of writing. For example, if in countries that use Latin script the sequence of events occurs from left to right, in those using Arabic or Hebrew script the logical sequence occurs from right to left. If in an advertising communication, for example, you want to emphasize the before and after, in Europe it will start from left to right and in Arab countries the direction is from right to left.

*Material productions* of a society transmit, reproduce, update and improve the knowledge and skills in a community. They include artistic production such as art, music and dance; intellectual productions such as articles, books and movies; physical productions such as factories, tools and machinery, as well as the products we consume such as food, clothing and furniture; and service productions such as education, healthcare and tourism.

*Symbolic productions* and sacred elements of culture determine the relationship between the physical and the metaphysical world. The importance of the metaphysical world varies in different cultures. In some cultures it is present in everyday life while it is denied in other cultures. Culture and religion are strictly connected, with noticeable differences between cultures sharing different religious beliefs. One main example concerns food restrictions and habits. Although traditional societies have been more involved in symbolic thought compared to modern ones, even the latter maintain symbolic behaviours and objects. They can be, for example, numbers (lucky and unlucky), lucky objects to be kept at home or in the car, or gifts on particular occasions, such as rings. Throughout this book the strength of the symbolic dimension will be described, especially in marketing communication strategies.

The last two components can be defined as 'the human component of the environment' (Herskovits, 2010). They incorporate two elements: the objective and the subjective. The first includes tangible objects and cultural artefacts, which can be artistic products, objects of everyday life, architectural aspects, and everything that is material. The subjective element includes norms, rules, values, ideas, habits, and whatever can take on a symbolic meaning.

Culture, therefore, challenges the basic strategies of approaching the market, the relationship with customers, the definition of the marketing mix, the management of commercial relations and the human resources management within the company. One principle in analysing the culture codes is that the only effective way to understand why people act in a specific way is to ignore what they say. This is not to suggest that people intentionally lie or misrepresent themselves. The point is that, when asked direct questions about their behaviours, people tend to give answers they believe are rational. Moreover, 'fish can't see water', that is, people cannot perceive the extent to which their culture is affecting their lives.

However, changing the level of aggregation studied changes the nature of the concept of 'culture'. Societal, national and gender cultures, which children acquire from their earliest youth onwards, are much more deeply rooted in the human mind than occupational cultures acquired at school or organizational cultures acquired on the job. Culture can be reflexive: a simulation, where cultural tradition increasingly exists mainly as a reflexive and conscious practice realization of some idea of culture. Culture, then, could be said increasingly to take the shape of hype, a simulation of a possibly imaginary or purified version of that particular culture. Culture is also hybrid. It must be seen as an amalgamation of various inputs from other cultures locally adopted and changed to form a new composition.

Douglas and Craig (2009) identify five main profiles of the concept of culture. First, culture as *Artifact*, because work provides a framework for understanding the cultural meaning of consumer goods and consumption partners. Brands serve as cultural marketers, reinforcing status boundaries and helping to denote social identities. Artefacts and objects are instruments of cultural identification; moreover, they produce cultural behaviours. Second, culture as *Communication*, because language is an important element of culture, not only in communication within a culture but also in categorizing cultural content and in retaining information relating to that culture. Third, culture as *Value Orientation*, that is, the impact of a society's value orientation on consumer behaviour. In particular this is connected to the horizontal dimension (individualism-collectivism) and society's vertical dimension (power distance). It is important in product evaluation and in considering the emotional content in communication messages. Fourth, culture as *Country*, because it is the unit of space for samples, surveys and experiments, providing a practical and convenient domain for data collection. Actually, secondary and industry data are available on a country basis; the official language(s) is also a facilitator and a cultural construct. Fifth, *Culture and Subculture*, which exist as ethnic, socio-demographic and so on within countries (for example, think of Belgium, Switzerland, Spain, USA, Canada etc.). Subcultures can create distinctive interests, values, and consumption and purchase behaviours.

In conclusion, culture is a journey. It evolves and arrives in different places compared to where it started. Actually, new generations never have exactly the same reference culture as previous generations.

Culture can be seen as a 'toolkit' of symbols, stories, rituals and worldviews that people use in varying configurations to solve problems and organize their life (Swidler, 1986).

According to Bhagat et al. (2012), cultural patterns evolve when some ecological and demographic factors are present. In particular:

a. a group of people who need to work cooperatively in order to survive;
b. as a consequence, a system of language, symbols, codes and ways of communication is developed, and a sense of collective identity begins to grow;
c. interactions among the members of this collective are of an enduring nature; they begin to develop ties of emotional bonds;
d. the culture of traditional societies, such as those in China, India, Greece and Italy have existed for thousands of years, resulting in strong heritages that are not easily changed; newer societies (USA, Australia etc.) are more prone to accept change induced by globalization.

Tight cultures are products of long-term and successful interaction among a group of people in a collective. Long-term association between members of a culture is vital for the development of a stable and mature culture. They do not easily accept changes in structural values pushed by globalization.

## 1.3  MARKETS AND CULTURAL COMPLEXITY

In the context of cross-cultural research, in addition to trying to understand some key features of the cultural theme, the studies of Ying Fan (2000), who attempted to classify Chinese culture, were considered as an example of the complexity of cultural influence. His analysis takes shape from the idea of national culture, which best reflects the values of the Chinese people and allows us to affirm that the value system of Chinese culture is so unique that it completely distinguishes China from any other Western or Eastern culture. This statement arises because Chinese culture, which we are comparing today, is composed of several elements: traditional culture, communist ideology and, more recently, Western values. According to this theory, the key to understanding Chinese culture and its values is Confucianism. After having fought and coexisted throughout history with other schools of thought, such as Taoism and Buddhism, Confucianism is in fact the philosophy of thought that is even more present today. It forms the basis of traditional Chinese culture, offering the basis of the rules of behaviour even to an outside observer. There are five basic principles of Confucianism: humility, moral correctness, good manners, wisdom and loyalty.

For example, it is noted that one of the main mistakes still made by non-Chinese companies concerns the language. Unpreparedness from this point of view can generate problems not only in the daily management of the foreign branch of the company, but in all its activities, from advertising to the management of local personnel. Even more subtle, and therefore of greater importance, are the differences in meaning that different cultures can give to the same object. For example, the colour red used in Western countries to indicate a warning sign can convey a different meaning when used in China, where red is also a symbol of success (Trompenaars and Woolliams, 2003). Culture is not simply another factor to be included among all the elements that influence marketing policies, but the context in which all life and business dynamics act must be considered. Culture therefore challenges the basic strategies of approaching the market, the relationship with customers, the definition of the marketing mix, the management of commercial relations and the management of human resources within the company.

From a Western, or rather European perspective, China appears as a world in which many aspects have yet to be discovered and in which culture plays such a significant role that understanding it becomes a necessary step for the company's success. Although there are many political, social and economic differences between the People's Republic of China and other territories where Chinese culture dominates (e.g. Hong Kong and Taiwan), it is still possible to identify the key values that unite the Chinese population. This is because culture provides a basic identity and the values it contains are unique and resistant, as they are derived from a millenary tradition that has remained virtually unchanged. As mentioned above, contemporary culture in the People's Republic of China is made up of three main elements: traditional culture, communist ideology and, more recently, Western values.

If for other peoples it is good always to keep in mind that culture changes in time and with time the perception that one may have of certain traditions, what emerges from Chinese cultural studies is that the set of Confucian values has remained almost unchanged over the course of history and still influences everyday life, coexisting with new systems. For example, economic reforms and opening up to the West have not only changed the cultural environment but have also contributed to partially restructuring the value system. All this helps to explain the differences in the behaviour of individuals in private and economic contexts.

It is also necessary to have a clear idea of what culture is not, especially when dealing with realities that are very different from one's own, as can happen in business. First of all, we can say that culture is relative; there is no right or wrong culture, as people from different cultures simply perceive the world in different ways. Secondly, culture does not isolate the behaviour of the individual, but places him or her within the community in which he or she acts.

For example, in the United States or in many European countries, children acquire values such as family values in the context of Christian culture, while in China there is a strong attachment to the family unit, but the context is completely different, because it is related to the values of Confucianism, transmitted through parents, teachers and friends.

Especially for those who may face work and life situations in close contact with other nationalities, it becomes essential to go beyond the first impact, to break through the surface of what could seem the complete vision of a culture, by going to the core. To better explain this phenomenon, anthropological studies often refer to this dynamic using the metaphor of the iceberg: what are seen on the surface are the most commonly recognized characteristics, but what really constitutes a culture is the part of the iceberg under the water's surface. It is there that all the rules and values that structure and influence behaviour, decision-making processes and attitudes are contained. It is necessary to look more carefully and openly at diversity to understand more easily the mechanisms at work within another culture. In the case of business activities, considering the Chinese reality, an intercultural perspective is fundamental, that is, 'the ability of the individual to manage a set of knowledge, skills and personal attitudes, in order to operate successfully with people of different cultural backgrounds both in a national as well as a foreign context' (Johnson et al., 2006).

The most significant values for Chinese culture are those of the family, considered to be a fundamental element in society; those of simplicity as opposed to extravagance in everyday life; humility and perseverance; saving face according to the principles of 'mianzi'; collectivism, which is expressed in the connection between people within specific contexts such as family, professional and cultural contexts, governed by the phenomenon of 'guanxi'. Alongside these values linked to the Chinese tradition, we also find a more modern component, which brings together the idea of success, wealth, social position, individualism and personal freedom. Above all, the last two traits are typically Western and they go against traditional Chinese thought, in which usually a group and collective idea tends to be preferred rather than choosing based on personal preferences.

With the arrival of Romanticism, culture begins to be identified as a more abstract component, linked to traditions and daily habits, and in contrast with the material and more tangible changes of society. From this moment on, sociological and anthropological studies begin to flourish, up to the first decades of the twentieth century in which there are hundreds of definitions of the term 'culture'.

Almost everyone is a member of multiple cultures, including political, family, religious and professional cultures and each one influences consumer behaviour. Thus, cultural behaviour can be different within the same community, because the combination of subcultures that each person shares could be different. The same could happen considering different subcultures defined by geographical or historical conditions. In several European countries there are subcultures in regions located in the north and the south of the country, as in Italy, France, UK and Germany. In Spain we can identify the Catalonian subculture and the Basque one; in Switzerland there are four different subcultures, the German, French, Italian and Ladin ones; in Belgium there are the Vallon and Flemish subcultures; the United States is an extraordinary example of a mixture of subcultures due to the country's immigration story.

We should also consider the emic and the etic perspective (Steers and Osland, 2020). The emic approach investigates how local people think, how they perceive and categorize the world, their rules for behaviour, what has meaning for them, and how they imagine and explain things. The etic (scientist-oriented) approach shifts the focus from local observations, categories, explanations and interpretations to those of the anthropologist. The etic approach realizes that members of a culture often are too involved in what they are doing to interpret their cultures impartially. Not only do you need to understand the emic perspective of the culture in question, you also must be able to detach yourself emotionally from that culture in order to arrive at an objective description. Most people from outside a culture do not have an emic perspective about it; they have an ethnocentric perspective, interpreting behaviours and beliefs in light of their own culture. The same happens to companies entering a market dominated by a different culture; they try to assume an ethnocentric approach both because it is a mental attitude and because it is considered an efficient and cost-saving way to replicate their business strategy everywhere. Unfortunately, it can be really ineffective.

In various societies there are numerous behaviours and cultural traditions that have lost their original function and survive in the form of symbolic acts, which are part of the cultural baggage of that specific society. It is these customs that have led to the constitutions of various institutions (family, school, political and legislative systems, etc.). Institutions therefore create social norms of behaviour that can be more or less changeable depending on the level of closure or opening of a given society. Furthermore, institutions can undergo change at a different pace than change in social customs and habits, which is generally more rapid. In different societies, habits vary. For example, in Western societies, especially in the United States, there is a tendency to give greater emphasis and importance to the legal and contractual aspects of an agreement, while in Eastern societies relationships and personal trust prevail. Culture conditions the way of acting in a situation of contractual definition. In China and the Far East in general, an alternative is sought that can offer a dignified solution for both parties, while in Western countries a more authoritarian attitude prevails, defined by the power relationship between the parties.

A further point should be considered in analysing cultures, a crucial perspective: cultural relativity. Every culture is perceived and, therefore, described and judged, in comparison to one's own culture. The point is that, when examining how people from different cultures relate to one another, what matters is not the absolute position of either culture on an objective scale, but rather the relative position of the two cultures considered. It is the relative positioning that determines how people view another. It can be said that every culture is ethnocentric to some extent. For example a German manager could complain that an Italian manager is disorganized, chaotic and never punctual. The same complaints could be made by an Italian manager about an Indian one. Also an Italian manager could complain that a German manager is rigid, inflexible and obsessed with deadlines, unable to adapt as the situation changes. An Indian manager could say the same of an Italian one.

Cultural differences and codes have points of view at different levels. For example, from a Chinese point of view, northern Italians or Scots are people with a Western culture. Going one step further, the Chinese can distinguish a European culture from an American one. Most Chinese people cannot isolate and understand a British culture from an Italian one. What is quite impossible from a Chinese point of view is to recognize that a Scottish culture is different from an English one and a northern Italian culture is different from a southern one. The last distinction can be perceived by a closer cultural point of view. Therefore, the point of view of the observer defines the level of the perception of cultural differences.

In conclusion I think that too much emphasis has been placed on identifying and describing differences between cultures and people rather than focusing on the universals that bind people together. Probably we should also find the commonalities if we want to create collaboration and comprehension, not forgetting differences, but using differences and commonalities to design better cross-cultural marketing strategies.

Modernization theories of the 1960s raised the idea of an emergence of a unique world culture following the maturity of developed countries' markets (Robertson, 1992). Consumer behaviour theorists were supposing that consumers in all parts of the world were becoming more and more attached to Western goods as status symbols, and in the process, were also adopting Western consumption values. Ted Levitt (1983) argued in his article 'The globalization of markets' that new technology would lead to homogenization of consumer wants and needs because consumers would prefer standard products of high quality at a low price to more customized high-priced products. This argument is, specifically, based on the classical microeconomic theory which imagines the consumer essentially taking two types of decision: the type of product to purchase and the quantity to purchase, and the solution would be enough to maximize utility and satisfaction of needs. However, this assumption limits the study of consumer behaviour, assuming that people tend to spend their income in a rational way and with the mere intention of maximizing profit. The concept of the rational consumer is increasingly regarded as unrealistic and places consumers outside a cultural context (Suerdem, 1994). The socioeconomic phenomena identified and assumed to be the cause of consumer behaviour convergence are modernization, urbanization, rising education levels, changing demographics, and convergence of national wealth.

Modern societies are characterized by rapid communication and transportation, urbanization, industrialization and bureaucratization; the term 'modern' refers to anything that has, more or less, replaced something that was considered the traditional way of doing things. Although modernization is an important force of change and development, it does not directly imply a convergence of value or the emergence of a global culture. For example, Asians view modernization as involving technology, behaviour, or material progress, without cultural implications (Fu and Chiu, 2007). As Mooney (2002) stated, 'The expectations were that with increased openness and capitalism in China, the Chinese would turn to Western values. Instead, they are rediscovering the teachings of Confucius, which for centuries have been the moral guidance of Chinese people. China wants to become modern while retaining its core values'.

# 2
# Methods for a cross-cultural analysis

Culture can be used as an explanatory variable depending upon the ability to 'unpackage' the culture concept; it is therefore appropriate to view culture as a 'complex multidimensional structure rather than as a simple categorical variable' (Clark, 1987). Culture can be described according to specific characteristics, such as behaviour patterns, norms, attitudes, and personality variables, or categorized into values or dimensions. These characteristics are based on observations, and many of these are found in dimensional models derived from large surveys.

Over the years, several research projects have been conducted in order to understand the triggering factor of these mental artefacts in order to provide companies with supportive tools in the formulation of international strategies. Generally, they have identified it with the aleatory concept of culture, very difficult to define.

There are five main explanatory models of culture used in the business literature and practice context: the Hall model, the Hofstede model, the Schwartz model, the Lewis model, and the GLOBE model. While Edward Hall bases his analysis on the dimensions of cultural context and of time and space perception, the other four base their analysis on interaction and behaviours.

We must consider that rather than having a single cultural identity, many consumers in today's global environment are bicultural, having internalized two distinct sets of sociocultural values and practices. So, in order to interpret their surroundings and determine appropriate actions, the two cultures switch as they move from one cultural context to another (Briley, 2009).

Conceptualizing and operationalizing culture is important because the concept has become a central focus of research in consumer psychology and behaviour. Although hundreds of culture measures have been developed, significant problems have been ignored, especially in consumer research (Sun et al., 2014). For example, Erin Meyer (2015) proposes an eight-scale map to compare the world cultures in how they influence business behaviour.

1. *Communicating*: low-context vs. high-context;
2. *Evaluating*: direct negative feedback vs. indirect negative feedback;
3. *Persuading*: principles-first vs. application-first;
4. *Leading*: egalitarian vs. hierarchical;
5. *Deciding*: consensual vs. top-down;
6. *Trusting*: task-based vs. relationship-based;
7. *Disagreeing*: confrontational vs. avoids confrontation;
8. *Scheduling*: linear-time vs. flexible-time.

National differences can be explained by examining cultural dynamics in terms of key drivers that influence how people interact and act, including attitudes, feelings and rules. People's behaviours are predictable in certain ways; they are characterized by different mental pro-grammes, replicated over the years, which lead to the representations of the same behaviours naturally and not noticed in similar situations. Every human being has a mental programming which is characterized by three levels, both unique and shared with others. The first level is shared by almost all humans and is the biological operating system of the human body. It is called the *universal* level and includes a set of expressive behaviours such as aggressive and laughing behaviours. The second level is shared with a restricted cycle of people usually belonging to the same category or group. It is labelled *collective* and includes the language, the physical distance maintained from other people to feel comfortable, the deference shown to elders and the way of perceiving general human activities such as eating, sleeping and so on. It represents the subjective human culture which is strictly related to all the elements listed earlier. The third and last level is unique and differs for every human being. It is the deepest level, and it corresponds to the *individual* personality. Thus, it is known as the individual level and includes a set of behaviours present in the same collective culture. It manifests itself in different degrees through symbols, heroes, values and rituals.

Against this backdrop, symbols are identified with gestures, words, objects and pictures that lead to a specific meaning shared by people belonging to the same culture. They are always changing and are likely to be replicated by other cultures: new symbols easily replace old and include dress, hairstyles, status symbols, words in a language and/or jargon.

Heroes, instead, are human figures identified as models of behaving who own characteris-tics highly prized in a culture. In the television era, outward appearances are becoming more and more important in the selection of heroes: Barbie, Batman and Snoopy are examples of heroes in the United States.

Rituals are those collective activities considered socially essential within a specific culture despite their technical superficiality in achieving the desired objectives. They include the way of communicating or, in a broad sense, the language used in talk and text both in daily interaction and in communication beliefs. Rituals are also particularly evident in business and political meetings, often organized for specific custom purposes such as reinforcing group cohesion. Other examples in daily life are the ways of greeting people or paying for purchases.

Trompenaars and Hampden-Turner (1997) identified six cultural dimensions regarding the analysis of the behaviours and value patterns of 55 countries. Specifically, the scholars defined the dimensions as expression of dichotomies between: (a) universalism and particularism; (b) communitarianism and individualism; (c) neutral and emotional; (d) diffuse and specific; (e) achieved and ascribed status; and (f) time as sequence and time as synchronization and human–nature relationships.

The first dichotomy refers to the people's way of judging other people's behaviours. It generally represents the contraposition between the compliance with rules and procedures as opposed to relationships. Universalism is about finding and adhering to universally agreed general rules and standards leading to abstract behaviours and a resistance to rules' exceptions, that may weaken them in order to avoid a system collapse. Conversely, particularism is about finding and focusing on exceptions of present circumstances: relationships are more important than rules that often lose their role and power.

The second dichotomy identified by Trompenaars strongly affects international management, especially decision-making, negotiations and motivation. In communitarian cultures, plural representation is preferred. The decision-making process requires mutual consent, extending the timeframe.

The third dimension has to be considered as the key element in intercultural communication. It refers to how people express their feelings to everyone else and how they exchange each other's ideas and messages. Members of neutral cultures keep their feelings controlled by showing emotions in a conventional way and they predominately use verbal communication through paper, film and conversation, they get upset if interrupted while talking, and they usually use a monotonous and self-controlled tone of voice. Non-verbal communication is avoided, thus, eye contact, touching and gesturing are a kind of taboo. Members of affective cultures (for example South European nations), on the other hand, magnify their emotions by scowling, laughing, smiling, grimacing and doing everything more loudly. They often rely on non-verbal communication, favouring eye and physical contact with other people and using a varied tone of voice together with gestures.

In specific-oriented cultures, also defined as low-context cultures, managers separate the task relationship that have with a subordinate and isolate him/her from dealing with others by providing him/her with a specific case. People belonging to specific-oriented cultures tend to analyse objects, specifics and other elements before considering how these are interrelated. In diffuse-oriented cultures, instead, people look at relationships and connections before considering each separate element. Everything is connected to everything and thus, a mental subdivision between work and the rest of life is not possible in doing business.

Cultures and societies also differ in how status is accorded to people: achieved status is obtained on the basis of people's achievements and performances; ascribed status, on the other hand, is defined through other ways related to the virtue of age and seniority, gender, social class, education and other similar qualitative characteristics.

Another key distinctive element of culture is the perception and management of time. Synchronic cultures are characterized by people who prefer effectiveness over efficiency and do more activities at the same time by choosing to get things done rather than doing the right things. At the other extreme, sequential cultures are characterized by people who do not track activities in parallel since they favour efficiency over effectiveness. They consider time as a defined sequence that has to be respected. People have to complete the first stage in order to start the second one.

Finally, Trompenaars et al. (2004) investigated the role people assign to the natural environment they are in. In their daily life, people are strongly affected by their own idea of nature. Inner-directed people are those who consider the human being as being able to control nature by imposing their will on it. Hence, companies are conceived of as machines obeying the will of their operators. In contrast, outward-oriented individuals consider the human being as part of nature and the organization as a product of nature which owns its development to the nutrients in its environment and a favourable ecological balance.

In light of the above, all the cultural models explained above facilitate the identification of the main cultural aspects that can potentially affect people's way of doing business and perceiving products. Indeed, they are often used as the basis of all international studies, especially in the emergent field of cross-cultural marketing, due to the different consumer needs and expectations that are arising as a consequence of the way of communicating or dealing with society and its members. In the following chapters we will go deeper to analyse the main cross-cultural models used in the business management approach to international cultural differences of markets.

With increased wealth people have no need to make either/or decisions; in a post-scarcity society consumers have more choices that make them less rational and impulsive in their buying behaviour, and the freedom to express themselves is based in part on their national value system. With more discretionary income, expenditure on education and the media is expected to increase among populations. Higher education makes people better educated and more affluent; as a consequence their taste will also become sophisticated, which means that populations are expected to become more and more aware of value preferences.

With regard to the influence of education on consumer behaviour, better-educated consumers are assumed to be better informed, but the information process is another aspect affected by culture; in fact the way consumers around the globe search for information is different in relation to individualism/collectivism and high/low power distance cultures. The idea of consciously searching for information to make an informed buying decision is more valid in individualistic, low power distance and high uncertainty avoidance cultures, like Western cultures. This is in contrast to a more collectivist and high-power distance culture where the opinion of one's closest friends is still valued as one of the most important sources of information, as with Asians.

According to the social phenomena just analysed, it is possible to assume that convergence follows economic development, but at the macro level, which means only dealing with aspects of consumption, health, social welfare, possession of means of communication, education levels, infrastructure, and so on. Economic development, in this sense, allows for the entrance of global brands in old and new developed countries, but the spread of global symbols does not imply the existence of a global consumer culture; on the contrary, what people possess does not converge with the usage of the same goods, as each consumer has his or her own personal way of utilizing their belongings. It can be assumed that globalization is the reason for the revival of local cultural identities in different parts of the world, instead of causing homogenization (Giddens, 2000). The emergence of a middle-income society in newly developed countries may be an explanation for this economic phenomenon, as the cultural values of a country are reflected in the different choices of products and brands. The interesting aspect to discover, in this historical moment, is what people do with their incremental income in order to live a comfortable life, and how they use new products in their daily life.

In every culture people make use of what we can call 'alibis'. Alibis give 'rational' reasons for doing things. Alibis make people feel better about what they do because they feel logical and socially acceptable. At a personal level, an alibi often has credibility even if it is not the reason why someone does what they do. Therefore, companies need to consider both the cultural codes and the alibis; they are highly instructive for shopping and luxury purchases.

According to research commissioned by P&G, women repeatedly said that they shopped to buy goods for themselves and their families and that they liked going shopping because it gave them the opportunity to discover the best products to purchase. This was the alibi. Going deeper, the researchers found the American culture code for shopping was *reconnecting with life*. Shopping was, above all, a social experience to be done with friends, to encounter a variety of people and learn what was new in the world, filled with discovery, revelation and surprise. In France the same search led to another culture code for shopping: *learning your culture*. French people consider shopping an educational experience in which older family members pass knowledge down through the generations. They explain why it is important to buy bread, wine and cheese at the same time (because they will be consumed together) or why certain colours and textures go together while other do not. In this sense, the same happens in Italy, where shopping is a school of culture (Rapaille, 2006).

Different culture codes can also be identified in luxury shopping. For example, most of the favourite American luxury items are functional. Americans seek luxury in things they can use: huge homes, top automobiles, professional-quality kitchens, Jacuzzi hot tubs, and so on. The luxury threshold is frequently the price. The American culture code for luxury is *military stripes*. Other cultures find luxury in things that are less functional. The Italian culture, a culture imprinted strongly by its veneration of great artists, defines luxury through artistic value. Something can be defined as luxury if it is highly refined, elegant, and well designed. It might be a necklace, a handbag, a suit, but never a refrigerator. Luxury in France represents the freedom to do nothing, to own useless things, providing beauty and harmony, without any practical function. For example, a very expensive scarf draped on the shoulders of a woman. The British use luxury to underscore their sense of detachment. They join very exclusive clubs where they can show one another how unimpressed they are about their own status. Another example concerns alcohol. In France and in Italy people drink wine for its taste, not because of its alcohol content, while for Americans, as well as for some Scandinavian countries alcoholic drinks have a functional aim: they make you drunk.

Culture is becoming increasingly reflexive. Individual actors (consumers, marketers) are aware of the social structure dynamism: engage in constant self-monitoring of action (consumers' choices, marketers' use of culture). A reflexive culture is therefore one in which marketers and consumers are aware of cultures and cultural symbolism, and monitor and modify their action accordingly, which consequently feeds into the dynamic change process of culture and globalization (Askegaard et al., 2009).

## 2.1  EDWARD HALL: CONTEXT, TIME AND SPACE PERCEPTIONS

The anthropologist Edward Hall (1981) distinguished patterns of culture according to context, space, time, and information flow. Despite the fact that Hall did not develop country scores, his findings show a certain robustness for cross-cultural studies: the context concept is useful for understanding consumer behaviour across cultures; differences between cultures with respect to the relationship between man and nature still are viewed as unique; his important study of time (1984) as an expression of culture provides an explanation of differences in behaviour and language, while in his study of space he developed the concept of *proxemics*, a description of how people behave and react in different types of culturally defined personal space (1969).

According to Hall, there are three types of relationship between man and nature: mastery-over-nature (man is to conquer nature), harmony-with-nature (man is to live in harmony with nature), and subjugation-to-nature (man is dominated by nature). The first one describes the Western world, where man is viewed as separate from nature, and in some cases, the human's relationship to nature is that it should be conquered and controlled for human convenience. The view of Western culture is that it is people's responsibility to overcome obstacles that may stand in their way. The East Asian experience of nature is one of communion, of exchange, characterized by a subtle intimacy. The Asian reverence of nature can be seen as an intimate relationship, which involves living in harmony with the world and experiencing identification with nature. In Chinese culture, particularly, the word used for nature is *daziran*, which literally means 'great spontaneity, infinity of spontaneity', expressing something that human beings are not capable of controlling or dominating. Other cultures, such as Africans, see people dominated by nature and supernatural forces that play a dominant role in religion. This subjugation involves the belief that nothing can be done to control nature.

The context orientation developed by Hall divides cultures into high-context and low-context communication cultures. In high-context communication or messaging, most of the information is either part of the context or internalized in the person; very little is made explicit as part of the message, and it could be defined as inaccessible to outsiders. In contrast, the information of a low-context message is direct and unambiguous; low-context communication cultures demonstrate positive attitudes toward words. Argumentation and rhetoric in society are found more in low-context cultures, whereas societies with a high-context culture are characterized by symbolism or indirect verbal expression. Another characteristic of a high-context culture is homogeneity, thus their members have more in common with respect to cultural heritage. This means that homogeneous cultures can rely on shared symbols more than heterogeneous ones. The use of linguistic code in sending messages is typical of low-context explicit cultures, while linguistic code is only one part of communication in high-context cultures, encompassing only part of the message. Sometimes linguistic code can contradict the real message, which is sent by context codes. This happens in many Far East cultures, where the meaning of 'yes' (linguistic code) can be 'no' if you can read the context codes. Consider, for example, that an event is usually infinitely more complex and richer than the language used to describe it. At least five sets of different categories of events should be taken into account: the subject or activity, the situation, one's status in the social system, past experience, and culture. In a high-context communication most of the information is either in the physical context or internalized in the person, while very little is in the coded and explicit part of the message. In a low-context communication, the mass of the information is vested in the explicit code. In a continuum scale, American, German Swiss, German and Scandinavian cultures are at the bottom of the (low) scale, while Chinese and Japanese cultures are at the top (high). Both of those countries have a great and complex culture requiring deep knowledge and careful attention to the context to be understood (Figure 2.1).

Compared to German Swiss and Japanese cultures, Italian and French cultures are a mixture of high and low-context institutions and situations. It is not always possible for the foreigner to predict in what proportions they will be found or in what order they occur. In all the high-context systems, the forms that are used are important. To misuse them is a communication in itself. Obviously, the paradox in investigating a high-context culture using low-context methods and vice versa analysing a low-context culture with high-context methods should be avoided.

Japan represents a typical example of a high-context culture. Rarely will the Japanese correct other people or explain things deeply to them. They usually say yes even if they think no and they are highly respectful of positions of authority; they prefer to deal with people with a similar role or of similar importance. In China, four different tones are used when someone is speaking. In this case, the knowledge of the exact pronunciation and tone to use is critical in order to understand completely what the speaker wants to communicate. A foreigner should know all these characteristics, otherwise they could create a situation of embarrassment, making an upsetting situation. In my first experiences in China, discussing common projects with Chinese colleagues, I frequently misunderstood the message that they sent me, despite the fact that I am Italian, in the middle of the high–low-contexts scale. For example, when they say 'it could be possible', I felt quite happy, considering that my proposal could be accepted. But the real high-context meaning was 'not possible', because 'no' could be an unkind answer that my colleague did not want to give me. I wasn't able to read the context in which the answer was given to me.

**Figure 2.1**  Continuum of high–low-context cultures

Conversely, low-context cultures attach great importance to ownership, being highly territorial, and they are used to creating boundaries with neighbours. Not surprisingly, the responsibility is diffused throughout the system and activism and demonstrations are viewed as the last most desperate act in a series of escalating events. For example, low-context people are more willing to manipulate laws by building the law they want and systematically influencing precedents. In addition, equality in treatment is not afforded, as it depends on the expertise of the lawyer. However, the way business is conducted is also different. German managers, for instance, are not satisfied with their job up to the point at which they know everything about consumers in order to match their needs and requests perfectly. They are monochronic-time oriented and their daily life is dictated by schedules and planned in detail from the beginning to the end. This is usually linked to the Western approach of time management where delays, last-minute changes or cancellations are frowned on. Doing one thing at a time, they tend to reduce the polychronic tendencies in order not to waste time by organizing events in all their aspects and giving priority to meeting dates.

According to Hall (1981), one of the functions of culture is to facilitate selection of information to which people are exposed, protecting the nervous system from information overload: the screening function. In this sense culture designates what the people pay attention to and what they ignore.

Edward Hall (1984) also divides cultures by their organization of time. Therefore, there are Monochronic and Polychronic cultures. Monochronic cultures are considered low-context, while Polychronic are considered high-context. In Monochronic cultures, such as German, North European, US American, events are scheduled as separate items, one thing at a time, and a person does not begin a new activity before finishing the previous one. The rule to be followed is that actions should be planned accurately and efficiently. By scheduling, they compartmentalize, making it possible to concentrate on one thing at a time, but also reducing the importance of the context. Scheduling selects what will and what will not be perceived and attended to. What gets scheduled constitutes a system for getting priorities for both people and functions. In Polychronic cultures, such as Mediterranean, Asian, or South American, people are involved in several things at once. The actions are continuously adapted to the emerging situation following the rule of flexibility. It doesn't matter if you do not complete an action whenever you judge it to be more important to do something else. Polychronic cultures are oriented to people. If you value people, you must hear them out and you cannot cut them off simply because of a schedule. On the other hand, Monochronic cultures are oriented to tasks, schedules and procedures. Both M-time and P-time have strengths as well as weaknesses. In a very dynamic environment Polychronic cultures are able to face change and adapt behaviour and tasks to the situation, while Monochronic cultures are quite rigid and unable to adapt easily to change. On the other hand, Monochronic behaviour is more efficient in accomplishing tasks in a relatively stable environment.

There are some cultures that can be both Monochronic and Polychronic in different social situations. Some German students in an international class I taught told me they were surprised by the behaviour of their Italian mates, who were absolutely Monochronic concerning lessons and university duties, but totally Polychronic during their free time when they met outside the university. The perception of time changed according to the social situation and the need for scheduling. The Italian students considered that during their free time they should change their approach to time and be very flexible (not accurate) in respecting any scheduled agreement, while the German students kept their cultural Monochronic attitude in any situation.

For example, the Chinese concept of time, even if not schedule or result oriented, is characterized by a keen sense of the value of time. In fact, the Chinese frequently thank other people for their time and consider it precious; on the other hand, they expect a liberal amount of time to be allocated for the repeated consideration of details and for the careful nurturing of personal relationships. According to the Chinese point of view, the reason they require time is to attain a degree of closeness that is great enough to build common trust and intent to better deal with future relationships. The time concept is of fundamental importance and has to be carefully considered by all foreign companies aiming to enter the Chinese market, with new or existing products.

In a business situation a Monochronic salesperson establishes quick customer relationships because they tend to think in short time intervals, considering the process as a relationship through business, whereas in a Polychronic culture the salesperson tends to create a long-term personal relationship with the customer, considering the process as business through a relationship. Also working time is affected by culture: M-time is perfectly scheduled so working time has a clear beginning and a clear end, while P-time leads to an extension of official working time. Frequently in Polychronic cultures workers and managers are asked to give extra time, while this is quite rare in Monochronic cultures.

Time perception defines the rhythm of life in every culture; what is long-lasting and what is not is a relative perception that a culture shapes in different situations:

- *waiting*: the perception of time during the period of waiting for service or a product (in a queue, at the cashier, etc.);
- *concentration*: the level of concentration culturally required by a certain activity (reducing the time perception);
- *age*: time has a different perception at different ages;
- *mood and emotions*: mood changes the perception of time; emotions give different value to time; different cultures are exposed to emotions differently.

Time can also be conceived as linear or circular. The linear time concept causes people to see time as linear and segmented like a road or a ribbon extending forward into the future or backward to the past. It is also tangible: people speak of time as 'being saved, spent, wasted, lost, made up, accelerated, slowed down, crawling and running out'. These metaphors should be taken very seriously as they express the way in which time is used as a measuring instrument and a means of controlling human behaviour by setting deadlines or objectives. The circular time concept emphasizes cyclical and repetitive aspects of time: seasons and rhythms. In these cultures, the adaptation of humans to time is seen as a viable alternative; it is not perceived as racing to a linear future, but as coming around again in a circle where the same opportunities, risks and dangers will represent themselves in other life's periods.

The second pillar of the Hall model is what he calls Proxemic (1969). It is the cultural perception of space and its management. The space between people, the space of conversation, the space of homes and the sense of privacy change across cultures. The perception of private space and its invasion is very narrow in some cultures, for example in German and British cultures, and much less in others, such as in the United States, where the definition of private space provides much clearer signals, in accordance with a low-context culture. This is represented for example by an open or closed door. A closed door represents the desire for privacy, while in Europe a closed door simply delimits the relevant space, while it is the distance between people that identifies the condition of privacy. In Chinese culture it is difficult to think of a private space; the living conditions are very collectivist and crowded, but there is a distance of respect between people as they relate to each other. It is not considered polite or respectful to touch someone, while in Mediterranean countries not touching someone is a sign of coldness and detachment.

In Mediterranean countries, people spend a lot of time outside the home in open spaces, owing to the ways of socialization, which takes place outside the home, where space is generally reduced, compared to the Nordic countries and the USA. This is obviously also affected by climate. The outdoor stalls of public places, places of strong sociality, are very frequent in Mediterranean countries compared to Nordic ones. The different perception of space is also seen in the choice of cars. This happens in Europe where cars are smaller than in the US, both for the perception of minimum personal space, and for a different urban structure, with much smaller spaces. In Europe the organization of urban space includes pedestrian areas, where the spatial relationship between people is contiguous, while in the USA it is preferred to dedicate a lot of space to cars (roads, parking lots, etc.) where the contiguity between people is separated. Overall, therefore, there are more public spaces in Mediterranean countries for relationships between people, and more private spaces in Northern Europe and the USA.

Proxemics defines the space in shops, which are medium-large and small in Europe and Japan, and always large in the USA.

**Figure 2.2**    Italian Renaissance garden

The available space increases the availability for crowding and distance. The result is a twofold idea of the concept of individualism in southern and northern Europe and the United States. If it is believed that these cultures, compared to oriental ones, have a greater individualism, as we will see later in Hofstede's model (2001), this does not mean the same thing. There is a Mediterranean individualism, related to the expression of one's individuality, that takes shape in people's houses, which are all very different from each other, in the personalized and differentiated products, in the lifestyles, and in the local subcultures, which stem from historical-cultural reasons in particular in Italy, but not exclusively. There is an individualism of achievement and a search for personal success, of the Protestant ethic (Weber, 2010) typical of Northern Europe and the USA. The concept of individualism must therefore be seen in the context of differences of manifestations. Hofstede therefore makes it a single concept that does not fully explain the cultural differences it implies.

The idea of space is very different in European culture compared to that of the Far East. In particular, the perception of emptiness in Europe is given by the absence of physical elements (objects or living beings), while emptiness in Japan is perceived as full of space. To get an idea of the different perceptions of space, just think of an Italian Renaissance garden or a Japanese Zen garden (Figures 2.2 and 2.3).

In Mediterranean cultures, people do not normally feel comfortable being alone. The presence of other family members or friends is necessary for feelings of relaxation and conviviality; it is an element of serenity. In this we understand how the COVID-19 pandemic has affected in a different way, all other conditions being equal, both in terms of spread of the virus and in terms of social suffering, the populations of Southern Europe compared to those of the North, who are more accustomed to managing loneliness.

Human beings' sense of space is a synthesis of many sensory inputs: visual, auditory, kinaesthetic, olfactory, and thermal. So, people living in different cultures live in different sensory worlds.

The contextual effects on culture and consumption can be enlarged to include other aspects, such as the affluence of a society, level of education, degree of urbanization, climate, or even the polit-

**Figure 2.3**    Japanese Zen garden

ical system. Moreover, a number of contextual factors can be identified as influencers of consumer behaviour. These include income, economic growth, population, health and religion. Douglas and Craig (2009) include ecological context, societal affluence and religion as three main contextual factors to be taken in account.

The *Ecological* context encompasses physical factors such as climate, terrain, navigable waterways, access to the sea, as well as biotic factors such as the nature of vegetation and animal life, arable land, water availability, minerals, and other resources (for food and lodgings). They heavily influence the production of goods and the purchasing behaviour of people. The *Affluence* of a society has a powerful impact on culture and on mediating its role in consumer behaviour. GDP per capita has been found to be correlated with national value orientation and with the individualism–collectivism factor. Social, economic and political institutions also play an important role in forming cultural patterns and behaviour. For example, in some Western societies there are social hierarchies and social class structures, formed by a combination of occupation, wealth and birth, or there is a caste system, as in India. The *Religious* context has a strong influence on cultural values and consumption patterns; some religions, such as Islam, Judaism and Hinduism, are very normative in prescribing rules for consumption behaviour, regarding food, beverages and dress.

Sometimes contextual factors act unpredictably as some of them prevail in a way that is accelerated by unforeseen events, resulting in surprising and unexpected behaviour, precisely because the importance of one factor was less evident than others. For example, the COVID-19 pandemic led to a completely unpredictable change in shopping behaviour due to a sudden prevalence of the 'health' factor, which no study had been able to predict or anticipate before the change took place.

According to Adair et al. (2009) the fundamental elements of Hall's concept of culture as communication can be distilled into four main components. First, *communication style*, which is about which messages are sent directly or indirectly and the extent to which people rely on explicit or implicit meaning. Second, *relationship context*, which is about the degree to which people attend to the nature and strength of a relationship and how the relationship influences communication and interaction patterns. Third, *time context*: monochronic and polychronic alternatives identify the way in which people attend to time and how time influences their communication and social interaction. Fourth, *space context*, relates to the degree to which people use space, called proxemics, in social interaction. Therefore, the low–high context is not just about whether we say or do not say things but it also refers to how we use different kinds of information in our environment when we communicate and interact with others.

## 2.2 GEERT HOFSTEDE: SIX DIMENSIONS OF NATIONAL CULTURE

Geert Hofstede (2001; 2011) developed a model of six dimensions of national culture for 75 countries that helps to explain basic value differences. Although the model was developed to explain differences in work-related values, over time it has increasingly been used for comparative cross-cultural studies and provides useful explanations of cross-cultural differences in consumer behaviour.

The research project which forms the basis of Hofstede's model started in 1966 for IBM, with the aim of discovering the causes of different behaviours exhibited by international managers coming from different countries and cultures, even if they shared a strong common company culture. These different behaviours created misunderstandings and mistrust in several relationships and communications. Therefore, IBM developed this international research in order to better understand the situation. Hofstede and other colleagues collected a huge amount of data (88 000 employees in 72 countries) concerning the different cultures and they formed the basis for the model. The data has been updated every year since.

Hofstede's six culture dimensions are (see Figure 2.4):

1. Power Distance, related to the different solutions to the basic problem of human inequality.
2. Uncertainty Avoidance, related to the level of stress in a society in the face of an unknown future.
3. Individualism versus Collectivism, related to the integration of individuals into primary groups.
4. Masculinity versus Femininity, related to the division of emotional roles between women and men.
5. Long-Term versus Short-Term Orientation, related to the choice of focus for people's efforts: the future or the present and past.
6. Indulgence versus Restraint, related to the gratification versus control of basic human desires related to enjoying life.

*Power distance* influences the way people accept and give authority. In a high power distance culture, such as an Asian culture, everyone has his or her rightful place in a social hierarchy. Inequality can occur in a variety of areas: (a) physical and mental characteristics; (b) social status and prestige; (c) wealth; (d) power; and (e) laws, rights and rules.

It investigates how people perceive and manage the inequality and distance between bosses and subordinates. Indeed, the index has been measured through employees' interviews on (a) how they perceive the boss's decision making and the extent to which it can be evaluated either as a paternalistic or a consolatory approach and (b) the frequency of feelings of fairness in the expression of disagreement with their managers.

In China, in particular, this is justified by a Confucius rule in society according to which there are strong dependency relationships between 'ruler and subject, father and son, elder and younger brother, husband and wife', and even between friends. This represents inequality (more versus less), but defined from below, not from above. It suggests that a society's level of inequality is endorsed by the followers as much as by the leaders. All societies are unequal, but some are more unequal than others. In societies where the Power Distance Index (PDI) is low, privileges and status symbols are frowned upon, so the people tend towards understatement in buying products and brands with a strong status value, while where PDI is high, privileges and status symbols are expected and popular. The PDI has strong connections with organizational, political, and family aspects of the culture. Low PDI leads to flat organizational pyramids, a small proportion of supervisory personnel, good champions for innovations, manual work having the same status as clerical work, and subordinates expecting to be consulted. On the other hand, in countries having high PDI there are tall organizational pyramids, where managers rely on formal rules, subordinates expect to be told, innovations need good hierarchical support, and information is constrained by hierarchy.

*Uncertainty Avoidance* deals with a society's tolerance of ambiguity. It indicates to what extent a culture programmes its members to feel either uncomfortable or comfortable in unstructured situations. Uncertainty avoiding cultures try to minimize the possibility of such situations by strict behavioural codes, laws and rules, and disapproval of deviant opinions. Research has shown that people in uncertainty avoiding countries are also more emotional and motivated by inner nervous energy. Conversely, uncertainty accepting cultures are more tolerant of opinions that are different from what they are used to; they try to have fewer rules, and on a philosophical and religious level they are empiricist, relativist and allow different currents to flow side by side. People within these cultures are more phlegmatic and contemplative, and not expected by their environment to express emotions. Extreme uncertainty creates intolerable anxiety, and society has developed ways to cope with it. These ways belong to *technology* (includes all human artefacts), *law* (all formal and informal rules that guide social behaviour), and *religion* (all revealed knowledge of the unknown). Uncertainty can create authoritarian situations, because of the need to escape from freedom. Actually, freedom implies the responsibility to decide and uncertainty in the behaviour of oneself and of others. Actually, strict rules reduce uncertainty as well as reducing freedom. Cultures having a low Uncertainty Avoidance Index (UAI) present low brand loyalty, and attraction towards new and innovative products. In high UAI countries there is belief in specialists and expertise (this can be important in choosing testimonials for advertising), fear of new products, and strong brand loyalty.

*Individualism* on the one side versus its opposite number, *Collectivism*, as a societal, not an individual characteristic, is the degree to which people in a society are integrated into groups. Collectivism does not mean a negation of the individuals' well-being or interest; it is simply assumed that maintaining the group's well-being is the best guarantee for the individual. On the individualist side we find cultures in which the ties between individuals are loose: everyone is expected to look after him/herself and his/her immediate family. On the collectivist side we find cultures in which people from birth onwards are integrated into strong, cohesive in-groups, often extended families (with uncles, aunts and grandparents) that continue protecting them in exchange for unquestioning loyalty, and oppose other in-groups. Hall's distinction between high and low-context cultures can be considered to be an aspect of collectivism versus individualism (Gudykunst et al., 1988). High-context communication fits the collectivistic society, and low-context communication is typical of the individualistic society. People living in countries having a low Individualism index (IDV) accept living in apartments or flats, with human companions, use social networks and social media as their main source of information, and rely on social and family/friends networks, whereas people in a high IDV culture live in detached houses with private gardens, with cats and/or dogs, prefer security with home and life insurance, and engage in do-it-yourself for jobs around the house.

*Masculinity* versus its opposite, *Femininity*, again as a societal, not as an individual characteristic, refers to the distribution of values between the genders, which is another fundamental issue for any society, to which a range of solutions can be found. Men's values from one country to another contain a dimension from very assertive and competitive and are maximally different from women's values, which are modest and caring. Masculine societies have a preference for achievement, heroism, assertiveness and material rewards for success. For them, advancement, earnings, training, and up-to-datedness are important. On the other hand, feminine societies stand for a preference for cooperation, caring for the weak and quality of life, where a friendly atmosphere, cooperation, and a secure position are important. The assertive pole has been called 'masculine' and the modest, caring pole 'feminine'. The women in feminine countries have the same modest, caring values as the men; in the masculine countries they are somewhat assertive and competitive, but not as much as the men, so that these countries exhibit a gap between men's values and women's values. In feminine cultures the gender roles tend to overlap, while in masculine societies they tend to be separated. In countries with a low masculinity index (MAS), buying decisions and shopping are shared between partners, homemade products are quite popular, vacations are taken in motor homes, and there is less confidence in advertising. In cultures with a high MAS, purchase decisions are dominated by showing off, there is more appeal in foreign goods, and engine power and dimensions of cars are important.

*Long-Term Orientation* stands for the fostering of virtues oriented towards future rewards, in particular, perseverance and thrift, and having a sense of shame. It refers to the extent to which a culture programmes its members to accept delayed gratification of their material, social and emotional needs. Its opposite pole, *Short-Term Orientation*, stands for the fostering of virtues related to the past and the present, in particular, respect for tradition, personal steadiness and stability, and preservation of 'face' and fulfilling social obligations. Actually, this last definition is a little bit controversial because in China (with very high long-term orientation) preservation of 'face' and fulfilling social obligations are very important, as well as respect for tradition. In societies with a long-term orientation (LTO) the control systems in managerial analysis are short-term oriented. The 'bottom line' (results of past month, quarter, or year) is a major concern. This situation is supported by 'rational' reasons, but the perception of what is considered rational is heavily affected by the culture. In societies characterized by low LTO, a small amount of income is saved, investment concerns mutual funds, and immediate gratification of needs is expected. In culture having a high LTO, a large part of income is saved, the gifts given to children focus on their education and finance, in business the building of long-term relationships and market position is important, and investment in real estate is preferred.

*Indulgence* versus *Restraint* focuses on aspects not covered by the other five dimensions but is known from the literature on 'happiness research'. Indulgence stands for a society that allows relatively free gratification of basic and natural human desires related to enjoying life and having fun. In countries with a high Indulgence score (IRI), there is a higher percentage of people declaring themselves very happy, there is a perception of personal life control, higher birth rates in countries with an educated population, and more people actively involved in sport. In societies with a low IRI, lower importance is attached to leisure, people are less likely to remember positive emotions, there is a lower birth rate in countries with an educated population, fewer obese people, and stricter sexual norms in wealthy countries. These conditions, both in high and low IRI countries, are important for marketing communication strategies.

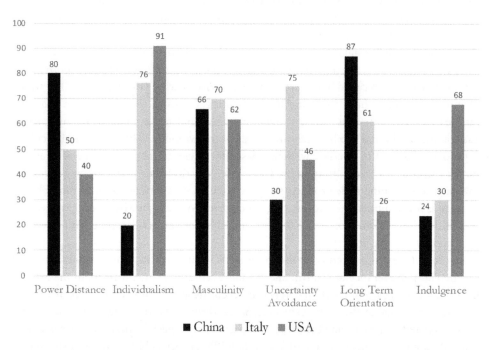

**Figure 2.4**    Example of country comparison based on Hofstede's six factors

Hofstede (2001) argues that there are three reasons national culture is crucial for understanding managerial actions. First, for its political importance: nations organize formal and informal institutional and legal systems. Second, nations are important sociologically, as a point of identification for their citizens. Third, and most important for Hofstede, national culture is important psychologically because it is imprinting in our brains as collective programming and conditions us to interpret situations and find solutions according to inherited cultural schemes.

The Hofstede model was and is hugely popular among the scholars as well as the practitioners of business management. It has been cited more than 7000 times in academic journals, and Hofstede's cultural indices have been used in over 600 empirical studies (based on Taras and Steel, 2009). Its success could be due to the great amount of data collected and continuously updated, to its clear and simple structure, and to its easy comprehension and easy use in developing strategies and actions in human resource marketing. More important than the scale of the study, quite attractive for practical applications in business management, especially for HRM, was the framework it introduced. Based on the survey data, Hofstede put forth a new and parsimonious conceptualization of culture, accompanied by measurements and indexes. The remarkable contribution of Geert Hofstede includes conceptualizing culture as a national-level construct capturing a set of shared values and measuring culture empirically through self-reports of value statements. For managers and marketers this approach has proven fruitful (Adair et al., 2009).

However, several criticisms have been made by scholars. McSweeney (2002) argued that the limited characterization of culture in Hofstede's work, its confinement within the territory of states, and its methodological flaws mean that it is a restricter, not an enhancer of understanding particularities. The identification claims are fundamentally flawed and the attribution of national-level actions/institutions to national cultures is an easy but impoverishing move. If the aim is understanding, then we need to know more about the richness and diversity of national practices and institutions – rather than merely assuming their 'uniformity' and that they have an already known national cultural cause. Both outside and within the management disciplines there are rich considerations of the characteristics of individuals, organizations, societies, nations and regions. Simplistic dichotomous explanation must be avoided, and classificatory systems, such as global–local, individualistic–collectivistic, masculine–feminine, foreign–domestic, vertical–horizontal, Western–Eastern and so on must be used with some caution (Askegaard et al., 2009). They are easy to be used, simplifying the complex reality, but they can also distort it.

We do not intend to argue that using a few dimensions provides a complete description of cross-cultural differences. However, we argue that Hofstede's framework constitutes a simple, practical and usable shortcut to the integration of culture into studies. In spite of some criticisms to his dimensions, the argument that they capture cross-country differences has received extensive support (Lynn and Gelb, 1996). Thus, there is wide support in the literature for the use of this conceptualization and operationalization of culture. Measuring these dimensions at the individual level should constitute an important contribution to cross-cultural research. While operationalizing culture remains a challenge, our multi-method approach constitutes a contribution towards capturing this elusive concept.

## 2.3  SHALOM SCHWARTZ: VALUES AND CULTURE

Shalom Schwartz (2012) develops the concept of values considering that they are beliefs that become infused with feelings once activated. They refer to desirable goals that stimulate actions. They become standards or criteria, guiding the selection and/or assessment of actions, people and events. Values are classified by importance through the creation of a set of value priorities that characterize them as individuals. Values transcend determined activities and situations, making them different from norms and attitudes connotative of each person. For instance, integrity and honesty are values important in various circumstances such as school, work and family. Therefore, any behaviour or attitude has implications for several values relevant in the context and important to the actor.

Schwartz describes six implicit main characteristics:

- *Values are beliefs* linked to affect. When values are activated they become instilled with feeling.
- *Values refer to desirable goals* motivating action. People are motivated to pursue what they consider to be important values, for example social order, justice and helpfulness.
- *Values transcend specific actions and situations.* In the workplace or in the school, in business and in politics, obedience and honesty values may be relevant.
- *Values serve as standards or criteria.* They lead the evaluation and selection of strategies, actions, people and events.
- *Values are ordered by importance.* Values form an ordered system of priorities that characterize people as individuals.
- *The relative importance of multiple values guides action.* Any attitude or behaviour typically has implications for more than one value.

Schwartz (1992, 2006) defines ten values in terms of the goals they express. They are self-direction, stimulation, hedonism, achievement, power, security, conformity, tradition, benevolence and universalism.

In particular, *self-direction* defines the goals of independent thought and the actions of choosing, creating and exploring. The values contained in it are creativity, freedom, independence and curiosity. *Stimulation* concerns excitement, novelty, and challenge in life. Its values come from the need to maintain an optimal and positive level of activation. *Hedonism* concerns pleasure or sensuous gratification, enjoying life, and self-indulgence. *Achievement* refers to personal success through demonstrating competence according to social standards and expectations. *Power* is the social status of prestige control and dominance over people and resources. It is based on authority, wealth, and social power. *Security* is composed of safety, harmony, and stability of society and relationships. *Conformity* relates to restraint of actions, inclinations, and impulses that may upset or harm others and violate social norms. *Tradition* aims to promote respect, commitment, and acceptance of the customs and ideas provided by a culture. Tradition and conformity share the goal of subordinating the self to socially imposed expectations, immutable from the past. *Benevolence* preserves and enhances the welfare of those persons with whom one is in frequent personal contact and a relationship. It derives from the basic requirement for smooth group functioning. Benevolence and conformity both promote cooperation and support social relations. *Universalism* values understanding, appreciation, tolerance, and protection for the welfare of all people and for nature. This contrasts with the in-group focus of benevolence values. Universalism combines an open mind, social justice, equality, a world at peace, a world of beauty, unity with nature, wisdom, and protection of the environment.

Although the theory distinguishes ten values, it postulates that, at a more basic level, values form a continuum of related motivations. This continuum gives rise to a circular structure. Schwartz's studies have assessed the theory with data from hundred of samples in 82 countries around the world. The samples include highly diverse geographic, cultural, linguistic, religious, age, and occupational groups, with representative national samples from 37 countries. In these analyses the opposition of self-transcendence (universalism, benevolence) to self-enhancement (achievement, power) and of openness to change to conservation values is universally present (Figure 2.5).

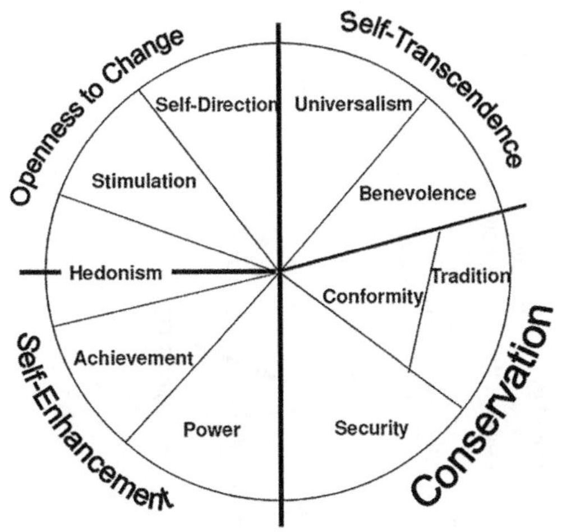

*Source:* Schwartz (2012).

**Figure 2.5** Theoretical model of relations among ten motivational types of value

Schwartz (2009) says that the prevailing values emphasized in a society may be the most central feature of culture. In this view, culture is outside the individual. It is not located in the minds and actions of individual people. Rather, it refers to the pressure to which individuals are exposed by virtue of living in a particular social system. He identified seven dimensions, starting from his research about values: two kinds of autonomy, embeddedness, egalitarianism, hierarchy, harmony, and mastery. First, he defined the nature of the relation and boundaries between the person and the group. The polar location on this cultural dimension is called *autonomy* vs. *embeddedness*. In autonomy cultures, people are encouraged to express their own preferences, ideas, feelings and abilities. There are two types of autonomy: *intellectual* and *affective* autonomy. The first encourages people to pursue their own ideas independently. The second encourages people to pursue positive experience affectively, including pleasure, and an exciting and varied life. In cultures dominated by embeddedness, people are considered to be embedded in the community. The meaning of life is expected to be developed through social relationships, identifying with the group, and participating in its shared way of life. The dimension of *egalitarianism* seeks to induce people to recognize one another as moral equals who share basic interests as human beings. Cultural *hierarchy* relies on hierarchical systems of ascribed roles. It defines the unequal distribution of power (Hofstede, 2001), roles and resources. *Harmony* emphasizes fitting into the social and natural world in order to appreciate and accept rather than to change, direct or exploit; as for example a world at peace, unity with nature, and protecting the environment. *Mastery* encourages active self-assertion in order to master, direct and change the natural and social environment to attain goals concerning ambition, success and competence.

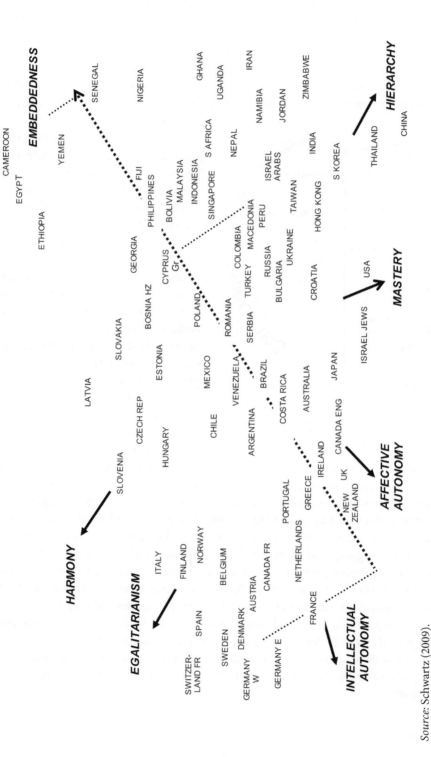

*Source*: Schwartz (2009).

**Figure 2.6**　Schwartz's map of cultures

Considering some examples, culture in Denmark emphasizes harmony, intellectual autonomy, and egalitarianism, while it is low in embeddedness and very low in mastery and hierarchy. In contrast, in Jordan, mastery, embeddedness and hierarchy are highly emphasized. Reading the map (Figure 2.6), eight cultural areas can be identified: West Europe, English-speaking countries, Latin America, East Central and Balkan Europe, Orthodox East Europe, South Asia, Confucian area, and Africa and Middle East. Obviously various countries present a different position, meaning that their profile can be closer to or further from the reference dimensions. For example, Italy is closer to harmony than Germany, and Greece is closer to autonomy than Belgium. In particular, according to Schwartz (2009), West European culture is the highest in egalitarianism, intellectual autonomy and harmony, and the lowest in hierarchy and embeddedness. The English-speaking culture is high in affective autonomy and mastery and low in harmony and embeddedness. American culture differs from the others by emphasizing mastery and hierarchy. The Confucian culture is pragmatic, entrepreneurial, but combines an emphasis on hierarchy and mastery with a rejection of egalitarianism and harmony. In African and Middle East cultures, meaning in life is based on social relationships and protecting the group by mean of embeddedness rather than individuality and autonomy. South Asian cultures emphasize fulfilling one's obligations in a hierarchical system. East-Central and Baltic Europe differs from East and Balkan Europe; the former is somewhat higher in harmony and intellectual autonomy and lower in hierarchy, while the latter is more conservative and in-group oriented, therefore lower in egalitarianism and autonomy. The culture of the Latin American region is close to the worldwide average in all seven orientations. It is higher in hierarchy and embeddedness compared to Europe, but it is lower if compared to African and Asian cultures.

At one extreme, embeddedness-oriented cultures are based on the idea that the human being is embedded in collectivity, finding the meaning of life through social relationships and through the sharing of his/her life with others. At the other extreme, autonomy-oriented cultures consider the human being as an autonomous entity who seeks to express his/her attributes and finds meaning in his/her uniqueness. Autonomous-oriented cultures are affective, that is, 'A cultural emphasis on the desirability of individuals independently pursuing affectively positive experience (pleasure, exciting life, varied life)' or intellectual, that is, 'A cultural emphasis on the desirability of individuals independently pursuing their own ideas and intellectual directions (curiosity, broadmindedness, creativity)' (Roe and Ester, 1999).

It can be understood how cultures referring to embeddedness are keen to buy considering the social value of the products and social respect, while, on the other hand, in cultures where autonomy is high there is less brand loyalty and more individualism in purchases.

## 2.4 RICHARD LEWIS: TRI-PARTITE MODEL

Lewis (2010) examined the cultural characteristics of 85 nation-states on six continents. He highlights the numerous layers within most national cultures: regional, professional, generational, educational, and those deriving from different religions, genders and social class. The question regards the way in which two types of culture, the national one shared in society and the corporate one, created by an organization or a company, can relate to each other and which kind of reciprocal influence they activate. National culture is a blueprint for survival of a nation. Corporations and other commercial organizations are interested in, and strive for, survival, even prosperity. They may achieve this by aligning the corporate culture with that of the country, or they may not do this, suggesting a new cultural approach that will create a cultural market innovation partially promoted by the company, and partially imposed by the national culture.

A corporate culture character is formed with several main components:

- *nation-state traits*, which are usually influential at the beginning of the story of the company;
- *historical factors*, considering in which historical period it has been established;
- *founder personality*, in the extent to which the corporate culture reflects their image;
- *regional characteristics*, concerning the national subculture in which the company is situated;
- *religion*, which lays down rules for the behaviour of each community, regarding how to conduct business.

Including masculine and feminine, as well as individualism and collectivism characteristics described by Hofstede (2001), Lewis developed a tri-partite model about national cultural types. It has three cultural poles (Figure 2.7): linear-active, multi-active and reactive (Lewis, 2010).

*Linear-active* people (Hammerich and Lewis, 2013) tend to be task-oriented, highly organized planners; they do one thing at a time. They prefer direct discussion, depending on facts they obtain from reliable sources. Speech is for information exchange, and conversations consist of taking turns in talking and listening. Linear-actives do not fear confrontation,

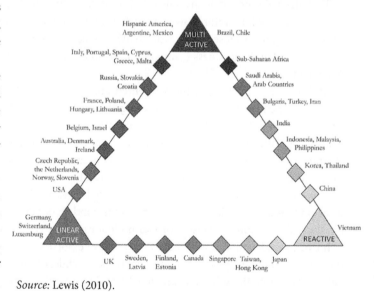

*Source:* Lewis (2010).

**Figure 2.7**     The Lewis model of different cultures

following logic rather than emotion. Linear-actives believe that good products make their own way and sometimes fail to see that sales are based on relationships in many parts of the world. The term 'linear-active' refers to cultures which emphasize 'linear' qualities such as punctuality, step-by-step planning, single-mindedness, observation of deadlines, quick response to written communication and completion of action chains. They are very active in supporting this goal with an elaborated system of strategies embedded in a complex texture of processes.

*Multi-active* people are emotional, loquacious and impulsive. They attach great importance to family, feelings, relationships, and people in general, to compassion and human warmth. They like to do many things at once and are poor followers of agendas. Conversation is roundabout and animated as everyone tries to speak and listen at the same time. In business, relationships and connections are very important. They prefer face-to-face communication, information obtained directly from people and trade in rumours. Although they have limited respect for authority in general, they nevertheless accept their place in their own social hierarchy. Multi-actives are often flexible and frequently change their plans, which in themselves are not as detailed as those of linear-actives. Improvisation and handling unexpected events are strong points. In business they use charisma and rhetoric and negotiate truth. They are diplomatic and tactful. The majority of people in the world belong to this category.

In a *Reactive* culture people are receptive and good listeners. Reactive describes a psychological stance of the Asian mindset and intention. Reactive listeners exercise their ability to adapt to linear-active and multi-active people. For example, the Japanese stress their qualities of punctuality, factuality and planning when dealing with the Germans, while they adopt a more flexible, people-oriented approach, cultivating friendship, when confronted with multi-active Spaniards or Italians. When negotiating, reactive cultures ask others to speak first. By speaking second, they are able to modify the variance between their opinion and that of the other side. They are not passive (the opposite of proactive), but aim to avoid possible pseudo-conflicts due to different degrees of self-assertion. In a reactive culture the preferred mode of communication is *monologue*–pause–reflection–monologue, while in linear-active and multi-active cultures the communication mode is dialogue. Reactive people tolerate silence and consider it a very meaningful and refined part of the discourse.

Linear-active, multi-active and reactive people live in their different worlds. In order for relationships to be harmonious and effective a certain amount of congruity is to be required. Globalization as a business concept has been developed in the United States, a linear-active culture. The business theories coming from that concept are heavily affected by that culture. But multi-active and reactive cultures (Italians, Arabs, Japanese, Chinese, French, etc.) do business in a different way. Therefore, it is extremely important to be able to understand and adapt business modes to the different type of culture you are facing in doing business.

The new economic geography indicates routes to the East, not only because of the rapid growth of China in the first part of the twenty-first century, but also because of the traditional importance of Japan and Korea and the new development of Vietnam. This new balance modifies the dominance of the linear-active culture as the business reference culture. It is increasingly necessary to acquire a multi-polar business culture in a world in constant movement from West to East, and in the future probably also from North to South. Since the world is a globe, the movement is circular, not linear, and therefore endless.

Unfortunately, all cultures are to some extent ethnocentric, viewing their worldview as normal and that of others as inaccurate. Each culture has a list of qualities that it considers positive and that other cultures consider wrong and inaccurate. So what one culture considers positive can be perceived as negative by another culture. Lewis (2010) and Hammerich and Lewis (2013) identify a list of rules for dealing with reactive and multi-active cultures, considering the views of linear-active business (Washington Consensus). In reality, linear business people used to ask others to adapt to them, and so now they should make the main effort, discovering that the world is not just bizarre, but culturally different.

Lewis's suggestions can be used as examples concerning how linear-active business people see and judge other cultures, too. In particular, referring to reactive culture, he suggests the following: speech is to promote harmony, good listening is important, never interrupt, never confront, never disagree openly, never cause anyone to lose face, suggestions – especially criticism – must be indirect, be ambiguous to a certain extent, so as to leave options open, prioritize diplomacy over truth, utilize networks, observe hierarchy and power relationships. Referring to multi-active culture, he suggests the following: speech is for opinion, not only for information exchange, let the people talk at length and then replay fully, be prepared to discuss several things at once, be prepared for several people talking at once, display feelings and emotions, what you consider truth is flexible and situational, be diplomatic rather than direct, socialize enthusiastically, think aloud, seek and give favours with key people, body language and tactility are acceptable, reputation is as important as profit, accept unpunctuality, remain relationship oriented.

## 2.5   THE GLOBE PROJECT

The GLOBE project (House et al., 2004) is an important research project concerning culture, leadership and organizations, reporting the results of ten years of work around the world, involving many scholars from many countries. GLOBE is an acronym for the Global Leadership and Organizational Behaviour Effectiveness research programme. The project includes 62 countries in all continents, and it is based on nine core cultural dimensions, some of which are similar to Hofstede's factors (2001), while others are different. The cultural dimensions close to Hofstede's model are: *uncertainty avoidance, power distance*, and *collectivism I* and *II*. Collectivism is divided into two parts; collectivism I concerns the degree to which societal institutional practice encourages collective distribution of resources and collective actions. Collectivism II is the degree to which individuals express pride and loyalty in their organizations or families. Different dimensions are: *gender egalitarianism*, the degree to which a society minimizes gender role differences; *assertiveness*, the degree to which individuals or societies are assertive, aggressive and confrontational in relationships; *future orientation*, the degree to which individuals or societies engage in future-oriented behaviours such as planning, investing etc.; *performance orientation*, the degree to which a society encourages its members in performance improvement and excellence; *humane orientation*, the degree to which individuals or societies encourage fair, altruistic, friendly and caring behaviour.

GLOBE analyses which specific leader characteristics are universally endorsed and which of them are culturally rooted in different cultures worldwide. The authors discovered that 29 characteristics are universally shared regarding the idea of leadership, while 35 are specific to different cultural approaches. They identified six different leadership styles:

- Charismatic/Value-Based leadership, positive towards performance orientation, collectivism II, and gender egalitarianism, while negative concerning power distance;
- Team-Oriented leadership, positive towards uncertainty avoidance and collectivism II;

- Participative leadership, positive towards performance orientation, gender egalitarianism, humane orientation, while negative concerning uncertainty avoidance and power distance;
- Humane Oriented leadership, positive towards humane orientation, uncertainty avoidance, and assertiveness;
- Autonomous leadership, positive towards performance orientation, while negative concerning humane orientation and collectivism;
- Self-Protective leadership, positive towards power distance and uncertainty avoidance, while negative towards gender egalitarianism.

The GLOBE project grouped the 62 national cultures into a set of ten regional clusters in order to identify similarities and differences among the societies, to understand the extent to which each cultural cluster is associated with a specific leadership behaviour, and to help manage the complexity of multicultural operations. The ten clusters describe European, American, African, and Asian societies. In particular in Europe the GLOBE project identifies five clusters:

a. *Anglo Cluster*, which includes English-speaking countries in Europe, North America, Africa (South African white sample) and Oceania.
b. *Latin Europe Cluster*, including Italy, Portugal, Spain, France, Switzerland (French and Italian-speaking), and Israel.
c. *Nordic Europe Cluster*, which includes Sweden, Norway, Denmark, Finland and Iceland.
d. *Germanic Europe Cluster*, which includes Germany, the Netherlands, Austria and Switzerland.
e. *Eastern Europe Cluster*, including Hungary, Russia, Kazakhstan, Albania, Poland, Greece, Slovenia and Georgia.

In the Americas, as USA and Canada are included in the Anglo cluster, there is only one cluster remaining, the *Latin American Cluster*, containing all the South and Central American countries plus Mexico. In Africa there are two clusters: the *Middle East Cluster*, including Mauritania, Western Sahara, Morocco, Algeria, Tunisia, Libya and Egypt, and the *Sub-Saharan Africa Cluster*, containing Namibia, Zambia, Zimbabwe, Nigeria and South Africa (black sample). In Asia two clusters have been identified: the *Southern Asia Cluster*, covering Iran, Pakistan, India, Turkmenistan, Balochistan, Afghanistan, and the *Confucian Asia Cluster*, including China, Japan, Taiwan, Singapore and South Korea.

Considering such a cluster division, an observation can be made that the analysis can appear Western centred and rooted in Europe, where the researchers identify five clusters, while in big continents such as Asia and Africa they divided all the countries into just two clusters. The suspicion is that as they are mostly European and Anglo-American, they perceive the differences among European cultures in a very sophisticated way, while they do not perceive the other continents with the same degree of accuracy.

Crossing the nine cultural dimensions and the nine cultural clusters, the GLOBE project gives value content to the clusters (House et al., 2004), as can be seen in Tables 2.1 and 2.2. The first matrix concerns the societal culture practices, while the second concerns the societal culture values.

**Table 2.1** Cultural clusters classified on societal culture practice

| Cultural Dimensions | High-Score Clusters | Mid-Score Clusters |
|---|---|---|
| Performance Orientation | Confucian Asia, Germanic Europe, Anglo | Southern Asia, Sub-Saharan Africa, Latin Europe, Nordic Europe, Middle East |
| Assertiveness | Germanic Europe, Eastern Europe | Sub-Saharan Africa, Latin America, Anglo, Middle East, Confucian Asia, Latin Europe, Southern Asia |
| Future Orientation | Southern Asia, Sub-Saharan Africa | Middle East, Anglo, Nordic Europe, Latin America, Confucian Asia, Eastern Europe |
| Humane Orientation | Southern Asia, Sub-Saharan Africa | Latin American, Anglo, Middle East, Confucian Asia, Nordic Europe, Eastern Europe |
| Collectivism I | Eastern Europe, Nordic Europe | Anglo, Middle East, Confucian Asia, Eastern Europe, Sub-Saharan Africa, Southern Asia |
| Collectivism II | Southern Asia, Middle East, Eastern Europe, Latin American, Confucian Asia | Latin Europe, Sub-Saharan Africa |
| Gender Egalitarianism | Eastern Europe, Nordic Europe | Anglo, Middle East, Confucian Asia, Eastern Europe, Sub-Saharan Africa, Southern Asia, Latin America, Latin Europe, Germanic Europe |
| Power Distance | | Anglo, Middle East, Confucian Asia, Eastern Europe, Sub-Saharan Africa, Southern Asia, Latin America, Latin Europe, Germanic Europe |
| Uncertainty Avoidance | Nordic Europe, Germanic Europe | Anglo, Middle East, Confucian Asia, Sub-Saharan Africa, Southern Asia, Latin Europe |

*Source:* House et al. (2004).

**Table 2.2** Cultural clusters classified on societal culture values

| Cultural Dimensions | High-Score Clusters | Mid-Score Clusters |
|---|---|---|
| Performance Orientation | Latin America | Anglo, Southern Asia, Sub-Saharan Africa, Latin Europe, Nordic Europe, Middle East, Germanic Europe, Eastern Europe |
| Assertiveness | Confucian Asia, Southern Asia | Sub-Saharan Africa, Latin America, Anglo, Middle East, Latin Europe, Southern Asia, Eastern Europe, Nordic Europe |
| Future Orientation | Southern Asia, Sub-Saharan Africa, Latin America, Middle East | Anglo, Nordic Europe, Latin Europe, Confucian Asia, Eastern Europe |
| Humane Orientation | | All 10 clusters |
| Collectivism I | Latin America, Middle East, Southern Asia | Confucian Asia, German Europe, Sub-Saharan Africa, Latin Europe, |
| Collectivism II | Latin American, Anglo | Latin Europe, Sub-Saharan Africa, Southern Asia, Nordic Europe, Middle East, Eastern Europe |

| Cultural Dimensions | High-Score Clusters | Mid-Score Clusters |
| --- | --- | --- |
| Gender Egalitarianism | Germanic Europe, Nordic Europe, Anglo, Latin Europe, Latin America | Eastern Europe, Sub-Saharan Africa |
| Power Distance | Middle East | Anglo, Middle East, Confucian Asia, Eastern Europe, Sub-Saharan Africa, Southern Asia, Nordic Europe, Latin Europe, Germanic Europe |
| Uncertainty Avoidance | Nordic Europe, Germanic Europe | Anglo, Middle East, Confucian Asia, Sub-Saharan Africa, Southern Asia, Latin Europe |

*Source:* House et al. (2004).

The use of regional clusters can be a great help in the selection and training of managers who work in global environments, facilitating managers to acquire the skills necessary for effective leadership in a different cultural environment, especially for expatriates. In reality, the role and number of expatriate managers is shrinking, just as, like a normal life cycle, the number of skilled local managers is constantly growing. However, expatriate managers can be used by a company for limited periods of time, especially in the first period of company establishment in culturally distant markets.

The research also explores another connection to local cultures: the *climatic* clustering of societal cultures (House et al., 2004). This approach is particularly new in the field of management, even if it is quite classic in the anthropologic approach to different cultures. Even Hofstede (1984) identified physical climate as the primary force influencing societal cultures. Unfortunately, he made very limited tests about the linkage between the physical climate and national cultures. Physical climate consists of a set of important variables, such as temperature, humidity, rainfall, altitude and pressure. GLOBE researchers suggest the following major clusters of world climates (Table 2.3): (1) *Tropical humid* climate, high temperatures, plentiful rains, short dry season; (2) *Tropical wet and dry* (savanna) climate, distinct wet and dry seasons, high temperatures varying across months; (3) *Tropical and subtropical desert and steppe* climate, very low rainfall, extreme daily temperature variations; (4) *Subtropical humid* climate, uniform distribution of precipitation throughout the year; (5) *Mediterranean* climate, combination of hot summers and cool, wet winters; (6) *Maritime* climate, significant precipitation through the year, possible storms, low variation of temperature throughout the year; (7) *Continental* climate, summers hot and winters cold, snow, significant yearly and daily variation in weather.

**Table 2.3**  Relation between climatic regions and cultural clusters

| Cultural Cluster | Climatic Cluster |
| --- | --- |
| Eastern Europe | Continental |
| Latin America | Tropical |
| Confucian Asia | Continental |
| Latin Europe | Mediterranean |
| Nordic and Germanic Europe | Maritime |
| Anglo | Maritime |
| Sub-Saharan Africa and Middle East | Desert |
| Southern Asia | Tropical |

According to the GLOBE research, physical climate can influence different socioeconomic behaviours. Other scholars have discussed this topic. Landes (1998) argues that positive physical climate shapes the dimensions of social culture in support of development. In contrast, Hofstede (1984) argues that adverse physical climate shapes the dimensions of social culture that support development. He suggests that colder weather creates survival challenges that lead to technological development, urbanization, mass literacy, and ultimately shape the middle class. My opinion is that the direct connection between climate and economic behaviour could be risky, as well as the direct connection between cultural clusters and climate clusters. The first risky connection could be evaluated as a logical leap: in fact, climate certainly affects culture and culture affects business and managerial behaviour, but it is quite difficult to demonstrate a direct connection (Figure 2.8).

As we have seen, scholars differ in this consideration. As for the second risky cluster connection, it seems quite bizarre to consider Latin America as tropical, from southern Chile to Panama, as well as considering the Anglo cluster as maritime including the United States, Canada and Australia, where there are many different climates. In conclusion, the GLOBE project offers some interesting points of view on the cultural contents of a social culture and offers a useful way to read the world map of

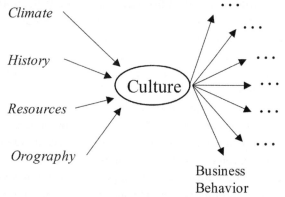

**Figure 2.8**   Influence relationship of climate on business behaviour

cultures. However, it seems centred more on Western countries (Europe plus North America). In my opinion, in some cases, such as in the theory of climate influence, it appears imprecise in forcing the cultural cluster model to adapt to the climate cluster hypothesis, guided and supported above all by a robust, quantitative analysis, perhaps devoid of an equally robust qualitative analysis.

# 3
# An anthropologic approach

Many contemporary cultural anthropologists are still interested in the different ways in which people living in different places act and understand their lives, but they often believe that it is not possible to understand such ways of living by dealing exclusively with the local context. On the other hand, it is believed that local cultures should be analysed in their regional context or even in global political and economic relations.

The anthropologist is often an uninvited guest, who stays for a long time and who, inevitably, establishes links with the people who inhabit and constitute his/her field of research. Anthropology is based on relationships, thriving on relationships between observers and observed, and there is no relationship that, for better or for worse, does not end up involving an individual (Aime, 2008). Going to the field, the anthropologist observes, looks, listens, tastes, touches and smells. His/her knowledge is built first of all on sensory bases, before coming to be translated into theories, models and paradigms.

Cognitive anthropology places context centre stage in its analyses by virtue of its contextual orientation. Cognition is explained through actual behaviour, as it occurs in a specific task context, using two key concepts for the analysis of reasoned behaviour: practical thinking and bricolage (Tadajewski and Wagner-Tsukamoto, 2006). Practical thinking relates to an intellectual, theoretical plane of reasoning and yields practical know-how for problem solving by being based on an application-oriented concept of reasoning, learning and intelligence that proposes that knowledge is acquired in daily life through learning-by-doing, that is, through trial-and-error. Bricolage, on the other hand, relates to a technical, practical plane where knowledge is generated through actual practice and problem-solving behaviour in everyday life. Translating such findings into consumer behaviour would seem to indicate that in order to understand problem solving in the everyday world, the concepts of rational problem solving and the concomitant diagnoses of irrational behaviour need to be re-examined, considering the cultural context. Cognitive anthropology develops a different, yet complementary, understanding of consumer cognition in comparison to a psychological approach.

Social anthropology takes as its objectives both accurate description of context and accurate understanding of how those contexts are interpreted and experienced by participants. It adopts a methodology of ethnographic immersion. This enables the capture of elusive, ambiguous and tacit aspects of research settings. Social anthropology, having taken into account recent developments in post-modern and critical thought, can contribute to the study, practice and teaching of marketing in three categories. First of all, the concept of the symbolic in marketing can be critically elaborated. Second, ethnography can be used to defamiliarize taken-for-granted circumstances and reveal suppressed and alternative possibilities. Third, new or unheard voices and forms of information can be resuscitated and used to sensitize

managerial processes; and cognitive, affective, epistemological, ideological and ethical considerations can be linked in the same framework (Linstead, 1997).

It is not the individual that interests the anthropologist, but rather his being part of a group
of individuals with whom he has affective, sexual, commercial, work, political, etc. relationships. It is these relationships, together with those established with their environment that
become the object of study, those that together define themselves as culture. The anthropological gaze must necessarily be holistic, totalizing, it must take into account the various elements
of a society and a culture in order to be able to analyse even just one. It deals with people and
their behaviour in relation to the cultural, historical, environmental and economic context.
The system of values to which a behaviour deriving from a different culture refers appears
strange and irrational in an ethnocentric view on the part of the observer, but clear and absolutely rational when referred to that system of values.

The anthropologist is specifically trained to study national character, or the differences
which distinguish our national group from another. They should be able to provide measures
for distinguishing the subtle differences among a Swede, a Dane and a Norwegian; or between
a Frenchman and an Englishman; or a Brazilian and an Argentinian. The anthropologist is also
a specialist in the study of subcultures. They would be able, in a city like New York, to differentiate the patterns of living of such disparate but rapidly homogenizing groups as Puerto Ricans,
Afro-Americans, Italo-Americans, Jews, Polish-Americans and Irish-Americans.

A more subtle area of special interest to anthropologists is the silent language of gesture,
posture, food and drink preferences, and other non-verbal cues to behaviour (Hall and Hall,
1959).

There are at least three kinds of situation in which the knowledge of the anthropologist has
been employed in marketing: specific knowledge; awareness of themes of a culture; sensitivity
to taboos.

Considering the first area, for example, a field in which the anthropologist has specific
knowledge that other social scientists are not likely to have, is that of clothing and fashion. In
marketing situations, the anthropologist has often been able to combine his/her special knowledge of the needs of the body for clothing of various kinds at different ages, his/her sensitivity
to what technology makes possible and his/her awareness of fashion. The special knowledge
of the anthropologist has been called into play where there are special sub-cultural groups to
which the marketer wishes to address themself. Anthropologists are the only social scientists
who have systematically studied gift-giving and gift-receiving.

Marketers may unwittingly violate a taboo, whether cultural, religious or political, especially
in selling overseas. Blue, for example, is the colour for mourning in Iran and is not likely to
be favourably received on a commercial product. Green is the nationalist colour of Egypt and
Syria and is frowned on for use in packages. Showing pairs of anything on the Gold Coast of
Africa is disapproved of. White is the colour of mourning in Japan and, therefore, not likely
to be popular on a product. Brown and grey are unacceptable colours in Nicaragua. Purple is
generally disapproved of in most Latin American markets because of its association with death
(Winick, 1961).

It seems at least bizarre to consider management, which is a social science, as a bearer of
values and therefore of universal rationality and behaviour in whatever cultural sphere it acts.

Yet this has been done for decades. As Montesquieu ironically states, if triangles were asked to describe God, they would do so with three sides. The management has basically described its deities mainly with the number of faces of a single culture, that of the United States. With the same number of sides, international markets where there are very different cultures in consumers and organizations have been analysed. The touchstone was often given by the American approach to business, considered as the correct approach to which different cultures should have adapted. There was therefore no reason to develop an anthropological approach.

Anthropological research is based on the inductive method, that is, it starts from observed elements, data, particular facts, and then reaches general considerations. It is a participatory observation. There is a tendency to favour the qualitative method, which allows a series of cultural aspects to be grasped, based on perception, difficult to translate into quantitative data, even if used to complete the process of detecting phenomena.

Even as the world is becoming globalized, many nations have increasingly voiced their claim to 'a right to culture' in international businesses. It is predicted that national culture will be a critical factor affecting economic development, demographic behaviour, and general business policies around the world. Anthropologists' interest in cultural studies grew out of academic purposes but has been extended to business applications as well. The results of anthropological study on culture have been widely applied in various fields of the business world. In the business world, a profound understanding of cultural values in general and specific individual cultural characteristics in particular can lead to greater success in the global market and economy. On the other hand, cultural misunderstandings can be counterproductive for individual development, organizational effectiveness, and profits, because cultural factors influence people's motives, brand comprehension, attitude, and intention to purchase (Tian and Borges, 2012).

The anthropological approach is a very effective way to assess the impact of culture on international marketing.

This is the method that should be used in intercultural analysis. It develops in long visits to hypermarkets, in different points of sale, from luxury ones to street ones, in markets, observing the behaviour of customers, the arrangement of goods, the game of shopping. The prices of goods are negotiated for a long time, building and analysing a rich and complex commercial relationship, a ritual in many cultures, which must end with mutual satisfaction or with a clear refusal.

Using this anthropological approach, I have interviewed many people, university colleagues, entrepreneurs, managers, employees, expatriates, ordinary people, and traders. I went to restaurants, inns, hotels and houses, eating everything I could try. I have visited museums in order to understand the different cultural description of the beauty, the cultural idea of the art; I read novels by local writers, books about the history of nations; I have visited companies and universities, places of power and leisure, I have walked and travelled for a long time, aware of reaching only a very small part of the whole. An untiring curiosity guided me in this adventure. On those visions that remain limited and partial, on this unsolvable insufficiency of elements, yet rich in discoveries, I am trying to describe the dimensions and the characteristics of marketing in different cultures.

## 3.1    GENERAL CONSIDERATIONS

The cross-cultural situation is liquid, *panta rhei*, Heraclitus would say. So, the boundaries should not be drawn with precision, because, beyond the intrinsic difficulty of the operation, they would be denied in a month or a year.

It is dynamic and it is altered over time thorough the interaction with people with different backgrounds. It is composed of a combination of elements that manifest themselves differently in accordance with the country of reference: it is the product of the past and the basis of the future continuously evolving. It depends upon the generation change and on the speed of socioeconomic change. China is a terrific example of rapid change.

The analyses made by Hall, Hofstede, Schwartz, Lewis and the GLOBE researches, as well as the studies of different scholars, present many common points and sometimes a reciprocal influence, as is normal in research fields.

The dichotomy of individualist culture and collectivist culture has had considerable success and insights from many scholars. They argue that in individual cultures the private self as separate and distinct from others is encouraged, whereas attachment to others is strengthened in the collectivist culture (Triandis, 1989). Triandis does not equate culture with nation per se but compares individualism and collectivism of persons from one country to persons from another country. Nevertheless, from a practitioner point of view the national-culture concept has great attraction because it simplifies the complexity, even if it is not accurate. The question is what can be scientifically correct and what can be useful for marketing strategy? It is a diffi-cult balance that should be defined in each specific market situation.

As a result, in Chinese society for example, it is completely natural to recognize hierarchy; moreover, one's social status must be clear so that others can show proper respect. In this sense, famous brands serve that purpose, they allow the owner to affirm his or her social status, otherwise to express respect and honour to a gift recipient. Conversely, in low power distance societies, authority can have a negative connotation; the focus is on equality in rights and opportunity, and children are raised to be independent at a young age, avoiding becom-ing dependent on anybody else. This aspect is also related to the Individualism/collectivism dimension. In individualistic cultures, people want to differentiate themselves from others, they are 'I' conscious and want to express private opinions. In collectivistic cultures, identity is based in the social network to which one belongs, people are 'we' conscious and their identity is based on the social system. Asia, Africa and Latin America are more collectivistic; in Italy, according to data, people in the north appeared to be individualistic, but Italians as a whole are collectivistic (Hoppe, 1992).

The long/short-term orientation is another shared dimension; it is also called 'Confucian work dynamism' (Hofstede and Bond, 1988) because it samples a domain of values formulated by Chinese scholars. The resulting size referred to a long-term versus a short-term orientation in life. Long-term oriented companies tend to focus on achieving long-term results. This type of culture reflects elements of Confucian philosophy: a good person adapts to circumstances and saves and invests for the future. Perseverance, thrift and the pursuit of tranquillity are important goals.

Schwartz's model is less used in quantitative cross-cultural studies than Hofstede's, but it is attractive for marketing research because, through value types, it describes imaginary consumers in terms of abstract preferences such as pleasure, sensual gratification, arousal, novelty, challenge or hedonism. The GLOBE study measures the desired and the desirable of respondents, probing them about organizations and societies in which they live or work as it is and as it should be. Originally, it was concerned with leadership issues, although later the questions were meant to clarify Hofstede's dimensions. The Lewis model refers to Hofstede's and Hall's concepts of cultural factors.

The appropriate number of cultural dimensions has always been a matter of controversy. While some scholars believe that having many dimensions (more than seven) is confusing and not useful (Hofstede, 2006), others believe that we need more cultural dimensions to better explain the variance among different cultures (Triandis, 2001). It is possible to reduce the number of dimensions to just four or five, but we believe that this reduction weakens their explanatory power. At any rate, there may be a trade-off between the simplicity of a classification system and its explanatory power. Maleki and de Jong (2014) propose nine exclusive clusters: Individualism versus Collectivism; Power Distance; Uncertainty Avoidance (UA); Mastery versus Harmony; Traditionalism versus Secularism; Indulgence versus Restraint; Assertiveness versus Tenderness; Gender Egalitarianism; and Collaborativeness.

Cultural dimensions are human constructs. Although they are based on objectively existing phenomena, they are not the phenomena themselves but ways of describing them. One and the same reality can be explained and presented in different ways, through different constructs (Minkov, 2007). The five models just presented overlap in some ways, but they vary with respect to sampling and type of questions used. They are different with respect to the level of analysis – individual versus cultural level – and the dimension structure. However, they all gave predominant emphasis upon characterizing cultures in terms of shared values, shared beliefs, or shared sources of guidance (Smith, 2006).

The five models can therefore be applied for different purposes: the Hall model is more connected to a marketing use, centred on cultural communication; the Hofstede model is considered more useful in predicting behaviour; the Schwartz model is useful for studying both individual-level values and culture-level values; the Lewis model can be used to analyse communication patterns; and the GLOBE value dimensions may prove more useful in predicting the impact of cultural variables on leadership and process organization.

Cultural models are increasingly applied in international business, marketing, and advertising research. These models may lose credibility by improper application as often such studies are not based on sufficient conceptual insight into the various cultural dimensions. New models are quickly embraced without proper analysis of the conceptual content. Frequent mistakes found are applying culture-level data to individuals and confusing the desirable and the desired. Loss of credibility of cultural models is also caused by using the same labels for different concepts (de Mooij, 2013).

# 4
# Case studies part I

**CASE STUDY 4.1    ITALY AND INDIA**
PRIVATE BANK AND SOFTWARE DEPARTMENT

*Anilkumar Dave*

## INTRODUCTION

The first private bank in Italy has its roots in 1886, when its founder (nephew of the Minister of Finance) along with six other brothers and cousins, founded a legal entity in a small town between Turin and Milan to 'carry on trade as the banking discounts, advances, current accounts, buying and selling of securities, etc.', as shown in the deeds. In 1949 the bank changed its name, becoming a *Società per azioni* (limited company) and began a path of steady growth, expanding to more than 300 branches in the first decade of the 2000s under the control of the same family. Over the years the bank has acquired small local institutions in the North East and South Italy and has established operating companies in various businesses such as leasing, consumer finance, asset management companies, and non-life insurance.

Being small sized in the national landscape and run by conscientious management (strongly linked to its birth town), the bank decided in the mid-1990s to move quickly towards digital transition. Considering the cost of the infrastructure and the level of technology efficiency (i.e. connectivity, mobile devices, digital divide), it was indeed a bold move, smarter and faster than other larger competitors. Fortune favours the brave. In less than five years the bank's e-commerce platform was the gold standard and the reference point for all other banks. New and more ambitious projects quickly came up: the shift to the Euro currency, the Y2K upgrade, the e-banking facility. The shortage of software developers and skilled staff such as DB programmers, servers/host managers, and back-end developers was not helping the bank protect itself from competitors' recovery and this was going to become the Achilles heel for a bank that was appointed 'digital pioneer'. Indian programmers' fame reached Italy after their roaring success in North America, UK and Australia: this could have been an interesting opportunity to explore.

# THE CROSS-CULTURAL AND CROSS-TECHNOLOGIES ISSUE

## FALLING IN LOVE, MARRIAGE AND HONEYMOON

Synergy India is a private limited company incorporated on 18 September 1996. It is classified as a non-government company and is registered at the Registrar of Companies, Chennai-India, with the description of its main activity stating 'Data processing including processing or tabulation of all types of data; Provision of such services on (i) an hourly or time-share basis, and (ii) management or operation of data processing facilities of others on a time-sharing basis; on a fee or contract basis'. The speed of programmers and, most of all, their cost compared to Western standards were the best motivation for starting to work together. The first projects were quite simple, and cost-effectiveness was absolutely incomparable to previous rates. Standard requests were sent to Indian Program Managers through relatively simple forms and documents; the source files were sent overnight, and the local (Italian) techies consequently uploaded and updated them. Both the teams were thrilled: from the Indian side the dream of visiting, sooner or later, the country of Ferrari, Venice and pizza, not as a tourist but for professional reasons (i.e. paid by the company); from the Italian side the excitement on interacting (maybe with some language obstacles) with such an exotic country and mimicking what the American and the Brits were doing, bringing such a small bank to the forefront of international collaborations on technology projects.

The expansion of the bank and the race towards e-banking and digital services necessitated increased speed of delivery and a larger workforce on specific projects. Project managers were used to flying over to Italy and India to look after the developers' team and acting as an interface between the two organizations. For a pilot project on a card emission system (aka From-host-to-web) an Italian computer science graduate of Indian origin (second generation) was hired to look after the project development and to interact directly with programmers and Project Managers both on admin and tech issues. The graduate was given a year to develop the project and demonstrate feasibility of such a revolutionary approach. The demo was a success and could have enabled the customer to self-issue a credit card (on the VISA circuit). But it was (like many innovations) too early, and in 1998 the digital infrastructure and connectivity were still at the very beginning of the boom and not yet accessible to the mass market or to retail customers. On the other hand, the pilot project gave a clearer picture on how to handle international projects and also revealed some critical points that needed to be fixed

## RELATIONSHIP CRISIS

Statistics say that marriages face problems after an average time of seven years. The bank and Synergy India anticipated these statistics. Looking at the pilot project, the sensation was of Indians managing the Italian projects in the same way as they had managed the American ones:

- Language is not an issue (Italians must learn English if they want to interact with Indians and not vice versa).
- Timing is not a problem (as in the US the time difference allows working days/hours to be gained).
- Software outsourcing rocks (Business Process Outsourcing (BPO), Enterprise Resource Planning (ERP), Customer Relationship Marketing (CRM) are routine software projects).

As in personal relationships, what is left unsaid is sometimes worse than explicit words. The above listed points were the first battlefield as the workload increased and the deadlines became tight; technology was not the only issue, the cross-cultural elements were even harder and critical.

- Language was a barrier: although technical English is commonly used in the software industry, personal relationships were affected by the language difference, and the empathy or 'chemistry' part of team building was almost absent. Communication is the soul of team building and informal interaction sometimes helps solve problems more than formal emails or exchange of documents.
- The time difference was not that easy to handle: paradoxically four hours' difference made interaction possible only for a half-day shift and in some cases the number of extra hours worked by Italian technicians were shrinking the cost benefit. Delays from one side or the other were doubling delivery time, and live interaction on the phone (if needed) was costly and inefficient.
- Software outsourcing of customized applications did not follow the same process as for standard ones: without a detailed requirements analysis, the trial-and-error approach led to misunderstanding and missed milestones. Silly problems like metric systems transformation, graphic user interface, hardware settings, and comments on code lines seemed mountains to climb.

## I'M LEAVING YOU 'CAUSE I LOVE YOU

At a certain point it became clear that, to keep the partnership alive, the relationship needed to move to the next level. On top of this the visa procedure between the two countries was lengthy and it was difficult to get the duration extended for a period longer than 90 days (from both sides). Moreover, from the very beginning of the partnership the bank decided to keep some software developments in-house, thus hiring local programmers. The new millennium paved the way for quicker development of applications and raised the bar on digital banking services: slowly the dilemma was between 'reducing cost' or 'increasing efficiency'. The time for a farewell was near, and the cultural gap was pushing it, but the business figures and cost reduction attractiveness were still pressing... We should remember that at the end of the day, the best bank is the one that is more money-conscious than its competitors! Another key aspect of the software industry in the late 1990s and early 2000s was the full addiction of customers to their IT providers and tight dependence on external software development: in some cases, the distinction between who was the customer and who was the service provider was also unclear.

Another (interesting) element was the rise of new opportunities in Europe and in particular in those countries that were starting the process of entering the European Union, which were culturally closer to Italy and to which travel would be easier. Of course, efficiency and the level of programming would not have been the same as in India. Still, Synergy India was an option that was not easy to leave. Last but not least, the bank was about to ride its dot.com bubble and those were the best years ever to do so. No time to lose.

## AN OPEN RELATIONSHIP

In a bold move the bank decided, once again, to be first mover on a new business model approach. By the early 2000s, at the edge of the digital boom (but just before the burst of the bubble… but that is another story…) there were three driving factors of the IT department consolidation:

- Keep sensitive software programs/infrastructure and ICT application in-house and possibly with an in-situ team;
- Keep going with a cost-effective outsourcing process for non-sensitive modules;
- Take advantage of cost reduction to sell new services backed by low-cost brain power.

The cultural aspect was one of the common links of all three priorities as you need cultural chemistry to gain trust and share sensitive content, you need cultural affinity to work together, and you need cultural matching to be seen as one bank.

Such awareness led the bank to launch a massive reorganization of the IT department. A Cerberus-like entity was created: three 'heads' in three different countries, all part of the same body and with a unique management team. The Italian branch of the IT department was in the HQ town and in charge of sensitive programs (i.e. servers, DB administration, host programming, financial transactions) involving local software competences (a massive hiring process was carried out within three years). The bank CEO decided to buy Synergy India to have exclusivity (and full control) of its services and to make their Indian colleagues feel an integral part of the bank or, making it clear that the bank was upgraded from 'customer' to 'owner'. The visa problem was still there but the bank's IT management team asked for guest houses, English training courses, get-together events and more Project Managers to look after the Indian projects. Last but not least, the third head of Cerberus was the brand new software team set up from scratch in Romania. This team supported the development of customer care software and prepared for BPO services as a result of being able to learn the Italian language easily and their geographical proximity, furthermore taking advantage of funds provided to support the process of application for membership of the European Union. Cost benefit, outsourcing opportunities, priorities diversification, geographical localization, cultural mix, all in one department.

# CONCLUSIONS

Love affairs are indecipherable, but all the stories have one thing in common: compromise. Cultural barriers are even more difficult, and both of the parties need to compromise ... if it is not because your customer is paying you and asking for that, maybe it's because your owner and majority shareholder wants you to do so. The experience with the bank was very interesting but with many pros and cons. I still ask myself if this could have happened in a big bank or in a less pyramidal organization. After a certain probation period the bank launched a new digital platform and e-banking services, maintaining the momentum and the legacy of a cutting-edge, technology-driven company. A multicultural team in a multinational company is common practice but in a smaller environment it has to be tackled in a serious and structured way. The 2010s crisis convinced the bank to move one step forward, thus spinning off all the IT activities and launching a 100 per cent owned company able to go on the market also to serve other customers. A new business 'culture' with new cultural issues to tackle. Love and cultural integration are never easy and most of the time they follow unknown paths but, as Henry Ford said, 'coming together is a beginning, staying together is progress, and working together is success' and it can be even greater if contributed from the perspective of different cultural backgrounds.

## QUESTIONS FOR DISCUSSION

1.  Which were the main cross-cultural 'mistakes' of the company and of the Indian programmers?
2.  Which would be the main actions that should be done in advance in order to avoid the cultural problems?

## CASE STUDY 4.2      UK AND CHINA
## MACALLAN SINGLE MALT WHISKY

*Juliette Wilson and Beverly Wagner*

# INTRODUCTION

The Macallan is a single malt whisky made by the Macallan distillery which was founded in 1824 and one of the first distillers in Scotland to be legally licensed. It is the number one whisky in the world by value. It is the most iconic and profitable of a portfolio of brands owned by the Edrington Group and is the key brand in their portfolio. It is unique for a number of reasons. The most notable is that it is marketed at a very high price point and is never discounted, even for the entry level 12-year-old The Macallan. Over 50 per cent of Macallan's business is made up of products that sell at over $100 a bottle. Increasingly the engine of their business is ultra-prestige whisky, which is whisky that sells at over $5000 a bottle, up to the highest recommended retail price of a bottle selling at $80 000.

Macallan have 7.5 million consumers around the world who have consumed The Macallan in the last 12 months, the bulk of these drinking 12-year-old or 18-year-old The

Macallan. Their key markets around the world are the USA, China, Russia, Taiwan, the UK, Hong Kong and Singapore. This is a diverse market profile and presents key challenges associated with managing a global brand of getting the right balance of global consistency and local adaptation and content. China is one of their biggest markets and is their fastest-growing market.

This particular case has been chosen for a number of reasons. First, it will aid discussion of strategies underlying the effective management of global brands. Focusing on two culturally distinct markets, the UK and China, it highlights an approach to global branding that mixes global and local strategies. It discusses the similarities and differences in consumption of this product in this market and how this affects all aspects of the marketing mix. There are also parallels between the strategic approaches to marketing for this brand and other high end luxury products. When devising a marketing strategy for the brand, the competitor set is other luxury products rather than other single-malt whiskies.

**Figure 4.1**   Macallan 12-year-old and 18-year-old bottles

Within the alcohol category the primary competitors are ultra-premium malts, fine wine and champagne. Within the Chinese market, The Macallan also competes with premium Baijiu.

When discussing the Chinese market for whisky, account needs to be taken of the regional influences of Taiwan and Hong Kong. Taiwan has always been the biggest whisky market in Asia and The Macallan has been absolutely dominant within Taiwan. This is the same in Hong Kong, where The Macallan is dominant. Also any discussion of the UK and Chinese markets for whisky needs to acknowledge that the focus is really on key cities within China, such as Beijing, Shanghai, Guangzhou and Shenzhen, and London in the UK.

## THE CROSS-CULTURAL ISSUE

The issue is an exploration of the effective management of a global brand taking account of cultural diversity between two markets. In this case one of these markets is the home market, the UK, and the other the fastest-growing market, China. The case data is drawn from an interview with Glen Gribbon, Marketing Director, The Macallan at Edrington Group, in March 2021, company presentations, and data drawn from their website: https://www.themacallan.com/en. Analysis of the different dimensions of the brand offer between the UK and China draws on Hofstede's dimensions of culture (Hofstede, 1979, 1980, 1982, 1983).

# MAIN FINDINGS

## PRODUCT ATTRIBUTES

The Macallan brand covers a range of single malt whiskies, all produced in Scotland and marketed throughout the world. They are one of the world's leading single malt whiskies. The sherry oak casks they are matured in determine up to 80 per cent of The Macallan's final character and flavour, and so the oak cask is the most prominent factor in ensuring and delivering the quality and style of the single malt. All Macallan whiskies take 100 per cent of their colour from the wood in which they are matured. There are a range of single malt whiskies produced under The Macallan brand, from 12-year-old single malt, to 78-year-old and various limited collections. Their core business is the 12-year-old and 18-year-old whiskies which are marketed at a significantly higher price point than other single malt whiskies in the market. Their other whiskies are seen as ultra-prestige products.

There is no local adaptation of product attributes to local palettes, rather the focus is on global consistency. Scottish whisky is a legally protected product and as such the product needs to be the same across markets. The reputation of The Macallan is built on a product of outstanding quality and distinctive character. Therefore, the company needs to ensure quality and distinction in every aspect of their marketing mix: from the processes used for the product from production through to the end customer; the people involved in these processes; and their marketing strategies and relationships with their end customers, both direct relationships and those mediated through retail and on trade, in restaurants and bars.

The demand for The Macallan whiskies outstrips supply so they are always stock constrained. This varies depending on the product, but it is the situation for all their products. This means that their marketing strategy differs from other alcohol products. Glen described the challenges associated with this:

> For example, last year we launched a range of products called the red collection – 40, 50, 60, 71, 74 ,78-year-old whisky. The start point is that there is a small quantity and there are more people around the world that we know would like to buy these bottles than actual bottles. It is not a selling process in the traditional sense of the word. It is more about us deciding who should get access to those bottles and it is an incredibly difficult thing to do. For the red collection last year we could have sold 3–4 times the number of bottles that we had available, so the real challenge is to manage the relationships in a way that … a lot of these individuals know each other.

## CONSUMER PROFILE

The Macallan have a model to define who their global consumer is. They cluster potential consumers into typologies, driven by their overarching motivations, the choices that they make depending on what is important to them at a particular point in time and the cultural world they are in. The Macallan consumer 'family' is attitudinally similar consumers separated by differences in wealth and their relationship with the brand. At the highest level of brand engagement The Macallan's focus is on whisky experts and status experts where the competitive set is other high-end whisky and other luxury products and experiences. This profiling directs how they create their content and how they plan their business. With consumers of whisky there are more similarities than differences, even within a market like China, which is culturally very different.

Of the 7.5 million Macallan consumers, 30 per cent are women. There are slight differences in their typical consumer profile in the UK and China although this is changing. In China the consumers have traditionally had a slightly older age demographic. This is in part because of the importance of business entertaining as an occasion in China, but as discussed below, this is changing. This transition in China is coming into line with what is happening in the rest of the world. A key difference is that the Chinese market moves at a greater pace than the rest of the world and so when change starts to happen it happens much faster than in other parts of the world.

London is the global hub for high-end whisky, and the key geographic focus in the UK market. A great many Chinese consumers will buy whisky in London and will ship it back to multiple homes around the world.

## SALES CHANNELS

A key difference between the two markets lies in the sales channels used. The Macallan is sold through a variety of sales channels: as bottles through speciality retail; e-commerce; auction sites; and on-trade in bars and restaurants.

E-commerce is evolving around the world as another channel that sits alongside physical retail and on-trade. The Chinese consumer is embracing e-commerce far faster than other parts of the world and is very comfortable buying whisky through e-commerce. The big Chinese e-commerce platforms are a much more important part of The Macallan's business now than ever before.

This can create challenges, as Glen describes:

> Edrington never discount on price and a lot of these platforms are very discount orientated. Chinese consumers are tuned to look for discounts – it is the way that people shop. It makes it difficult at certain times of the year such as the big celebration periods, and there's lots of them. The fact that we don't participate in discounting is culturally challenging.

The trade in the UK, and London in particular, is much more developed in terms of specialist whisky retailers, with mainstream retailers and e-commerce a much smaller part of the business, although as at-home consumption is much more established in the UK than in China, they do need to have some presence in mainstream retailers as well as specialist retailers even though it is not a priority channel for them.

The on-trade and restaurant trade is also much more developed in the UK than in China, although it is not as part of business entertaining, unlike China, as this is far less important in the UK as an experience or as a motivation.

Mixology and cocktails are also a really important part of The Macallan's sales in the UK and are much more established in London than in China. In China, the on-trade market is geared around the status of the visibility of The Macallan brand rather than its use as a mixer with other products. Culturally it is consumed in conjunction with local food and drink products, as noted by Glen:

> In Shanghai you can go into a restaurant with a bottle of 18-year-old Macallan on the table which is £250 a bottle and it will be green tea that people are drinking with it as that is the cultural norm. Having the bottle on the table in China is still a big status moment – the visibility of what you drink is important and that is not as big an issue in the UK.

Another growing sales channel for super-premium whisky is through auction houses such as Sotheby's and Bonhams. Online whisky auctions, for example whisky auctioneers, are a grow-ing segment. London is a global hub for whisky collecting and investing. The Macallan don't actively participate in this sales channel as they don't put bottles into auction, but they do occasionally buy for their archive. Glen talked about how important this channel is becoming:

> Last year Sotheby's sold a bottle of 1926 Macallan for £1.5 million! Macallan dominates that auction channel, so a lot of these individuals will go to that auction channel to get what they want to get. This means that whisky is now in an asset class in the same way as fine art and fine wine, but there are not that many people in the world who are prepared to pay £1.5 million for a bottle of whisky or even £80 000. So, when people get access to the whisky other people know, so our challenge is managing that relationship when supply is so scarce.

Some of Edrington's biggest investors and collectors are Chinese individuals. These col-lectors don't always want to be known, so it is a different type of relationship they have with them. Edrington decide on an allocation of bottles of The Macallan that will be sold through their private client network. They agree on an allocation and then their private client managers open up conversations around levels of interest. They need to take ac-count of whether they can physically get the bottles to people. They don't sell everything through one-to-one selling as they want these bottles to also appear in trade or even bars.

The Macallan have invested in a beautiful new estate on their Speyside site which in-cludes a fishing beat, and they sell experiences around this. They sell two-day experiences for £50 000, but it is less about the transaction and more about a conversation around creating a complete experience for these individuals like nothing else they will be able to buy. These have to be personalized and have to be different. This is reflective of the super-premium category they sit within.

## CONSUMPTION EXPERIENCE

There is a real difference between the Chinese and the UK market in terms of how whisky is consumed, in terms of the occasion or experience. The product might be the same, the content might be the same, the presentation and packaging might be the same, but how people consume it is very different. In Asian markets the traditional whisky experience has been what is called traditional trade, business entertaining, and is very male oriented. This is changing as China evolves and changes and a younger middle class develops. Demographically there is great interest in whisky among women globally, especially in China, but it is consumed in a completely different way, in a more modern environment, or at home.

An important part of the consumption of whisky historically has not been at home. Gifting is an important part of Chinese culture. The motivations for buying The Macallan are to drink it, to gift it, to collect it, and to invest in it. This is for all their brands. In China gifting is more important than it would be in other parts of the world. Where they do tailor their proposition is around gifting, so in the New Year, they will develop very specific content to support that gifting period within China.

## BRAND COMMUNICATION

The content plans for marketing for the UK and China are very similar. The timings vary slightly, but fundamentally it is the same content. The innovation plans are exactly the same, with some timing movements in the UK, so in whisky there is a consistent global approach with the brand presented in the same way everywhere. The one change they do make to content is that they include translations, which is an incredibly difficult thing to do. For example, one of their main assets is a film called 'The Turning Point', which has a final line of 'make the call'. It has been very complicated to try and find the right Chinese expression for this.

On the website they talk about the brand today and in the future through the lens of what's happened in the past. Legacy is a very important aspect of the brand to the Chinese market, but how this is communicated is important. The past is evoked through stories about founders, but discussed in a modern way rather than focusing on tradition, about the sentiment of the individuals rather than who they were or that moment in time. That content resonates very effectively in China.

Some brands take a very devolved approach to brand management, where there is lots of local content and local innovation. The Macallan take a very centralized approach. The team in Scotland manage all product innovation. They provide all the content. The aim is to connect in culturally relevant ways whilst maintaining their Scottish roots.

For their social content, 60 per cent is global content that cannot be adapted, 20 per cent is global content that can be adapted for local channels, and then 20 per cent is genuinely local content, but even this is defined quite tightly in terms of what it should look like. Local adaptation includes translation, taking account of cultural resonance, understanding of local occasions and events, and engagement with local celebrities. Therefore what you see in China should broadly be what you would see in any other market around the world.

There are different marketing models for the 12-year-old The Macallan in comparison to their ultra-prestige whiskies. With a 12-year-old The Macallan it is much more like traditional marketing – simplicity of the messaging, reason to believe and so on.

The Macallan have a big marketing team in China. They don't do a lot of content creation, they don't do any innovation, they work well with the global assets they provide, but a lot of what they focus on is experiential marketing. In China, drinking whisky with your meal has been an important part of the business entertainment experience. So they hold lots of dinners and big events and these are a more important part of their model in China than anywhere else in the world. They tend not to do that elsewhere.

# CUSTOMER RELATIONSHIP MANAGEMENT (CRM)

The Macallan have a global CRM or direct to consumer programme where they sell bottles of whisky direct to consumers and they have strong relationships with these individuals, especially Tier 1 and Tier 2, which are their super-premium customers. A lot of them are in China. In other parts of the world they use people who are part of the global team to manage the relationships but in China local management of those relationships works better.

There are also lots of data restrictions in China that mean that they aren't able to manage the data in the way that they would in other parts of the world, so they have to be very respectful of that. Investing in whisky is a hugely growing segment in China and a big part of their business.

The core The Macallan business is 12-year-old and 18-year-old whisky and then there is ultra-prestige, which is $5000 a bottle, and the marketing models are very different. For the ultra-prestige the direct to consumer is a much bigger part and they have private client relationship managers to do this. They structure this with different tiers depending on how often you buy, how you engage with the brand, and your net worth.

In London this is managed through an individual who is part of Glen's team. In China that wouldn't work as well. They are much more reliant on Chinese individuals who are based in China. That localization of the relationship management is much more important. It is not all about the local relationship as lots of wealthy business people are travelling all around the world, but the local relationship is more important in China, for example understanding the cultural nuances of business entertaining is difficult to do if you are a UK individual who hasn't spent a large part of their life in China. In the direct to consumer space this is definitely one of the differences between the two markets.

# CHALLENGES

A key challenge in China for the big volume whisky brands is contraband. The Macallan don't suffer from this in any major way. They go to extreme lengths to make sure their packaging is very difficult to refill, that they don't have a lot of empty bottles in circulation. Once confidence is lost that you are buying the genuine article it can become problematic very quickly.

There is a different shape to the business in the two markets in terms of seasonality, which can make marketing difficult. In the UK, the Christmas period is still incredibly important for alcohol brands. For mainstream alcohol brands, 40 per cent of their sales can be made over a two-month period. The Macallan is less seasonal in the UK, but there is still a difference in seasonality between the two markets. The fact that The Macallan is never discounted on price and that it is relatively expensive in comparison to other single malts takes some of the seasonality out of market.

# DISCUSSION AND CONCLUSIONS

Table 4.1 summarizes the key differences between the home and Chinese market for The Macallan. This is a truly global brand where there is no differentiation in terms of product attributes such as flavour, branding, packaging or suggested use. Where differences occur, it is in terms of the brand occasion, consumer profile, some aspects of the brand communications, sales channels and customer relationship management.

**Table 4.1    Differences between home and Chinese market**

| Different Product Dimensions | UK | China |
|---|---|---|
| Product Attributes | Clear understanding of product attributes from core consumers. | There is no local adaptation of product attributes to local palettes, rather the focus is on global consistency. Chinese consumers show clear understanding of product attributes. |
| Consumer Profile | Clear consumer profiling in terms of differences in wealth and relationship with the brand. Split 70:30 in terms of gender. | Clear consumer profiling in terms of differences in wealth and relationship with the brand. Similar profile to the UK although slightly older and more male although this is changing. |
| Sales Channels | Specialist retailers and restaurants and bars. Mixology important in London. Buying for investing through auction houses growing in importance for super-premium brands. | Importance of e-commerce as a channel. Buying for investing through auction houses growing in importance for super-premium brands. |
| Consumption Experience | Business entertaining with whisky is not important in the UK market. Consumption at home is more prevalent as is consuming as a social occasion in bars and restaurants. | Traditional trade has been in business entertaining and gifting and is very male oriented. This is changing to more at home consumption by a younger, more female demographic. |
| Brand Communication | 60:20:20 approach to brand communication with a focus on consistent messaging globally. 60% is global and is the same across all markets. 20% is globally adapted to local markets and 20% truly local. | 60:20:20 approach to brand communication with a focus on consistent messaging globally. 60% is global and is the same across all markets. 20% is globally adapted to local markets and 20% truly local. Local adaptation includes translation, taking account of cultural resonance, understanding of local occasions and events, engagement with local celebrities. |
| CRM | Global relationship management team based in the UK. | Local management of relationships in China by those with an understanding of cultural nuances. |

Using Hofstede's cultural dimensions (Hofstede, 1979, 1980, 1982, 1983) helps to high-light differences and similarities between the two markets and further explains the ra-tionale for the mix of global and local marketing strategies. These are summarized in Table 4.2.

**Table 4.2    Hofstede's cultural dimensions, UK and China**

|  | UK | China |
| --- | --- | --- |
| Power Distance | 35 | 80 |
| Individualism | 89 | 20 |
| Masculinity | 66 | 66 |
| Uncertainty Avoidance | 35 | 30 |
| Long-term Orientation | 51 | 87 |
| Indulgence | 69 | 24 |

*Source*: https://www.hofstede-insights.com/country-comparison/china,the-uk/.

China's high-power distance is shown through clear hierarchies and acceptance of in-equalities. An example of this is the importance of the role of gifting in Chinese culture as part of business relationships. The collectivist culture in China is reflected in the types of occasions when The Macallan is used. There is a higher prevalence of use of The Macallan as part of shared eating experiences and less of an emphasis on individual experiences such as home drinking, as in the UK.

Both cultures have relatively high masculine cultures. These societies are driven by competition, achievement and success, and success is visible. This resonates with the global marketing strategy for The Macallan. In China, this success is also seen in the pri-oritization of work over family and leisure and consumption experiences that reflect this.

Low uncertainty avoidance in both countries reflects comfort with ambiguity, adap-tation and entrepreneurship. The importance of complex story-telling in building up the understanding of the brand, the 'six pillars' of the brand and the appeal to multiple senses resonates with this cultural positioning.

The high score for China in Long-Term Orientation reflects a pragmatic culture that is willing to adapt traditions to changed conditions. Although The Macallan discuss the im-portance of legacy and their founders, this is done in a modern way, with less of a focus on tradition and more about the sentiment of the individuals involved.

The low score for indulgence in China reflects a more restrained society. There is less emphasis on leisure and the gratification of desires. This is important to consider when examining experiential consumption opportunities and the focus of marketing messaging. As discussed above, some of their biggest investors and collectors are Chinese individuals but these collectors want to remain anonymous, so The Macallan have to manage their relationship with them in a way that is sensitive to this.

## QUESTIONS FOR DISCUSSION

1. Whisky drinking in China is changing from an older, male business where the focus is on entertaining, the dining experience and gifting, to a much younger experience focused on drinking in cool bars, buying through e-commerce, and collecting, but not necessarily large levels of investing. How does a brand like The Macallan which has been in China for many years manage that transition?
2. What cultural aspects are particularly important to take account of with The Macallan's 60:20:20 marketing communications model? What aspects might be different in the UK and Chinese markets?
3. This study uses Hofstede to analyse the different dimensions of The Macallan brand offer. Using an alternative framing, compare your findings with those presented here.

---

## CASE STUDY 4.3     UK AND GERMANY
### BMW AND MINI

*Anne-Flore Maman Larraufie*

# INTRODUCTION

In 2000, Monika Lampe, Director of Change Management at BMW's Mini plant in Oxford, UK, faced a daunting challenge. BMW had just divested Mini's former parent company, Rover Group, which it had operated at a loss since it acquired Rover in 1994. In deciding to keep Mini in the BMW family, BMW was committed to turning Mini around, retooling the factory and successfully launching a new, innovative and cost-efficient model.

Tasked with integrating two very different BMW and Rover cultures, expectations and experiences, Ms Lampe noted that,

> The legacy of Rover and the work culture [is] very much 'us and them'. There [is] a blame culture within the plant and, to be honest, people used to leave their brains at the gate ... We [have] to create a culture of success. We [have] to change the processes, attitudes and behaviour and to empower staff and involve them in the process.[1]

As Ms Lampe began to draft her change management plan, she knew she would have to effectively bridge a cultural gap between German and British staff as well as address fundamental differences in approaches to automotive manufacturing in each of these countries.

# HISTORY AND CULTURE OF THE FIRMS

## BMW HISTORY

BMW (Bayerische Motoren Werke AG) was created in 1913 by Karl Friedrich Rapp. BMW's early automotive manufacturing course was diverted by World War II when it was enlisted to produce aircraft engines for the German military. This drew the ire of Britain's Royal Air Force, which bombed BMW's factories. With its infrastructure demise, particularly given the loss of its manufacturing base to East Germany, BMW only resumed automotive manufacturing operations in 1951.

Although it targeted a booming market, BMW's re-launch had a rocky start, and it was almost taken over by Mercedes Benz in 1959. Having hit bottom twice in the nascent stages of development, BMW has since ascended to a position of prestige and profit. Key to its success has been innovation, a management style focusing on 'independence, self-fulfilment and the pursuit of new goals', and the creation of a top quality brand image.[2]

The 1990s saw BMW strengthening its global leadership and image by investing in new factories in the United States and releasing major style enhancements. Prior to its 1994 merger with Rover, which encompassed the Rover, Mini, Land Rover and Triumph brands, BMW fielded a joint venture with Rolls Royce in 1990.

## ROVER, MINI AND THE BMW-ROVER MERGER

The Rover Company was founded in 1877 as a partnership between John Kemp Starley and William Sutton, both of whom were bicycle builders. Rover has ever since been considered the heart of Britain's automotive industry.

The Rover Company entered into production in 1903 with the Imperial Rover, a car deemed luxurious for its time. In 1932, Rover introduced a new company strategy and produced a long series of small, inexpensive cars and a smaller number of expensive luxury vehicles. That strategy changed again with the advent of World War II. Civilian production halted and Rover built engines for aircrafts and tanks. Post-war, Rover found a niche market for a civilian light Jeep-style four-wheel drive vehicle. This niche was developed into Land Rover, which today serves as a luxury sport utility vehicle exported globally.

In January 1994, BMW began to search for growth strategies. It turned to the UK and capitalized on Rover's poor financial state and broad portfolio of companies. In March 1994, BMW purchased Rover for £1.7 billion. Determined not to repeat Ford's failed transition strategy with Jaguar (which used a very hands-on approach), BMW still struggled with strengthening Rover despite using a very hands-off approach in its management of British staff.[3]

Rover continued to lose huge amounts of money, costing BMW £600 million per year.[4] Still, BMW did eke out some wins from the acquisition: it used the off-road technology from Land Rover to develop its own BMW branded 'sport activity vehicle'. After adapting the technology, BMW sold Land Rover for £1.8 billion to Ford Motor Company's Premier Auto Group. In May 2000, BMW sold the remaining Rover operation, save Mini, to Phoenix Group, a private equity firm, for £10 and the assumption of Rover's debt from BMW.[5] BMW felt it needed to develop a car to replace the smaller Rover-branded cars, yet remain clearly differentiated from their very upscale Roundel Marque. The ensuing restructuring strategy led to a dramatic redesign and manufacturing effort for the Mini brand, with BMW aimed at eventually selling 200 000 Minis per year.[6]

# CULTURAL ISSUES

As Ms Lampe began to prepare her change management plan in expectation of her first formal meeting with Bernard Moss, the head of the Transport and General Workers' Union in Oxford, she knew the meeting was going to be challenging. Mr Moss was a very powerful union boss and competent manager from all reports. Nevertheless, major changes were needed at the factory to reverse the poor performance plaguing the company. Ms Lampe saw three central issues that needed to be addressed during the meeting. They were: (1) determine the management structure inside the factory; (2) develop a culture of innovation within the company; and (3) implement a winning operational plan.

Each was essential to executing a successful recovery plan. Not only that, but she owed it to her superiors in Munich. Ms Lampe knew she had to get Mr Moss's buy-in on the recovery plan or risk a lengthy and costly stalemate. Relying on her past multicultural experience, she also knew that key cultural issues would underlie each issue. In a past expatriate assignment, she had been exposed to a groundbreaking research methodology on cross-cultural relations, The GLOBE Study[7] and a Cultural Orientation Indicator test she had taken (study comparisons of British and German culture are presented in Appendices 4A.1–4A.3). She now began to go through the data and identify what she thought would be the underlying cultural dynamics for each of the issues.

## MANAGEMENT STRUCTURE

Ms Lampe identified this largely as a participatory leadership, power distance and collectivist issue. Being a German and BMW long-time employee, Ms Lampe appreciated a somewhat flat leadership system. She was naturally inclined to implementing a more flexible management structure. BMW was characterized by a collection of relatively independent factories; within each were a myriad of autonomous departments with individual responsibility for their particular areas. Managers were free to make their own plans and had a great deal of say in their performance measures. Additionally, she preferred, as the GLOBE study indicates most Germans and British do as well, a very participatory leadership style. She expected to have managers at all levels engaged with their subordinates and involved with day-to-day operations. Now Ms Lampe had to look at the data in front of her and try to put herself in the shoes of her Mini managers. Would this system work for them? Would she get the performance and dedication she needed to get the company and the factory turned around?

Ms Lampe's research and knowledge of the history of Mini provided her some key information. Rover and Mini's corporate culture were somewhat different from the GLOBE study's general characterization of British culture. Although Germans and English were both in the mid-range of power distance, the extent to which the less powerful expect and accept that power is distributed unequally, the Mini company culture was very different.[8] Decisions would be made at the highest level, and then directed and implemented to lower-mid-level managers and finally to the workforce itself. Each department head would report to a superior up the entire chain of command. Managers would be directly accountable for the performance of their departments, and their bonus systems would be directly matched to their ability to meet a series of performance measurements dictated from higher management.

From what Ms Lampe could tell, this was a very high power-distance approach to management. In addition, in studying her Cultural Orientation Indicator (COI) (Appendix 4A.3), Ms Lampe saw that the British workforce tended to be more individualistic than their collectivist German counterparts. Ms Lampe had to make a decision. She believed she had two potential choices: (1) maintain a very hierarchical management structure that seemed to be at odds with the British culture and BMW, but to which the Mini workforce was accustomed; or (2) implement a new, flatter structure that may be a better fit for both the British and German cultures but would cause a large culture shift within the Mini corporation.

## INNOVATION CHALLENGE

Ms Lampe quickly caught onto the conventional wisdom that the Rover and Mini brand had been stuck in the 1970s as far as innovation was concerned. Little had been done in the past two decades to improve the Mini. The BMW management believed in the Mini brand, but knew it needed a major overhaul. BMW, as a German auto manufacturer, was renowned for its engineering excellence and new technology innovation. Ms Lampe needed somehow to instil this same spirit of innovation and strategy in her managers and workforce. However, her research using cultural data on future orientation, the degree to which cultures focus on long-term organizational objectives and planning, seemed puzzling again.[9] The Anglo culture was not exactly known for its lack of future orientation; in fact, the data indicated that both German and English cultures were very similar with regard to this cultural indicator. In looking at the historical evidence, it was Ms Lampe's view that the former managements' adherence to tradition at the expense of innovation was what led to Rover-Mini's serious performance issues. Little had changed at the factory in 20 years. Machines were in disrepair and the factory itself was in need of serious renovation. Rover-Mini clearly lacked an innovative spirit and in fact was in a creative 'rut'.[10]

Rover-Mini's corporate culture was at odds with what seemed to be the norm in English culture and quite different from German and BMW culture. Clearly something needed to be done to motivate the factory management and workforce to develop a culture of innovation in line with BMW's corporate culture. Ms Lampe knew this would be a challenge and would seek Mr Moss's input in developing a plan to change the workforce culture. The factory also needed a significant amount of capital investment to renovate. This was a risky proposition in a merger where success was not assured. However, if BMW was to get Mini's workers to buy into the operational plan, BMW needed to show commitment to the success of the company, and so would have to invest large sums of capital to make this happen.

## OPERATIONAL PLAN IMPLEMENTATION

Ms Lampe believed this to be the most important and difficult element of her change strategy to overcome culturally. Upon viewing the COIs (Appendix 4A.3), she saw that German culture tended to have a more direct communication style than Britain's. In addition, she noticed that the British generally tended towards a more inductive style of reasoning, in contrast to a typical German deductive approach. BMW's operational plans typically relied on direct guidance and attention to key processes that needed to be fixed.

In developing a plan, BMW relied on proven operational practice and theory to improve plant operational efficiency.

Ms Lampe wondered if simply stating the overall operational goals and systems would provide the managers with the kind of guidance they sought. If her managers were more 'low-context', they might need demonstration of the practices that addressed each problem to demonstrate how each fitted into the overall operational picture she had in mind. In appealing to a more inductive thought process, the best method might be to get the workers to identify the problems that were evident. From this exercise, they would surely come to the conclusion that BMW's plan would solve the problems at hand. Ms Lampe believed this had the potential to engender a workforce that supported and believed in the recovery plan.

## THE CHALLENGE AHEAD

After analysing the culture and history of BMW and Mini, reviewing performance statistics, observing employee behaviour and interviewing staff, Ms Lampe was ready to draft her change strategy and present it to Mr Moss. Key to BMW's success at Mini would be replacing a traditional hierarchical mindset with one focused on teamwork, innovation, continuous improvement and one that was more reflective of the 'energetic, youthful and fun image' of the Mini. She realized she needed to vest a likely reticent work staff in BMW's lofty production and cost-cutting goals for the plant to successfully negotiate a contract between German managers and union officials.

## BMW AND MINI: OUTCOME

### WORKING IN GROUPS

To develop a culture of innovation, meet production goals and cut costs, Ms Lampe knew she had to break up a traditional hierarchical structure and develop a new rewards system aligned with BMW's goals for Mini. BMW launched WINGS (Working in Groups), which created hundreds of self-managed teams of between eight and fifteen employees tasked with solving production problems and generating new ideas. Employees received external training in working as part of a team. To emphasize the importance of the groups and provide them uninterrupted time in which to meet, BMW halted the production line for 90 minutes a month while the teams met.

The production duties of one member from each team were halved to allow that individual to focus on developing their team members and team dynamics. WINGS created less distance between employees and management decisions and 'placed continuous improvement and the achievement of plant improvement targets directly into the hands of the team members', noted Heike Schneeweis, HR Director at BMW.[11]

WINGS also provided a forum for employees to vent concerns about 'noise factors, such as having a drinks cooler too far away from the track. If we take away the noise in the system – the things that frustrate people – they are much more able to submit ideas that affect the car', explained Nicola Scott, a subsequent Head of Change Management at the Oxford Plant.[12]

## REWARDING INDIVIDUAL CONTRIBUTION

WINGS helped bring collectivist values at BMW into a traditionally individualistic Mini culture. BMW then structured a rewards system that bridged the gap and supported individual ideation and an inductive thought process. To qualify for a new bonus system, employees were required to submit an average of three successful ideas per year, totalling a savings of at least $1250, in addition to hitting standard production and quality targets.

BMW rewarded both individual concepts (e.g., turning off lights in an unused part of the plant at a saving of $3642 per year) and group concepts (e.g., halving the number of sound-proofing foam blocks used in each car with no adverse effect at a saving of $235 000 per year).[13] BMW launched a database to capture the ideas and provide feedback as to whether an idea was accepted, or why it was not.

## MANAGEMENT STYLE – IMPLEMENTATION

In implementing and gaining buy-in for the new flat structure and ideation platform, BMW both brought in external temporary management and removed barriers between German managers and employees. BMW fielded 13 contractors with strong automotive industry management experience: most were British. Employees identified with a common culture shared with these former senior industrial managers and they were able to implement WINGS successfully on the shop floor. They also helped obtain buy-in from the union for the ideation-based bonus ties and other key contract amendments such as the introduction of a German-style working time account (e.g., workers continued to be paid during plant closures for retooling or production downshifts, but up to 200 hours had to be made up later).

BMW also introduced a 'Back to the Track' programme, which significantly increased the amount of time managers and directors spent on production lines working in tandem with employees. Combined with the WINGS programme, Alan Buckingham, a process area manager at Oxford, noted the message received by workers was, 'Here is the empowerment to go and do things ... Go to the manager but treat him as a support function'.[14]

## CONCLUSION

BMW's culturally intelligent processes for change management saved $9.4 million in costs in 2002.[15] Of 14 086 ideas submitted by the Mini staff, more than 11 000 were implemented.[16] BMW was also able to exceed its 2002 production goal by 40 000 Minis, making more than 160 000 cars that year.[17]

### QUESTIONS FOR DISCUSSION

1. Using the data included in the appendices and the information included in the story, define the two cultural profiles (UK and Germany) and the possible critical points in the common work.
2. Suggest solutions in order to reduce the cultural gap-related problems.

# APPENDIX 4A.1  COUNTRY RANKINGS FOR LEADERSHIP SECOND ORDER LEADERSHIP SCALE

**Table 4A1.1**     Charismatic leadership

| Country | Scale | Band |
|---|---|---|
| UK | 6.01 | B |
| Germany (Former FRG {WEST}) | 5.84 | C |

*Notes*:
Scale = Second Order Leadership Scale identified by a second order factor analysis of the 21 first order leadership scales.
Band = The band width is equal to 2*SED.
SED for the charismatic/ value-based scale was .1149.

**Table 4A1.2**     Team oriented leadership

| Country | Scale | Band |
|---|---|---|
| UK | 5.71 | C |
| Germany (Former FRG {WEST}) | 5.49 | C |

*Notes*:
Scale = Second Order Leadership Scale identified by a second order factor analysis of the 21 first order leadership scales.
Band = The band width is equal to 2*SED.
SED for the team-oriented scale was .1214.

**Table 4A1.3**     Participative leadership

| Country | Scale | Band |
|---|---|---|
| Germany (Former FRG {WEST}) | 5.57 | B |
| UK | 5.88 | A |

*Notes*:
Scale = Second Order Leadership Scale identified by a second order factor analysis of the 21 first order leadership scales.
Band = The band width is equal to 2*SED.
SED for the Participative scale was .1431.

**Table 4A1.4**     Humane leadership

| Country | Scale | Band |
|---|---|---|
| UK | 4.90 | B |
| Germany (Former FRG {WEST}) | 4.44 | C |

*Notes*:
Scale = Second Order Leadership Scale identified by a second order factor analysis of the 21 first order leadership scales.
Band = The band width is equal to 2*SED.
SED for the humane scale was .2222.

**Table 4A1.5**     Autonomous leadership

| Country | Scale | Band |
|---|---|---|
| Germany (Former FRG {WEST}) | 4.30 | A |
| UK | 3.92 | B |

*Notes*:
Scale = Second Order Leadership Scale identified by a second order factor analysis of the 21 first order leadership scales.
Band = The band width is equal to 2*SED.
SED for the autonomous scale was .3022.

**Table 4A1.6**     Self-protective leadership

| Country | Scale | Band |
|---|---|---|
| UK | 3.04 | G |
| Germany (Former FRG {WEST}) | 2.96 | G |

*Notes*:
Scale = Second Order Leadership Scale identified by a second order factor analysis of the 21 first order leadership scales.
Band = The band width is equal to 2*SED.
SED for the self-protective scale was .1301.

# APPENDIX 4A.2 COUNTRY RANKINGS FOR CULTURE SOCIETY IS NOW SCALE

Table 4A2.1    Performance orientation: Society is now

| Country | Scale | Band |
|---|---|---|
| Germany (Former FRG {WEST}) | 4.25 | B |
| UK | 4.08 | B |

Notes:
Higher scores indicate greater performance orientation.
Scale = Globe questionnaire scale.
Band = The band width is equal to 2*SED.
SED for Performance Orientation was 0.3153.

Table 4A2.2    Future orientation: Society is now

| Country | Scale | Band |
|---|---|---|
| UK | 4.28 | B |
| Germany (Former FRG {WEST}) | 4.27 | B |

Notes:
Higher scores indicate greater future orientation.
Scale = GLOBE questionnaire scale.
Band = The band width is equal to 2*SED.
SED for Future Orientation was 0.3138.

Table 4A2.3    Assertiveness: Society is now

| Country | Scale | Band |
|---|---|---|
| UK (most assertive) | 4.55 | A |
| Germany (Former FRG {WEST}) | 4.15 | A |

Notes:
Higher scores indicate more assertiveness
Scale = GLOBE questionnaire scale
Band = The band width is equal to 2*SED.
SED for Assertiveness was 0.3241.

Table 4A2.4    Collectivism I - Societal Emphasis: Society is now

| Country | Scale | Band |
|---|---|---|
| UK | 4.27 | B |
| Germany (Former FRG {WEST}) | 3.79 | C |

Notes:
Higher scores indicate more collectivism while lower scores indicate more individualism.
Scale = GLOBE questionnaire scale.
Band = The band width is equal to 2*SED.
SED for Collectivism I: Societal Emphasis was 0.3222.

**Table 4A2.5**    Gender Egalitarianism: Society is now

| Country | Scale | Band |
|---|---|---|
| UK | 3.67 | A |
| Germany (Former FRG {WEST}) | 3.10 | B |

*Notes*:
Higher scores indicate greater female orientation, medium scores indicate an equal orientation and lower scores indicate greater male orientation.
Scale = GLOBE questionnaire scale.
Band = The band width is equal to 2*SED.
SED for Gender Egalitarianism was 0.3245.

**Table 4A2.6**    Humane Orientation: Society is now

| Country | Scale | Band |
|---|---|---|
| UK | 3.72 | C |
| Germany (Former FRG {WEST}) | 3.18 | D |

Notes:
Higher scores indicate more humane orientation.
Scale = GLOBE questionnaire scale.
Band = The band width is equal to 2*SED.
SED for Humane Orientation was 0.2630.

**Table 4A2.7**    Power Distance: Society is now

| Country | Scale | Band |
|---|---|---|
| Germany (Former FRG {WEST}) | 5.25 | B |
| UK | 5.15 | B |

*Notes*:
Higher scores indicate greater power stratification.
Scale = GLOBE questionnaire scale.
Band = The band width is equal to 2*SED.
SED for Power Distance was 0.2658.

**Table 4A2.8**    Collectivism II – In-Group Collectivism: Society is now

| Country | Scale | Band |
|---|---|---|
| UK | 4.08 | C |
| Germany (Former FRG {WEST}) | 4.02 | C |

*Notes*:
Higher scores indicate greater collective orientation.
Scale = GLOBE questionnaire scale.
Band = The band width is equal to 2*SED.
SED for Collectivism II: Family Collectivism was 0.5044.

**Table 4A2.9**     Uncertainty Avoidance: Society is now

| Country | Scale | Band |
|---|---|---|
| Germany (Former FRG {WEST}) | 5.22 | A |
| UK | 4.65 | B |

*Notes*:
Higher scores indicate greater uncertainty avoidance.
Scale = GLOBE questionnaire scale.
Band = The band width is equal to 2*SED.
SED for Uncertainty Avoidance was 0.3201.

## APPENDIX 4A.3  COI® GAP ANALYSIS

The gap matrix in Table 4A3.1 highlights the critical cultural gaps one needs to bridge when dealing with the cultural environment of the selected countries.

**Table 4A3.1**     UK and Germany gap analysis

| Lampe Orientation | United Kingdom | Germany |
|---|---|---|
| Environment | | |
| **Constraint** | Control | Control |
|  | Constraint | Constraint |
| Time | | |
| **Single-focus** | Single-focus | Single-focus |
| **Fixed** | Fixed | Fixed |
| **Future** | Past | Past |
|  | Future | Future |
| Action | | |
| **Being** | Being | Being |
|  | Doing | Doing |
| Communication | | |
| High Context | Low Context | Low Context |
| **Direct** | Indirect | |
| **Expressive** | Instrumental | Instrumental |
| Informal | Formal | Formal |
|  | Informal | |
| Space | | |
| **Private** | Private | Private |
| Power | | |
| **Hierarchy** | Hierarchy | Hierarchy |
|  | Equality | |

| Lampe Orientation | United Kingdom | Germany |
|---|---|---|
| Individualism | | |
| **Collectivistic** | Individualistic | Collectivistic |
| | Collectivistic | |
| **Universalistic** | Particularistic | Universalistic |
| Competitiveness | | |
| Cooperative | Competitive | Competitive |
| | Cooperative | Cooperative |
| Structure | | |
| **Order** | Order | Order |
| Thinking | | |
| Deductive | Inductive | Deductive |
| Systemic | Linear | Linear |

# References – Part I

Adair, W.L., Buchan, N.R. and Chen, X.P. (2009). Conceptualizing culture as communication in management and marketing research. In C. Nakata (ed.), *Beyond Hofstede*. London: Palgrave Macmillan, pp. 146–80.

Aime, M. (2008). *Il Primo Libro di Antropologia*. Turin: Einaudi.

Almeida, P. (1996). Knowledge sourcing by foreign multinationals: Patent citation analysis in the US semiconductor industry. *Strategic Management Journal*, 17(S2), 155–65.

Askegaard, S., Kjeldgaard, D. and Arnould, E.J. (2009). Reflexive culture's consequences. In C. Nakata (ed.), *Beyond Hofstede*. London: Palgrave Macmillan, pp. 101–22.

Bhagat, R.S., Triandis, H.C. and McDevitt, A.S. (2012). *Managing Global Organizations: A Cultural Perspective*. Cheltenham, UK and Northampton, MA, USA: Edward Elgar Publishing.

BMW History (n.d.). Accessed at http://www.bmw.com/com/en/index_narrowband.html.

Brady, C. and Lorenz, A. (2001). End of the road: BMW and Rover: a brand too far. *Financial Times*.

Briley, D.A. (2009). Cultural influence on consumer motivations: A dynamic view. In C. Nakata (ed.), *Beyond Hofstede*. London: Palgrave Macmillan, pp. 181–97.

Carter, M. (1996). Britain's Bavarian bulldog. *Director*, January, pp. 28–33.

Clark, L.A. (1987). Mutual relevance of mainstream and cross-cultural psychology. *Journal of Consulting and Clinical Psychology*, 55(4).

Cova, B., Giordano, A., Pallera, M., Fuschillo, G. and Sala, M. (2012). *Marketing Non-convenzionale: Viral, Guerrilla, Tribal, Societing e i 10 principi Fondamentali del Marketing Postmoderno*. Gruppo 24 Ore.

De Mooij, M. (2013). On the misuse and misinterpretation of dimensions of national culture. *International Marketing Review*, 30(3).

Douglas, S.P. and Craig, C.S. (2009). Impact of context on cross-cultural research. In C. Nakata (ed.), *Beyond Hofstede*. London: Palgrave Macmillan, pp. 125–45.

Dunning, J.H. (1988). The theory of international production. *The International Trade Journal*, 3(1), 21–66.

Edwards, C. (2004). Productivity drive. *People Management*, pp. 14–15.

Fan, Y. (2000). A classification of Chinese culture. *Cross Cultural Management: An International Journal*, 7(2), 3–10.

Fu, J.H.Y. and Chiu, C.Y. (2007). Local culture's responses to globalization: Exemplary persons and their attendant values. *Journal of Cross-Cultural Psychology*, 38(5).

Giddens, A. (2000), *Runaway World*. New York: Routledge.

Gudykunst, W.B., Ting-Toomey, S. and Chua, E. (1988). *Culture and Interpersonal Communication*. Thousand Oaks, CA: Sage Publications.

Guilford, J.P. (1959). *Personality*. New York: McGraw-Hill.

Hall, E.T. (1960). The silent language in overseas business. *Harvard Business Review*, 38(3), 87–96.

Hall, E.T. (1969). *The Hidden Dimension*. New York: Anchor Books.

Hall, E.T. (1981). *Beyond Culture*. New York: Anchor Books.

Hall, E.T. (1984). *The Dance of Life*. New York: Anchor Books.

Hall, E.T. and Hall, T. (1959). *The Silent Language* (Vol. 948). New York: Anchor Books.

Hammerich, K. and Lewis, R.D. (2013). *Fish Can't See Water*. Chichester: Wiley.

Herbig, P.A. (2000). *Handbook of Cross-Cultural Marketing*. Binghampton, NY: Haworth Press.

Herskovits, M.J. (2010). *The Human Factor in Changing Africa*. Whitefish, MT: Kessinger Publishing.

Hofstede, G. (1979). Value systems in forty countries: Interpretation, validation, and consequences for theory. In L.H. Eckensberger, W.J. Lonner and Poortinga, Y.H. (eds), *Cross-Cultural Contributions to Psychology*. Lisse: Swets and Zeitlinger.

Hofstede, G. (1980). *Culture's Consequences: International Differences in Work-related Values*. Beverly Hills, CA: Sage Publications.

Hofstede, G. (1982). Dimensions of national cultures. In R. Rath, H.S. Asthana, D. Sinhaand and J.B.H. Sinha (eds), *Diversity and Unity in Cross-cultural Psychology*. Lisse: Swets and Zeitlinger.

Hofstede, G. (1983). Dimensions of national cultures in fifty countries and three regions. In J.B. Deregowski, S. Dziurawiec and R.C. Annis (eds), *Expiscations in Cross-cultural Psychology*. Lisse: Swets and Zeitlinger.

Hofstede, G. (1984). *Culture's Consequences: International Differences in Work-related Values*. Thousand Oaks, CA: Sage Publications.

Hofstede, G. (2001). *Culture's Consequences*. Thousand Oaks, CA: Sage Publications.

Hofstede, G. (2006). What did GLOBE really measure? Researchers' minds versus respondents' minds. *Journal of International Business Studies*, 37(6), 882–96.

Hofstede, G. (2011). Dimensionalizing cultures: The Hofstede model in context. *Online Readings in Psychology and Culture*, Unit 2. Accessed at http://scholarworks.gvsu.edu/orpc/vol2/iss1/8.

Hofstede, G. and Bond, M.H. (1988). The Confucius connection: From cultural roots to economic growth. *Organizational Dynamics*, 16(4), 5–21.

Hoppe, M.H. (1992). A comparative study of country elites: International differences in work-related values and learning and their implications for management training and development. PhD dissertation, The University of North Carolina.

House, R.J., Hanges, P.J., Javidan, M., Dorfman, P.W. and Gupta, V. (eds) (2004). *Culture, Leadership, and Organizations: The GLOBE Study of 62 Societies*. Thousand Oaks, CA: Sage Publications.

Kluckhohn, C. (1951). *Values and Value-Orientations in the Theory of Action: An Exploration in Definition and Classification*, In T. Parsons and E. Shils (eds), *Toward a General Theory of Action*. Cambridge, MA: Harvard University Press, pp. 388–433.

Kroeber, A.L. and Parsons T. (1958). The concepts of culture and of social system. *American Sociological Review*, 23, 582–3.

Kuckhohn, F.R. and Strodback, F.L. (1961). *Variations in Value Orientation*. London: Greenwood Press.

Johanson, J., and Vahlne, J.-E. (1977). The Internationalization process of the firm: A model of knowledge development and increasing foreign market commitments. *Journal of International Business Studies*, 8(1): 23–32.

Johanson, J. and Vahlne, J.E. (2009). The Uppsala internationalization process model revisited: From liability of foreignness to liability of outsidership. *Journal of International Business Studies*, 40(9), 1411–31.

Johanson, J. and Wiedersheim-Paul, F. (1975). The internationalization of the firm: Four Swedish cases. *Journal of Management Studies*, 12(3), 305–22.

Johnson, J., Lenartowicz, T. and Apud, S. (2006). Cross-cultural competence in international business: Toward a definition and a model. *Journal of International Business Studies*, 37, 525–43.

Landes, D.S. (1998). *The Wealth and Poverty of Nations: Why Some are so Rich and Some so Poor*. New York: Norton.

Levi, J. (2003). BMW turns to experts to help steer Mini on to right track. *The Daily Telegraph*, p. 32.

Levitt, T. (1983). The globalization of markets. *Harvard Business Review*, May–June.

Lewis, R. (2010). *When Cultures Collide*. Boston, MA: Nicholas Brealey Publishing.

Linstead, S. (1997). The social anthropology of management. *British Journal of Management*, 8(1), 85–98.

Lynn, M. and Gelb, B.D. (1996). Identifying innovative national markets for technical consumer goods. *International Marketing Review*, 13(6).

Mackintosh, J. (2003). Good ideas pay dividends: An employee suggestion program at BMW's Mini plant saves millions annually. *National Post*, 7 April, BE4.

Maleki, A. and de Jong, M. (2014). A proposal for clustering the dimensions of national culture. *Cross-Cultural Research*, 48(2).

Malinowski, B. (1944). *A Scientific Theory of Culture and Other Essays*. Chapel Hill, NC: University of North Carolina Press.

McSweeney, B. (2002). Hofstede's model of national cultural differences and their consequences: A triumph of faith – a failure of analysis. *Human Relations*, 55(1).

Meyer, E. (2015). *The Culture Map: Decoding How People Think, Lead, and Get Things Done Across Cultures*. New York: Public Affairs.

Minkov, M. (2007). *What Makes Us Different and Similar: A New Interpretation of the World Values Survey and other Cross-cultural Data*. Sofia: Klasika i Stil Publishing House.

Mooney, P. (2002). Learning the old ways. *Newsweek*, 27 May.

Rapaille, C. (2006). *The Culture Code*. New York: Crown Business.

Robertson, R. (1992). *Globalisation: Social Theory and Global Culture*. Thousand Oaks, CA: Sage Publications.

Roe, R.A. and Ester, P. (1999). Values and work: Empirical findings and theoretical perspective. *Applied Psychology*, 48(1), 1–21.

Rugman, A.M. and Verbeke, A. (2003). Extending the theory of the multinational enterprise: Internalization and strategic management perspectives. *Journal of International Business Studies*, 34(2), 125–37.

Schwartz, S.H. (1992). Universals in the content and structure of values: Theoretical advances and empirical tests in 20 countries. In M.P. Zinna (ed.), *Advances in Experimental Social Psychology*, Vol. 25. Academic Press, pp. 1–65.

Schwartz, S.H. (1999). A theory of cultural values and some implications for work. *Applied Psychology: an International Review*, 48(1), 23–47.

Schwartz, S. (2006). A theory of cultural value orientations: Explication and applications. *Comparative Sociology*, 5(2–3), 137–82.

Schwartz, S.H. (2009). Culture matters: National value cultures, sources and consequences. In C.-Y. Chiu, Y.Y. Hong, S. Shavitt and R.S. Wyer, Jr (eds), *Understanding Culture: Theory, Research and Application*. New York: Psychology Press, pp. 127–50.

Schwartz, S.H. (2012). An overview of the Schwartz theory of basic values. *Online Readings in Psychology and Culture*, 2(1), 2307–919.

Smith, P.B. (2006). When elephants fight, the grass gets trampled: The GLOBE and Hofstede projects. *Journal of International Business Studies*, 37(6), 915–21.

Soares, A.M., Farhangmehr, M. and Shoham, A. (2007). Hofstede's dimensions of culture in international marketing studies. *Journal of Business Research*, 60(3).

Steers, R.M. and Osland, J.S. (2020). *Management Across Cultures*. Cambridge: Cambridge University Press.

Suerdem, A. (1994). Social de(re)construction of mass culture: Making (non)sense of consumer behavior. *International Journal of Research in Marketing*, 11(4).

Sun, G., D'Alessandro, S., Johnson, L.W. and Winzar, H. (2014). Do we measure what we expect to measure? Some issues in the measurement of culture in consumer research. *International Marketing Review*, 31(4).

Swidler, A. (1986). Culture in action: Symbols and strategies. *American Sociological Review*, 51(2), 273–86.

Tadajewski, M. and Wagner-Tsukamoto, S. (2006). Anthropology and consumer research: Qualitative insights into green consumer behavior. *Qualitative Market Research: An International Journal*, 9(1).

Taras, V. and Steel, P. (2009). Beyond Hofstede: Challenging the ten commandments of cross-cultural research. In C. Nakata (ed.), *Beyond Hofstede*. London: Palgrave Macmillan, pp. 40–46.

Tian, K. and Borges, L. (2012). The effectiveness of social marketing mix strategy: Towards an anthropological approach. *International Journal of Business Anthropology*, 3(1).

Triandis, H.C. (1989). The self and social behavior in differing cultural contexts. *Psychological Review*, 96(3), 506.

Triandis, H.C. (2001). Individualism-collectivism and personality. *Journal of Personality*, 69(6), 907–24.

Trompenaars, F. and Hampden-Turner, C. (1997). *Riding the Waves of Culture: Understanding Cultural Diversity in Business*. London: Nicholas Brealey.

Trompenaars, F. and Woolliams, P. (2003). *Business across Cultures*. Chichester: Capstone.

Trompenaars, F., Prud'Homme, P. and Trompenaars, A. (2004). *Managing Change Across Corporate Cultures*, Vol. 3. Chichester: Capstone.

Usunier, J-C. and Lee, A. (2013). *Marketing Across Cultures*. Harlow: Pearson.

Watkins, J. (2003). A Mini adventure. *People Management*, pp. 30–32.

Weber, M. (2010). *The Protestant Ethic and the Spirit of Capitalism*. New York: Oxford University Press.

Wikipedia (2006). BMW. 8 March. Accessed at http://en.wikipedia.org/wiki/BMW.

Winick, C. (1961). Anthropology's contributions to marketing. *Journal of Marketing*, 25(5), 53–60.

Zucchella, A. and Siano, A. (2014). Internationalization and innovation as resources for SME growth in foreign markets: A focus on textile and clothing firms in the Campania Region. *International Studies of Management & Organization*, 44(1), 21–41.

# PART II
## TOWARDS A CROSS-CULTURAL MODEL OF MARKETING STRATEGY

# 5
# Evolution of international markets

International markets represent the frontiers of global development, and not grasping the potential they offer to the development of European MMNEs means putting the survival of the companies themselves at risk. These markets are often culturally very distant from national ones and therefore pose, as already mentioned above, a triple challenge to companies: (1) to contribute to their formation so that the offers of medium-sized international companies can be understood and exploited; (2) to develop ways of intercultural education, coherent with their cultures; (3) to build completely new models of international development of MMNEs, adapted to the changes that have occurred in world economic scenarios.

The geography of international markets has changed a lot over the past twenty years. There have been cyclical developments, relating to periods of crisis and economic recovery, but above all some basic conditions have changed, which produce a long-term rooting in the markets. These changes, after long years of substantial stability, from the second post-war period to the end of the twentieth century, create completely new conditions that interrupt and modify the trends that dominated the second half of the twentieth century.

In particular, with regard to the area of marketing that this book deals with, a trend that seemed unstoppable has changed speed, characteristics and direction: the globalization of markets. Since the early 1980s, with Levitt's (1983) article predicting the unstoppable globalization of markets, the phenomenon of market unification and homogeneity had seemed an unstoppable trend. This prediction had aroused enthusiasm and criticism, but still it seemed that nothing could stop it. It was the powerful advance of the Washington Consensus. This seemed to become inevitable after the US–USSR dualism ended in the late 1980s. In ten years, therefore, what many economists had predicted seemed to come true: the end of opposing and rival systems, the homogenization of society and consumption patterns. But the easy snapshot of that moment turned out to be only temporary (Oppenheimer, 2007). At the beginning of the new millennium a new reality was to have appeared, whose main trends, relating to the evolution of international markets (Rugman, 2012), can be summarized as follows.

First of all, *new national players* have appeared on the international markets, some rapidly occupying an important space, others in search of the never achieved maintenance of a potential promise of growth. China and Vietnam are certainly among the first, and to a lesser extent Russia has joined Japan and South Korea as key economic players. The latter are Brazil, South Africa, Mexico, India and others. This evolution can also be read through the evolution of international intergovernmental economic groups that have moved from the G-7 (Canada, France, Germany, Japan, Italy, United Kingdom, United States) to the G-8 with the addition of Russia, up to the G-20 (Saudi Arabia, Argentina, Australia, Brazil, Canada, China, France, Germany, Japan, India, Indonesia, Italy, Mexico, United Kingdom, Russia, United States, South Africa,

South Korea, Turkey, European Union), where also, as in the case of the European Union, the economies of some nations are considered twice, individually and as a whole. The evolution of these groupings describes a situation of liquid globalization (Baumann, 2005), where there is no definite prevalence, where continuous change, variable plurality and inhomogeneity seem to dominate.

*New balances of economic and market strength* have been formed, highlighting how multi-dimensionality has become the key to interpreting the world, from North America (USA and Canada), to Europe (European Union), India, China, South-East Asia (Vietnam, Singapore, Thailand) and Australia, to North-East Asia (Japan and Korea). The plurality of forces that act on different levels of comparison of development and consumption models and not simply of acceptance of a single dominant model, make mutual influence possible and frequent, which leads to the construction of new models, different from previous ones and different from each other. The reciprocal influence, in fact, does not lead to a homogeneous and unique solution, but favours the modernization of consumption models that follow different paths. The Chinese consumer, for example, acquires Western models which he/she immerses in Confucian culture by creating a new pattern of values and consumption choices, just as a European consumer acquires oriental influences and inserts them into his/her cultural reference framework.

Some *innovative purchasing and consumption cultures* have been strengthened alongside more traditional ones. In particular, high context cultures (Hall, 1981), typical of the Confucian area, as well as the Mediterranean, have increased their importance with the economic growth of South-East Asia and China. The need to deepen the knowledge of the cultural context of business activities, both B2C and B2B, has become a fundamental rule for the development of one's business in the fastest-growing markets. They did not replace low-context entrepreneurial cultures (USA, Germany, Northern Europe), but created a new approach to international markets, with the need for cultural learning not usual in the past, dominated by US management theory. Again, entering international markets requires a variety of approaches.

The shift of the *market axis to the East* is very evident. Obviously, the East defines a group of nations and a geographic area, and not a direction. Shifting the market axis is a frequent historical condition, albeit over long periods. Only considering the last century has the axis shifted westward in the USA–Europe binomial, now it moves towards the Far East (Fujita and Krugman, 2004). The geography of the markets is not stable but follows the speed of growth and development that is generated in some areas for different reasons and causes, but which constitute new wealth. The wealth of nations determines the poles of attraction for international businesses.

*New competitive players* come into play, find success in their home markets and subsequently expand into traditionally more developed markets. Until 2013, among the top 25 global brands in value (Brand Finance, 2021) there were only one Korean, one Japanese and one Chinese; the rest of the brands included one German, one Dutch, two British and 17 Americans. In the 2021 report, among the top 25 there are a Korean, a Japanese and 11 Chinese, of which five are banking and six linked to the digital world. The rest consists of one German and nine American brands. It is an extremely clear sign of the growing importance of the new Chinese brands on the market, which have exceeded American brands in number of appearances, although the latter occupy the top four places in the ranking.

This multipolar evolution, where America and China confront each other directly, but where there are other important realities, even if not large, such as the European Union, India and Russia, and other minor regional economic powers, creates the conditions for *strong competition*, but also for an *inevitable collaboration*. The relationship plans with the market are therefore different. A plan concerns competitive rules, protectionist actions, and defences against competitive advantages created in conditions of non-parity of rules. Another plan concerns the collaborations and intertwining dictated by the conditions of global economies, which lead to integrated production, collaborations for product development, and international distribution between the same nations that on the other level seem hostile. Everything is made more complex by the framework of international finance, which introduces further links and dependencies that are reflected in the market actions. The continuous search for a balance in which the weights continue to vary is therefore a condition of normality.

Finally, it is necessary to consider the influence that the two megatrends of the new millennium exert on the markets: the spread of digitization and the growth of the sustainable economy. Digital transformation is a long-standing challenge faced by businesses and consumers that is not over yet, but that has changed purchasing habits, processes and decisions (Quinn et al., 2016). It also designs an international market that has no limits; it is not global, or it is only partially global, but it is certainly without borders. This is creating social, fiscal and legal repercussions in the markets that give rise to increasingly worried criticism and the demand for greater control, aspects that concern decisions that are still in motion. Environmental sustainability represents the most important epochal challenge for various societies, first of all economically advanced nations (Belz and Peattie, 2009). Sensitivity to ecological issues has grown exponentially on two fronts that surround companies and heavily influence their behaviour, consumers and governments. In some countries and in some cultures the issue has mainly become a question from consumers to producers; let's define it as bottom-up. A sometimes underground social movement, sometimes sensationally evident, asks for product solutions linked to environmental sustainability. This happens especially in European and North American countries. In other contexts, where the form of government is not liberal or it is in a very limited way, preventing or hindering social protest movements, it is governments that oblige companies to respect the environment, a process that we can define as top-down, as is happening in China, where the environmental situation has been bent to the need for economic development, creating unsustainable health risk situations that have been tried to be remedied in recent years.

International markets are therefore assuming a liquid state, continuously variable, changing geography and characteristics, and expanding the intercultural challenge. The marketing approach to the various international markets finds complex challenges that highlight the task of social responsibility.

## 5.1 STRATEGY: STANDARDIZATION OR ADAPTATION?

Global strategy is defined as the way a company competes in the global market and plays a vital role on determining the performance of a business in the global market. By conceiving a global strategy, management articulates sourcing, R&D and manufacturing, and marketing must be coordinated worldwide. 'Because marketing assumes the role of interacting directly with the customers marketing strategy is probably the most important component of a firm's global strategy (Zou and Cavusgil, 1996). Levitt (1983) maintained that communication, transportation, technology and travel would eradicate country differences and lead to universal needs that companies could satisfy by standardized products.

As a result, there is a difference between multinationals and global companies.

> The multinational corporation operates in a number of countries and adjusts its products and practices in each—at high relative costs. The global corporation operates with resolute constancy—at low relative cost—as if the entire world (or major regions of it) were a single entity; it sells the same things in the same way everywhere. (Levitt, 1983).

The biggest advantage of this approach results in economies of scale that lower the price and allow high quality products. The battlefield concentrates on lowering the prices, while proposing high quality products.

Contrasting opinions state that an effective global strategy requires not a single approach, such as product standardization, but a differentiated strategy, while Hamel and Prahalad (1994) maintain the need for a diversified portfolio and believe that 'a global strategy requires several product varieties, so that investments in technologies, brand names and distribution channels can be shared'. Quelch and Hoff (1986) emphasize the importance of being responsive to local market conditions. Bartlett and Ghoshal (1991) maintain that 'globalizing and localizing forces work together to transform many industries, and success depends on whether a business can achieve global efficiency and national flexibility simultaneously'. Competing with multiple strategies in the same global industry is more successful than adopting a single approach.

There is a pre-internationalization phase in which the focus is establishing a strong position in the domestic market, and the strategy adopted in the domestic market determines the direction of internationalization. In the initial phase exports are usually the chosen pattern and manufacturing and R&D are centrally controlled. The costs of entering a new market have to be evaluated considering to which degree a standardized approach can be followed. The choice comprehends choosing which products can be marketed and to which degree the domestic marketing mix can be followed. Cavusgil and Zou (1994) find a positive relationship between product adaptation and an export venture's performance. Many scholars agree that global marketing strategy plays a critical role in determining a firm's performance in the global market and that the success of the companies in the twenty-first century will depend on whether they can compete effectively in world markets.

The question to be investigated is if in the new culturally distant markets, such as China, Vietnam and India, the standardization strategy should always be adopted, or whether adaptation is the more suitable solution in certain industries (Zhang and Yanqun, 2012).

Past studies have been mainly focused on the analysis of globalization's effects on consumer behaviour and preferences. Some scholars have identified globalization as a driver for a future consumer convergence, while others see it as a phenomenon able to reduce the divergence between countries up to a limited point. At one extreme, standards and consumers' needs would converge, arousing the creation of global markets with standardized products. Cultural differences and national or regional preferences would disappear, leading to the extinction of corporations defined as multinational, that is, companies that adjust their products to each country they operate in while favouring the stabilization of global companies that would standardize their offers in all the markets by creating a global product identical in each and every market.

Companies would be able to benefit from scale economies in all the commercial aspects such as distribution, production, marketing and management, by favouring the elimination of gaps in qualitative variables such as business conduct and in quantitative elements such as prices, margins and profit gaps (Levitt, 1983).

Globalization would lead to the creation of a global market free of distinctions in terms of preferences and tastes, enclosing the success of a company in its efficiency over management, marketing, distribution and production.

At the other extreme, scholars have rejected this thesis, showing that globalization favours convergence on only some dimensions, such as the state of economy. By this line of reasoning the occurrence of unpracticable aspects dictated by the culture leads to a concurrent divergence and convergence of consumers' preferences and behaviours. Differences in terms of consumption are stable and still diverging, except in isolated cases, eliminating the historical myth of presence of a global target characterized by the same preferences and needs such as the global teenagers' target (Mooij, 2003).

Accordingly, the use of national wealth differences as a benchmark to identify markets' divergence loses its explanatory role, rather favouring other dimensions able to capture all its inner aspects. Thus, the degree of proximity between countries become predictable thanks to the ability of culture to justify the differences in terms of consumption and tools to attain marketing efficiency towards the adaptation of cultural values mostly influencing all aspects of marketing, from promotional campaigns to inner strategy. For instance, Asian countries consider it to be an aim of marketing to create relationships and trust between company and consumers.

Global products, introduced for the first time by pilot companies in terms of advanced marketing research applications such as household and cleaning products, soft drinks and cigarettes, could be identified as a homogeneous product category. Indeed, not recalling intrinsic cultural meanings, they are characterized by global advertising defined merely as the cause of current differences in usage.

Nowadays, the debate is all about whether companies operating at an international or global level should standardize their marketing strategies and programmes, offering an essentially uniform marketing mix to all the markets in which they operate around the world, or whether they should tailor and adapt the marketing mix to local needs, valuing varying cultural and behavioural dimensions and differentiating them in each market of the global arena. Using as a base the theories explained above, companies selling at least in one foreign market have to select their best fitting strategy combining as much as possible both firm and consumer needs.

The starting point of all the marketing activities is the formulation of a product strategy since this is the first element that people see and interact with and it greatly affects the consumer's decision. It represents the expression of the company's mission and vision. It includes all the decisions concerning the design, technology, usefulness, value, convenience, quality, packaging, branding, warranties and after sales services. Generating divergent feelings among consumers, it plays a key role in the international scenario where companies take on different typologies of strategies aimed at capturing new and cross-cultural consumers.

As a result, companies formulate a new marketing strategy taking into account new variables such as consumer behaviours and different tastes, and decide whether to implement a product standardization strategy or an adaptation strategy.

A product standardization strategy implies the creation of a global product intended for a global consumer who looks for high-quality products at a low price and implies a reduction to zero of all the differences in terms of targeting, branding and product attributes.

A product standardization strategy is facilitated by the similarity between countries in terms of the economic and infrastructural stage, regulatory environment and competitive intensity and it is positively related to the degree of globalization and technology advancement.

However, it is particularly challenging in culturally distant markets since it can undermine the company's foreign market position due to the presence of barriers which tend to disallow the perfect convergence of tastes and preferences. Barriers are created by singular traditions, norms of behaviours and local value systems, which shape the way business is conducted in each nation (Dimitrova and Rosenbloom, 2010).

Adaptation allows the satisfaction of consumer needs and the enforcement of the company's competitive position by the creation of tailored products and broad product lines. Requiring a balance between local autonomy and central coordination, it needs a wide investigation of local market differences such as the state of the economy, the stage of the product life-cycle, the competition, the distribution, the legal restrictions, the physical environment and the level of cultural proximity. Indeed, the composition and characteristics of the local market strongly affect the importance of home demand and the company's perception, interpretation and response to buyer needs.

In certain cases, companies are even forced to change their product to be allowed to sell a domestic product as an original made in the international environment due to the presence of mandatory restrictions. In this case, companies are forced to modify their offer in order to sell products in foreign countries due to legal, political, economic, technological and other unpredictable restrictions.

Political adaptations depend on the foreign trade and tax policy, the level of political stability and corruption, the government and labour policy and the trade restrictions. Where trade is restricted, the export of the good in its original state may be either blocked as soon as it physically enters the market or counterfeited shortly thereafter.

Sometimes, companies also have to alter their products because of different body shapes: Asian fitting is the most relevant example. Compared to Westerners, Asians have a different nose shape, forcing eyewear companies to reshape their products, changing the nose pads of glasses. Asians also have different shaped feet, making it necessary to reshape the shoes when making Asian sizes. The Chinese have smaller, streamlined and wide-soled feet compared to Westerners, with a low instep, causing a shift in the curve of the size's scale.

Companies can spontaneously decide to adapt their products to the local market. Alterations can be implanted in all the product features, from the design to the branding, in relation to local needs. Often, companies alter the products' original design in order to meet functionality requirements which vary in countries according to social, environmental and technology concerns. Indeed, age distribution, career and lifestyle attitudes, emphasis on safety, health consciousness, cultural barriers and population growth rate lead to taste alterations across countries. A younger target with a contemporary lifestyle would be likely to appreciate glamour and stylish products more than an old-fashioned target. In particular, the level of education and the gender gap, in particular, affect the production of specific goods categories such as luxury products and, for instance, high-end footwear due to the loss of the traditional feminine way of purchasing.

In the same vein, environmental concerns such as weather and climate differences, environmental policies, pressures of NGOs and climate change, could totally overturn the target's requests and the product functionality in turn, favouring design or packaging alterations. At other times, companies add or remove design features, looking for the particular properties that local consumers are interested in. For instance, Coca Cola is sweeter and less gassy in America than in Italy and it has different flavours, such as Cherry Coke.

Companies usually make this decision for economic and brand awareness reasons. Basically, they desire either to increase the company's position in the marketplace, improve the company's local distribution system or improve its image by matching consumer preferences as far as possible. It requires great flexibility, organization and goodwill resources to combine local responsiveness and global efficiency's goals simultaneously, and also often to modify the other correlated marketing mix dimensions. Not surprisingly, the costs of adapting to local markets are very high since companies have to replicate activities already performed in the home market and modify them in relation to local requests. The replication costs are particularly evident in those industries where adaptation is forced due to the presence of national standards: companies have also to replicate test and certification procedures.

Summarizing, the selection of a product adaptation strategy is favoured when companies have to deal with cultural differences, contrasting consumer preferences intended as the patterns of decision outcomes according to consumers' characteristics, different product use conditions, a high level of market competition, both economic and technological turbulence, and a strong level of compliance between headquarters and subsidiaries.

In the real world, companies are rarely able to totally adapt strategy to the local market by applying a pure brand adaptation strategy. They usually choose between the exportation of the domestic product with some adaptations, the creation of a standardized product adjusted for transnational targets and the desired creation of a new product conveyed to the foreign market. Therefore, after consideration of the main issues concerning the social-cultural, political, economic, legal, environmental and technological dimensions, companies decide on their most suitable strategy.

Although the investigation of the political, economic, legal, environmental and technological states of affair is likely to change across sectors, the socio-cultural dimension is almost static and embodied in the country's essence. This is exactly why the former are easily predictable through strategic tools such as the PESTELE (Political, Economic, Social, Technological,

Environmental, Legal, Ethical) analysis, one of the most employed, while the latter require an accurate and deeper analysis (Figure 5.1).

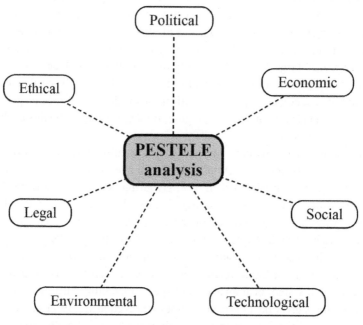

**Figure 5.1**      PESTELE analysis components

An example of successful adaptation is an American company, Häagen-Dazs. Its mooncakes are an example of how the brand has adapted culturally while retaining its global identity. Häagen-Dazs created the 'premium ice cream' category with its rich ice cream made with exotic ingredients such as Belgian chocolate and vanilla beans from Madagascar. It reinforces the message of indulgence through its prizewinning advertising campaigns and new flavours. Just as Starbucks was expected to fail in a nation of tea drinkers, Häagen-Dazs was expected to flop, as dessert in China was just fruit. In carving out a brand identity specific to China, Häagen-Dazs decided not to compete with incumbent ice cream brands, and instead aligned itself with Western icons of luxury. Despite the traditional lack of dairy products in the Chinese diet, venturing on to the mainland in 1996 the company introduced a completely different set of challenges. One of the most appealing was to direct the brand at the local hunger for luxury goods that were markers of economic status. Luxury brands such as Louis Vuitton and Cartier lined the high-end shopping areas of Shanghai and Beijing. With increased buying power and a diminishing stigma on displays of wealth, the upper-class Chinese appeared well situated to appreciate Häagen-Dazs's themes of indulgence and self-gratification. The strategy was simple: high-end real estate and service reminiscent of a five-star hotel. Patrons were served on Wedgwood tableware by highly trained staff in an ambience that suggested a European patisserie. The extensive all-dessert menu had the word 'Indulgence' on the cover.

# 6
# Acquainted and non-acquainted markets

We consider an *Acquainted Market* to be a market in which the knowledge of consumers and customers has reached a sufficient level to make them able to understand, and correctly evaluate, the differences in quality present in the offers proposed by the various competitors (Chang et al., 2010). Acquainted markets are generally developed, differentiated and segmented markets. Small and Medium-sized Enterprises (SMEs) mainly target these markets, in particular medium-sized enterprises, which cannot deal with mass markets due to their wide extension and the general characteristics of the needs to be satisfied they require, which are far from the targeted skills the SMEs possess. Typically, such companies are successful in niche markets, where customer expertise, knowledge and experience are accumulated in sufficient size to understand and appreciate the value proposal they offer (the product characteristics and components of the marketing mix), which contains elements of great complexity. In fact, the value perceived by customers in an offer depends on the level of knowledge (Grewal et al., 1998) and on the experience they have accumulated over time on products and brands, in other words it depends on their ability to recognize the differentiation elements of value and higher quality (Hong and Sternthal, 2010) contained in the proposals of the MMNEs (Medium-sized Multinational Enterprises), compared to the mass market products generally offered by the MNEs (Multinational Enterprises), therefore able to attribute an adequate perception of value to the proposals of the MMNEs operating in international contexts.[1]

In acquainted markets, many skills are acquired and learned using and consuming products, from the simplest to the most complex, in a learning process that normally lasts for years, built through the acquisition of knowledge that is formed both individually and collectively. This can be defined as a 'social experience of value' (Sridhar and Srinivasan, 2012). This socio-individual path facilitates the evolution from a mass market, based on an offer characterized by high standardization, to a niche market, where specificity and differentiation dominate, according to a cyclical development that has covered the history of markets. Internationally, MMNEs have found very different and widespread levels of expertise among customers, due to the different levels of development of each single national market, as is evident, for example, in the case of China and India. European MMNES come from their home markets, where they draw the sources of their competitive advantages, where there are very sophisticated customers who are extremely knowledgeable about products and brands, in other words they are acquainted customers and consumers. Companies, in their continuous process of internationalization, should now face new markets characterized by inadequate knowledge, if compared with the complexity of the offer they propose.

Whether or not there is an informed and acquainted market influences the decisions of the MMNE with respect to the times and objectives of the entry mode and process. For many MMNEs, this means implementing a second-mover strategy (Carpenter and Nakamoto, 1996), first waiting for other companies, usually large multinationals, to help build the basic knowledge that consumers need to correctly perceive the value contained in the various offers. In B2C markets, the main players are mainly large multinationals. In many cases, indeed, huge investments of resources are needed to create and shape these 'new' markets. As large multinationals acquire a presence and gradually consolidate it, a learning process about products and brands begins that influences consumer behaviour.

For example, in a country like China, where the consumption of coffee has no tradition and consumers have very little knowledge of the product, the spread of a basic offer promoted by large multinationals such as Starbucks allows the birth and growth of the coffee market. Subsequently, other smaller companies, such as the MMNEs Illy or Lavazza, can come into play as quality niches become real, offering products with higher quality characteristics at a higher price, but acceptable, because they are assessed more competently by the consumer. However, coming from a very sophisticated market like the Italian one, MMNEs are unable to create the basic skills and knowledge about coffee in China for two reasons: (a) their limited size for such a large market does not allow them to have enough resources available to create a social experience of the value of coffee; (b) the excessive refinement of their offer makes it unsuitable for markets still in the learning phase. Therefore, they log in as a second-mover. The literature on internationalization underlines the need to acquire sufficient knowledge on foreign markets, especially from the direct experience acquired in operating across borders. However, little is discussed about the need for markets to understand the offer of companies and its development through the education of the market itself. Fewer still are the insights into which ways to follow to educate the market more quickly.

Knowledge of foreign markets can be classified (Eriksson et al., 2015) in three ways: institutional competence, business competence, and internationalization competence. The first, institutional competence, refers to knowledge of foreign culture, institutions, norms and social regulations. Business competence refers to knowledge of consumers, competitors and market conditions in specific countries. The last type, internationalization competence, concerns the company know-how in terms of resource adaptability and about the competences needed to undertake international operations. While the first two help the company to be vigilant about the opportunities and problems that can be generated in the overseas markets, the third skill allows the company to take appropriate actions to open new markets (Zhou, 2007).

MMNEs should therefore develop the three abovementioned skills in order to enter foreign markets with a reasonable hope of success. So far, the literature has mainly described conditions on the company side, but there is no study of conditions on the market side. In fact, it is assumed that the flexibility of the company should be at a maximum and that it can and must be fully adapted to market conditions. This, as reality shows, is not entirely true. Although the greatest effort to adapt to market conditions is responsibility of the company, it cannot distort its nature, its skills and competences, the sources of its competitive advantages, according to a logic of zero-based strategy. Its product and market culture, combined with its average size and often with entrepreneurial characteristics of governance, limit its total adaptability:

in other words, to achieve its objectives, the company requires the presence of a sufficiently educated market for its offer. Therefore there are two dynamic positions: (a) the position of the company that tries to adapt as much as possible to the market, approaching offer conditions that are understandable to customers; (b) the position of the market that acquires competence, approaching an increase in the company offer compatible with its culture of quality.

Customers increase their experience over time through purchasing behaviour. As their expertise grows, specific and sophisticated segments of customers in search of high-end goods and services increase in the market. Consumers' approach to products that require a high degree of experience in new uneducated markets is limited and reduced by diverse cultural habits, by simplified and elementary marketing policies by distribution companies, and by greatly simplified price–quality comparison. The highest quality products, when they do not base their attractiveness above all on the value, knowledge and reputation of the brand, require experience and competence from the customer; this clearly has obvious implications for MMNEs' entry strategies and entry modes in emerging markets.

The entry of MMNEs into the new B2B markets, not educated to the complexity and perfor-mance of industrial goods normally offered in developed markets, is explained by the presence of their traditional customers who already operate in those markets and who also require their regular suppliers in new realities that are developing. The first comers are therefore still mul-tinationals offering mass products and representing educated customers of MMNE B2B; for industrial customers a critical factor is represented by maintaining the same configuration of the supply chain and the value chain that they have designed in the markets of origin.

Medium-sized enterprises that are specialized suppliers of large multinationals, by necessity have to locate in markets not acquainted by the direct request of their customers, who are multinationals that are investing in those markets. It is therefore not a question of a free and autonomous decision to enter a new market, but rather of the need to serve a large strategic customer, and following it wherever it is located. In this sense, the acquainted market of MMNEs is delocalized to an emerging country, through a consolidated clientele acquired for some time in a traditional market.

The process of internationalization of the MMNEs of the B2B sectors shows how this is mainly driven by the need to follow customers and subsequently trying to expand their pres-ence in the market once they are more acquainted with their products. Therefore, in the case of B2B markets, large client companies decide to enter as first mover and MMNE suppliers follow them, with a second level decision. This explains once again why MMNEs tend to play a second mover role in emerging markets. In a first phase, large B2C companies open up and create new markets by generating space for B2B companies (development of the supply part); subsequently, as consumers acquire more experience and knowledge, they end up generating further demand in specific high-end niches (demand side development) for B2C MMNEs.

The choice of the moment of entry seems to have a profound influence on the performance of MMNEs: early entry would not find a market, just as late entry would encounter formidable competition and very little space. In this perspective, MMNEs' exploration of new markets, aimed at specific high-end niches, requires a deep understanding of how fast the process of spreading the acceptance of high quality and consequently of higher prices is, both by end consumers and B2B customers, moving from a cost-focused strategy to a performance-oriented one.

In summary, what emerges from the research in the field highlights that MMNEs enter culturally distant and new markets in four different ways:

- In B2B markets, following existing customers (especially big multinational companies) who enter new markets as mass producers; in this case the big first mover multinational companies represent the educated market for MMNEs;
- In B2B markets, when potential local customers become 'acquainted' (mainly due to changes in consumer markets, which in turn have become 'acquainted' and require higher quality products) by improving MMNEs' offering, once the most sophisticated supply needs are perceived in terms of quality and performance;
- In B2C markets, when consumers are able to perceive the different quality and performance offered by MMNEs, having been educated and informed about products and brands;
- in B2C markets activating a process of exploration and adaptation to the new cultural context of the market.

Markets therefore need to be explored more in terms of customer knowledge and experience and consumer behaviour. Exploration requires a set of international information of an institutional, entrepreneurial and socio-cultural nature, especially in the case of emerging and culturally distant countries. The cultural distance between the country of origin and the country of destination significantly influences the company's decision to internationalize and its economic performance. In particular, MMNEs suffer a lower level of internationality than MNEs due to their structure and size.

Therefore, the theme of acquainted markets often has two faces, the market one and the company one, both of which address the need for mutual learning. This reference framework strengthens the hypothesis of a future international scenario in which large and medium-sized enterprises can play a more significant role. Some global trends taking place in the high-end product sectors, along with growth in the learning of the markets, are driving an increased presence of both types of companies.

## 6.1   MIRRORING AND MIRRORING BACK

The MNE and the MMNE are different both in the way they look at the modes (how) and the actions (what) that they implement in the international context. Basically, strategic drivers reflect the stock of resource availability and the models of exploitation. The size effects can be observed at two levels: first is the stock of resources to invest to gain new foreign, overseas markets (not limited to marketing and sales but also manufacturing and logistics); second, the organizational capabilities to combine quickly and to move faster than MNEs, typical of smaller and entrepreneurial firms. The evidence from the field (Pontiggia and Vescovi, 2013) confirms the challenge and difficulties faced by MMNEs to explore and implement new business models. The mere imitation of international modes from MNEs is not feasible and sustainable and confirms a tendency to replicate models and routines and to deploy them from the home organization to overseas units. Economies of replication and scarce resources suggest and explain these traits in the internationalization behaviour of MMNEs. The question is: how do the companies (MNEs and MMNEs) move to international markets that are culturally different?

Globalization can be seen as a test for the international managerial and economic models and theories. Some globalization changes concern the size of emerging markets and the speed of the development of new consumers' models and behaviours. And it's not only size, but deeper changes are connected to social and cultural differences. Moreover, global and large markets are emerging on the supply of new products and services, at least those that are new for a large segment of the demand. Customers are involved for the first time in buying and consuming that is completely new for them, of which they have no previous experience. This is the competitive challenge faced by many European firms when they enter the Chinese, Indian and South Asian markets.

International business scholars have conducted substantial research on many different issues: the internationalization process (Dunning, 2001), multinational companies' strategy (Kogut and Zander, 1995; Rugman and Verbeke, 2003) and foreign direct investment. Some research has shown the link between innovation and internationalization. An example is the so-called 'reverse innovation' effects: developing products in emerging countries and then distributing them globally. The flow of innovation (i.e. in term of product or delivery system) is moving from developed countries to emerging countries and the other way around. But in tracking the innovation flow among different countries the observation mainly concerns the experiences of MNEs or the so-called Emergent Countries Multinational Enterprises (ECME). Less evidence has been studied on MMNEs, largely diffused in Europe, and how their business models are innovated by the internationalization process in new economies. Large markets for consumer goods with a high potential growth look attractive for the international development of MMNEs. A first dimension is linked to the cultural, linguistic and institutional differences between a firm's country of origin and other countries to which it may internationalize (Johanson and Vahlne, 1997). These differences can increase the 'liability of foreignness'.

In the Uppsala model, a widely diffused explanation of the process companies use to enter international markets, the process of internationalization is described as a gradual and incremental acquisition, integration and use of knowledge about foreign markets. The contribution from Johanson and Wiedersheim-Paul (1975) describes internationalization as a slow and incremental process described by four distinctive stages. Each phase shows different degrees of involvement in the foreign country:

1.  no regular export activities;
2.  export via independent representatives;
3.  establishment of an overseas sales subsidiary;
4.  overseas production/manufacturing units.

Johanson and Vahlne (1997) developed a model that looks at internationalization as causal cycles in which knowledge about foreign markets and market commitment are affected by the firm's current activities and commitment decisions. In the Uppsala model, internationalization is modelled as a process of incremental resource commitments, driven by increasing experiential knowledge (Johanson and Vahlne, 2006). The process starts from domestic markets, moves on to culturally and/or geographically closer countries, and then moves to culturally and geographically more distant countries. Foreign activities move from exports to foreign direct investment (Figure 6.1).

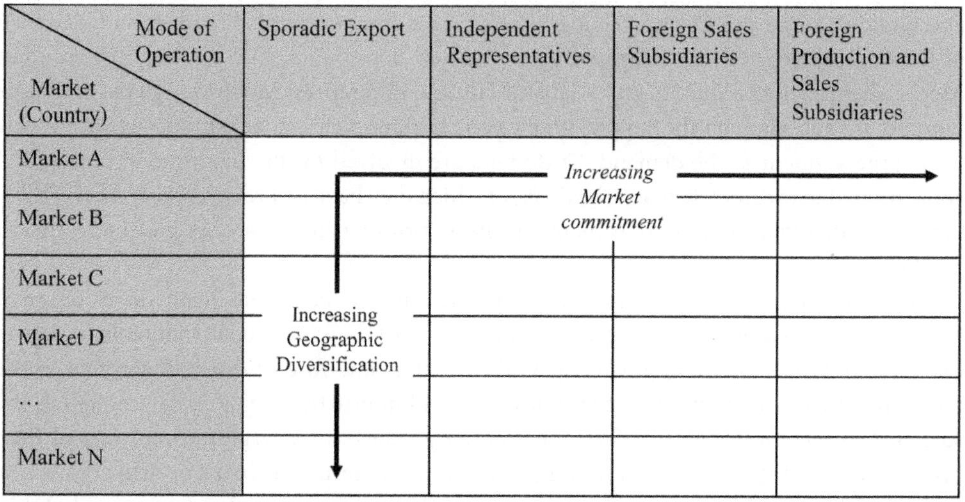

| Market (Country) / Mode of Operation | Sporadic Export | Independent Representatives | Foreign Sales Subsidiaries | Foreign Production and Sales Subsidiaries |
|---|---|---|---|---|
| Market A | | | | |
| Market B | | | | |
| Market C | | | | |
| Market D | | | | |
| ... | | | | |
| Market N | | | | |

*Increasing Market commitment* →

*Increasing Geographic Diversification*

*Source*:　Adapted from Dervillée et al. (2004).

**Figure 6.1**　　The Uppsala model

Despite the recent updates of the Uppsala model, other researchers criticize the sequential internationalization approach as they consider it too deterministic (Reid et al., 1987). Turnbull (1987) argues that the internationalization process cannot be generalized across industries as it is influenced by the environment in which companies operate, whereas Andersen (1993) stresses that the model is unclear with respect to the congruence between theoretical and operational mode. In particular, the Uppsala model is challenged especially in the context of emerging markets: for example, in the case of China the empirical evidence of Alon (2003) shows that the model does not seem to fit the majority of the sample of MNEs operating in that market. Therefore, it is relevant to define the main characteristics of emerging markets, which are presented in the following paragraph.

Dunning's (1988) OLI (Ownership–Location–Internalization) paradigm is the most widely known theory of the multinational firm. It explains that MNEs overcome the costs and disadvantages of competing with domestic rivals in a host country by using a source of advantage that exploits internalized asset transfers and access to global value chains. Much of the rationale for FDI (Foreign Direct Investment) is based on this paradigm. Insufficient home markets, global competitive pressures, and/or government policies spur decisions to internationalize from firms who, naturally, wish to protect or increase their profitability and/or capital value. These firms then choose to engage in FDI (as opposed to exporting or licensing) based on the belief that they can exploit existing firm-specific competitive advantages abroad (i.e., asset-exploitation).

A widely debated criticism of this model is its ineffectiveness to explain new firms and the dynamic nature of competitive advantage. Other approaches suggest that international expansion oriented to acquire new capabilities (asset-augmentation by exploration) requires a different framework than expansion designed to exploit existing capabilities (asset-exploitation). The process by which companies create value from international knowledge was initially conceptualized as a linear sequence and though no circular effects are revealed.

Knowledge transfer tended to be internalized within the firm to avoid the transaction costs associated with market contracts in knowledge assets. Johanson and Vahlne (1997) developed a model of the internationalization process suggesting that firms incrementally increase their international commitments via a gradual process of acquisition, integration and subsequent utilization of knowledge related to operating abroad. Firms may supplement their existing technical capabilities by expanding internationally and such expansion would allow them to access new technology, skills, or knowledge. Empirical evidence shows (Almeida, 1996) that firms may be increasingly motivated to expand internationally with the primary intention of acquiring valuable knowledge that resides abroad, rather than to exploit existing competencies.

International expansion provides learning opportunities through exposure to new markets, internalization of new concepts, assimilation of ideas from new cultures, and access to new resources. A company has a collection of valuable options that permit it to move real economic activities or financial flows from one country to another. The diverse environment facing a company going international exposes it to multiple stimuli, allowing it to develop diverse capabilities and providing it with broader learning opportunities than are available to a purely domestic firm. The most unexpected the situation is, the most stimuli the company receives. This is true especially when the company faces a different cultural context. This situation affects entry mode decisions. Also, contextual factors moderating market entry can be regarded as a relevant theme for entry mode research.

In a foreign and culturally distant market any indirect presence seems negatively to affect the possibility of gaining access to information and knowledge. If exporting strategies provide faster access to a foreign market, this hinders the learning process; it seems to lower the probability that an international presence may generate some sort of innovation. In many cases it also makes the adaptation to the emerging market's needs difficult. Foreign direct investment, by establishing subsidiaries and internalizing markets for proprietary asset exchange, enables firms to minimize transaction-related risks and gather benefits of direct contact with the evolution of markets' needs (Rugman and Verbeke, 2003).

Proponents of the so-called *standardization* approach view the globalization trends as a tendency toward a greater market similarity and higher convergence of consumer needs, tastes and preferences. This line of thought claims that standardization is further facilitated by the growth and emergence of global market segments. Typically, the benefits of a strategy based on standardization are: significant economies of scale in all value-adding activities, particularly in research and development, production and marketing; the presentation of a consistent corporate/brand image across countries, especially in light of the increasing consumer mobility around the world; and reduced managerial complexity due to better coordination and control of international operations (Winter and Szulanski, 2001). Strategy standardization suffers from an oversimplification of reality and a contradiction of the marketing concept. It should be remembered that the goal of the firm is not cost reduction through standardization, but profitability through higher sales accrued from a better exploitation of the distinctive consumers' needs across countries.

In contrast we see an *adaptation* approach. This states that the increasing globalization trends do not affect the deep differences between countries. Consumer needs, use conditions, purchasing habits, commercial and delivery infrastructure, culture and traditions, laws and regulations are still too different to implement a unique approach. Firms' marketing and competitive strategy needs to be adjusted to the idiosyncratic and specific conditions of each foreign market.

A third approach offers a contingency perspective to the replication/standardization versus adaptation debate. This states that standardization or adaptation are two ends of the same continuum, where the degree of the firm's marketing strategy standardization/adaptation can range between them; in other words, they are not a discrete choice. Second, the decision to standardize or adapt the marketing strategy depends on the specific market at a certain time or period. Third, the appropriateness of the selected level of strategy standardization/adaptation should be judged and measured on its impact on company performance in international markets.

For example, Jonsson and Foss (2011) clearly explain how the IKEA international strategies have not been an exact replication as recommended by the replication-as-strategy literature. IKEA try to get the advantages of both format standardization with local adaptation. The acquisition and internal transfer of the knowledge that results from such learning is coordinated and systematized through organizational means. These include dedicated units that are responsible for intra-firm knowledge sharing, as well as organizational principles, such as corporate values that stress the importance of co-workers questioning existing solutions and continuously engaging in knowledge sharing.

The general picture that emerges is that a firm is especially oriented to imitate, in terms of market entry and consolidation. There is a broad tendency to replicate the business models from the domestic configuration towards new markets, but at the same time some pitfalls are recognizable: a sort of 'competences trap', which constitutes an obstacle to innovation from internationalization. Firms show they are less prone to mirror back using knowledge generated in their international investments.

In the *mirroring/mirroring back* model (Pontiggia and Vescovi, 2014) the company develops its original business model in its home market and, normally following the Uppsala model, the company uses the same business model in foreign markets that is similar to the home one. The same happens when the company decides to enter such a distant market as China, even if the characteristics are totally different. So, the company enters the *Mirroring* phase, replicating the original business model. After the first period, the performances of the company are not as good as expected and the business model seems not to be working as in other foreign markets, so the company enters the *Exploration* phase, trying to understand if the market is acquainted enough to be able to properly analyse and appreciate the offer. As a temporary solution, the company can decide to wait for the moment when the new market will be acquainted, keeping the offer the same as in the other markets. This is obviously risky, first because the market can mature in a different way compared to the others, and second because other competitors can exploit the situation of 'absence'. Alternatively, the MMNE can start the *Adaptation* of the business model and the offer to the characteristics of the market in order to be successful. Therefore, the company develops new models and new solutions; in other words, it develops strategic innovation by mean of the *Mirroring Back* phase, in which it introduces innovation acquired through the experience it had in the new foreign market to the original business model it had in the home market (Figure 6.2).

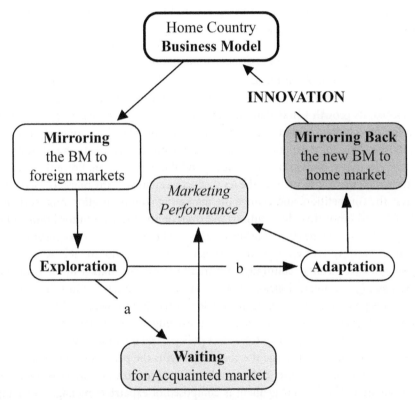

**Figure 6.2**     Mirroring-mirroring back model

The process of internationalization can run two paths (Figure 6.2): adapting or waiting. The mirroring-mirroring back process including four main steps: (1) *Mirroring*/entry strategy-export; (2) *Exploring*/looking for the acquainted market, local organization; (3) *Adapting*/modifying the offer and the business behaviour; and (4) *Mirroring* back/new business model.

Phase 1, which identifies with the *mirroring*/entry strategy-export defines a simplified access to the new market, simply by exporting existing products that have been designed in other markets (usually the home market); the key role is the importer. There is no direct presence of the company. On one hand the company tends to simplify the approach to foreign markets, because of limited resources availability (human, financial, knowledge), relying on the experience previously obtained in international markets. The company wants to minimize or even ignore possible differences encountered in the new market following a strategy we might call a 'hope strategy', hoping that the new market is very similar to the others. On the other hand, the importer exclusively plays a sales management role, since this is their competence, managing the logistics and distribution and placing the product in the best stores, but not offering any support to strategic marketing. However, this role is fully consistent in a traditional acquainted market where the consumer has great expertise regarding the product and established consumption patterns. Having no expertise in strategic marketing, the importer is acting as a 'cap of knowledge' to the new market, not being able to formulate marketing suggestions to the company, especially if it is middle-sized, which is facing a blind market very different from the known markets. For the company, the importer has an extremely effective role in the case of traditional acquainted markets, and a severely limited role if it is not an acquainted market.

Phase 2, *Exploration*/looking for an acquainted market, is entered by the company after some presence on the market, typically 3–5 years, when the company realizes that its expansion is blocked, its growth is less than the rate of market development and that the strategy of mirroring has obvious limitations in the expansion of sales. The company is looking to increase its knowledge of the market in order to fit the marketing mix to the consumer expectations. It works in two dimensions: the market and the organization. From the market point of view the company tries to identify the level of acquaintance of the market, select the target and analyse the competition, and change the marketing communication mix, such as developing flexible and innovative distribution, and overcoming the distributor limits in terms of market expansion. It switches to a multi-channel sale. The company develops a direct presence in the market, most often by means of expatriate managers who are able to read the local market, but who are strongly culturally anchored to the home market of the company. The company is taking a strategic decision about what the key markets are in which to invest for the future. This phase requires a strategic decision in relation to two possible alternatives: (a) wait and see if the market assumes the conditions existing in traditional markets, maintaining the mirroring strategy; or (b) move towards a policy of adaptation to the market, changing its business behaviour. At this stage the company begins the process of internationalization, that is, it begins to take on an international culture. The organization choice is still dominated by the headquarters, so the management is composed of expatriate managers or temporary managers coming from the home market.

In phase 3, *Adaptation*-modifying the offer, the company takes the decision to change its offer or business model in the foreign market, compared to the initial strategy of mirroring. It is evident that the business model derived from the home market is not working. At this point the alternative, after exploring the market, is to adapt its offer to the specific situation, by changing the starting model, and changing the business behaviour, to make it compatible with the specific conditions of the market, which are very different from the home market. The company decides to adapt its offer to the local market in a non-marginal way, changing the product content and characteristics, the product design, and the brand. At this point it breaks the glass wall that culturally prevents a radical innovation. It lays the groundwork for the next phase. Management are recruited locally, because it is more important to increase the market sensitivity than the link with the company.

Stage 4, *Mirroring Back*/new business model, is characterized by an increasing internationalization of the company, which constructs a new business model or changes the existing business model according to the new market, which takes on the characteristics of second home market. For the management it becomes more important to understand the market than to understand the company. A bond with the importer remains, but it is driven by an organization composed of the managers of the company, sharing strategic alliances with other actors (local and/or international) to cope with the market challenges. The development of specific products for new markets and distribution choices are modelled using innovative solutions. The communication and branding strategies are strongly localized. The product often follows a logic of 'good enough' and not of 'absolute top quality' that is typical of the acquainted markets. In this phase the company learns from its experience in the new market and brings to the first home market some of the strategic models, readjusting them. Therefore, the company enters a state of continuous mirroring back between first and second-home market, producing strategic innovation. At this stage, the process of internationalization conceptually passes from the extension of the domestic market (mirroring) to the development of a new market (adaptation), to the learning from the new market (mirroring back). The mirroring phase of internationalization should be as short as possible.

International development in culturally different contexts may offer some knowledge, which contributes to change and to innovate (sometime deeply) the original business models. This innovation in terms of a single component or all the elements of the business model produced by the internalization works only if some transfer mechanisms are designed to internally explore and exploit the knowledge acquired in the new markets.

There are three main managerial implications:

- Entering new, large markets means not only increasing sales and revenues, but opening the strategic innovation 'window', which could be really important in terms of innovation, growth and learning. But learning is leverage by direct action coherent with the *mirroring back* effort.
- Entrepreneurs and managers should choose to enter culturally different markets also for the indirect but strategic benefits arising from the internationalization.
- The managerial decisions concerning international investment should be coherent with the *mirroring back* perspective. The second order effect is to increase the probability of strategic innovations of the business models.

Passing the *Mirroring* phase means for the company starting a cultural and strategic innovation process, reaching the *mirroring back* phase.

## 6.2  MANAGING UNEXPECTED SUCCESS

Entering very different cultural markets through a mirroring process should be unsuccessful rationally, since the contextual conditions of the internal market or a traditional market of the company, in which the business model used was developed, are different from those of the new market of reference. In most cases this occurs in the early stages of market entry (mirroring).

In the subsequent exploration phase, the company can discover potential opportunities for success that it had not foreseen, regarding aspects and components considered secondary, but which acquire a completely new and higher importance according to the typical values of the cultural context of the new market.

The exploratory phase therefore becomes fundamental not only to understand the causes of a failure due to a too ethnocentric replication of the business model, but also to understand the causes of success. These causes perhaps do not depend on the casual consistency of the original business model to the new market, which the company understands is not an *Acquainted Market*, but from the emergence of new competitive advantages that depend on the diversity of the cultural context and that were previously not considered important or were considered irrelevant in the domestic market. In this case, the *Adaptation* to the new cultural conditions present in the new market does not request the change of the offer (marketing mix), but, because of variation of the importance of the motivations for the purchase, the company should focus on the characteristics of the product or on the reasons for unexpected purchase or even just not imagined as crucial to success. This often results in a different positioning and communication strategy.

A well-known example concerns the extraordinary success achieved by Ferrero in China with the Rocher product. Rocher is a round wafer praline covered with milk chocolate and chopped hazelnuts, with a filling of Nutella and one toasted hazelnut, wrapped in a film of golden foil. The product was launched in the early 1980s in Italy and Germany, enjoying success as a sweet snack to offer to guests. Since the late 1980s, Rocher has been exported to the Chinese market with far greater success (Figure 6.3).

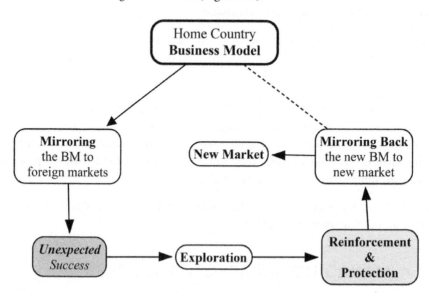

**Figure 6.3**    Managing the unexpected success

The attraction of Ferrero Rocher in China is due to many factors: gold is an emblem of wealth and prosperity; a praline packaged in the form of a gold nugget contains desires and hopes of luck and success: it is no coincidence that Ferrero Rocher are given as gifts on important occasions, such as weddings or birthdays, or holidays, such as Chinese New Year. In fact, on anniversaries, the Chinese custom is to give a 'red envelope' that contains money. But this is an impersonal gift, which is not opened out of respect, to which the Rocher packaging is added, or a more festive and personal auspicious relationship. The product is given or shared more as a symbol of luck and prosperity than for its taste characteristics. It should not be forgotten that the Chinese do not love very sweet things. Despite this, Rocher has conquered a vast market. The price range is very high for a praline, transforming it into a luxury product suitable for an important and challenging gift. Moreover, diffusion has been facilitated by the particular relationship of knowledge and collaboration (guanxi), typical of the Chinese market, that Ferrero was able to build with its distributors (Ranfagni and Guercini, 2014).

## NOTE

1.   The dimension of an MMNE that is considered in this book is not the one defined by the European Union (50–250 employees) because I consider this to be too small if compared to the companies acting in the international market. That definition of size seems to be referring to the internal market of each European country. What should be considered as a Medium-sized Multinational Enterprise should be one that has 200–2000 employees to be able to compete internationally.

# 7
# Case studies part II

## INTRODUCTION

The Islamic religion invites the faithful to be modest and to avoid ostentation; clothes and beauty products must therefore guarantee a dignified behaviour free of excesses. Modesty affects all aspects of life and calls for decency, humility and moderation in speech, attitude and behaviour.

The *hijab* is worn exclusively by women and is considered the symbol of Muslim identity. In fact, a woman with her head covered shows respect for the community and for the code of moral conduct. Not being precisely defined by the sacred text, the *hijab* takes on different forms: from the *gallebaya* and *abaya* of the Arab world, to the *chador* and *ruwsari* (foulard) of the Persian world, from the *salwar kamiz* of the Indian subcontinent to the *burqas* of Asia and Africa.

Women can choose the *hijab* based on circumstances; today the choice in terms of fabrics and colours is very vast, so much so that the more traditionalist women consider it a lack of modesty.

In the more liberal Islamic countries, such as Egypt and Turkey, recently the veil, not compulsory for women, is becoming more and more a trendy 'accessory'; since, in fact, 2005, when many movie and TV stars started using it, their example has been imitated by millions of girls. In other countries, such as Saudi Arabia, Qatar and Iran, however, the question does not arise as the use of the *hijab* is mandatory.

The Euromonitor International study 'Doing Business in the Halal Market' highlights how, in countries belonging to the Organization for Islamic Cooperation (OIC), women's clothing absorbs most of the revenues generated by the fashion industry; in 2016, women's clothing generated a third of the sector's revenues (34 per cent), followed by men's clothing (27 per cent), footwear (21 per cent), junior clothing (12 per cent) and, finally, accessories (3 per cent).

## MODEST FASHION

The term *Modest Fashion* identifies a simple fashion that respects the values and principles of the Islamic religion. Sober dresses that hide the shape of the body by sliding loosely over them, covering the arms and body, but trendy and colourful; this is the essence of Modest Fashion.

Muslim consumers around the world spent $266 billion on clothing and footwear in 2016, 11.9 per cent of the world's spending on these products. If this market were a nation, it would be the third largest fashion spending nation in the world after the United States ($494 billion) and China ($285 billion).

The countries with the largest number of Muslim consumers currently are Turkey ($39.3 billion), United Arab Emirates ($22.5 billion), Indonesia ($18.8 billion), Iran ($17.1 billion), Saudi Arabia and Qatar ($16 billion) and Nigeria ($14.4 billion).

The Islamic fashion industry is growing so rapidly that in the World Report on Islamic Economy 2014 Thomson Reuters and DinarStandard introduced a special indicator, the 'Modest Fashion Indicator' (MFI), which assesses the health and development of the Islamic fashion ecosystem in 72 countries. The indicator bases its assessment on specific factors, such as the number of suppliers in relation to the size of the country (export of clothes to OIC countries), the perception (number of new items and events), and the social impact (price index clothing and work ethic index).

The first European magazine dedicated to this type of clothing was born in Italy, entitled *Modest Fashion*, which announced that in 2016 Modest fashion generated a turnover of $300 billion and estimated that, by 2018, this business will reach over $400 billion. This growth forecast is linked to the fact that 62 per cent of the Muslim population is made up of young people under 30 and that Muslim customers already represent 11 per cent of world spending on clothing today. The opportunity may also be valid for SMEs, companies addressing market niches, looking for alternative channels to resist the impact of globalization.

The Muslim market is promising, and is one that Western fashion houses certainly cannot ignore, but there are no brands entirely dedicated to this consumer target. And it is a market where, unlike sectors such as Islamic finance and *halal* food, there is no certification capable of establishing precise criteria that companies wishing to invest in this market can adhere to.

## WOMEN'S CLOTHING IN QATAR

Qatar's culture appears to be one of the most conservative in the Gulf countries, second only to that of Saudi Arabia. Qatari women are provided with education, from elementary school to graduate studies, on female-only campuses; any form of approach and interaction with male individuals who do not belong to their family is also prohibited.

Weddings are organized by the bride's parents, who have the opportunity to see her future husband, a strictly Qatari citizen, only for a few minutes before the ceremony; no type of physical contact in public between spouses is allowed and women manifest considerable discomfort in the presence of men who are not part of the restricted family circle.

To overcome this problem and to alleviate anxiety for women attending public places, various shopping centres, parks and museums organize 'family days', days in which men can only enter as companions of their own family.

This extreme sense of modesty obviously translates into the way women appear in public and, therefore, into clothing; the *abaya* is the female symbol of Qatar and represents a strong sense of belonging to a people; it is a wide coat that reaches to the feet and is generally dark in colour.

Wearing the *abaya* is also a cultural choice; it is the symbol, in fact, of a social status that is considered enviable, that of a citizen of Qatar: a privileged minority of about 300 000 people who are among the richest in the world.

For each occasion, women wear a different *abaya*: sober in the workplace, or embellished with coloured rhinestones or Swarovsky crystals for the evening, while the younger women tend to prefer bright colours over the classic black. To meet these different needs, the number of shops entirely dedicated to the sale of traditional clothing is particularly high; in many cases they are single-brand stores of well-known brands and *abaya* designers, which just a few years ago were non-existent in the emirate.

Under the traditional dress, women are free to choose what to wear; they are not, in fact, obliged to wear loose and opaque clothes. The practice for those women, mostly Westerners, who prefer not to adapt fully to local customs, is not to wear the *abaya*. This choice, however, is not willingly accepted by Qatari citizens, who perceive this Western behaviour as a threat and as a sort of cultural invasion.

In this regard, some Qatari women have organized the 'One of us' campaign, also supported by the Qatar Tourism Authority, with which they propose, in addition to the ban on exposing knees and shoulders in public, the extension of the dress code that is valid for residents also to foreign women, or the use of the *abaya*, in order to preserve traditions.

# THE SUCCESS OF MADE IN ITALY FASHION IN QATAR

Particularly important is the passion that Qatari women show for Italian high fashion brands. Precisely in order to attract this very rich and relevant market target, every year, in Doha, at the Hotel St Regis, there are fashion shows covering collections prepared for the occasion by Italian fashion houses such as Renato Balestra, Gattinoni, Lella Curiel, Sarli and Antonio Grimaldi. Voluminous evening dresses are shown in chiffon and lace, sparkling with embroidery and studded with Swarovski, that the most famous names of Made in Italy couture create specifically to meet the tastes of Qatari ladies. These are strictly closed-door fashion shows, in which men, including designers, are not allowed, not even backstage.

In this way, the few hundred privileged people who have the opportunity to participate in these exclusive events of Italian fashion, after having deposited their *abaya* in the wardrobe, can show off, away from male eyes, miniskirts and décolleté, tight-fitting dresses, sensational jewels and refined make-up, according to an all-Western style.

On the occasion of the 2016 fashion show, Gattinoni paid homage to Sheikh Mozah, second wife of Emir Hamad bin Khalifa al-Thani, a woman of extreme beauty and charm, with a dress that reproduced her face; Lella Curiel instead proposed refined dresses with embroidery inspired by Islamic culture.

The sheika Mozah, defined by *Forbes* magazine as the most powerful woman in the Arab world, is a true style icon; her clothes, in Western style but adapted to Islamic traditions and accompanied by a turban, which has become her hallmark, are celebrated by fashion magazines all over the world. They are admired in Paris and New York, but they are loved above all by the Arab girls who see in her, more than in Westernized icons like Rania of Jordan, an inspiration and a model of elegance.

Mozah's passion for fashion, and in particular for Italian haute couture, would have been the main motivation that prompted Qatar to buy Maison Valentino in 2012. After spending tens of millions of dollars on her wardrobe (just think that every state usually visits Mozah who changes into six or seven dresses in a single day), the Emir of Qatar Hamad bin Khalifa al Thani decided to invest over 700 million euros in the Permira fund, thus conquering 100 per cent of the Italian fashion house.

Mozah, on the other hand, is a much admired and celebrated figure for her elegance and social commitment; in fact, especially in clothing, she has always returned an image of herself as respectful of local customs as she is oriented towards a 'Western friendly' style, promoting, on numerous occasions, a deeper point of contact between the Islamic world and the Western world.

# THE FASHION MARKET IN UAE

The presence of international brands is booming in the UAE, thanks to the high disposable income of both the local Emirati population, expatriates who have moved to work in the UAE, and tourists from all over the world: these factors place the United Arab Emirates among the markets in which there is the highest percentage of so-called big spenders.

The United Arab Emirates is today a global destination for international leisure tourism, but also for business tourism: the result is that international brands dominate shopping centres and 95 per cent of the most important brands in the world are distributed in the Emirates. Italian products, thanks above all to their high quality, are always the first choice for those with a high income.

It is not easy, however, except for the big brands, to succeed in establishing an Italian product by focusing on quality; given the high presence of products of Asian origin at low prices, and since the local currency has always been linked to the US dollar, importers and wholesalers focus on quantity, rather than incurring the costs necessary to favour imports of niche products.

However, consumers still expect to be able to choose from a wide range of models and variations; design, therefore, is key to gaining market share in the Emirates. Customers ask for new products and new ideas, and they constantly ask for new products.

The products of the most important brands are marketed in the most important shopping centres in Dubai: Saks Fifth Avenue, Bin Hendi and Harvey Nichols, to name just a few. The Italian high fashion product constitutes a status symbol for the wearer and, for the locals, represents a sign of distinction. The UAE is a market to which access is still very difficult today if not driven by a strong brand or a large investment in communication.

The progressive development of the Dubai Design District (D3) is worth noting: it is an area completely dedicated to design, art and fashion, with the aim of stimulating the growth of the entire fashion chain, from design to production, to retail. With more than half of the major international retailers having outlets in Dubai and a third of Middle Eastern luxury shopping taking place there, D3 aims to attract world-class fashion houses; the goal is to enable local talent to interact with international trend-setters to create a global market, transforming Dubai into a true fashion capital.

In 2015, an organization for the development of the Islamic fashion industry, the Islamic Fashion and Design Council, was created in Dubai, which today has eleven offices around the world. Its founder, Alia Khan, is one of the most influential women in the Muslim world and, following her passion for fashion, she created the Islamic Fashion Council to support brands that want to propose a 'correct Islamic' style.

There has been an exponential increase in demand for this type of clothing globally. Despite the levels of demand, however, Alia Khan argues that there is an absence on the part of Western producers, little awareness and ability to attack a market that is still unexplored, but which offers enormous opportunities; hence the need for careful study, aimed at understanding Muslim consumers' culture and aimed at satisfying their needs.

This gap is partly due to the fact that there are no religious norms or sources that describe the characteristics that a dress should possess to be defined as 'modest'; in fact, there are no Islamic dresses, it is simply a new style that the fashion world is currently developing and, for this reason, the idea is spreading that modest fashion must lose its strong religious connotation to be observed mainly from a cultural and entrepreneurial perspective.

Muslim women who, fascinated by the world of Western fashion, wish to combine elegance with the sobriety imposed by their faith, however complain about a lack of market offer, a deficiency that translates into the impossibility of developing a fashion that is culturally appropriate to their values.

## DOLCE & GABBANA *ABAYA* LINE

Modest fashion hasn't been completely ignored by all brands. Brands such as Zara, Mango and H&M, following the example of their progenitor DKNY, have launched their own 'Ramadan Collection', lines specifically dedicated to the Islamic market, but for which an in-depth study of the market has not been carried out and therefore they are unable to meet the new needs of this target consumer entirely.

The first to launch, at an international level, a high fashion collection for Islamic women were the Italians Domenico Dolce and Stefano Gabbana, who, following the example of the low-cost brands mentioned above, decided to seize the extraordinary opportunities offered by a market that is still partially unexplored and therefore with little competition.

In January 2016, the D&G brand launched the line dedicated to Muslim customers on Style.com/Arabia, the online edition of *Vogue*. This was a rather sober entry into the market, which did not include fashion catwalks or spotlights, for what was called the 'Dolce & Gabbana Abaya Line', from the name of the long traditional dress.

The collection was created by re-adapting the style of the two designers in a *halal* key, that is, respecting the principles and rules dictated by the Islamic religion in terms of clothing; *abayas* in shades of black and beige with touches of colour, lace inserts and floral applications, are the undisputed protagonists of the collection.

Obviously, there was no lack of *hijab* veils in very light fabrics and dark tones to cover the garment, enlivened by floral motifs and polka dots that reflect the decorations of the dresses. All were combined with glasses, jewellery, accessories and even cosmetics, especially for the eyes, specially made by Islamic women.

In addition to an obvious commercial purpose, the launch of the new line was also a cultural operation with the aim of dispelling certain prejudices and giving Islamic women the

**Figure 7.1**  D&G Abaya Line

freedom to choose what to wear, responding to their hitherto little listened to desires.

D&G also used a global event to highlight the new line dedicated to the Islamic market, namely the state visit of US President Donald Trump to Riyadh, the capital of Saudi Arabia. During the presidential trip, what particularly attracted the attention of the international fashion press was the sober and respectful elegance of the clothes sported by his wife Melania, signed by Dolce & Gabbana.

In particular, in the first stop in Riyadh, the First Lady showed off long black trousers, with strictly covered arms and embellished with golden details, which echoed the traditional *abayas* given a modern look. This was an unprecedented gesture, given that until then the First Lady and the heads of government had always opted for chaste looks but never so similar to local customs. The innovative choice of Melania, on the other hand, was particularly appreciated by the Gulf countries and was interpreted as a great sign of respect, even if the woman presented her head uncovered, which was a condition that had been agreed.

## THE CRITICISMS OF D&G

Although the launch of the *halal* collection took place online, as the new line brought with it a number of cultural implications, its debut sparked a lot of criticism and discussion from the Islamic world.

First of all, the Middle Eastern press criticized some practical aspects of the collection, namely the fact that the models chosen by the fashion house were distinctly Western and, therefore, were notably physically different from Arab women, who tend to be shorter and more shapely, with dissimilar somatic characteristics.

The Saudi creative designer Nabila Nazer also appreciated the initiative and intentions of the designers Dolce and Gabbana, but did not spare her criticism of the contents, inviting the two Italian creative designers to study the market more in depth instead of just customizing a traditional *abaya*. In fact, she argues that adapting an *abaya*, reinterpreting it according to one's own style, is neither a novelty nor, least of all, an initiative capable of having significant effects on the market or of revolutionizing, even in a small part, the lives of Muslim women.

Immediately after the launch of the 'Dolce & Gabbana Abaya Line' there were a number of mixed reactions online; hundreds of thousands of women, especially those under 25, thanked the designers for having finally created a line designed to meet their needs and entirely dedicated to them. On the opposite side, the more conservative one, however, after having launched the hashtag 'nothanksD&G' on social media, people argued that wearing the *hijab* has nothing to do with fashion, but that it is exclusively about faith in Allah: wearing designer veils with the sole purpose of appearance would therefore be immoral and one would lose sight of the essence of the meaning of the traditional headdress.

The Islamic Fashion and Design Council, on the other hand, supported the role of the two designers, expressing their admiration for Dolce and Gabbana as, aware of the risks they were running, they chose to undertake a difficult path to dedicate luxurious and elegant garments to thousands of women, created by the skilful talent of two pillars of high fashion and enriched by the prestige of Made in Italy. This also underlines the social implications that the D&G initiative is creating, first of all the fact that seeing the 'Abaya Line' in magazines and advertising campaigns is helping to familiarize Westerners with Islamic culture, thus dispelling the widespread prejudice that leads to identifying Arab women exclusively with strict veils and submission.

Despite having supported the initiative of the Italian brand, the Islamic Fashion and Design Council also deems it necessary to carry out a more in-depth study of the culture of this particular target of consumers. It suggests that it is necessary to create ad hoc collections totally oriented towards *modest fashion*, which therefore are not limited to embellishing or reinterpreting classic tunics, but which aim to create new clothes, for a Western taste but respectful of Islamic traditions and culture.

# BOYCOTT DOLCE & GABBANA

Paradoxically, the harshest criticisms of the Dolce & Gabbana collection came not from the most conservative circles of the Arab world, but from France. The first heavy attacks on the boom in 'Islamic fashion' were initiated by the French family minister, who categorically rejected the possibility that Islamic women, outside their home countries, could continue to wear their traditional clothes. The choice to wear the *hijab* even beyond the borders of their homeland would in fact express, according to his point of view, the condescension to submission and the denial of the desire for emancipation.

The French feminist philosopher Elisabeth Badinter also expressed her disagreement, urging women to boycott the D&G brand, calling 'irresponsible' those brands that produce clothes that legitimize what she considers negative symbolism of the Islamic world.

Answering to heavy attacks on brands that are slowly shifting their focus to the Islamic world, Alia Khan, as a spokesperson for the Arab fashion world, says European countries should approach the issue of Islamic fashion less aggressively, realizing that what they see as a threat to their culture represents instead a remarkable profit opportunity for the fashion industry, adapting to a different cultural context.

He also pointed out that the use of the headdress was a constant in the Western world until a few decades ago; just think of figures like Grace Kelly and Audrey Hepburn, who in the 1950s with their head scarves became style icons, an emblem of elegance and refinement.

## QUESTION FOR DISCUSSION

1. Should the fashion industry be globalized or localized?
2. How can culture influence fashion?
3. Which marketing strategies should the fashion houses follow?

**CASE STUDY 7.2    HIGH-END ITALIAN FURNITURE IN JAPAN**
APPROPRIATE FURNITURE FOR THE HOME

# INTRODUCTION

Japan is the home of minimalist design: Japanese architects are committed to making their structures simple and essential. A traditional Japanese house is mainly made of wood and with a tatami flooring system, which is a rectangular woven straw mat. Wood is a light material that responds well to earthquakes and embodies the concept of the transitory; its irregularities and textures are considered to be of high aesthetic value.

The tatami, on the other hand, is used to cover the floor as it adapts well to the climate. It allows air to circulate freely and the sensation of walking on it with bare feet is very pleasant. For the Japanese, the tatami represents grass and therefore when you sit on it, it conveys a feeling of union with nature.

The interior of traditional Japanese houses is not made up of anterooms and rooms with fixed destinations, but of habitable spaces according to the needs of the moment. While in European houses the walls clearly divide the rooms from each other, in the traditional Japanese house the subdivision appears more nuanced, with defined spaces and separated by sliding doors, shōji. The furnishings present are few and favour this flexibility of adaptation: the built-in wardrobes isolate the only two fixed spaces, which are the kitchen and the bathroom. The bathroom is the symbol of the differences between Japan and the West: in Japanese homes the bathroom is separated from the toilet and is often small. For many, bathing is a religious experience, while for others it is curative; both aspects are closely linked to the rite of purification: one does not immerse oneself in hot water just for a matter of hygiene but also to purify the soul.

One of the fundamental aspects to take into consideration for European companies operating in the furniture sector in Japan is the size of the living spaces of Japanese houses, since this is clearly a factor that influences the demand for furniture and furnishing accessories by the Japanese consumer.

On average a Japanese house ranges from 50 sq m to 70 sq m; however, the dimensions may vary depending on the type of apartment and where it is located. In urban centres there are a greater number of apartments inhabited by one person and a fundamental social factor in Japan plays on this trend: new singles. Since 1973, the decline in the number of marriages has been 33 per cent and today young professionals avoid marriage too early to focus on their careers. Consequently, the construction of single-family homes is the construction sector with

**Figure 7.2    Japanese house interiors**

the highest growth. 1R is short for 'one room' house, and there are no walls separating the bedroom from the kitchen.

Typically, a studio apartment ranges from 13 sq m to 20 sq m. When you enter a Japanese studio apartment, you will usually find, beyond the entrance, a kitchen counter on the left and, opposite, the small bathroom. Unlike traditional Japanese houses, these studios have a bathroom and toilet in the same room due to their small size. Unlike the 1R, the 1K, where 'K' stands for kitchen, is a studio apartment where the kitchen is separated from the bedroom by a wall. Clearly, in these types of studio, space is precious and furnishing needs tend to move towards more practical elements. For example, furniture with drawers and containers is very popular for this type of apartment.

Luxury apartments in a city like Tokyo differ mainly in the premium price, the careful design, and the location; however, this does not mean that they are necessarily even bigger than normal. Most of the luxury apartments are around 100–120 sq m in size.

When it is necessary to furnish small living spaces, the choice falls mainly on small and above all functional furniture and accessories, which can be combined and used in various ways. Different living areas can be used for different purposes, but the same platform can also serve as a sitting surface, desk, dining table, and so on.

The position and shape of the furniture is also a choice not to be underestimated if you live in small spaces. In this case, corner sofas and/or wall units certainly help to take advantage of all the available space. By placing the pieces of furniture towards the corners or the wall, the floor will be clearer and consequently the house will also seem more spacious.

Based on the principle of making the room appear larger, Japanese consumers also wisely choose furniture based on height: the lower and wider the cabinet, the more it can offer a wider view of the room. Tables, beds but also sofas, are low in height to keep the eye line low.

In modern Japanese homes, the kitchen and dining room are one space. In Japan, the number of kitchens with counters that are used for quick meals, such as breakfast, is growing. When designing the interior of a house, the kitchen is designed and built with a built-in refrigerator, oven and microwave.

Finally, in the interior of Japanese houses white prevails, a colour that gives life to the space. The whiter the furniture, the more it blends in with the walls without creating a sense of oppression. In addition to white, the Japanese often choose wooden products, the same colour as the floor, in order to eliminate the boundary between them, as if to create a fusion.

The competitors of high-end furniture made in Italy in the Japanese market are the following companies: Armani Casa, Cassina, Minotti, Poltrona Frau and Molteni. Japan represents a strategic market for them, but their marketing strategies are very different.

# ARMANI

In 1988 the Armani group entered the Japanese market. In 2019 the new Armani Casa section opened in Tokyo. Armani Casa in Japan caters to both B2C and B2B markets. As for B2C, the target audience is high-income people, mostly wealthy men and professionals aged between 30 and 70 who are looking for furniture to furnish their homes or offices. In addition to the private customer, sales are aimed at B2B customers such as hotels, healthcare facilities, real estate studios, and so on. There is a greater male presence among Armani Casa customers, as the Armani brand in Japan has always referred to masculine elegance. Armani Casa offers the same collection all over the world and therefore there is no particular product line designed especially for the Japanese market.

Within the Armani Casa collection, wallpaper is the item that is the most successful. Armani wallpaper is characterized by soft colours and therefore, being inconspicuous, it is suitable for Japanese homes, where colours such as white and wood prevail. Very often it has a natural themed design that reflects the Japanese world. The wallpaper is extremely functional for sound insulation and moisture absorption, particularly optimal for the summer season. Each wallpaper has a name that reflects the title of a work or a Japanese city such as 'Ginza', 'Fuji', 'Sagano'.

Armani Casa lamps have the same success as wallpaper: they have different shapes and motifs that echo Japan, such as lanterns, fishing bells, but also architectural elements such as the roofs of temples. The lamp is one of the least expensive products but at the same time it is one of the few that fully express the Armani style. The lamp works especially for professionals who turn to Armani to furnish their workspaces.

In the Armani Casa collection, sofas and beds are among the pieces of furniture that least meet the needs of Japanese consumers. The reason lies in their size, which is too large and therefore unsuitable for Japanese living spaces. The same goes for sofas, which are also too large. In Japan, the most common apartment is the one in which the kitchen, dining room and living room occupy a single area, and people need to optimize the spaces and above all to make them balanced. A large sofa would take up too much space in the kitchen area, making it difficult to fit in other furniture.

Another key aspect to consider is that the Japanese market is highly competitive in terms of customer service. Armani Casa currently offers only shipping, payment and return services. One of the weak points in terms of service concerns the products of the Armani-Dada kitchen selection. The design of the kitchens is entirely entrusted to an Italian team working from Italy: the customer from Japan sends information about the characteristics of the type of kitchen he has in mind for his home and the team then proceeds with the realization based on these details. Given the distance between the two countries, the company is not expected to send personnel to take care of the measurements of the kitchen area; the customer has to wait for the product to arrive in Japan and then rely on an external company for assembly. Therefore, the entire logistics process presents a high level of risk and a low level of service for the customer.

The brand's communication is limited to a few articles published in fashion magazines preferring, even in Japan, to organize exclusive events for the most loyal customers. The strengths of Armani Casa are: the value of the brand, the sense of luxury that the brand conveys, and the level of quality. The weaknesses are: creativity and product innovation.

# CASSINA

Cassina is an Italian company founded in 1972, specializing in high-end design furniture. Cassina has been present on the Japanese market for 30 years with Cassina IXC, a joint venture with the Unimat group that distributes its products in five highly prestigious show-rooms in the most important cities in Japan. Inside the Tokyo store, the positioning of the furniture and furnishings is not accidental. The first thing you see as soon as you enter the store is the crockery department, located near the main entrance, which represents the first step for new customers to the world of high-end furniture. For customers looking to improve their home with luxury and quality products, the prices of Cassina glasses and plates are relatively low: it is 'affordable luxury'.

The Cassina brand is normally known to the Japanese elite who do not require invest-ment in advertising or social media. Cassina allocates its resources to events and parties, with an exclusive invitation list for customers, old and new. The key points of Cassina's success in the world and in Japan are twofold: high quality and excellent customer ser-vice. Cassina furniture is extremely resistant and handed down from generation to gen-eration: the quality is excellent. In Japan, when a customer wants to furnish their home with Cassina furniture, the company sends an employee to check the dimensions of the house to make sure that the furniture is suitable for the living spaces; they also check the dimensions of the elevators and stairs to make sure they do not sell a sofa that can't be taken to the upper floors. It should be emphasized that this service is included in the price of the furniture. In addition, Cassina repairs or replaces the furniture regardless of the sales date.

# MINOTTI

Minotti is an Italian company recognized internationally as an interpreter of a modern classic lifestyle concept in the furniture sector. It was founded in 1948. The constantly growing sales are mainly made abroad: the main market of the company is Japan. The strategy adopted in Japan was to open as many single-brand showrooms as possible; as Japanese consumers appreciate the brand, they want to see the complete collections and settings and prefer to have products, finishes and colours in one space. Minotti focuses heavily on market research and on the choice of a partner to collaborate with on site, be-cause 'selling furniture is not like selling cars, you need to be rooted in the territory, have a deep knowledge of local customs and, obviously, have specific design skills, therefore a local partner is of fundamental importance for the success of a showroom'.

In Japan, the close collaboration between Minotti and partner Sukeno has led to the opening of many stores. Research is another aspect in which the company invests in order to develop new coatings, fabrics and leathers every year, both to offer aesthetic innova-tions and to guarantee excellent quality. Continuity of advertising and communication has also created significant benefits. In 2019 Minotti won the Wallpaper Design Award in the 'Best reflective space' category with the Tape sofa, signed by the Japanese designer Oki Sato.

# POLTRONA FRAU

The Poltrona Frau company was founded in 1912 and opened its first flagship store in Tokyo in the Aoyama fashion district in 2018: the opening of the showroom consolidated the collaboration with its Japanese partner IDC OTSUKA. The name Poltrona Frau in Japan is synonymous with the highest quality leather, in fact the company is also known for covering the interiors of luxury cars such as Ferrari, Infiniti and Alfa Romeo and the first class seats of airlines such as JAL, Singapore Airlines and Etihad. The strength of Poltrona Frau is its continuous renewal, maintaining the artisan quality of Made in Italy but proposing new design ideas. The modular sofas are those that seem to best meet the needs of Japanese customers who in recent years, in addition to quality, have also sought functionality in the furniture products they buy. The company benefits greatly from online shopping.

# MOLTENI

The Molteni company was founded by Angelo and Giuseppina Molteni in 1934. The company is now divided into four main brands: Molteni & C (home furnishings), Dada (kitchens), UniFor and Citterio (office furnishings). In 2015 Molteni opened its first flagship store in Tokyo; the project was born in collaboration with Arflex Japan, a historic local distribution company. In 2017, the company opened its second flagship store in the city of Osaka. The strategy was not to offer a standardized range of products, but to study each context in which the company operates to meet specific market needs. In the case of the Japanese market, the group is successful because of the sustainable and certified quality of its products. The key is to maintain the aesthetic quality but with a low impact on waste production. The use of wood from certified plantations, recyclable and renewable materials, and non-toxic water-based paints are all elements that contribute to the company's success in the Japanese market. Molteni's collaboration with internationally renowned designers such as the Japanese Yasuhiko Itoh is also important. He has always maintained: 'Japanese and Italian culture are similar in the love for wood and its artifacts in all shapes and forms'.

## QUESTION FOR DISCUSSION

1. Comment on the different strategies followed by the companies and choose the two companies you consider are using the best strategies for the Japanese market, explaining why.

**CASE STUDY 7.3　　　HOTELS FROM ISRAEL TO CENTRAL EUROPE**
LEONARDO HOTELS CHAIN MARKETING STRATEGY

*Enav Friedmann, Merav Weiss-Sidi and Idan Tschisik*

# INTRODUCTION

In 1998, David Fattal established the first hotel in the 'Fattal' chain of hotels in the city of Eilat, in Israel, under the name 'Meridian'. Since then, Fattal has set up hundreds of hotels, branded in various forms, within the Fattal chain. The 'Leonardo' brand was established in 2005 and it functions as the European division of the Fattal hotel chain. Today, Leonardo operates 24 hotels throughout Israel and over 160 in Central Europe.

Following the economic downturn experienced by Germany in the early 2000s, David Fattal decided to expand his chain and establish a hotel in Germany under the Leonardo brand. With the help of business ties that he had developed in the region, Fattal identified the potential that Germany offered in 2004, after the country rebounded from the economic crisis. With the help of Daniel Roger and Yoram Bitton, he decided to enter the German market using Israeli management: Yoram Bitton, who was familiar with the European market, as Regional Manager for Central Europe, and Daniel Roger, CEO of Leonardo Europe. The first hotel of the Leonardo chain outside Israel was established in Germany. Subsequently, additional hotels were established throughout Germany and Central Europe. Some of the hotels in Israel that were operating under the name Fattal were rebranded as Leonardo to promote the new brand. Penetration into the European market was a great challenge for the Leonardo chain, which at the time was only operating in Israel. To deal with the challenge and difficulties that arose as a result, the company took a series of significant steps regarding several different aspects (branding and value proposition, elements in the 'product' itself, marketing etc.) to bring about the success of the company overseas, adapting it to the new customers.

# CHARACTERISTICS OF ISRAEL AND EUROPE CUSTOMER SEGMENTS

Following the move to Europe, the hotel chain had to determine which customer segment to target and how. The hotel chain management conducted an analysis of both types of customers, Israeli and European, which revealed the main differences in their characteristics. Israeli customers regard the hotel as the objective of their vacation. They like to stay at the hotel, spend time in the pool, eat in the dining room (all you can eat for breakfast), and love the all-inclusive format. Their primary interest is leisure, and they regard the hotel as the main element of their vacation. By contrast, German customers consider the hotel as a means to achieve other goals, for example, business.

In Israel, the customer segment the chain targeted consisted of families, young couples, groups of friends, and groups of employees. In preparation for penetration into Europe, David Fattal was advised by his business connections to launch a hotel chain with a German urban business style, to capture the largest possible market share. The reason that Fattal chose this particular segment was that he saw in it the greatest expansion potential and recognized that there were almost no urban business hotels at the 3+ to 4+ star level.

In an interview, Sandra Drahr, VP of Marketing for Central Europe, noted that about 70 per cent of Leonardo's current patrons were business customers:

> When I arrived, in 2007, the hotel was not branded as the sexiest hotel in Europe, so we had to show openness. The business segment is a large part of the hotel market in Europe, and therefore it is the one we targeted. Another reason was that our hotels were not in the suburbs or in areas close to the sea or in resort towns, but in the city centre. The rest of the customers came for weekend trips, performances, or sporting events.

Based on these considerations, the marketing message in the marketing plan was aimed mainly at the business customer segment. It was decided that the hotel would be branded as a European-style urban business hotel, with a European character to all intents and purposes. The targeting of the business customer segment turned out to have been extremely wise, as evidenced by the fact that the Leonardo chain already has more than 160 hotels throughout Europe.

## ADJUSTMENTS AND CHANGES IN THE TRANSITION FROM THE ISRAELI TO THE EUROPEAN MARKET

Because of the difference between the Israeli and German customers and their needs, management was forced to rebrand the hotel chain in Europe. For the Israeli customer, the Fattal chain was branded as a leisure hotel chain, with the exception of two business hotels, in Rehovot and Beer Sheva. Following the understanding of the chain managers that the European customer is different from the Israeli one, the Leonardo hotel chain was branded as a European urban business hotel chain.

The hotels were designated according to the classic European standard at the 3+ to 4+ star level, and they offered exactly what European business customers demanded, including an excellent location in the city centre, high standard of cleanliness, order, reasonable level of breakfast, and a high level of service. In an interview, Leonardo CEO for Central Europe, Yoram Bitton noted that the chain had to completely change its style and branding from the one in Israel, and 'reinvent itself in Europe as a purely European urban business network'.

Initially, in Germany, the chain was run entirely in a Central European way thanks to the many years of experience that Biton and Roger had in managing hotels there. Subsequently, the chain made adjustments and changes that the company imported from Israel and from Israeli business culture, as detailed next.

## BRANDING AND POSITIONING THE VALUE PROPOSITION

After penetration into the German market, the marketing plan of the Leonardo chain was fully adapted to the Central European customer. At the same time, an important part of this plan was imported from Israel.

The marketing plan of the Leonardo chain in Germany focused mainly on the customer. Compared to other hotels in Europe, where everything is done in a purely cold and professional manner, the Leonardo hotel chain decided to emphasize its high standard of quality, but at the same time, to create a family and friendly feeling for customers so that they 'feel good' (the motto of the chain) while staying at the hotel. Customers were made to feel that they were more than a regular customer, yet another number, another wallet. Rather, they were made to feel like friends of the hotel, and even part of the family of the hotel. As Sandra Drahr said in the interview: 'the moment you book a room at one of the hotels of the Leonardo chain, you become part of the family'. These values were imported from Israel, which has a collectivist culture and where family and community are supreme values.

In an interview, Sandra Drahr said that the marketing message of the company begins with the company logo (the Vitruvian man), where the person is at the centre; it continues with the attitude toward customers and their reception at the hotel; and it ends with check-out, when the customer is satisfied and usually returns to the hotel. Sandra said:

> German customers are treated as if they were more than customers, like family and friends, which differentiates Leonardo from the rest of the hotels in Europe. Customers prefer our hotels over those of our competitors for this reason, that at our hotels the customer is in the centre and receives full attention. We do this in a slightly warmer way than our competitors. This approach came mainly from the Israeli character of the Israeli managers, who give the senior executives (Europeans) this family feeling, and this feeling simply percolates all the way down, through the junior managers, the employees, and finally to the customers themselves ... In hotels in Europe, every chain has very clear and strict rules for their employees on how to deal with customers. For example, how to greet them, what sentences they should say at the reception, on the phone, etc. We, at Leonardo, don't have these rules. Of course, one should be polite, sociable, inviting, and clear. We regard each guest individually, and this is how we adapt ourselves to him. The message is 'be who you are' because we are one big family, and we see the customers as our guests who come to our home. As a result, customers, staff, and employees all connect, and this is basically what our customers like – not to be yet another number but to feel invited to our home and be part of the concept called 'Leonardo'.

## THE 'PRODUCT' ITSELF (HOTEL SERVICES)

In Israel, the standard of hotels is completely different from that in Germany as the Israeli customer's hotel experience is fundamentally different from that of the Central European customer. Therefore, the chain administrators had to make many adjustments for the European customers to satisfy them and to contribute to the success of the chain in Europe.

First, the standard of the rooms was adjusted to the 3+ to 4+ star level, in the European style. This meant basic rooms that are not large, but that are clean, tidy, and meet the customers' needs. All this was done to target the appropriate segment of potential guests:

the German business customer. In Israel, by contrast, the rooms are larger and more luxurious, to match the needs of Israeli customers, who spend most of their vacation in the hotel (they are mainly families, young couples, and groups of friends who come to the hotel for vacation purposes only). Moreover, for the hotels in Europe, special attention was paid to giving the hotel a business character. Therefore, conference rooms and business meeting rooms were created, and in general the hotel was made suitable for hosting large business conferences.

Second, the atmosphere at the hotel was made to suit the Central European business customer. In Germany, the atmosphere in hotels is calm and quiet, compared to that of hotels in Israel, where the environment is noisier, aimed at recreation and leisure. This change was intended to attract the business traveller, who seeks a quiet refuge from tedious work and long meetings.

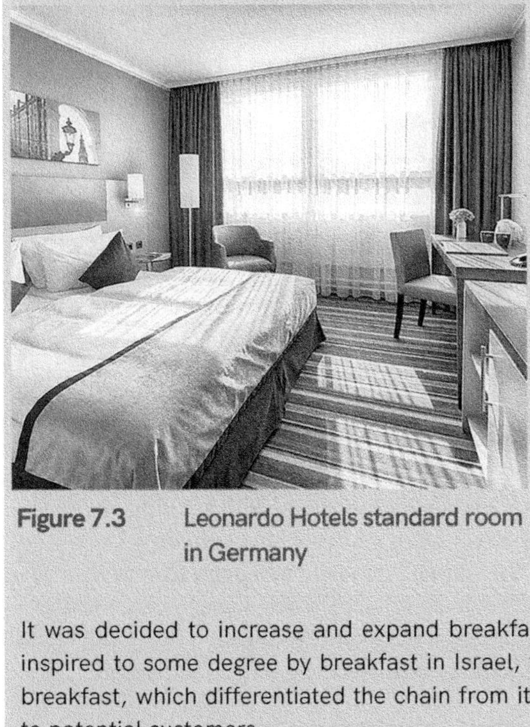

**Figure 7.3** Leonardo Hotels standard room in Germany

Breakfast is a good example of how the hotel chain paid great attention to the smallest detail in penetrating the European market. In Israel, breakfast is a central experience in hotels. The Israeli customer has many expectations of breakfast at the hotel, and often this is the standard by which the level of the hotel is determined. In Europe, by contrast, the status of breakfast at a hotel is lower, and at times quite marginal. The Leonardo management understood that breakfasts in hotels in Europe are quite minimal, and therefore they tailored their breakfast to the European customer. But this was not the end of the considerations of Leonardo management.

It was decided to increase and expand breakfasts in the European hotels of the chain, inspired to some degree by breakfast in Israel, to add a dimension of abundance to the breakfast, which differentiated the chain from its competitors and provided added value to potential customers.

## DIGITAL MARKETING TAILORED TO VARIOUS SEGMENTS

To capture the image of the potential customer that the chain wishes to attract and whom the chain wants to contact, management is assisted by the digital marketing department and the technological means available to it. In Israel, customers are approached by promotions, discounts, and club memberships. This method has proven to be highly effective in reaching Israeli customers, who by nature are more attracted to discounts, limited time promotions, and booking last-minute vacations at discounted prices.

By contrast, the German customer is less focused on incentives in the form of promotions and discounts, but sees greater value in utilitarian transactions. 'The Israeli customer is moved more by emotion, compared to the European customer, who operates more out of common sense'. This is what Dan Ogen, the chief digital officer (CDO) of the Leonardo network said. Dan claimed that Israeli customers like last-minute deals and discounts because they act more emotionally, whereas European customers are more utilitarian and are looking for added value (for example, points earned on a certain card that works with Leonardo, the German railway company, and the airlines). Dan noted that three campaigns were running in parallel: annual, seasonal and continuous. Continuous advertising was designed to keep Leonardo in the minds of customers at all times. The seasonal and annual campaigns were designed to produce 'peaks' that expose the network to a greater extent in the short term. In addition, Dan and the eight employees working under him, regularly perform marketing research tests in targeting the potential customer base: 'It's okay to fail. The main thing is that we find what works well and use it, and what doesn't work well, we toss'.

## MANAGEMENT AND HUMAN RESOURCES

The people who guide the ship and navigate the waters are the network managers. They also deploy work methods imported from Israel and adjust them for Germany. For example, in an interview, Yoram Bitton, CEO for Central Europe, said that when the position of a senior manager is created by the chain, Leonardo management examine the character traits of the candidates with the help of a graphologist, who analyses their handwriting to detect certain character traits, skills and qualities of the candidate. In addition, the chain looks for managers whom they characterize as 'Israeli' - creative, with a strategic vision, with 'aggressive' management abilities, and brave. Yoram said that the combination of senior executives with an 'Israeli' character and junior executives with a 'European' character creates a mix that comes close to perfection: it combines the pedantry, order and discipline of the German character with the daring, creativity and aggressiveness of the Israeli character. Yoram pointed out that the chain reflects Israeli management mainly in digital marketing, yield management and the legal department - areas in which the chain management considers sophisticated and aggressive management to be important.

> European chains have a very large organizational structure, and there are a lot of people responsible for something specific. For example, if you have to make a decision, it takes a very long time until you reach the person who is responsible for making that decision, and even then, there are about 20 other people involved in making the decision. The process is very long and the structure and hierarchy is very 'conservative'. In contrast to the European structure, the way Israelis manage and lead the company is simpler and passes through fewer people. There is an internal circle of senior executives from Israel who are very involved in the company. This is not customary in Europe, and in my opinion, it is one of the reasons why Leonardo is so successful.

> For example, David Fattal is involved in so many things, he knows the people, is close to them, and trusts them.

Sandra Drahr added that:

> if you are part of this team, you are inside. You have a wide range of options to make your own decisions, to start your own project. This makes decision making faster and more flexible, better suited to market needs. According to the Israeli mindset, you are part of the company, you are inside, and once you are inside you cannot leave anymore, which is why I've been with the company for 14 years. This is very unusual in the hotel industry.

The fast decision-making process and the flexibility in management differentiates Leonardo from its competitors, who usually react more slowly to changes in the business environment.

From the point of view of human resources, the differences between Israel and Central Europe are enormous. Personnel in hotels in Germany consist of staff members who studied the profession at university (have a bachelor's degree in hospitality management). In Israel, hotel personnel consist mostly of temporary workers, discharged soldiers, and employees who have not been previously trained or educated for the job.

When the first Leonardo hotel was established in Germany, local employees set a high European standard and proved to be far more effective than the average Israeli worker. As David Fattal, the owner of the company, said: 'I was surprised to see that the receptionist, in addition to his job at the front desk, cleans windows, pours beer at the bar, and does all sorts of other chores'.

It is clear that German employees take their job more seriously than Israeli employees do, and as a result, are more committed to the position in which they begin their career in the hotel industry. Furthermore, in Israel there are functions that are not required in Europe. In Europe, for example, there is no need for a security officer, a lifeguard, entertainment staff, and a kashrut supervisor, which reduces hotel expenses relative to Israel.

## SUMMARY AND CONCLUSIONS

Over time, it can be seen that the penetration of the Leonardo hotel chain into Central Europe proved to be highly successful, and at present the chain has about 160 hotels at more than 75 destinations in 15 Central European countries. The chain has been defined as one of the leading and fastest-growing hotel chains in Europe.

Leonardo penetrated Europe by completely adapting itself to the European customer. In addition, it brought with it the Israeli managerial aspect, which is manifest in creativity, 'aggressiveness', strategic vision, and risk-taking. This has led to Leonardo standing out, compared to its various competitors in the industry, and to the success of the network across Europe.

After many interviews with senior executives of the company, an unequivocal conclusion was reached that the mix of management deployed by the company, which combines Israelis and Central Europeans, aimed at understanding the market, has led to the success of the chain in Europe. Thanks to their managerial qualities and ability to make appropriate adjustments and changes that are well suited to the European customer in various areas, the company was able to become a successful hotel chain and win the hearts of the European customers.

## QUESTIONS FOR DISCUSSION

1. The challenges faced by the Leonardo hotels' management in its entry into the Central European market in characterizing the target audience:
   A. What is the difference between the Israeli audience and the German (Central European) audience?
   B. How did the Leonardo hotels' managers in Europe outline the solutions in the design of the marketing strategy?
   C. Why do you think the strategic plan was successful?
2. A strategic plan for Leonardo hotels:
   A. What are the differences in the product and service that Leonardo hotels had to adjust in penetrating the Central European market (to Germany)?
   B. How did the Leonardo hotels' managers adapt its marketing system to the European audience? Give an example.
   C. What are the differences and adjustments of Leonardo hotels' services in the transition from Israel to Europe, and how have they been expressed in the tactical plan (4Ps\7Ps)?
3. Write at least three characteristics of the Leonardo hotels' services, and how do cultural aspects come into consideration when recruiting new employees and managers in Europe?
4. Summary:
   A. Make a list of five key differences in the Leonardo hotels' marketing activity in Israel compared to Central Europe: write an explanation about this adaptation to the culture of the target audience.
   B. Summarize in your own words in a short paragraph: what can be learned from the case regarding the entry of services into a new market in the international sector?

# References – Part II

Almeida, P. (1996). Knowledge sourcing by foreign multinationals: Patent citation analysis in the US semiconductor industry. *Strategic Management Journal*, *17*(S2), 155–65.

Alon, I. (ed.) (2003). *Chinese Economic Transition and International Marketing Strategy*. Westport, CT: Greenwood Publishing Group.

Andersen, O. (1993). On the internationalization process of firms: A critical analysis. *Journal of International Business Studies*, *24*, 209–231.

Bartlett, C.A. and Ghoshal, S. (1991). Global strategic management: Impact on the new frontiers of strategy research. *Strategic Management Journal*, *12*, 5–16.

Baumann, Z. (2005). *Liquid Life*. Cambridge: Polity.

Belz, F.M. and Peattie, K. (2009). *Sustainability Marketing*. Glasgow, UK and Hoboken, NJ, USA: Wiley and Sons.

Brand Finance (2021). Global 500 ranking. Accessed at https://brandirectory.com/rankings/global.

Carpenter, G.S. and Nakamoto, K. (1996). Impact of consumer preference formation on marketing objectives and competitive second mover strategies. *Journal of Consumer Psychology*, *5*(4), 325–58.

Cavusgil, S.T. and Zou, S. (1994). Marketing strategy–performance relationship: An investigation of the empirical link in export market ventures. *Journal of Marketing*, *58*(1), 1–21.

Chang, T.J., Chen, W.C., Lin, L.Z. and Chiu, J.S.K. (2010). The impact of market orientation on customer knowledge development and NPD success. *International Journal of Innovation and Technology Management*, *7*(4), 303–27.

Dervillée, F., Rieche, M., and Zieske, A. (2004). Internationalization and Foreign Market Entry Mode Choice – An Alternative Approach: The Kristianstad 3° Model.

Dimitrova, B. and Rosenbloom, B. (2010). Standardization versus adaptation in global markets: Is channel strategy different? *Journal of Marketing Channels*, *17*(2), 157–76.

Dunning, J.H. (1988). The theory of international production. *The International Trade Journal*, *3*(1), 21–66.

Dunning, J.H. (2001). The eclectic (OLI) paradigm of international production: Past, present and future. *International Journal of the Economics of Business*, *8*(2), 173–90.

Eriksson, K., Johanson, J., Majkgård, A. and Sharma, D.D. (2015). Experiential knowledge and cost in the internationalization process. In M. Forsgren, U. Holm and J. Johanson (eds), *Knowledge, Networks and Power*. Basingstoke: Palgrave Macmillan, pp. 41–63.

Fujita, M. and Krugman, P. (2004). The new economic geography: Past, present and the future. In R.J.G.M. Florax and D.A. Plane (eds), *Fifty Years of Regional Science*. Berlin and Heidelberg: Springer, pp. 139–64.

Grewal, D., Krishnan, R., Baker, J. and Borin, N. (1998). The effect of store name, brand name and price discounts on consumers' evaluations and purchase intentions. *Journal of Retailing*, *74*(3), 331–52.

Hall, E.T. (1981). *Beyond Culture*. Anchor Books.

Hamel, G. and Prahalad, C.K. (1994). *Competing for the Future*. Harvard, MA: Harvard Business School Press.

Hong, J. and Sternthal, B. (2010). The effects of consumer prior knowledge and processing strategies on judgments. *Journal of Marketing Research*, *47*(2), 301–11.

Johanson, J. and Vahlne, J.-E. (1997). The internationalization process of the firm: A model of knowledge development and increasing foreign market commitments. *Journal of International Business Studies*, *8*(1), 23–32.

Johanson, J. and Vahlne, J.-E. (2006). Commitment and opportunity development in the internationalization process: A note on the Uppsala internationalization process model. *Management International Review*, *46*(2), 165–78.

Johanson, J. and Wiedersheim-Paul, F. (1975). The internationalization of the firm: Four Swedish cases. *Journal of Management Studies*, *12*(3), 305–22.

Jonsson, A. and Foss, N. (2011). International expansion through flexible replication: Learning from the internationalization experience of IKEA. *Journal of International Business Studies, 42*, 1079–102.

Kogut, B. and Zander, U. (1995). Knowledge, market failure and the multinational enterprise: A reply. *Journal of International Business Studies, 26*, 417–26.

Levitt, T. (1983). The globalization of markets. *Harvard Business Review*, May–June.

Mooij, M.D. (2003). Convergence and divergence in consumer behaviour: Implications for global advertising. *International Journal of Advertising, 22*(2), 183–202.

Oppenheimer, M.F. (2007). The end of liberal globalization. *World Policy Journal, 24*(4), 1–9.

Pontiggia, A. and Vescovi, T. (2013). Medium size multinational firms internationalization strategies: When size matters in Chinese markets. *Proceedings EURAM Conference 2013*, Galatasaray University, Istanbul.

Pontiggia, A. and Vescovi, T. (2014). Medium size multinational firms internationalization strategies in China. In R. Taylor (ed.), *The Globalisation of Chinese Business: Implications for Multinational Investors*. London: Chandos, pp. 80–108.

Quelch, A.J. and Hoff, J.A. (1986). Customizing global marketing. *Harvard Business Review, 64*, 59–68.

Quinn, L., Dibb, S., Simkin, L., Canhoto, A. and Analogbei, M. (2016). Troubled waters: The transformation of marketing in a digital world. *European Journal of Marketing, 50*, 2103–33.

Ranfagni, S. and Guercini, S. (2014). Guanxi and distribution in China: The case of Ferrero Group. *The International Review of Retail, Distribution and Consumer Research, 24*(3), 294–310.

Reid, S.D., Rosson, P.J. and Modes, M.E. (1987). *Managing Export Entry and Expansion: Concepts and Practice*. New York: Praeger.

Rugman, A. (2012). *The End of Globalization*. London: Random House.

Rugman, A. and Verbeke, A. (2003). Extending the theory of the multinational enterprise: Internalization and strategic management perspectives. *Journal of International Business Studies, 34*(2), 125–37.

Sridhar, S. and Srinivasan, R. (2012). Social influence effects in online product ratings. *Journal of Marketing, 76*(5), 70–88.

Turnbull, P.W. (1987). A challenge to the stages theory of the internationalization process. In S.D. Reid, P.J. Rosson and M.E. Modes (eds), *Managing Export Entry and Expansion: Concepts and Practice*. New York: Praeger, pp. 21–40.

Winter, S.G. and Szulanski, G. (2001). Replication as strategy. *Organization Science, 12*(6), 730–43.

Zhang, L. and Yanqun, H. (2012). Understanding luxury consumption in China: Consumer perceptions of best-known brands. *Journal of Business Research, 65*(10), 1452–60.

Zhou, L. (2007). The effects of entrepreneurial proclivity and foreign market knowledge on early internationalization. *Journal of World Business, 42*(3), 281–93.

Zou, S. and Cavusgil, S.T. (1996). Global strategy: A review and an integrated conceptual framework. *European Journal of Marketing, 30*(1), 52–69.

# PART III
## CROSS-CULTURAL MARKETING CHOICES AND DECISIONS

# 8
# Cross-cultural marketing research

Market research can undergo important variations in structure, due to the influence of various cultures that can modify the response conditions of respondents, in the case of questionnaires, and to the diversity of meaning in culturally different contexts that the questions may assume, not only because of difficulties in translating the questionnaire but because of completely different cultural references. Furthermore, the scales of evaluation of opinions or judgements can have totally opposing logics in different cultures. This chapter explores the aspects of diversity that influence marketing research and can lead to errors in various cultural contexts.

## 8.1 CULTURAL ATTITUDE TOWARDS MARKETING RESEARCH

Culture, and the influence that cultural values have on attitudes and behaviour, is an important topic in cross-cultural consumer research.

The precise definition of the marketing research problem is more difficult, and more important, in cross-cultural marketing research than in domestic marketing research. Unfamiliarity with the culture and environmental factors of the countries where the research is being conducted can greatly increase the difficulty of attaining comparability (Malhotra et al., 1996). Many international marketing efforts fail not because research was not conducted, but because the issue of comparability was not adequately addressed in defining the marketing research problem. As a practical way of attaining comparability, it has been suggested that the researcher should isolate and examine the impact of the unconscious reference to their own cultural values.

Evaluation of secondary data is even more critical for cross-cultural studies than for domestic projects. Different sources report different values for a given statistic, such as GDP, because of differences in the way the unit is defined. Measurement units may not be equivalent across cultures. In France and in Italy, for example, workers are paid a thirteenth monthly salary each year as an automatic bonus, resulting in a measurement construct that is different from other countries (Douglas and Craig, 1983).

Market research can be either primary data (newly obtained data) or secondary data (previously acquired data). Primary data can be obtained from personal interviews, surveys, focus groups, observation, or experimentation. Each has distinct cultural influences and potential dangers when used in an international setting. For example, telephone or email surveys work poorly and give poor results when used in countries with low telephone or web penetration; shopping mall-intercept interviews may provide biased results because of the skewed demographics of mall users as in many countries only the affluent upper class are able to afford products in shopping malls.

The accuracy of secondary data may also vary from country to country. Data from highly industrialized countries like those in Europe are likely to be more accurate than those from newly emerging countries. For example, many countries attempt to attract foreign investment by overstating certain factors that make the economic picture look better than it is. On the other hand, there may be some countries that understate certain factors, making their economic situation appear worse so that they can indicate a need for more foreign aid. Statistics could also be manipulated for political reasons. For example, a study conducted by the International Labour Organization found that the actual unemployment rate was over 10 per cent in Russia compared with the official reported figure of 2 per cent. Still, in other countries where there is a lack of sophisticated data collection systems, estimates rather than precise readings are reported. Business and income statistics are affected by the taxation structure and the extent of tax evasion. Population censuses may vary in the frequency and year in which the data are collected. In most European countries a census is conducted every ten years, whereas in the People's Republic of China, there was a 29-year gap between the censuses of 1953 and 1982.

Because the researcher is often not familiar with the foreign market to be examined, qualitative research is crucial in cross-cultural marketing research. In the initial stages of cross-national research, qualitative research can provide insights into the problem and help in developing an approach by generating relevant research questions and hypotheses, models, and characteristics which influence the research design. Thus, qualitative research may reveal differences between foreign and domestic markets. Focus groups can be used in many settings, particularly in industrialized countries. Not only should the moderator be trained in focus group methodology but they should also be familiar with the language, culture and patterns of social interaction prevailing in that country. The focus group findings should be derived not only from the verbal contents but also from non-verbal cues such as voice intonations, inflections, expressions and gestures. In some cultures, such as in the Middle or Far East, people are hesitant to discuss their feelings in a group setting. In these cases, in-depth interviews should be used.

Yaprak (2008) reviewed the development of culture theory in international marketing and provided recommendations such as to define culture better and to overcome ethnocentrism. Some recommendations can be added for the purpose of improving international marketing and consumer behaviour research (De Mooij, 2015):

- Before embarking on any cross-cultural research, we need to understand the concept of culture and the working of dimensional models.
- When using comparative data at national level, only countries can be compared, not individuals.
- If researchers want to measure culture together with other phenomena, their samples must be matched properly.
- When developing dimensions from self-assembled scales, labels should be used that are different from those of existing models.

- Before setting hypotheses, the conceptual content of the dimensions used must be properly studied. If countries are compared with respect to appeals in advertising, hypotheses can be set by first analysing cultural relationships of product category-related consumer motives or other national-level data on attitudes or behaviour.
- The researcher has to be careful not to formulate ethnocentric questions and not to use lists of values or advertising appeals developed in one specific country for cross-cultural comparison.

Language may also be a problem that is not immediately obvious. For example, India has 14 official languages spoken in different parts of the country; knowing which one to use where is a major concern. Every language has multiple dialects and its own slang and idioms; idioms in each Spanish-speaking country can be significantly different from its neighbours; one should not blindly use the same translation of a questionnaire for all countries, even if people in those countries speak the same language (Kaynak and Herbig, 2014). The same situation can be found in English-speaking countries.

The respondents can be sensitive to certain aspects of the interviewer's background: care should be taken to bridge that distance. For example, in some cultures, it may be necessary to use female interviewers to interview women. Important aspects of the interview and its setting include thematic relevance and sensitivity, cultural relevance, social desirability, capacity to reach depth, length, and structure. The relevance of the topic, and hence the need to emphasize the relevance of the interview through initial rapport building may vary across cultures. In certain cultures, some questions may be sensitive or taboo, and thus require special interviewer training. Courtesy norms, such as greeting respondents or accepting hospitality from them, are likely to vary across cultures. In some cultures, such as Japanese or Chinese cultures, people do not talk much or are slow in giving their responses.

The cooperative respondent sometimes gives responses that he/she believes will please the interviewer rather than stating his/her real opinions or feelings. This is often viewed in a variety of cultures as being polite; those in Latin cultures tend to go overboard and tell you what they think you would like to hear rather than what they really think, especially if it is negative. This is called the 'courtesy effect' (also known as hospitality bias or social acquiescence). This phenomenon is particularly common in Asia, but is also present in countries such as Poland. When Japanese consumers are asked directly for their opinions about a new product being tested, they are much more reluctant to criticize the new product than are consumers in the West. For the Japanese culture, as for the high context ones, right and wrong are relative values.

Respondents in the Netherlands or Germany are reluctant to divulge information on their personal financial history; it is said that the Dutch are more willing to discuss sex than money. Privacy issues abound, especially in Europe. One of the European Union's directives on data privacy states that respondents cannot be asked sensitive questions without prior written permission. The European Union also has legislation in place restricting the use and sale of consumer research data in Europe. This limits what can and cannot be asked (Herbig, 2000).

The growth of the e-commerce industry has increased the complexity associated with conducting cross-cultural studies. Internet research techniques are now, for some companies, the dominant medium through which they conduct their marketing research. The internet raises distinctive cross-cultural and equivalence issues whilst it mitigates some of the problems outlined with some of the traditional techniques, such as sample equivalence (Slater and Yani-de-Soriano, 2010).

Considerable culture bias occurs in marketing research; what may be viewed undesirable in one culture may be viewed as an accomplishment in another. Researchable problems within one culture may not be researchable within another because of societal taboos and different levels of abstraction. Major problems regarding cross-cultural marketing research include unwilling respondents, unwillingness to provide current and truthful information; locating knowledgeable sources; taboos about discussing personal or family matters; private matters not discussed with strangers; political questions; limitations of infrastructure; sampling problems; language, slang, idioms, or dialects; literacy rates; and education levels.

## 8.2    THE EQUIVALENCE PROBLEM

The need for comparability gives rise to a host of methodological issues concerning research design and data collection.

Traditional approaches in marketing research aiming to establish equivalence across cultures have typically devoted attention to just one aspect of it, namely, linguistic equivalence. Most tests on marketing and marketing research have numerous examples of mistakes that have been made when words and phrases have been used without appropriate translation. While it is true that words have different meanings in different cultures, cross-cultural equivalence is more than just linguistic equivalence.

Market research projects are, at best, photographs of the market and not the market itself. On the other hand, it is important not to underestimate the power of the process of designing images of reality. Scientific market research provides marketing decision makers with an image of the actual or potential market, consumer behaviour and the competition. In addition, it is important to consider that international market surveys should not be constructed by simply replicating domestic research, because of the presence of cross-cultural variance in several factors such as the nature and scope of researched market information, the ways of collecting it, the accuracy of the data, as well as the criteria of reliability of the data. Before searching for information, it is vital to search for meaning which relates to examining potential cultural influences at each step of the research process: questions, survey methods, interviews and questionnaires and informants (Usunier and Lee, 2013).

More specifically, the main difficulty in cross-cultural market research is establishing equivalence at the various stages of the research process. Craig and Douglas (2005) individuated different types of cross-cultural equivalence which is a vital consideration for cross-cultural marketers, these are: conceptual equivalence, functional equivalence, translation equivalence, measurement equivalence, sample equivalence and data collection equivalence.

Concerning *conceptual equivalence*, a basic issue in cross-cultural research is the determination of whether the concepts have similar meaning across the different countries. Actually, the same construct may be relevant across cultures, but interpreted or expressed in different ways.

Generally speaking, conceptual equivalence is an obstacle to the direct use of constructs that have been specifically designed for low-context cultures.

As for example, every 'risk-perception' construct could be broken down into several sub-dimensions, including financial, physical, performance, psychological, social and time or convenience risk, then it is possible to vary the emphasis placed on these sub-dimensions across cultures. In some contexts, people may attach more value to the social risk of buying a car because they are mostly status-oriented, whereas in other cultures people are more concerned with physical safety due to the high rate of accidents. Further, there is a distinction between the perception of the risk and the attitude toward perceived risk, which may vary (Weber and Hsee, 1998). For these kinds of reasons, it is necessary to investigate the validity of the constructs in each target culture when cross-cultural consumer behaviour is studied. Moreover, the construct's validity is affected by both construct bias and equivalency issues. Bias occurs when the definition of the construct differs across cultures, influencing construct validity, and equivalency relates to the level of comparison or measurement of the construct (Douglas and Craig, 2006).

*Functional equivalence* focuses on whether the concepts have the same role or function across groups. This means that even if similar activities exist, they could perform different functions in different societies. Concepts which could be used in market surveys, such as preparing a meal, are not necessarily functionally equivalent across countries. Functional equivalence problems can be illustrated by taking the example of the consumption of coffee among cultures. Ordering a coffee includes a whole range of beverages that are enjoyed in very different social settings or in quite different forms. The function of an Italian espresso (Weiss, 2001) served in small cups of strong coffee drunk regularly in exchanges with colleagues and many times during the day, cannot be compared with that of the weaker American coffee, which is consumed in large cups and drunk mostly in transit or during leisure time. One of the best ways to investigate functional equivalence, before engaging in market decisions, is to examine the social settings in which a product is consumed, and local observation methods or focus groups could be employed for this purpose.

*Translation equivalence* focuses on whether the language is understood by respondents as having the same meaning in different cultures. Culture sets many implications for language and communication which requires sophisticated translation techniques which not always achieve full comparability of data. Translation equivalence can be divided into four sub-categories: lexical equivalence, simply provided by dictionaries; idiomatic equivalence, where an idiom is a linguistic usage natural to native speakers and most often non-equivalent even for regions within a country; grammatical–syntactical equivalence, which refers to the order of words, the construction of sentences and the meaning that is expressed in language; and experiential equivalence, which means that translated terms must refer to real items or experiences familiar to the target cultures, even if some concepts have no real equivalent translation in other languages. The back-translation technique is the most widely employed method for reaching translation equivalence in market research. This involves one translator translating from the source language into a target language, and another translator, ignorant of the source-language text, who translates the first translator's text back into the source language. Then a comparison is made to prepare the final target language questionnaire. It is fundamental to investigate translation equivalence before the launch of a new product, because in the event of misunderstanding or differences in perception it can lead to dangerous and wrong product evaluations.

*Measurement equivalence* takes into account the measurement reliability across cultures, which means the potential source of variations in the reliability of research instruments. For example, some types of questions are less likely to be plagued by measurement equivalence than others, as it should be easier to obtain measurement equivalence for demographic variables than for psychographic variables such as lifestyles. Measurement includes perceptual, metric, calibration and temporal equivalence. About perceptual equivalence, as emphasized in the first chapter, different cultural backgrounds influence individuals' behaviour and perception. When conducting research about sensory products or elements (e.g. packaging), perceptive clues are important for product evaluation, therefore questions must be formulated to allow interviewees to express their perceptual view and their first impression on the sensorial parts of the object (colours, smell, touch, etc.). If the scores given by respondents do not have the same meaning, it means that *metric equivalence* is not accurate. In fact, scores may differ across cultures for a variety of reasons, which include differences in the interpretation of numerical or verbal anchors, the avoidance of extreme responses, humility or social desirability (Van de Vijver and Poortinga, 1982). The validity of a rating scale in a cross-cultural context is affected by the equivalence of the scales and by the homogeneity of meanings. For example, the translation of scale terms in different languages can lead to misleading interpretations; it is not advisable to translate scales lexically (simply with dictionary-equivalent words); on the contrary, they should be translated for equivalence of meaning. Reaching equivalence of meaning may require the original wording to be 'decentralized' in order to obtain reliable and valid data for all the countries under survey. Metric equivalence of scale terms reveals that some languages have fewer terms to express gradation in evaluation, whereas others have a multitude. Therefore, the best solution is not simply to translate scale terms, but rather to start from local wording based on scales used by local researchers. The meaning of numbers across cultures may be another factor influencing score results. For instance, the numbers 2, 8 and 9 are considered lucky in China and as such may be chosen more frequently (Marchetti and Usunier, 1990). Moreover, in Italy the scale of grades used at school is 1–10, where 1 is the minimum and 10 the maximum, while in Germany the scale is 1–6, where 1 is the maximum and 6 is the minimum.

*Calibration equivalence* problems arise from the employment of units based on different computation systems. For instance, a typical problem relates to differences in monetary units, especially when comparing a high-inflation context where daily prices over a year change constantly with those of low inflation countries. Exchange rates and units of weight, distance and volume are other causes of calibration equivalence problems. Calibration equivalence also mixes with perceptual equivalence: for instance, according to the perception of a particular country, different classifications of the same colour are recognized, and this inequivalence might be of great influence in a product test or a packaging test. Temporal equivalence is similar to calibration equivalence, in terms of calibrating dates and time periods. For example, information spreads and ages at different speeds across countries, and it is therefore necessary to indicate on which date data were collected in order to make comparisons.

*Temporal equivalence* also deals with differences in development levels and technological advancement: certain differences are 'equivalent' to what others were 20 years ago. In this case, assessing time lags is necessary in order to make analogies. Considering the northern and southern hemispheres, temporal equivalence should be about seasonal equivalence. For many products the season of the year is really important for the consumer's perception and use. This is evident for ice cream, soda beverages, and so on. All the products that are connected to a specific season of the year are affected by different perceptions at certain dates according to whether consumers are above or below the equator.

*Sampling unit equivalence* relates to the choice of respondents. Selecting a unit of analysis is a key issue in the conceptualization of comparative research design, as the role of respondents in the buying decision process – organizational buying, family buying, information and influence patterns – may vary across countries. As well as when researching industrial products, it is important to compare the position, the role and responsibility of industrial buyers throughout different countries. The main problem in the cross-cultural sampling process is the selection of comparable samples across countries, as the characteristics of the whole population are inferred from a limited sample. In cross-cultural research, there are often two levels of sampling to consider: the first level is a sample of countries or cultures, and the second level is based on samples of individuals within the chosen countries or cultures. Reaching perfect comparability at either level is very difficult, which means that results might be considered an intrinsic limitation.

At the first level, samples are more often chosen to represent the markets of interest, or a selection of maximally different countries, in an attempt to compute the average influence of cultural values on certain consumption patterns. At this level, country characteristics, such as socio-demographic, economic and cultural variables, national wealth, legal system, individualism and level of national identity, may be related to the per capita consumption of a particular product or service. This type of information can guide strategic marketing decisions related to the selection of national target markets, including the identification of markets with low actual demand but high growth potential, and so on. Samples of cultures should not be confused with samples of individuals, as there is a risk of gross stereotyping when country characteristics are considered as individual characteristics. If individuals are of interest, researchers must also carefully design the within-country or culture sample. Often representative samples are chosen to reflect some characteristics of the population of interest, such as being representative of the primary purchasers of a product or users of a product category. The sampling method must be selected so that each national sample is fully representative of the population of interest. As sampling frames or lists are usually unavailable at the individual consumer level across cultures, non-probability sampling is the solution adopted in many countries. Screening criteria may also be necessary to ensure that the sample fits the characteristics of the population of interest. Different screening criteria might be used across countries to ensure the comparability among the samples. For example, a basic objective in China may be to sample respondents who had access to consumer markets, with screening criteria including an education level that would allow a literate information search and an income level that would allow consumption, whereas in countries like North America the objective may be to sample mainstream consumers with screening criteria including being a native English speaker, born in North America to

North American parents (Doran, 2002). Another problem is to secure equivalence in meaning. If the objective is to examine similarities and differences across cultures, cross-national comparability is important, and purposefully chosen non-probability samples may be better, as they allow the researchers to create homogeneous samples. Conversely, when the objective is to describe attitudes or behaviour within specific countries, within-country representativeness is important, and probability samples should be used to enable the researcher to estimate the sampling error.

In defining the initial procedures about finding equivalent national questions for a cross-cultural study, and searching for equivalent samples, it is still necessary to analyse response equivalence, which includes respondents' cooperation equivalence, *data-collection context equivalence* and response-style equivalence. These sources of error can create discrepancies between observed measurement and true measurement, but some basic precautions help to avoid the generation of data with a great deal of measurement error. Respondents' cooperation equivalence refers to secrecy or unwillingness of participants to answer interviewers' questions. The reasons for this could relate to the disclosure of personal data and privacy; sometimes participants simply do not want to be justify or explain their actions. This may lead to differences in response rate, or biased responses. This means that different survey methods should be employed in different cultures in order to avoid any kind of secrecy from the participants.

*Contextual equivalence* relates to elements in the context of the data collection process that have an influence on responses. Questions are never culture-free: there is inevitably a social and cultural context built into them. Any question that deals, directly or indirectly, with social prescription needs to be worded so that people can elaborate a response without feeling too embarrassed. This may mean further questioning some well-disposed and open-minded interviewees to ascertain their true view on the question. Social desirability may also be a factor, where individuals answer questions in a way that presents them or their country in a more positive light. People from collectivist cultures tend to express culturally appropriate or normative responses to promote a desired social image more often than people in individualist cultures (Lalwani et al., 2006).

*Response-style equivalence* is the final step. The four main concerns in relation to response-style equivalence are: yea-saying or nay-saying patterns (acquiescence/dis-acquiescence); extreme response style; non-contingent responding; and item non-response patterns. First, 'yea-saying' or acquiescence is the tendency to agree with items, and 'nay-saying' or dis-acquiescence is the tendency to disagree with items regardless of content. Second, extreme response style is the tendency to choose the most extreme response regardless of content, even when a response range is stetted to either use a narrow or wide range of categories around the mean. This could produce a bias in the standard deviation of data; it artificially increases in cultures where people tend to overreact to questions, compared to other cultures where people may tend to suppress their opinions, be they positive or negative. Third, non-contingent responding is the tendency to respond carelessly, randomly or non-purposefully. This may happen if respondents are not very motivated to answer the questionnaire. Fourth, item non-response is another typical source of bias in cross-national surveys, where respondents may be unwilling to respond to some questions, such as those relating to income or age. In order to achieve a consistent response equivalence in the collection of data, it is important to consider addressing only the relevant questions: those that can be understood in that specific context, as participants cannot respond to a barrage of questions alien to their knowledge and frame of reference.

Therefore, the content of the research must somehow be strictly controlled and must focus on really significant issues.

Moreover, informants' competence as insiders of that market has to be considered far superior to the researchers as outsiders, but the interview should be focused only on those who have something to say, making use of selective criteria to be included. Multiple methods may be used to elicit feedback from respondents, including a preliminary study using in-depth interviews, focus groups to identify the appropriate product categories and help define the interview, and, after the main study, follow-up interviews to clarify unclear issues and investigate new issues.

# 9
# Consumer behaviour and cultural factors

## 9.1    CULTURE AND CONSUMPTION

Since ancient times, consumption has always characterized the lives of people. Goods are crucial to our lives and they have always underlined the difference existing between individuals and between the different groups of society. Customers make purchasing choices according to the meaning that goods represent to the individuals within the same group. It is thanks to goods that they use that it is possible to outline the differences between many social groups and, in this way, goods become representative of their cultural profile. The sociologist McCracken (1990) in his work affirmed that consumption is the way in which cultures are daily displayed and expressed. Usually, customers are seen as a group of individuals very different from each other. Actually, behind their purchasing choices, there are hidden many different social dynamics, which come from a series of rules, codes and lifestyles. Customers are really influenced by the cultural and social context, so the purchased goods take on a different meaning that varies according to the ideals of the social group of belonging. It is possible to say that consumption is the element of identification of different social groups. Choices are not only driven by personal tastes, but also by external factors, such as family or work groups. Culture and consumption are closely connected. The first represents the ideals, rules and behaviours that enable an individual to make choices during his/her lifetime and, for this reason, the environment in which the individual grows indirectly affects his/her purchasing choices. If we want to understand the choices of a customer, we have to understand the social and cultural context beforehand in which they live. Family, ethnicity, generation, profession, everything in the life of an individual has its own role and influence. The elements that most influence the choices of customers can be divided into five groups: mentality, which includes values, aspirations and personality; style of life; cultural productions; informal social structures, such as family; and lastly, religious beliefs. They are basic elements of culture. Purchasing choices can be influenced by many other factors, such as situational, social, personal and psychological elements. However, the most influential factor is surely the cultural factor. So, if we want to understand the choice of a community or an individual, we must first analyse and study the society which has created their values, perceptions and behaviours.

The concepts of self and personality as developed in the individualistic Western world include the person as an autonomous entity with a distinctive set of attributes, qualities or processes.

The configuration of these internal attributes or processes causes behaviour. People's attributes and processes should be expressed consistently in behaviour across situations. Behaviour that changes with the situation is viewed as hypocritical or pathological. In the collectivistic model the self cannot be separated from others and the surrounding social context, so the self is an interdependent entity that is part of an encompassing social relationship (De Mooij and Hofstede, 2011). Individual behaviour is situational, it varies from one situation to another and from one time to another (Markus and Kitayama, 1991). For members of collectivistic cultures self-esteem is not linked to the individual but to relationships with others.

Therefore, the social and cultural context exerts a profound influence on the methods of consumption and the meanings associated with it. In the case of luxury goods, for example, the importance attached to the values of status and ostentation is evident compared to other values associated with the brand and the product. It is typical of collectivist cultures to emphasize visible possession, particularly in the younger sections of the population (Yu and Bastin, 2017). The resulting benefits are not of a utilitarian type, but fundamentally instrumental to the strengthening of social representation and prestige, to conform and at the same time to be accepted by the community. At the basis of this model of consumer behaviour in China, for example, are evident the principles of Confucian philosophy and *guanxi*, a term that indicates a type of interpersonal relationship, based exclusively on relationships of a utilitarian nature (Fox, 2008). Individuals, not subsisting autonomously, must necessarily relate to each other to achieve a specific goal. This exposes the principle of *wanglai* (exchange): each subject cannot refrain from returning the favour, on pain of losing face and their own *mianzi* (social prestige). Consequently, the status of a person in China depends on the extent and level of their *guanxixue*, that is, on their relational capital, capable of having a decisive impact on commercial relations and business relations (Huang, 2009).

As marketing efforts become increasingly globalized, understanding cross-cultural consumer behaviour has become a mainstream goal of consumer research. In recent years, research in consumer behaviour has addressed a broadening set of cross-cultural issues and dimensions. However, the need for a deeper understanding of the psychological mechanisms underlying cross-cultural differences continues to grow. As societies become more globalized, cultural boundaries will become more blurred and new hybrids of cultural values will emerge, along with an increased need to understand these phenomena better (Shavitt et al., 2009). Both individualist and collectivist consumers use brands for self-expressive purposes. They use brands, however, in different ways: collectivist consumers use brands to reassert their similarity with members of their reference group, while individualist consumers use brands to differentiate themselves from referent others.

Consumer behaviour and the consumer's journey (the journey made by the consumer for the moment of perceiving a need with (not) satisfaction) are deeply influenced by culture. Culture creates cultural symbols, rituals and hero profiles that embody the values of a society. Buying Behaviour and Consumer Journey are the results of culture, on the one hand, and of the marketing activities carried out by companies, on the other (Figure 9.1).

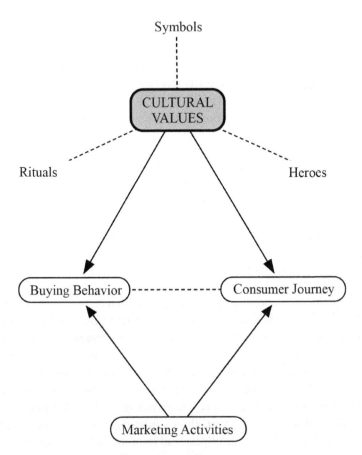

**Figure 9.1**     Cultural values and consumer behaviour

The relationship between values, symbols, rituals and consumer behaviour is a complicated one. As Mehta and Belk (1991) assert, 'rather than a result of the persistence of abstract Indian cultural values ... this [ritual] may be a strategy of aggregate identity preservation anchored in more concrete symbols'. Thus, rituals may not necessarily reflect the values of the culture where the rituals originate. Indian food may be eaten by Indian immigrants in the USA (a ritual), but food purity precepts are ignored (a traditional Indian cultural value). Instead, the rituals serve as an outward sign to secure one's identity.

## Values and Consumer Behaviour

Models of the diffusion of innovation or of new product adoption (Rogers, 1983) need to be generalized to include cultural variables. For example, cultures in which following tradition is considered a terminal value may have relatively slow adoption and diffusion curves. In contrast, cultures in which innovativeness is seen as an important value will have much faster adoption cycles.

## Consumer Symbols and Behaviour

Products can take on symbolic characteristics in a culture. For example, many food products become cultural symbols, such as Champagne in France, pasta in Italy or *würstel* in Germany. This can involve entire categories of products that take on different symbolic values in different cultures. The choice criteria and the purchasing behaviour of the same category of product can therefore be based on very different considerations like functional or symbolic value.

## Rituals and Consumer Behaviour

Consumer purchase models relying on scanner data which incorporate variables such as price, promotions or advertising may need to be generalized to include cultural variables. For example, if an item is being consumed as part of a ritual (e.g. espresso coffee to affirm one's belonging to an Italian culture), price and other variables might lose at least some of their significance.

## Heroes and Consumer Behaviour

For example, a specific culture could place a strong weight on certain subjective norms like the household elder's opinion, while other cultures may tend to place emphasis on other heroes, or on none at all. The relative weight of attitudinal and subjective norm components may also shift from one culture to another. For example, in Western cultures, group interests are not considered as important as they are in Eastern cultures (Luna and Forquer Gupta, 2001).

A very interesting example concerns ethnic cuisine. The mass-processing food industry present in the entire world has not been able to reduce or eradicate the popular gastronomic traditions. On the contrary, in recent years there has been an expansion of myriad ethnic cuisines coming from all over the world. Widespread fast food restaurant chains, which present foods of dubious origin, have unintentionally promoted the growth of the demand for healthy products and the interest of many customers has moved to natural, local and traditional food.

Inside the European Union, and even between the former Eastern bloc countries, there are cultural differences affecting product and brand choice. A study, based on Hofstede's theory, about cross-cultural variations in a number of clothing-related consumer behaviour phenomena in the Czech Republic and Bulgaria highlighted significant differences regarding consumer interest in clothing, preference for utilitarian, self-expressive and hedonic meanings of clothing artefacts, preference for well-known clothing brands, brand loyalty, and importance of clothing attributes (Millan et al., 2013). In Bulgaria, messages emphasizing one's high position in the social hierarchy may have a greater impact, whereas achievement and success themes may be more productive in the Czech Republic. Regarding the ascertained cross-cultural differences, advertising appeals tapping into consumer desires for self-expression through consumption may work better in Bulgaria than in the Czech Republic. Additionally, functional brand images may be more effective in Bulgaria.

The Hofstede model can be used in analysing the consumer behaviour in different cultures (De Mooij and Hofstede, 2011). In large, *power distance* cultures, for example, one's social status must be clear so that others can show proper respect and brands serve that purpose.

In the purchase process in *individualistic* cultures, parties want to get to the point fast, whereas in collectivistic cultures it is necessary to first build a relationship and trust between seller and buyer. This difference is reflected in the different roles of advertising: persuasion versus creating trust. In *masculine* cultures, household work is less shared between husband and wife than in feminine cultures, while men do more household shopping in the *feminine* cultures. Members of high *uncertainty avoidance* cultures express in their behaviour a need for purity related to several product categories such as food. *Long-term* orientation implies investment in the future.

Consumers across cultures attribute different brand personalities to the same brand. A commercial cross-cultural brand value study (De Mooij and Hofstede, 2011) that compared personalities attributed to highly valued global brands across cultures showed that a brand characteristic as 'friendly' is most attributed to strong global brands in high uncertainty avoidance and low power distance cultures; 'prestigious' is a characteristic attributed to global brands in high power distance cultures, and 'trustworthy' is most attributed to strong brands in high uncertainty avoidance cultures. In cultures of the configuration low power distance and low uncertainty avoidance, people attributed 'innovative' and 'different' to these brands. So consumers project their own personality preferences onto global brands.

How people acquire, organize and utilize information is related to their cultures. People of collectivistic high-context cultures, used to symbols, signs and indirect communication, will process information in a different way than people of individualistic, low-context cultures, who are more verbally oriented and used to explanations, persuasive copy, and rhetoric. Whereas in individualistic cultures of low power distance, people will actively acquire information via the media and friends in order to buy, in collectivistic and/or high power distance cultures, people will acquire information more via implicit, interpersonal communication and base their buying decisions on feelings and trust in the company. Ownership of luxury goods like expensive watches and jewellery is related to masculinity, and this relationship is stable over time.

Singh (2006) carried out research in France and Germany aiming to analyse the different propensity to adopt innovations using Hofstede's cultural values. Only three out of five factors were confirmed as predictors of the cultural propensity to accept innovation easily. For example, despite France having a higher individualism score, which should lead to innovation adoption, Germany has a higher level of innovative behaviour. This means that cross-cultural analysis of consumer behaviour cannot be done simply by applying the generic rules of cross-cultural analysis models, but should be carefully verified culture by culture. Actually many others factors can interfere in the behaviour that maybe are not included in the models. The modes proposed by Hofstede, Schwartz, Hall etc. should be used as frameworks that should be combined in order to analyse a specific culture and not as semi-automatic predictor tools.

Two cultural tendencies – concern for face and belief in fate – that are characteristic of Asian (vs. Western) consumers, in having contrasting effects on consumer tolerance, mean that Asian (vs. Western) consumers are more dissatisfied with social failures but less dissatisfied with non-social failures. These contrasting effects of culture are sensitive to pertinent contextual factors such as the presence of other consumers or a fate-suggestive brand name (Chan et al., 2009). Asian consumers' higher tolerance is confined to non-social failures caused by brands or products.

The search for a universal instrument that can describe consumers' decision-making styles across cultures seems to be problematic. Therefore, when designing global marketing, branding, and advertising strategies, companies ignore cultural differences at their peril.

## 9.2    CULTURE AND BUYING PROCESS

In the different phases of a consumer's purchasing process, the influence of cultural factors is strongly present, in relation to the different components that characterize and influence each single phase (see Figure 9.2). In particular, cultural context directly affects some factors that influence the different phases of the process, determining the diversity between culture and culture.

In the initial phase of *need recognition*, there is in particular one component that is affected by cultural differences, the hierarchy of needs for the creation of requests. Regarding the hierarchy of needs (Maslow, 1943), cultural evidence influences this hierarchy by questioning that the hierarchy[1] is the same in every culture and that it is necessary to satisfy the needs that are defined as most urgent on the scale, that is, all those at the bottom, compared to those considered less urgent, towards the top. The judgement of urgency, in fact, also depends on the cultural context, while Maslow considers the hierarchy as a natural and universal condition of the individual. The different levels of economic development can change the hierarchical order of needs. Furthermore, some cultures advise against giving priority to the needs of the lower part of the scale in favour of those of the upper part. In collectivist societies, for example, social needs may take precedence over more individual ones.

Furthermore, similar needs can be satisfied very differently and there are countless examples of them in different cultures, such as in food, clothing, family and social relationships, and so on. Therefore, the *wants* that derive from the perception of needs take on characteristics dictated by different cultures, as happens for tea and coffee, bread and rice, beer and wine, and so on. For example, the area of obvious needs represents a field that varies greatly in different cultures and that has different positions in each cultural hierarchy of needs (Usunier and Lee, 2013).

In the *information search* phase, the sources of information can be very different, for example, according to whether it is a collectivist or an individualist culture. People belonging to an individualistic culture prefer information from official sources, such as companies or third parties, in writing or through various media. People of a collectivist culture, on the other hand, prefer personal and group sources, such as friends or relatives. They seek less formal and more personal opinions; they welcome what is called the 'wisdom of the crowd' (Keen, 2007), that is, the reliability of the collective opinion of a group of individuals rather than that of a single expert.

In *evaluation of alternatives*, the role played by the widespread values in a certain society is preponderant, be they of a social or cultural nature. The former is about the importance of relationships with others, while the latter is about shared identity with the community to which an individual thinks he/she belongs. If the product does not match these values, it is difficult to insert it into the purchase set. For example, in Italy the purchase of coffee considers both social aspects, as it is a product that is offered to guests, and aspects of identity, since it is a product of cultural identity. When evaluating a coffee shop in Italy, the perceived quality of the coffee and the tradition of the point of sale are taken into account. Entering a coffee shop in China is based instead on the extraneousness to the tradition of that place, that is, on its ability to create an experience of escape, to immerse yourself in a Western reality.

In the *purchase decision*, the choice criteria can vary greatly between alternative cultures. For example, selection criteria in high context cultures tend to favour symbolic aspects of the product or brand, while low context cultures tend to favour functional criteria. In collectivist cultures, the criteria of choice are linked to the relationship with others, while the individualistic ones tend to favour personal advantage. In situations of high power distance, the choice must be linked to the social role covered by a person; in cultures with a high uncertainty avoidance it is preferred to maintain choices made previously with respect to brands and products, avoiding products and brands that are not already known or tested. Purchasing roles also change. In cultures with a high index of femininity, purchasing roles are more shared and collaborative, while in cultures with a high index of masculinity, roles are more clearly divided according to a diversity of responsibilities, separating those who deal with purchases related to family and home, such as food, from those who deal with products of greater monetary or social value, such as cars. Perceived risks are also different in different cultures. The social risk, for example, it is very strong in collective cultures, while the performance risk is very strong in individualistic ones.

There can be many differences in the *purchase* phase depending on the retail alternatives available and purchasing habits. There may be preferences for small shops, where a strong personal relationship between seller and buyer is sought, or for large shops, where the assortment is greater, but the personal relationship and the level of service is much lower. In Japan, for example, small shops are very frequent, while in the United States they are quite rare. This is the result of a culturally very different sales relationship sought by customers, attributable to high context cultures (Japan) or low context cultures (USA). There are cultural habits that favour frequent purchases of small quantities, also due to the difficulties of storing products in generally small homes, such as those in China and Japan. Other habits favour less frequent but more consistent purchases, for example every two weeks, in large hypermarkets in family situations where products can be stored in larger homes, such as in the United States and Europe.

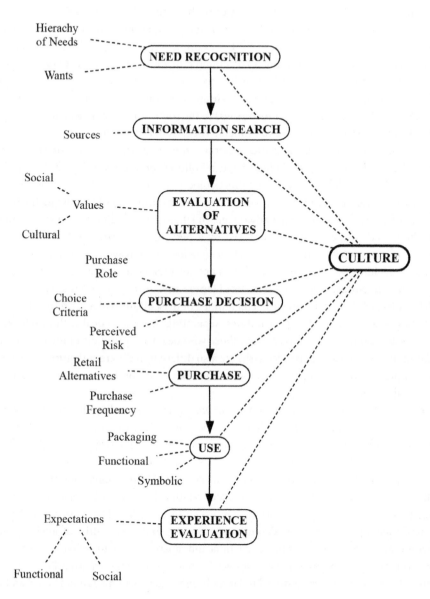

**Figure 9.2**      The consumer buying process and the culture influence

The ways to *use* the same type of product can be very different in different cultures. It may be necessary to adapt the package size to different conditions of use. For example, in China, where sweetness is not as appreciated as it is in the West, confectionery packages are smaller, as their use is more limited. Wafer biscuits are packaged in single doses, while in Europe they are in packs of 45, 125 and 400 grams. Packages of flavoured milk are reduced to single doses in bags to be used as a midday snack. The more functional use of products is typical of low context cultures, while the symbolic use is typical of high context cultures.

Finally, the *experience evaluation* of shopping is based on a hierarchy of values that can be very different between cultures. In collectivist societies and in those with a high power distance, such as China and Japan, and to a lesser extent in Mediterranean cultures, consumer satisfaction depends on the performance of the product with respect to social relations, linked to how much the product signals the social position of its owner or indicates its belonging to the group, its symbolic potential. In individualistic and low power distance societies, in contrast, as in the United States or in the Northern Europe, satisfaction depends more on the functional performance and the psychological relationship between consumer and product, that is, the relationship of coherence between the image of the product and the self-image of its owner.

In conclusion, at every stage of the buying process, cultural influence significantly affects consumer behaviour. Companies entering international markets must study this influence and its effects on behaviour to make the buying process as easy as possible for the consumer to pass through the various stages, achieving customer satisfaction.

## 9.3 OMNICHANNEL AND DIGITAL CONSUMER BEHAVIOUR: THE CUSTOMER JOURNEY

The explosive growth of innovative digital technologies over the past two decades has revolutionized the way customers browse for information, compare products and services, make purchases, and engage with firms and other customers. Customers today interact with firms and other customers through multiple online touchpoints in multiple channels and media (Nam and Kannan, 2020). The term 'customer journey' commonly refers to a process or sequence that a customer goes through to access or use an offering of a company. The concept places customers at its heart, making it a useful framework in assessing and evaluating customer experience within any product and service context. The analysis of customer journeys is useful in highlighting critical moments and touchpoints that are significant for the formation of the customer experience (Rawson et al., 2013). The recognition of the customer journey is a means to enhance and manage customer experience. Within a single economic market, customers tend to switch between different online and offline channels, resulting in omnichannel touchpoints playing a greater role. In addition, customers' use of technology-driven touchpoints (e.g., virtual agents such as Alexa and Siri) differs across global markets. Such differences have important implications for how firms approach each market, design their touchpoints, and acquire and retain customers. The journey has been described as a three-stage process (Lemon and Verhoef, 2016): pre-purchase, purchase, and post-purchase stages. Along the process all the touchpoints with the customer should be identified, using an omnichannel approach (Ieva and Ziliani, 2018), in order to communicate with him/her and improve the buying experience (see Figure 9.3).

In the *pre-purchase* stage, the customer perceives the need and its characteristics, being aware of it. Then the customer discovers brands/products that can be inserted in a set to be analysed, considering which ones are really available for reducing the discomfort caused by the need. The pre-purchase stage ends with the search for information about the alternatives included in the consideration step. In the *purchase* stage the customer chooses the brand/

product using the choice criteria considered suitable for the specific buying situation. The choice criteria are deeply influenced by culture, technology and social conditions. Then there is the order phase, which depends on how simple it is to order online or offline, followed by the payment solution, totally digital or partially physical (in the store). The purchase stage can include customer interactions with a platform during the purchase event. In the *post-purchase* stage the customer starts the usage experience, leading to the (non) customer satisfaction that engages the customer in a relationship with the brand. If the customer has been positively engaged by the buying experience, he/she can be the evangelist of the brand/product, using social media, word of mouth and every social communication he/she considers appropriate. Even the post-purchase stage comprises customer interactions with a platform after the purchase (Figure 9.3).

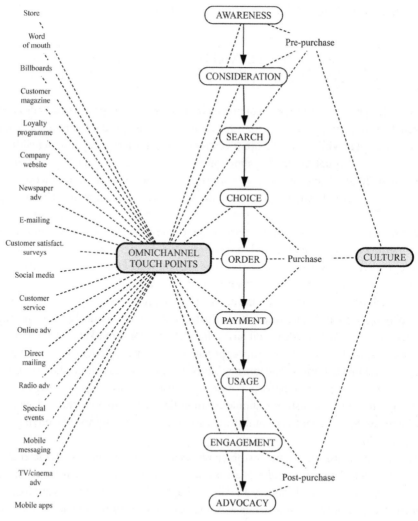

**Figure 9.3**     Customer journey, touchpoints and culture influence

As the options for touchpoints increase in the digital environment, consumers may be faced with choice overload, lack of confidence in their purchase, and dissatisfaction with their decision.

The company should analyse and use all touchpoints deemed useful to engage the customer during the journey. Customer touchpoint exposure and preference can be very different in different cultures. Lemon and Verhoef (2016) identify four main touchpoints (brand-owned, partner-owned, customer-owned, and social/external touchpoints) and acknowledge that the importance of different types of touchpoints may differ at each stage in the customer journey. Brand-owned touchpoints are those where customers' interactions are under the firm's control. Partner-owned touchpoints are those where customers' interactions are jointly managed by the firm and its partners. Customer-owned are customer actions that are part of the overall customer experience but that the firm, its partners, or others do not influence or control. Social touchpoints are those where customers' interactions are influenced by other customers.

To better understand the role of multiple touchpoints in the customer journey, firms try to determine each touchpoint's contribution to the purchase conversion. Researchers also note that touchpoints influence each other. For instance, customers' interactions with social touchpoints influence the use of other touchpoints and the effectiveness of other touchpoints on decisions in the customer journey.

There are some differences among countries in their customer journeys. For instance, Chinese customers' paths from awareness to purchase are distinctly different from the path of Western customers. According to a report published by the Boston Consulting Group (Biggs et al., 2017), one of the key differences between Chinese and Western customers' journeys is that Chinese customers interact with a myriad of touchpoints under the major online hubs (e.g., Taobao, Alibaba's marketplaces, Tmall), where news sites, games, videos, and ecommerce are all interconnected (see Figure 9.4), compared to Western consumers. They, on the other hand, interact with standalone touchpoints offered by different brands and platforms. Such differences may be due to sociocultural differences. In the West, customers shop online predominantly because it is more convenient and efficient than travelling to an offline store; therefore, e-commerce platforms in the West tend to be optimized for efficiency (e.g., Amazon's one-click purchase model). Western e-commerce platforms focus on helping customers shop quickly and easily, and they correspondingly invest more in building search functions, developing convenient payment processes, and improving delivery services. This is an individualistic and low context culture approach. In contrast, Chinese customers go online expecting to spend time discovering new products, browsing content, and interacting with friends, following a collectivistic and contextual approach. Consequently, e-commerce platforms in China are optimized for customer engagement by offering social communities, chat functions, various content, news, games and videos on top of e-commerce. Thus, e-commerce platforms in China are more likely to mix entertainment, community options, and social sharing in addition to listing product features and ratings, all personalized on the basis of customers' profiles (Nam and Kannan, 2020) (Figure 9.4).

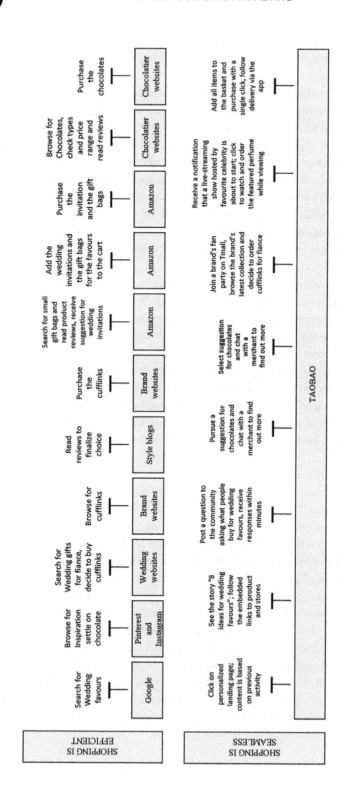

*Source:*   Biggs et al. (2017).

**Figure 9.4**   Chinese and Western online customer journey

Consequently, brands in the West tend to build a standalone site and interact with customers mainly through brand-owned touchpoints. In contrast, brands in China tend to set up a store on a centralized hub and focus more on engaging customers within the hub. Online and offline touchpoints are highly integrated throughout Chinese customers' journeys, as the platforms that Chinese customers use were designed to blur the lines between online and offline touchpoints (Biggs et al., 2017). As a result, Chinese consumers switch between online and offline touchpoints more frequently. Chinese companies focus on fostering richly detailed, qualitative feedback, whereas many Western companies focus on quantitative feedback such as star ratings.

There are also differences in how consumers see the importance of branding and social influence in their digital purchases. For example, Japanese customers are willing to pay more for premium brands but are reluctant to buy private label brands. Chinese shoppers view the brand and how the company views the brand more prominently than customers in the US and Europe. Likewise, the role of social influence in the customer journey is further amplified in Japan and China than in Europe. In China, Korea and Japan, influencer marketing through live streaming has become one of the most popular advertising strategies. Their influence on consumer brand and product choice is quite high, compared to the actual influence that web influencers have in Europe or the United States.

This is also the result of a combination of individualism/collectivism and the distance of power between different cultures. In collectivist cultures, the hedonic shopping experience is highly associated with other oriented role shopping (shopping for others), as opposed to the self-oriented gratification shopping (shopping as a special treat to oneself) that predominates in individualist cultures (Evanschitzky et al., 2014). In conclusion, the omnichannel customer journey, including online and offline touchpoints, as well as digital behaviour, are influenced by the cultural context in which the consumers are embedded.

## 9.4 CONSUMER RESPONSIBLE BEHAVIOUR IN CROSS-CULTURAL CONTEXTS

The state of current consumption that we are witnessing around the world is destructive and unsustainable; it compromises the ability of future generations to meet their basic needs (Varey, 2010). It also creates environmental problems such as reduced biodiversity, rising sea levels, extreme weather conditions, natural resource shortfalls, and soil degradation. Social features associated with products (e.g., environmental protection, support for human rights) are becoming important criteria in consumers' shopping strategies. Ethical consumerism, the practice of purchasing products or services that are produced in a way that reduces social and/ or environmental damage, has gained great attention in recent years.

The socially responsible consumer is one who takes into account the public consequences of his or her private consumption or who attempts to use his or her purchasing power to bring about social change. Roberts (1993) assumed that two elements operate in the definition of a socially responsible consumer: environmental concern and general social concern. He described this consumer as one who purchases products and services perceived to have a positive (or less negative) influence on the environment or who patronizes businesses that attempt to affect related positive social change (Han and Stoel, 2017). Sustainability consumption refers to patterns of acquiring, possessing, consuming and disposing of goods while keeping social, economic and environmental concerns in mind.

In order to analyse responsible consumer behaviour it is useful to consider the TPB (Theory of Planned Behaviour) model (Ajzen, 1991), which is one of the most influential social-psychological models for explaining human behaviour. According to TPB, the most powerful determinant of the actual behaviour is individuals' intentions to perform the behaviour. Behavioural intention is a function of the following three factors: attitude toward the behaviour, subjective norms, and perceived behavioural control. The TPB has been shown to represent a reliable (i.e. results exhibited both acceptable internal fit and external consistency with other findings) predictive model of intention to purchase sustainable products (Kalafatis et al., 1999). The theory of planned behaviour postulates three conceptually independent determinants of intention (see Figure 9.5). The first is the *attitude* toward the behaviour and refers to the degree to which a person has a favourable or unfavourable evaluation or appraisal of the behaviour in question. The second predictor is a social factor termed *subjective norm*; this refers to the perceived social pressure to perform or not to perform the behaviour. The third antecedent of intention is the degree of *perceived behavioural control*, which refers to the perceived ease or difficulty of performing the behaviour and it is assumed to reflect past experience as well as anticipated impediments and obstacles (Ajzen, 1991).

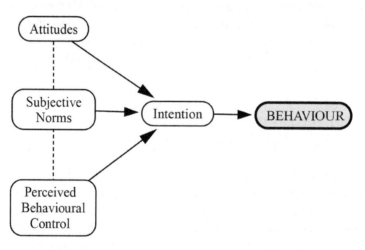

**Figure 9.5**    TPB model

The TPB intends to capture an individual's intention to perform a pre-established behaviour because the latter influences behaviour. All the three elements of attitude, subjective norm, and perceived behavioural control are influenced by behavioural, normative and control beliefs. The first entails attitude and links the behaviour to a certain positive or negative outcome. The second refers to the likelihood that the social group may accept that behaviour. The last entails the control of resources, which is sometimes influenced by second-hand information and friends (Ceglia et al., 2015).

It should be considered that an individual's cultural profile mediates both their behavioural intentions and their sustainable (or otherwise) consumption as well as disposal behaviours.

Sustainable consumption has different perceptions and leads to different behaviours in different cultures. Therefore, it needs to acknowledge profound differences between Western and non-Western consumers and contexts, for example. Differing economic, social, and particularly cultural contexts affect individual perceptions, motivations and behaviour (Nair and Little, 2016). Even in closely related national cultures such as the USA and Canada, differences in green consumption reflect differences in ethnic backgrounds and social norms (Ignatow, 2006). Clearly in countries where cultures are not closely related (e.g., Germany and Italy, China and India, Japan and Malaysia) the profound differences in ethnic origin, history and religion will influence green consumption. In multicultural countries with heterogeneous ethnic composition (e.g., Malaysia's three major ethnic groups – Malays, Chinese and Indian), this may result in within-country as well as between-country differences. In the West, sustainability was recently described as 'a transcendent societal mega-megatrend that realizes the implications of nearing load bearing and source availability limitations of our finite habitat in the man-made, socio-cultural evolution big bang in which we are living' (Varey, 2013). However, in non-Western contexts we observe that such realizations are some way off. The current 'big bang' is in hyper-consumption with no regard for tomorrow, supporting our call for research that increases understanding of non-Western consumers (Nair and Little, 2016).

For example, the significant difference in waste control between two countries, India and USA, can be explained by the long support in the traditional Indian moral economy. Subsistence may be one of the reasons, but the values have been oriented towards coexistence with nature and minimalist consumption practices. Jainism embodies such values at its best. Concepts like Mokshya, Nirvana and Maya are all such ideas that preach the futility of unnecessary consumption. On relatively more contemporary terms Gandhian political economy leverages on self-sufficiency and frugality as a basis for a self-reliant economy. However, the liberally global outlook has Indian consumers at a crossroads. While most Indians are culturally aware of such schemes of waste and spending control, the lure of consumption values seems to be overwhelming. Their Western counterparts are relinquishing material possession, after a sustained consumption spree. However, Indians have just started to value material possession. At this juncture, sustainability seems to be a negotiated value to Indian consumers (Nguyen et al., 2019). For example, due to their ability to deal with food shortages or religious constraints, Indian consumers could be more able to overcome some barriers to sustainable consumption than Swiss consumers, since the latter are surrounded by a longer history of favourable economic stability, in contrast to Indian consumers, for instance. Thus, cultural elements influence values and, in turn, sustainable behaviour.

Cross-cultural investigation on five countries (USA, Canada, Australia, Germany and Russia) confirmed that individualistic nations develop pro-environmental subjective norms and attitudes based on an ecocentric value orientation (Soyez, 2012). Otherwise, people in collectivistic nations develop pro-environmental subjective norms and attitudes based on an anthropocentric value orientation.

Also the social role that a culture assigns to the business varies by cultures, and it influences the responsible image of the companies/brands in the perception of customers. In research evaluating the extent to which consumers in France, Germany and the US are willing to support responsible organizations when shopping, interesting differences emerge (Maignan, 2001). Accordingly, French and German consumers may not view economic achievements as the primary social duty of businesses. Instead, these consumers may sense that businesses should use their economic resources to foster the well-being of society in general. Accordingly, corporate economic responsibilities may be viewed by French and German consumers as secondary to other corporate social responsibilities. French and German consumers allocated significantly less importance to corporate economic responsibilities than their US counterparts. Consequently, whereas US consumers perceive economic performance as a leading responsibility of businesses, French and German consumers view economic achievements as only secondary. This finding illustrates the communitarian dimension of the French and German national ideologies as depicted by Lodge (1990). In contrast, the individualistic nature of the US ideology comes out clearly in the study results since economic responsibilities – along with legal responsibilities – were rated as most important in the US. Altogether, the comparison of the differences in consumers' expectations of the firm in France, Germany, and the US points to the difficulty of implementing uniform communication programmes about social responsibility across borders.

Examining cultural differences in attitudes towards responsible tourist behaviours, Korean tourists had the highest total scale scores and were the most likely to agree that they would spend time before they travel studying or collecting information about the environment of the destination, the lifestyle of the local residents and environmentally friendly tours and places to stay. By way of contrast, the British gave the highest agreement ratings to the statements about following both social and nature conservation rules at a destination. The Australians overall gave the lowest levels of agreement on most statements, especially when compared with the Koreans. The Korean national cultural group had the highest levels of environmental concern (Kang and Moscardo, 2006). This is consistent with research into other Asian cultures, such as China (Chan, 1999) and Japan (Franzen, 2003). While this may seem to be at odds with actual levels of environmental degradation in the country, the issue might be one of knowledge and awareness, rather than concern. Collectivistic cultures that are high on the power distance, uncertainty avoidance and masculinity dimensions should be more concerned with following rules. It is possible that cultures have different sets and configurations of values in different contexts.

Considering MENA (Middle-East North-Africa) countries, evidence also suggests that in many occasions individuals believe that environmental preservation should be (mainly) the responsibility of a broad category, including not only other citizens, but also (and primarily) actors such as companies or public authorities (Yaghi and Alibeli, 2017). In this situation individuals might be unwilling to pay a premium price or to make a personal contribution to sustainable consumption behaviour, knowing that someone else will do it. Most of the MENA countries score high on power distance, which could explain the observed tendency to ascribe responsibility of global problems to governments (Elhoushy and Lanzini, 2020).

Culture and religion appear to share a similar concept, but the two value systems differ in locus. Culture generally comes from a geographic location, whereas religion transcends geographic bounds. Additionally, religious values are rooted in religious scripture that provides consistent insight into beliefs, whereas culture often represents a milieu of transitory beliefs that even incorporate religious beliefs. Relating to sustainable consumption, religious scripture discusses views toward sustainability and sustainability-related values, thereby suggesting that core religious beliefs may influence sustainable purchase and non-purchase behaviours. With differences among specific religious affiliations, James (2004) notes that Western religions (Christianity, Judaism, Islam) believe that God created nature and therefore God and humans hold a superior position to nature. Eastern religions (Buddhism, Hinduism, Taoism), on the other hand, follow a pantheistic view that God is in and through everything, including nature. Western religions follow the thesis that God created nature, God gave control of nature to humans, and therefore Western religions should be less apt to be environmentally friendly and more willing to alter the environment. Buddhists follow the pantheistic view that God exists in and through all elements of nature (Sarre, 1995). In other words, a highly religious Buddhist might believe that buying an environmentally friendly detergent or an organically grown apple shows respect for God because purchasing such items respects the nature in which God resides. There is a difference in attitude towards sustainability according to the level of religiosity. Less religious and atheist people show less interest in sustainability (Minton et al., 2015).

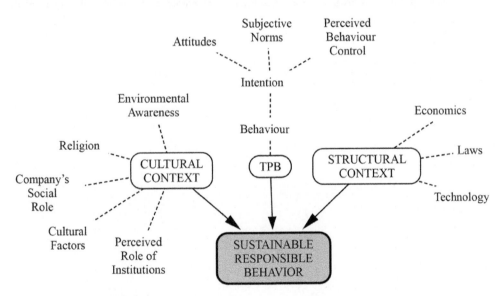

**Figure 9.6** Conceptual model of cross-cultural sustainable and responsible consumer behaviour

In conclusion, there are three main forces that influence sustainable and responsible consumer behaviour in an international context: (1) the specific cultural context; (2) planned behaviour; and (3) the structural local context (Figure 9.6). The *cultural context* depends on people's awareness of sustainable issues in a country, which becomes a cultural feature of a society.

Religion also plays an important role in its value and in its idea of the relationship between divinity, human beings and nature. As mentioned with regard to the United States and Europe, there are different cultural perceptions of the role that business and companies should play in society if they are to prioritize their economic or social goals. This is related to the judgement on the role of state institutions as a system of government in promoting a sustainable society. Finally, the classical cultural factors of Hofstede, Hall and Schwartz models such as collectivism, power distance, low context and so on influence consumer behaviour towards responsible purchasing behaviour. *Planned behaviour* is important in explaining the success or failure of rational consumer behaviour, as is sustainable behaviour. The *structural local context* concerns the economic situation, the wealth of a nation and the money available for the people to pay a premium price in order to adopt sustainable behaviour. The legal system can also favour the desired attitude of consumers, especially if environmental awareness is not widespread. Technology concerns the tools available to a society to pursue environmental sustainability behaviour, in recycling, in waste reduction, and so on.

## NOTE

1.  According to Maslow, each individual should satisfy a lower level before trying to satisfy a higher one, bottom-up: from physiological needs, fundamentally, to security needs, social needs, esteem needs, self-actualization needs.

# 10
# Cross-cultural branding

## 10.1    BRAND NAMES IN DIFFERENT LANGUAGES AND CULTURES

In the new culturally distant markets, some general conditions can be identified that concern in particular the building of the reputation of the brands of both MNEs and MMNEs, which suffer from limited recognition and reputation:

● the need to adapt products to the specific conditions of the local market in relation to functional (sizes and dimensions) and symbolic (colours and shapes) aspects;
● the need to explain the use and role of the product in daily life and in the values of the consumer's identity, linking them to the context of the local society (for example, in food products, the specific health purposes and properties and not simply the taste); the widespread and consolidated knowledge normally present in European markets may not exist and therefore cannot be taken for granted;
● the need to illustrate and make the consumer aware of the value components both in general terms of the product category and in those specific to the individual product.

In general, it is the construction of a product culture which, despite having a greater and faster ease of understanding among the higher income classes and more exposed to an international context, finds it increasingly difficult to move towards the middle classes and towards the mass market. It can be considered that there is an inevitable need, on the one hand, to adapt and increase the localization of the offer, and on the other hand, to form a purchasing culture closer to the models present on Western markets, since international offers of European companies rely on behavioural references and selection criteria culturally different from those of the target markets. In brand strategies this takes on completely original characteristics, which focus on four aspects that can be outlined as follows:

● valuable components of a brand for the local consumer;
● translation of the trademark according to the local language and culture;
● need for brand experience, reassurance and visualization;
● importance of brand leadership in a defined cultural context.

As Schulz (2002) suggests, the recent introduction of brands in China, for example, went through three main stages. The first phase concerns the concept of *globalization* proposed by Levitt (1983), according to which the organization that faces the market chooses to expand

and strengthen the global concept of brand and product in a similar way to what happens in markets where it is present for a long time. This is the strategy followed by large global companies in local markets, especially in large cities, where the cultural and structural distance is smaller than that in Europe, albeit significant. However, the market soon becomes saturated or overcrowded with competitors. This approach soon ends up showing its limitations.

The second phase is that of *think global, act local* (glocalization); this means using concepts and skills of production, logistics and process, developed in the markets of origin and applying them in the new market considering the available conditions, with respect to the market constraints present in communication (media availability), in distribution alternatives, and in merchandising (Swoboda and Elsner, 2013). The third phase concerns the concept of *think local, act local*, which involves the development of brand, marketing and communication policies specifically designed for the local market, maintaining the advantages deriving from knowledge, methods, techniques and managerial approaches developed in the markets of origin.

Subsequently, some companies have embarked on what can be called a fourth phase, which has no examples in previous international marketing strategies and policies, and which concerns *post-glocalization*. This is an international market strategy intending to build a brand personality that is born in the market cultural context of a specific country, keeping some global characteristics, and which ends up giving life to a new brand identity, with both global (ability to be accepted globally) and local (identity of country of origin) characteristics, which is then extended to other countries.

The reasons for the strength of a brand in culturally distant markets seem to be based on three fundamental elements that are not so far from those of European markets even if they take on different strength and characteristics. These three elements concern the brand according to: (a) the values that define it; (b) its history and a past of renown; (c) the rich cultural references to which it is connected.

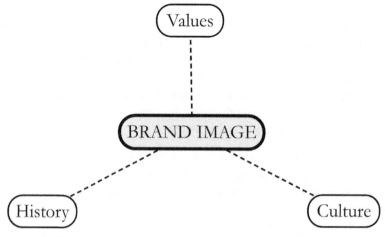

**Figure 10.1**    Key strengths of the brand in new markets

European companies can enjoy some significant advantages in building their brand image by relying on typical aspects of their market tradition. The risk that MMNEs often run is to take for granted the consumers' knowledge and perceptions, typically diffused in the markets of origin, but which do not find correspondence in the new international markets. Instead, it is necessary to offer a clear narrative path for the history of the brand and its consolidated values; solid cultural references are needed, which must belong to the origin of the brand, but should, at the same time, be understandable and consistent with those of the consumers in the culturally distant market.

A defined and clear key of values should be proposed, which captures a positioning space that is understandable for the target consumer, and which can be identified by them as important in defining the criteria and alternatives of choice. The new customer is interested in knowing the historical path of the brand, having no previous experience with it. Therefore, the history of the brand represents a proof of value given by its persistence over time; it proposes the tradition as essential value, assigning to its history the role of building a reputation that cannot already have been realized on the destination market, given its recent introduction. Many medium-sized European companies own brands with unique and extraordinary elements of history and cultural references. They should be able to make them known and to combine them with positive values for the local consumer. The study of the socio-cultural context is therefore an essential premise for the development of any marketing strategy in new and culturally different markets (Gao et al., 2006).

A completely new and critically important aspect is the need to translate the brand name. Until now, the problems of translating trademarks in an international market were related only to the meanings and phonetic similarities that were assumed in the country of arrival and which could bring unwanted identities to the trademarks, giving rise to almost grotesque cases and episodes. With the opening of the Chinese market, for example, the situation has changed significantly, because of greater specificities and of cultural and literal complexities (Zang and Schmitt, 2001; Hong et al., 2002). Developing a global brand can be the right solution according to an abstract marketing strategy, but it does not take into account the existing cultural differences. It maintains a pseudo-colonial approach, which cannot be applied in all markets, especially in those that do not accept or share elements of Western homogeneity.

Keller (2008) defines brand equity as composed of *awareness* and *image*. Awareness comes from *recognition*, correct identification and *recall*, and ease of remembering in the purchase conditions. The image is defined by the consumers' perceptions of the associations that the brand brings to their memory. Consistency with the cultural references of the country in which the brand is to be spread is understandably an important point in any context, but it assumes strategic importance in some countries such as China, Japan and Korea. A brand is made up of many identifying elements: the name, the logo, the signs, the colours, the graphic images, and the lettering, where the name remains the central element. Factors that influence the choice of the name are the indication of the benefits of the product or the characteristics of the company, the promised quality and the desired positioning, the links with the logo and with the packaging, the country-of-origin effect, the traditional values of the target market, the sense of patriotism, the beliefs and habits spread among the target consumers.

The alphabets of the various languages can be very different from the Latin one used in Europe, such as in China, Japan, Korea, Vietnam, India, Thailand and so on. And therefore, the characters, pronunciation and meanings of a European brand are not always understandable and clear. Familiarity with the Latin alphabet varies from culture to culture. The characters of Chinese writing have, for example, associated meanings in addition to specific sounds, and these can significantly influence the perception of the brand. Even if a name can be translated into Chinese characters, it does not mean that it still has an understandable meaning for a Chinese consumer, as the resulting sound or set of meanings may be meaningless. For example, the choice to translate Maxwell House coffee into *my family's brand* was not successful as coffee is not part of Chinese culture and therefore a meaning linked to tradition and family is not understandable or acceptable; a name without direct meaning and a sound reminiscent of a Western brand would make the product more credible. Later the name was replaced by *relative to wheat* (Maisiwei'er – 麦斯威尔), which helps an uneducated consumer to understand the product.

There are different approaches to the translation of a product name. Fan (2002) indicates three: (1) direct translation, a sound equivalent to the original without any specific meaning; (2) free translation, where the foreign name is translated with a correct meaning without retaining the original pronunciation; (3) mixed translation, in which a sound similar to the original is maintained, but a coherent meaning is added. When choosing a name, in some countries there is usually more emphasis on the meaning than the sound, although it is always good to be able to associate a sound similar to the original with a coherent meaning. The main references regarding the translation of the brand can be associated with the indication of the benefits of the product, the desired positioning of the brand and the cultural values that the brand embodies. Each Chinese character, for example, is associated with a syllabic sound and its meaning, while the characters of the European alphabet have no meaning in themselves and it is only their composition that carries a specific sound and meaning.

Names that have no direct meaning are foreign to Chinese culture, while they are not present in Western culture (e.g. acronyms, initials, surnames, etc.). An illustrative example can be Coca-Cola, whose Chinese translation is pronounced Ke-Kou-Ke-Le (可口可乐) and means *is good and makes you happy*; the solution links the brand to the characteristics of the product and to the results that can be obtained from its use: meanings are more important than sounds, even if in these cases their combination is obviously the best solution. In some situations, however, it is necessary to follow an opposite logic because it is more suitable for the product. For example, the Chinese translation of Nike makes no sense but sounds foreign and appeals to those who are sensitive to the Western lifestyle, while Reebok is translated as *bold step* (锐步), but it has no international flavour. It is therefore necessary to adopt a translation by carefully evaluating the target segment and its expectations.

From the research conducted on this topic (Vescovi, 2011), a reference model emerges for the definition of the brand. The model is represented in Figure 10.2 and includes five fundamental alternatives: (1) the similarity of sound; (2) the construction of meaning; (3) the search for cultural synchrony; (4) the integrated solutions between the different components; and (5) the maintenance of the original brand without any modification. Choosing to look for a brand that creates sonic similarities with the original brand maintains phonetic consistency and global recognition, but it is necessary to verify that the characters producing the sound have no negative or unintended meanings.

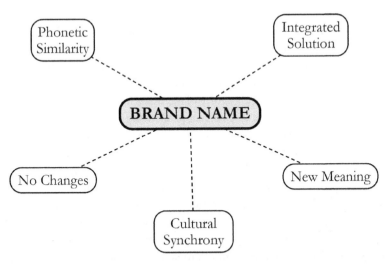

**Figure 10.2** Composition of the brand name in China

An international brand must therefore decide which image (Western or local) it wants to pursue, referring to the existence of an acquainted or not-acquainted market. A Western name benefits from the country-of-origin effect and is more consistent with the original, whereas a local name may have greater appeal because consumers find it more understandable and therefore easier to identify with. The creation of meaning therefore concerns a choice in which the original pronunciation of the brand is not maintained but is abandoned in favour of the construction of a message that is indicative of the positioning sought. At this point there is a complete makeover of the brand name, while the logo, colours and other graphics remain common. This is the case, for example, of Heineken beer, which in China has translated its name into *Xi-Li* (喜力), which means *happy strength*. As you can understand, every connection between the original name and the local choice is completely unrelated, letting the visual elements of the brand maintain the coherence of the image. The search for cultural synchrony concerns the identification of a name that has a positive value in the local culture and allows a reference to shared social identities.

Therefore, it is possible to create a brand name that can be partly distant as a sound and as a desired positioning to the original name, but which contains characters that are easily acceptable to the consumer, because they belong to his/her reference of traditional values. An interesting case is that represented by the Red Bull energy drink, which has been translated with the characters 红牛, pronounced *Hong-Niu*, which means *red cow*, since the cow represents a positive symbol in the Chinese horoscope that refers to work, robustness, meekness and opulence, while the bull is perceived much less positively and does not have the cultural value in China that it does in the West, where it is a symbol of strength and impetuosity. Integrated choice seeks to combine the three previous aspects. It is evident that this is the preferable choice in theory, but it is not always practicable since it may not be certain that the three previous requirements can coincide in a single name; moreover sometimes this choice makes the brand lose its Western connotations that in some cases may be necessary for the perception of its value.

Managers of international companies seem to be aware that brand translation is more important in some markets than in others. If the brand is translated, it is important to keep the original character of the logo in order to be perceived as an international brand.

An interesting case is that of Ikea, who translated their name into *Yi-Jia* (宜家), which means *appropriate home (family)*. This choice of name has a similar sound to the original name in the diphthong, creating a meaning of correct positioning, because it is perfectly in line with the brand's mission, which is an appropriate reference to Chinese culture in which home and family represent key values. Pal Zileri, a men's clothing brand, for example, has decided to rely on a phonetic-cultural translation. That is, it has chosen to use a name in Chinese characters that is as close as possible to the Italian pronunciation, but that uses the sounds present in Chinese phonemes and which, at the same time, conveys a positive meaning, the translation of which in this case is *flying dove*. Traditional Chinese culture, in fact, combines the presence of good and bad spirits with everyday human practices. The choice to acquire a meaningful translation with positive propitiatory connotations, such as that of a dove in flight, is therefore aimed at greater integration with the local culture to support marketing choices. The logo present inside and outside the stores is the same as the one used in Italy. Combining the two names, the Italian one and the Chinese one, helps the Chinese consumer to recognize the logo and memorize it.

In many Eastern markets it is also important to consider the good luck meaning of a brand. Chang and Lii (2008) underline the importance of the numbers considered lucky inserted in the brands, especially in uncertain markets. In China and in Japan, for example, the number 4 is connected to bad luck and death, while the number 8 means good luck and prosperity (see Table 13.6 in Chapter 13) as for example has been used by the Korean fashion brand *8seconds*.

Finally, another alternative pursued by Western companies is that of not adapting anything to the local market, keeping the original brand and spelling, insisting on the idea of globalization and of an international and Western product. This is for example the case with many luxury and high-end goods. This choice, while pursuing clearly definable advantages linked to the brand's global strategies, must also consider that the Latin characters of the name must in any case be translated into local language, both to allow it to be pronounced and to be written down when it is necessary to quote the brand name in the media. By keeping the original name unaltered, we end up entrusting the brand name to impromptu and uncoded translations, from time to time different, by editors who have little or no knowledge of the brand's values and strategies. This is bad in itself, but can become worse if the popular translation does not match the desired image placement.

The need for experience, reassurance and brand visualization are factors that take on considerable importance in the context of the international market precisely because of the relative training and inexperience that can characterize it. It is necessary to reassure the consumer through multiple brand reputation tests, which cross numerous perceptual aspects. First of all, in the graphic components of the brand and packaging, it is necessary to evaluate the cultural perception of colour, which differs markedly between Eastern and Western cultures (Aslam, 2006). This is also true in all physical representations of the brand, as happens in single-brand stores, which are so important in the strategies of communication, representation, reassurance and experience.

## 10.2   BRAND POSITIONING STRATEGY IN DIFFERENT CULTURES

More recently, in international markets there are three combined conditions that lead to a completely new situation with respect to brand diffusion and positioning:

- the presence of a cultural context (symbols, myths, rituals, values, etc.) very different from those commonly found in traditional markets;
- the existence of a system of writing, signs and meanings that are not always close to those of Europe;
- a rapid opening of the markets, and a consequent overload of information on brands and products, towards a population not used to the functioning of a modern consumer market.

Then there are other factors that influence brand choices and that concern the concept of quality, cultural similarity and global accessibility. The concept of quality in different countries is linked to the history of products and consumption, often centred on the reliability and durability of the product, typical benefits sought in a market of scarcity (durability) and low service (reliability). Cultural compatibility concerns the recognition of identity by the consumer in brands and products with characteristics and meanings that are understandable and acceptable in the specific cultural context of each destination country, in which shared values and symbols must be found.

Cultural compatibility is particularly important in a situation of significant difference with respect to the customs of European countries; this is becoming increasingly necessary as we move towards the sectors of consumer products and goods considered as commodities. Global accessibility is given by the demand for foreign brands and products available in a global context and not just adapted and available only for the local market. In some product categories, the consumer of a country does not want to be considered different from the consumer of the reference countries for the product category (fashion in France and Italy, cars in Germany, etc.), while demanding consistency with their own culture references hardly accepts European products that are not the same as those that can be found in Europe.

A brand is made up of many identifying elements: the name, the logo, the signs, the associated music, the colours, and so on. In the brand the name remains the central element. Other factors that influence the choice of the name are the indication of the advantages of the product or the characteristics of the company, the promised quality and the desired positioning of the brand, the links with the logo and with the packaging, the country of origin, the traditional values of the reference market, the sense of patriotism, and the beliefs and habits widespread among the target consumers. The literature highlights how difficulty in pronunciation can affect sales results as this hinders word of mouth. Rather than risking embarrassment when trying to pronounce the name, consumers may decide not to mention the brand at all.

The main factors influencing the creation of the brand can be associated with the indication of the benefits of the product, the positioning of the desired brand and the cultural values that the brand embodies. In addition to the previous principles of brand identity, there are other marketing factors that obviously have to be considered, such as the target, the product category, the effect of the country of origin, or the perception of good luck.

Regarding the product category, it is important to note that the type of industry can have an impact on the strategy used to adapt the name. Services and high-tech use direct transliteration, while research shows (Chow et al., 2007) how in hedonistic and high-end products, name variation can reduce purchase intent, damaging the symbolic image and the perception of European quality, while for a functional product it can also increase it.

As is known, the country of origin can influence customer evaluation as people link a stereotypical perception of the country of origin to the product. In many markets, brands referring to a country having a high reputation in the product category represent status, cosmopolitanism and modernity (Zhou and Belk, 2004), and it is therefore good to maintain this perception. An international brand must also decide which image (European or local) it wants to pursue. If a European name benefits from the country-of-origin effect and is more consistent with the original name, a local name may have more appeal because consumers find it easier to identify with it.

The brand manager must decide the main value on which to build the meaning of the brand with respect to the desired strategic positioning. In some cases, the trademark can be strongly related to the country of origin and it may be necessary to make this evident within the brand name. In other cases, the name may need to be more global, with no direct link to the country of origin or even connected to the local culture.

Another aspect concerns the importance of brand leadership. In many new markets there is a strong competitive position assigned by the consumer in a preliminary phase in the evaluation of the choice of the brand, which, for leading brands, is much more pronounced than in Europe. This is what we could define as the 'number one syndrome', and which concerns the need to refer to a simplified selection criterion among countless alternatives, not so easily distinguishable and partly unknown. These alternatives arrive on the market very quickly, so the consumer is unable to build a sophisticated capacity for choice, as exists, however, in the markets of consumer-based societies.

This attitude tends to strengthen already strong brands at the expense of new entrants, keeping offer innovation low. This favours large global companies and reduces the appeal for niche brands that are instead a widespread heritage of quality European manufacturing. For these brands it is therefore a question of finding, and bringing out, even partial or niche leadership positions and thus increasing their reputation in order to be perceived as leading brands.

The search for a certain leadership reputation is therefore fundamental, as is objective recognition to be presented to the market, and quality awards and references from highly reputable customers. This is a consequence of the paradox that European companies often face, the visibility of small companies in large markets.

A global brand with a local image represents a challenge that must be balanced and that can increase the brand equity.

## 10.3   COUNTRY OF ORIGIN EFFECT

A major marketing and branding challenge concerns the product/brand origin. This refers to the mental link that a purchaser creates in response to the sight of the label of a country and its products. This associative link is known as the *Country Of Origin* effect (COO) and it depends on both the country and the product that is designed, produced and/or assembled in it (Aiello et al., 2009). Therefore, it can refer to the country of assembly (COA), the country of design (COD), the country of a brand (COB), and the country of manufacturing (COM), known as 'Made-in' and being the precise identifier of the country of origin. In other words, it manifests itself when a customer assessing the level of quality associated with a specific country is more likely to have an accepting attitude toward the purchase of that country's products.

On this matter Haubl and Elrod (1999) noted that the qualitative perception of a product becomes more positive when the harmony between the brand and the country of production/manufacturing is recognized. They distinguished between uni-national products and bi-national products. The first category refers to those goods produced in the brand's home country, whereas the second category includes all products characterized by a country of production different from the brand's home country. Consumers' judgements about the quality of the product are more favourable when there is congruity between the brand name and COO. This condition is more difficult to attain in a global economy context, where the production of components and parts of a product are spread around the world for economic and technologic reasons. The brand–COO congruity is particularly apparent when two extreme scenarios are present: when a production is shifted to a country with a COM image that is worse than the domestic one and when it is moved to a country where the COM is judged to be a better country of production.

Therefore, the brand image is influenced by four main drivers as the national image of generic products, the national image of manufacturer, the country evoked by brand name and the country image diffused by the 'Made in' label. For instance, a French producer of perfumes should adopt a French name since its domestic country is associated with that specific goods category. According to Koubaa (2008), COO information greatly affects brand image perception. A favourable well-known COO has a positive influence on brand image perception, whereas an unknown COO impacts negatively on brand image perception. Consequently, consumers have different perceptions of the country in which goods are manufactured, which is evolving over the years. Hence, these perceptions are dynamic: the same country could be evaluated in a different way around the world, and its evaluation would be likely to change over time as a result of a country's improving or worsening status, for example. The country image is created and modified in consumers' minds on the basis of individual knowledge, experiences, exposure, and preferences towards a particular country. Obviously, a COO can be positive or negative. Sometimes the consumer does not want to buy products or brands coming from certain countries that he/she considers unreliable for different technological, manufacturing, social or political reasons.

A correct perception of the value of the country of origin is a fundamental support to the enhancement and affirmation of the brands of the MMNEs, which do not enjoy the global reputation of those of the MNEs and do not have sufficient resources to promote them (Elliott and Cameron, 1994; Koschate-Fischer et al., 2012).

The positive image of the country on product categories is certainly a facilitator of acceptance and represents a guarantee for the customer, reducing risks and worries in purchasing (Papadopoulos and Heslop, 1993). However, the new markets may not have a clear perception of a country's image, which is built over time through experiences of social consumption and credible information on the quality of the product categories, which are linked to socially widespread know-how in the country of origin (Baker and Ballington, 2002). The habit of European MMNEs is to refer, in some key sectors, to the renown of the so-called Made in Italy, Made in France, Made in Germany etc. labels. This is particularly true for some B2C macro-sectors (fashion, food, furniture, cars, cosmetics, etc.) and for the B2B macro-sectors (automation, machinery, components). Such a reputation is strong enough in *acquainted markets*, but can be very weak, if not absent, in *non-acquainted* ones, so referring to that reputation and relying on it does not lead to the desired result.

Building a country's image is a process that must be conducted in a coherent and collective way by companies and institutions. It should be noted that the image of the country varies from market to market. In a non-acquainted market, for example, the perception of the COO image of a foreign country cannot be the same as that in markets familiar with the products of that foreign country. This happens not in terms of distortion towards completely unexpected or unwanted meanings, an event that can happen, but is mainly due to the lack of knowledge of country-specific characteristics, or to their perception in a confused and superficial way. For example, some research (Checchinato et al., 2013) reveals a completely partial and confused perception of the image of Italian and French products in China. In fact, Chinese consumers understandably tend to build a simplified image, where the specificity of a country is absorbed by the homogeneous area of origin. In particular, it is difficult for them to distinguish between Italy, France, Spain, Portugal, Greece and other European countries, so they prefer to associate them with a 'Western' image at the beginning and 'European' afterwards.

Furthermore, the correlation between product and country is based on their recent market experience, so the first comer or market leader builds the image of the country. In China, the United States is therefore the country of coffee (Starbucks) and pizza (Pizza Hut), Sweden the country of furniture (Ikea), while Italy is the country of chocolate (Ferrero). MMNEs are particularly interested in the image of the country, as they have to rely on an image platform that supports their little-known brands, whereas leading companies are less interested in the COO effect, because they follow globalization strategies. Their brands, conversely, help build the country's image. In a non-acquainted market, strong brands are favoured over weak ones to a greater extent than in acquainted markets. This is what we have defined as the number one syndrome, which responds to the need to build a simplified choice criterion among countless alternative brands not so easily distinguishable by the consumer who has an unsophisticated ability to choose.

Identifying the leading brand as a reassuring purchase option has long been acknowledged to be important, but the diffusion of the brand in some markets is paramount, coupled with the reinforcing effect created in some countries by a collective culture, where the most diffused brand acquires the value of social belonging.

Kleppe et al. (2002) observe that to collect the image effects relative to the country of origin there must be a coherent correspondence between the cultural identity of origin, the political, social, economic and technological identity and the proposed product. In the case of Made in Italy or Made in France products, for example, it is useful to make the Italian and French identity and lifestyle known and appreciated as a factor in the positioning and reputation of the products. This action obviously involves cooperative behaviour between the companies of a country, which is not easily obtainable due to structural factors (limited size of the companies and lack of agreements and alliances) and cultural factors (strong individualism of entrepreneurs). Anyway, the company has a difficult social responsibility: to contribute to the education of the market. The new internationalization in non-acquainted markets requires strategic alliances and collaboration skills, without which success is very difficult.

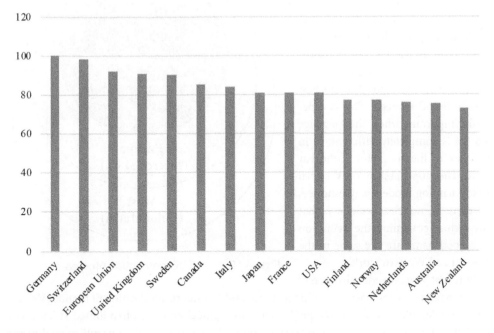

*Source*: Statista (2017).

**Figure 10.3**    Made-in country index

In many markets, brands from a specific country of origin with a high reputation for a particular product category represent status, cosmopolitanism and modernity (Zhou and Belk, 2004), and it is therefore positive to maintain their perception in the target market. This effect is even greater in emerging economies due to the positive symbolic meanings, such as modernity and high social status, that are associated with foreign brands. However, the country of origin is not always clearly perceived or distinct. While in Western markets French, Italian, German and Swiss products have a clear image, in the new markets there is a 'European' homogenizing factor which often reduces the particularities and distinctive elements of each single country. Sometimes brands from Europe are considered to be in a homogeneous category, without country differences. Even the European Union brand has a specific perception, which is valued very highly by consumers (Figure 10.3). The formation of stereotypes on the brand and product image can therefore concern a geographical area and not just a nation. In this sense, the effect concerns Western and European products and also Eastern products (Japan, Korea, etc.) compared with local ones.

In an increasingly specific approximation process, in new markets, in culturally distant markets, in poorly acquainted or partially acquainted markets, perception begins with the identification of a macro-cultural area of origin of the products (e.g. a macro-region such as Europe), then a country (France) and finally also a specific region or city (Paris), as shown in Figure 10.4.

If a European name benefits from the country-of-origin effect and is more consistent with the original image, a local name may have more appeal because consumers find it easier to identify with it. There is therefore no absolute best way to brand strategy. This is especially important when the language system is completely different, as in the case of the countries of the Far East. The applicability of Western brand naming models is questioned, as there is no clear evidence that the factors governing the definition of a good name are the same in the Eastern and Western world.

In recent years the globalization of

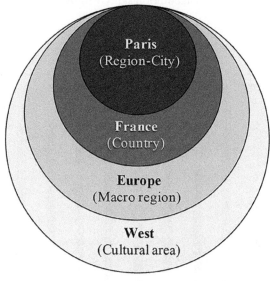

**Figure 10.4**     COO perception process

brands has been reconsidered, leading to a geographical micro-localization of brands (Vescovi and Gazzola, 2007), which adds quality value in a global context, often aimed at 'cultured' market niches, where the local, historical or cultural reference recalls concepts of quality and excellence, as often happens in Europe. Basically, in an educated market and where consumer knowledge of products is high, an attempt is made to reduce the anomie of the global brand, increasing differentiating attributes through local brand policies. This is more frequent as we move from mass consumer products to high-end products, where brand attributes and values become more sophisticated and refined.

Concerning COO, companies must also face another problem: the consumer often confuses the origins of the brand due to the communication strategies of local companies that adopt names and images with foreign characteristics and confuse the correct perception of consumers: this is *country sound branding* (Vescovi, 2013).

## 10.4    COUNTRY SOUND BRANDING

An aspect that links local market operators, with a COO of little value, to the exploitation of the position reached by other countries concerns the so-called *Country Sound Branding*. This is the creation of brands that, in the name of the brand, in their pronunciation, and in the look of the name, sound as if they are from specific countries that have a high reputation as a COO in that particular product category, but do not actually belong to these countries. It has already been said that in new markets, consumers are not fully educated with respect to the global market, and therefore they are unable to build realistic coherent images of the country. Even consumers from countries where products with a specific country image have traditionally been present for a long time are often unable to identify the COO correctly, therefore we can understand how difficult it can be for others.

There are often also no positive stereotypes to rely on (Ahmed et al., 2002). In newly formed markets, the knowledge of the countries of origin of the products is therefore often confused and uncertain, as it belongs only to a first familiarity and to a concept of general quality. For example, on the Chinese market, knowledge of Spain, Belgium, Denmark, Portugal and Finland is very limited, due to the cultural distance, the dimensional imbalance, due to a minority role played internationally by those countries, and due to the closure suffered for many decades of the Chinese market. It remains very difficult for a consumer to identify the qualitative specificities of the production of the various European nations, the excellence of 'Made in'.

Furthermore, it is almost impossible for a consumer from culturally distant countries to distinguish an Italian sounding brand from a French, Spanish, German or British one. Indeed, the cultural distance is such that the sounds and characters of the brands appear to the consumer's ears and eyes as 'Western' and not specifically belonging to any nation in the European galaxy. Some research (Checchinato et al., 2013) shows how a funnel-shaped perception exists, in which an origin of the global area (West) is first perceived, which is subsequently refined over time through a learning process to the sub-area (Europe) and that only after a process of repeated experience, study and understanding can it identify specific areas of the country (Italy). One can imagine how impossible it is to identify the regions of origin (Tuscany, Veneto, etc.).

In other words, in a new market the perception of the Country Of Origin (COO) is built through a learning process that requires time and coherent communication policies; it is by no means a starting point on which to base the reputation of a company that intends to extend its presence in a foreign market. The process of building a coherent and global image of the country of origin (COOI) is therefore not at all simple and perhaps not entirely possible, since the cultural and historical conditions of the destination countries in which it is perceived affect it, creating perceptual differences. In new markets, this image is more related to a supranational area with characteristics of homogeneity (e.g. Europe), which reduces the difficulty of perception and avoids the confusion between images that are not clearly defined in their diversity. Furthermore, in large markets such as China, the distinction between countries that are culturally and geographically very close to each other, as well as considerably smaller, such as Italy, France, Spain, and Portugal, can be very difficult. Consequently, we are only at the beginning of a learning process that can take many paths, but that does not always seem to be faced in a coherent way and with due perseverance by the European companies.

In distant markets, only partially educated on brands and products, sound branding actually strikes the consumer as an identifier of a macro-area of origin rather than a country of origin; a brand that sounds 'Scandinavian' to a European consumer actually sounds 'Western' to a consumer in those markets. The big European brands play an individual game in this context, understandably focusing more on strengthening their reputation than on promoting a concept of the country's image: they are brand nations much more than their countries of origin and find no advantage in promoting COOI not to favour minor competitors. They have inherent strength and don't always want to be associated with just one country; they are citizens of the world and they want to belong to their customers everywhere. They use the COO concept only when it can be consistent with their communication strategies.

The approach regarding the image of the country-of-origin changes enormously according to whether it is a medium–small or large company: in the first case it represents protection and promotion, in the second it is sometimes an obstacle. It is therefore clear (Balabanis and Diamantopulos, 2008, 2011) that the COO does not matter where the brands have strength. If we move from COO evaluation by big brands to COO evaluation by small brands, the COO effect is completely different. In the first case, the effect of individual brands on countries should also be considered, especially by big brands on small countries (i.e. Ikea–Sweden, Nokia–Finland, Skype–Estonia). Few studies have been done about the influence of cumulative COOs of small and big brands on the perception of other small brands. In this sense, stores play an important role in the construction of the image linked to a country as places of experience in the world of the brand. Often, in a logic of paradoxical globalization, this possibility is only partially exploited by the original brands and much more by the country-sound ones.

In general, we tend to consider the phenomenon of Country Sound Branding to be negative towards the original brands and the image of the country, since it evidently favours and maintains a level of ambiguity and lack of transparency for the customer. However, these judgements should be mitigated by some positive aspects that are taking shape in the new markets, those less competent regarding the brand and the product.

As previously mentioned, in the new markets knowledge of the COO is scarce and often confused, in particular for countries where there is no constant and repeated historical-cultural attendance, or which do not hold leadership roles on the international scene. Furthermore, it has already been said that the main European world brands do not deliberately support the country's image as a productive role of excellence, partly out of the desire to strengthen their role as a global player, and partly in order not to become drivers of potential COO competitors. We must therefore start from this framework to frame the positive role that Country Sound Branding can play.

Country Sound Branding can represent a COO image accelerator among consumers who do not recognize the image. The emergence and repetition of names and symbols referring to a specific country in certain sectors and product categories, such as fashion, furniture, food and drink, personal care, electronic products, automobiles, or luxury products, suggests and builds in the customer's mind a spontaneous link between the category and the country. It does so on several dimensions: first of all on the sound of the brand, we must not forget the great difficulty a distant language (where the distance is cross-cultural) has in assigning to different national contexts a name that appears simply 'Western', as it would also be difficult for a European consumer to distinguish a Chinese name from a Korean, Japanese or Vietnamese name; a second level concerns iconic symbolism, such as the national flag or the use of its colours, which are usually largely unknown and in this way made more familiar; the third dimension concerns the symbols and images of Country Sound Branding that increase the familiarity of places (Florence, Rome, Venice, Paris, London, Barcelona, Madrid, Munich, Berlin etc.), the ease of identification and positioning in the Western context or in the European specificity of a given country.

The phenomenon of sound branding is not only present in distant markets, but also in various European and more generally Western markets. Sound Brands can come from other European countries, or directly from the local market. There are many examples. In the first case we can mention MarcoPolo Bread (USA), and Costa Coffee (UK), which in their stores also combine the sound of the brand with a strong Italian atmosphere, both in the furnishings, in the images of places that line the walls, and in the product names. The same can be said of ProntoCaffè (Japan), a coffee chain widespread in the Far East. This evidently introduces and strengthens a direct link between coffee and Italy in the mind of the Asian customer. In the second case, among the many examples, we can mention Giormani Furniture (Hong Kong), where the colours of the Italian flag are reproduced in the logo; other cases involve Haier appliances, a German-sounding Chinese brand, Marie Dalgar cosmetics, a French-sounding Chinese brand, and 'Houppie!' clothing (Korea), with a British sound. The link with Made-in is strengthened, creating a platform of first knowledge and identification of the COO on which European companies that subsequently enter can rely and which, in the context of a more educated market (Pontiggia and Vescovi, 2013), are able to perceive and appreciate a qualitatively better offer, which otherwise would be difficult to understand. A growing diffusion of Country Sound Branding has the effect of increasing the perceived value of the image of the European country in the product categories concerned, and therefore has a driving role at the beginning of the brand entry process and in the introduction of education towards the Made-in image. Its undoubted initial usefulness is, however, temporary in its most positive phase.

In fact, if in an initial phase of market development, positive effects tend to prevail over negative ones, the undoubted positioning in general of lower quality and lower price of a Country Sound brand in the non-pioneering market phases can represent a reason for irritation or negative image creation for customers, which negatively affects the COO's overall image. In markets that end up appreciating the COO of European products, the European Sound brands could therefore enjoy an initial premium positioning that they do not deserve and therefore could subsequently cause distrust or disappointment for the image of the country that these brands recall.

On the other hand, in acquainted market conditions, which are aware of the Made-in value of a European country, the consumer is certainly more experienced and is often able to understand the original brand, as is happening in markets where there is a consolidated presence of European brands, albeit with some remaining grey areas. It can therefore be said that Country Sound Branding, obviously when it does not become a real counterfeit, mainly plays a positive role rather than a negative one in the initial stages of building the image of the country of origin, especially in newly opened markets having little competence in international brands. Paradoxically, Country Sound Branding, wanting to exploit the image, ends up strengthening it. After all, sound branding sometimes compensates for insufficient institutional intervention and the insufficient social role played by global brands in building the COO's image.

# 11
# Products and local cultures

## 11.1    CROSS-CULTURAL PRODUCT PERCEPTION

Product perception can differ greatly in different cultures. A cross-cultural analysis concerning the perception of luxury products, for example, carried out involving six countries (China, France, Germany, Italy, Japan, US), shows clearly that strong cross-cultural differences exist in the evaluation and meanings of luxury (Godey et al., 2013):

- Chinese respondents express a concept of luxury predominantly linked to 'prestige' and 'extravagance'. The general image of luxury as something unusual is confirmed for Chinese respondents by 'conspicuous', in fourth place. For both 'extravagant' and 'conspicuous', the Chinese interviewees' score was the highest of the six countries.
- French respondents have a traditional concept of luxury, predominantly hetero-referring and based on 'prestige', 'expensiveness' and 'elitism'.
- Italian respondents put 'exclusivity' in first place, followed far behind by 'elitism' and 'prestige', but we can also see a self-referred item, 'desirable', not far from them. Italians seem to have a well stratified image of luxury.
- German interviewees put in first place, far above every other adjective, 'exclusive', but in second place in the ranking is 'desirable', followed by 'expensive' and 'prestigious' with almost the same score. So, for German respondents, we can draw similar conclusions as for Italians.
- For Japanese respondents, 'expensive' is clearly the most appropriate adjective for luxury, followed by a group of four other adjectives linked with 'sophistication', 'prestige' and 'exclusiveness/elitism'.
- US respondents express a concept of luxury with the adjectives 'exclusive' and 'prestigious', but their vision of luxury appears well stratified too, because of the ranking of 'desirable' in third place and 'extravagant' just below.

International luxury companies should take into consideration the multifaceted concept of luxury in general, but also the main differences between countries in the continuum between the 'status' and 'emotional' dimensions of luxury. According to the authors' research, luxury companies cannot adopt a global strategy when addressing the six countries analysed.

Considering food products, for example, there is a great deal of research indicating the importance of the cultural context in the perception of quality. Danish, Lithuanian and Portuguese citizens were interviewed about the importance of several cues and dimensions in their evaluation of the perceived quality of bread, cookies, breakfast cereals, pasta and vodka (Krutulyte et al., 2009). The Portuguese and Lithuanians consistently gave a significantly higher average importance than did their Danish counterparts to all the cues and quality dimensions considered for all products. Such personal relevance of the foods may be perceived as a sign of a high involvement with food.

Dimensions and cues like taste and country-of-origin were the most relevant to Lithuanians. The cues and dimensions Portuguese found relevant were fairly different and more category dependent. Cues such as store type for bread, brand for breakfast cereals, pasta and vodka, country-of-origin (COO) for vodka, and price for cookies, pasta and vodka were more often assessed by the Portuguese as relevant for decision making at the point of purchase.

Looking at each of the countries studied individually, it can be seen that the Danes found price and label information important. This is in accordance with the low-context culture of the country. Danish respondents did not consider either cues or quality dimensions as a whole as important as did their Portuguese and Lithuanian counterparts. This could be taken as a sign of a relatively lower involvement with food purchase and consumption. The results obtained for the Danish sample also reveal that the importance they attach to different quality dimensions depended on the category of products in question. For example, it was important for this sample that bread, cereals and pasta were healthy and natural products, but vodka and cookies were not.

Another study has been conducted about how consumers evaluate the quality of beef in a purchase situation in four European countries: France, Germany, Spain and the UK (Grunert, 1997). Tradition and security, variation, atmosphere and social life, health, acceptance by family/children/guests, nutrition, demonstration of cooking abilities, and status are the most important purchasing motives in all four countries. Place of purchase and quality perception are related in all four countries, that is, the butcher is regarded as a sort of guarantor of high quality. This applies less in the UK than in the other countries, however. German consumers prefer dark meat, whereas Spanish consumers tend to prefer light meat. Information about country of origin and breeding and feeding has no effect on quality perception.

So, in different European countries there are some similarities in the perception of food products and also some differences. They seem to be related to the different cultural value of food and to the tradition in cooking in each country. If we refer to other cultures, the perception factors, and therefore the choice criteria, can differ more. For example, in China the judgement of food is not based above all on taste, as in Western countries, but on its health properties. Obviously, the Chinese consider taste important as well, but it is evaluated as a basic condition: if the food is not tasty it will be refused. But culturally, they ask why a specific food should be eaten in order to improve their health. Therefore, for European companies, it is important that they find a significant, reliable reason why their product should be consumed for its health benefits when they promote it to customers.

In conclusion, the main cultural factors that influence the perception of the product concern the personal involvement of the consumer with the specific type of object or service considered, the symbolic value it has in the community to which the person belongs, the information that is available on the product, the social value it holds, the specific use made of it in the cultural context in which it is used and, obviously, the cultural context itself that defines its perceived role (Figure 11.1)

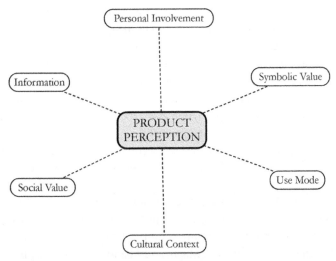

**Figure 11.1** Factors influencing product perception

## 11.2 PRODUCT ADAPTATION TO LOCAL MARKETS

Should the MNEs and the MMNEs adapt their products in order to make them more suitable to the demand of international customers and, if so, identify the specific factors submitted to adaptation, changes, their pervasiveness, and the reasons underlying the decision to adapt them? The adaptation dilemma is a decision to take when you have to cope with certain mandatory conditions; in other cases it is a discretionary choice of the company considering market opportunities and their strategic importance. MMNEs have to compete in international markets with limited resources and skills, which they normally overcome by using speed, flexibility and greater adaptability.

In the new international markets, there are macroeconomic, social and cultural aspects that are so specific and peculiar to those markets as to directly influence the purchasing behaviour of consumers and product expectations.

It is necessary to evaluate whether Western and European products should be subjected to forms of adaptation to make them more suitable for the demand of customers from other cultures and, if so, to identify the individual aspects subject to intervention, the changes made, the pervasiveness of the change and the reasons behind the decision to operate in this direction.

Over the years, the development of information technologies and the use of global communication campaigns have facilitated the phenomenon of shortening distances. It was thought that such a reduction would make it easier for European and Western companies to meet the demand for physically distant markets and initiate a process of progressive Westernization of markets.

The analysis of the current situation, instead, highlights a different reality. The most modern Chinese consumers, for example, have not embraced the Western lifestyle unconditionally: if on the one hand they are looking for cosmopolitan products capable of affirming their '*mianzi*' (reputation), on the other hand a kind of patriotism persists in them, which translates to a rediscovery of traditional values (Zhou and Belk, 2004).

It is not just physical distance that continues to play a central role in generating differences; four dimensions have to be considered (Ghemawat, 2001). The *cultural* dimension (Hofstede, 2006; Hall and Hall, 2001) influences the preference formation system: language, religion and social norms are the most important sources of differences between countries. The Chinese language, for example, uses ideograms (Alon et al., 2009), which are not only bearers of sound, but also of meaning (Amuso and Montagna, 2009).

There are also the *political-administrative*, *geographical* and *economic* dimensions that can act as an obstacle or favour the reduction of distances, depending on their impact on relations between different nations.

While it is true that Western products are often considered better than local products in many newly developed countries in terms of quality and relevance (Zhuang et al., 2008; Lin and Lai, 2010), it is also true that in many countries there is, especially in big cities, a strong desire to emulate the Western lifestyle (Magni and Atsmon, 2010), an aspiration that, however, tends to clash with the desire not to abandon one's traditions and culture. From this arises a continuous dialectical comparison between the desire for modernity and attachment to one's roots, and this aspect must be taken into careful consideration in the introduction and presence of European products.

In general, international product policy does not end its function with the choice of products to be offered on international markets, but it also deals with identifying the level of homogenization or adaptation required by the markets for each individual product. It is as if there was a contrast between a logic that imposes a forced and uniform extension of the marketing strategies on the most interesting international markets (globalization) and a logic of adaptation, in which the economic, socio-cultural and competitive specificity of every regional area are valued (Hultman et al., 2009), favouring an approach based on differentiation strategies (Vianelli, 2001).

It is difficult to take a position in one of the two extremes of adaptation and standardization, since the product itself, due to its physical characteristics and technical and economic constraints, cannot be adapted beyond certain limits, while other variables, such as price and communication in the first place, almost necessarily need to be calibrated on the specific cultural context to favour the meeting between offer and demand (Valdani and Bertoli, 2006).

A global approach is desirable when it is possible to exploit a strong brand and product image in the various markets (Bengtsson and Venkatraman 2008); it also guarantees cost containment due to production uniformity and economies of scale, resulting from the implementation of a standardized marketing plan. Conversely, a local approach is preferred when the regional contexts are such that they cannot meet the needs of consumers in the various markets in a single way (Bradley, 1999).

Companies are increasingly trying to reconcile the two solutions (Gupta and Wang, 2011), implementing partial globalization policies where it is possible to select transnational market segments and at the same time offering adequate and adapted goods thanks to international production sites and technological innovation (Valdani and Bertoli, 2006). Plausible alternatives are also 'standardization of core components' (Aulakh, 2003) and referral strategies (Shao and Ji, 2008), solutions that seek to reconcile standardization and adaptation, offering a wide range of specific products for each segment, using common and standardized components, which guarantee economies of scale to companies.

There are standardized products and global products. According to Onkvisit and Shaw (2004), the standardized product is originally designed for the home market and subsequently exported to foreign markets without major changes, except for the name and some aesthetic changes. Global products are instead designed for a global market rather than a specific country (Steenkamp and De Jong, 2010). They are characterized by satisfying the needs of buyers who share the same needs in terms of functions of use and conditions of use, thus addressing customers who are little influenced by the cultural and market context in which they live. The strength of the global approach in international marketing strategies is due to its relative simplicity of implementation and to cost containment. This is possible thanks to the concentration of marketing activities and to the exploitation of economies of scale (Tantong et al., 2010) and learning economies by the company, and greater bargaining power towards suppliers (Jeannet and Hennessey, 2001).

Cost savings also concern the elimination of adaptation costs, the lack of retooling of the systems, and the simpler management of warehouses. All this allows the company to be more competitive in terms of prices, therefore freeing up resources that can be usefully used, for example, in promoting the product.

A global strategy also offers advantages from the point of view of strengthening the brand and corporate image at an international level (Bengtsson and Venkatraman, 2008), given the uniqueness of the message spread out, extended to all intangible elements, from the guarantee offered to after-sales services: consumer loyalty is thus maintained even when the consumer moves from one country to another (Pellicelli, 2007).

The product categories particularly suitable for design according to a global approach are those of high-tech goods, which exploit the universal language of technology, products that are status symbols, aimed at young people at an international level, and all those products that evoke the 'Made-in' effect (Kumara and Canhua, 2010). Adapting products with a strong COO (country-of-origin) effect beyond a certain threshold would become counterproductive, as this would disperse the brand equity and identity of the products, losing the advantages of their country image.

An approach based on this logic, at times can also compromise the penetration of a product in a foreign market, invalidating its success: the attempt to control costs, through standardization, could make the product unsuitable for some markets, reducing demand, especially in the face of cultural diversity which may require extreme adaptations.

To prevent this from happening, an adaptation of the product is made in international markets according to the needs of consumers in the specific market. In addition to the stimuli coming from the market, there are also product adaptations deriving from a series of factors defined as country-specific; these are modifications that change depending on the country in which the company operates and that may refer to product safety regulations, rather than conditions of use, as well as specific cultural traditions and local consumption habits (Hultman et al., 2009).

The disadvantages that an adaptation strategy entails can be reduced by considering a different interpretation. The question relating to economies of scale can be reviewed first of all, arguing that the economies of variety guaranteed by adaptation, in the face of low-cost increases, allow solutions that are closer to what the customer is looking for, increasing the value in use and attraction of the product. Consequently, the client is willing to pay a higher price (Vianelli, 2001). This also allows you to stand out from the competition, to increase customer satisfaction and make the product less easy to be imitated.

So, the adaptation of the product is a decision to be taken when certain imperative conditions are met, while in other cases it is a discretionary choice of the company exploiting some opportunities found in the market.

Among the mandatory adjustments, the most important is certainly that of product approval (Cateora and Graham, 2007) relating to the regulations imposed by national governments: their violation effectively closes the possibility of access to the market. Other factors then concern the size of the products, whose characteristics are expressed by parameters such as size, capacity and volume, subject to the conditions imposed by the market.

The discretion and uncertainty that characterize optional adaptations are part of business strategies. Several authors have proposed different decision-making areas that can be taken into consideration when the dilemma arises as to whether or not to adapt the product to an international context (Yorio, 1983; Hibbert, 1990; Chryssochoidis and Wong, 2000; Usunier and Lee, 2013). A first decision-making area concerns the environmental factors linked to the single market/country, which concern aspects linked to technological, legal and cultural conditions. A second area evaluates the size of the product, which can facilitate physical distribution and reduce transport costs. Another aspect to consider concerns the changes that aim to improve the conditions of use in the various local contexts, with reference, for example, to climatic conditions, which can modify the performance and duration of a product. The perception of the product and the expected benefits can vary greatly in different markets, too. The physical characteristics of consumers and their cultural habits also influence adaptation decisions, as in the case of clothing.

Then there are products that also have a symbolic meaning, which must be carefully correlated to the culture of the country in which they are marketed. It is the local culture that defines the aspects that consumers consider fundamental and the perceived value, consequently the direction in which to develop adaptation. For example, this is often evident in food products, where the weight of cultural factors is often high. Failure to adapt the product can be associated with a low sensitivity to cultural differences, resulting in possible negative attitudes by potential customers.

To analyse the elements influenced by adaptation strategies, one can refer to the product component model of Cateora and Graham (2007). According to this model, the product is conceived as a multidimensional element, consisting of a series of basic characteristics which, related to each other, generate the set of utilities and benefits demanded by the customer. These components can be grouped according to perceptual or functional links that connect the different dimensions in three macro categories, incorporating the tangible and intangible attributes of each product.

The core is made up of the *basic components*, which represent the product in its concreteness, and which mainly concern the technical-functional, physical and aesthetic characteristics. On a broader level there are the *completion components* that combine the packaging and branding. Finally, the third macro-category concerns the *service support components*, such as the guarantee and the after-sales service (Figure 11.2).

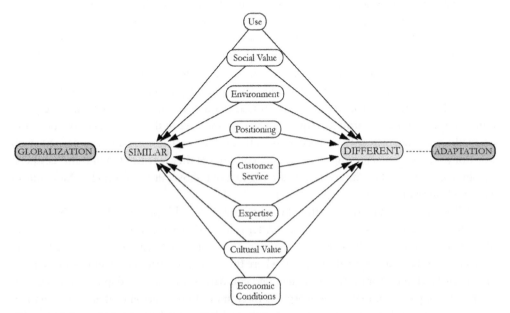

**Figure 11.2**   Globalization/adaptation conditions

According to some research in the Chinese market (Vescovi and Trevisiol, 2011), the first impression is that in international markets, although there are many strong cultural and structural differences, in reality they are not considered very different by European or Western companies, or at least not to such an extent as to initially justify an adaptation in their eyes. This is also confirmed by the reasons given to support the adaptation which, in fact, are not particularly linked to the cultural value system of the countries or to the different conditions of use. Compliance with local regulations and economic factors are in fact the main reasons. Local regulations act as a filter for the entry of foreign products into the market, above all to protect the local industry; the economic reasons are based on the fact that the adaptation is pursued not only aiming for greater adherence to specific market requests, but also with the logic of reducing production costs to allow the consequent reduction of the price, often a crucial element for competitive strategies in new markets. However, this shows that a different assessment is assumed in the definition of value, where the quality components of the product take on less weight than the price components, compared to what happens in Western markets, at least in an initial phase of development of the new markets.

The choice not to adapt the product can also be attributed to the desired positioning, considering the target customers that the company intends to address. High-tech or high-end products with strong symbolic content, such as luxury products, are less influenced by cultural differences between countries, as they appeal to a buyer who truly demands a global identity from them. Their value is given by not being different from their counterparts in other markets, since they have the role of state 'homogenizers'. Many European brands and consumer products, such as those related to cars, fashion, furniture and home accessories, play this role in world markets. This certainly does not apply to industrial goods, which are preferred for their superior technological quality and their ability to meet the needs of local entrepreneurs.

With regard to the aspects subject to adaptation, the data relating to the *core components* normally register rather marginal levels of adaptation, which do not alter the original design of the product. The elements that receive a more coherent form of adaptation, even if still far from strategic interventions, are the *functions of use*, the *design* and the *product platform*. This could be due to the need to operate in such a way as to simplify and contain costs: interventions aimed at redesigning the product require, in fact, an increase in the resources to be spent and an increase in management complexity, something that smaller companies in particular do not always succeed in achieving. The last core component that registers the fit is the 'aesthetic design' factor. Important interventions are highlighted above all in personal fashion and in agri-food companies.

*Ancillary services* aim to reassure the customer about the purchased good, helping to reinforce the company's *brand promise*. After-sales assistance procedures are particularly affected by adaptations. It is obvious that for companies that are heavily involved in the industrial-mechanical automation sector, where the company–customer relationship is much closer, the level of customization is higher, and companies are used to adapting these services on specific requests. In reality, adaptation is often more to the customer than to the market. The reasons behind the choice to adapt recall problems that have already been faced: the considerable physical distance imposes a need to create operational units in the area, with the consequent adaptation of the entire logistics process.

In conclusion, a framework is generally presented whose supporting elements can be identified in the following three points:

- product adaptation processes are significantly different in B2B and B2C markets;
- the local cultural system is underestimated as a factor of significant diversity in business relations;
- a life cycle of the market approach emerges, from standardized to *glocalized*;[1]

Regarding the first point, it can be highlighted that consumer goods, particularly in high-end sectors, maintain a global vocation, since their value is linked to universal recognition and contributes to the description of the international status of their owners. If they adapted, they would lose value and enter a losing battle with local products, based on convenience. For such products adaptation can only be of a less visible type (dimensions, labels, etc.). Going down from the top towards more intermediate positions, adapting becomes more important. Consumers recognize themselves less in the globalization processes of social status and appreciate the high value of money/product, but this is a difficult role for European brands to play.

In B2B, on the other hand, the ability to adapt is transformed into a competitive advantage, the economic-functional aspects prevailing over those of brand reputation and social Westernization. The adaptation therefore follows the rules established by market prices and by the conditions of use of machines and production systems. There are specific conditions to be addressed linked to individual customers and more general market conditions, often through productions located in the destination country and dedicated to that specific market or neighbouring and similar markets.

Regarding the second point, the underestimation of the local cultural factor seems to be dictated by the desire to simplify, beyond reality, any situation of complex diversity which for medium-sized enterprises, unlike large multinationals, would be difficult to manage, also taking into account the lack of adequate tools and interpretative skills. Seen from the headquarters of the companies, the markets are treated as similar, more because this will simplify their management than because this is really the case, and this puts these companies at risk, mitigated only by prudent low and progressive investment policies to reduce the extent of any losses. This leads to a vicious circle of investing little for fear of failure and therefore not investing enough in such large and diversified markets as China or India, making bankruptcy likely. In the best cases they remain in a precarious situation, in niches that are difficult to consolidate and so small that they cannot expect to be truly active on the market, but at most they have contacts with some specific local customers. Expat managers often complain about this lack of cultural understanding with the head office. Among these managers, there are those who do not connect with the local culture and shut themselves away in a professional activity, focused only on technical responses to various problems (they do not speak the local language, have no relationships with the local population outside work, etc.) and they risk remaining unrelated to both the market and business relationships, performing below the level required.

Finally, a life cycle of product adaptation in international markets by medium-sized companies seems to be emerging. Unlike multinationals, it is not market research that works for them, but market experience, which requires longer integration times and methods. By evaluating the length of time the companies are present in the international market, it appears that the longer they are present in culturally and structurally distant markets, the more the product adaptation grows. Therefore, as the knowledge of the country and the market increases, the ability to understand what should be localized reduces the fear of making wrong adaptation choices and the misjudgement of their value. It is an exploratory process that companies conduct based on their actions and experience. The canonical methods envisaged by marketing processes, requiring a careful study of the potential and conditions of the market they are going to enter, and identifying the product aspects to be adapted, which is typical behaviour of a large multinational with considerable resources, analytical skills and deepening skills, are not followed. Medium-sized companies seem to have a different approach: they enter the market through the opportunities created by customers. They are often large companies arriving on the international market that ask their suppliers to follow them so they can have a supply network they can rely on. Subsequently, these medium-sized companies acquire operational and market knowledge that allows them to increase the number of local customers, by adapting their offer to the market. They start by proposing to the customer a strategy that we could define as standardized, then, as their knowledge of the market grows, they localize their strategy by inserting elements of both international globalization and localization in a specific country.

Adaptation is not a problem for smaller companies which, in contrast, often gain a competitive advantage from it. Adaptation may perhaps be a problem for big companies, which are accustomed to greater standardization. The difficulty that culturally distant markets present concerns not only operational or structural adaptation, but rather cultural adaptation, which requires an approach that has different rules from those traditionally applied in international marketing behaviour. Sometimes companies prefer to oversimplify and not give importance to a market that they cannot evaluate with the traditional criteria that they use in international expansion. Paradoxically they take refuge in an inverted view: the international market seems to them very small and not very profitable when seen from Europe, as it would require a logical rethink. On the other hand, the more companies' international presence matures, the more they are able to adopt adaptation strategies.

## 11.3    PACKAGING AND CULTURES

Consumer preferences play an absolutely critical role in manufacturers' decision making, as packaging is an important element of the marketing mix, with a clear marketing function. Packaging can represent up to one third of the overall consumption utility of a product (Rokka and Uusitalo, 2008), and therefore can be decisive for the success of a product. Packaging influences a decision precisely when the consumer is completely focused on the purchase, often leading them to choose between competing brands.

Packaging has three main general functions: (1) containing and protecting the product; (2) making the use of the product as easy as possible for the consumer; (3) promoting the product and giving information. The first function is essentially functional and technical, while the other two concern marketing choices.

Regarding the use of the package by the consumer, it must be considered how similar products in different cultures can be used differently. For example, when it comes to food, there are important differences in packaging regarding the quantities that the products are bought in and their daily use. In addition, the space available in homes for the storage of products must also be considered. In many Japanese houses, unlike European and especially American ones, storage space is minimal, due to the small size of apartments in cities and their multifunctional use. A room, in fact, can be transformed into a living room, study and bedroom, depending on the time of day. This means, for example, that the dimensions of the food packages as well as the refrigerator have to be small. Small refrigerators are also present in Chinese homes, while in American ones they are very large, often double the size of European ones.

The packages of soft drinks, milk, meat, and so on that are found in the United States are therefore much larger than both European and Eastern ones. For example, Coca-Cola has different packaging in different countries. Having tried in the past to standardize on the 2-litre pack, in Europe they had to switch to the 1.5-litre pack, as the 2-litre pack did not fit into European refrigerator spaces.

As European sweets are very often considered too sweet for local taste in China, the packaging is small, suitable for limited use. Flavoured milk is often found in small plastic cartons, which can easily be stowed in a bag, to use as a snack with a straw during the day away from home.

Often packages are designed to be reused after the consumption of the product, so in this aspect different types of reuse related to different cultures must be considered. Actually the ways people reuse the packaging are very different in different cultures, relating to the management of the house.

Regarding the informational function of packaging, first of all it may be essential to consider that consumers of low-context individualistic cultures are more verbally oriented, but consumers of high-context collectivist cultures, instead, use symbols, signs and indirect communication such as sources of information.

In the context of product packaging, this may involve a different pattern of information selection in cultures whose direction or styles of writing and reading vary. One of the hallmarks of a culture is its language and the method of writing and reading. Hernandez et al. (2017) highlights the intercultural differences in the perception process (attention allocation and memory) due to the biasing effect of reading direction on the positioning of position-based stimuli in marketing. Cultures that write from left to right have a tendency to anchor to the left in comparative judgements and vice versa. Furthermore, through horizontal positioning, a consumer of a culture who reads from left to right generally sees the past as being on the left and the future displayed on the right (Ploom et al., 2020).

The colour in product packaging draws attention, but at the same time it is a source of information, on the basis of which consumers assess the general properties of products (e.g., smell and flavour), ingredients, potential quality and the experience of consuming the product. Colours influence a consumer's perception and behaviour as a physical reaction. When designing product packaging, it is crucial to consider that colours are context and object dependent (Amsteus et al., 2015) and can have different implications for a person's thoughts, feelings/emotions and behaviour. The contextual dependence of colours becomes essential when designing packaging for different markets in international marketing, as colours have different symbolic values, cultural meanings, associations and evoke positive and negative emotions/feelings (Aslam, 2006).

The purpose of the visual design element on the packaging – a picture, photograph or illustration – is to make the content of the packaging easily understandable to the consumer. Moreover, the shape of the package may have symbolic cultural values.

Packaging waste poses serious environmental problems. The production, use, disposal and recovery of packaging not only generates huge volumes of waste, but also consumes raw materials, water and energy, thus generating those emissions that are driving global warming. Therefore, any reduction in packaging waste contributes in many ways to the goals of sustainability and cleaner production. The environmental characteristics of packaging are becoming increasingly important in consumer choice; however, they are not perceived in the same way in all cultures (Figure 11.3).

We can observe some marked cross-cultural differences in the attributes of packaging identified as environmentally friendly: while over 50 per cent of French and German consumers have chosen 'reduced packaging', only a third of US consumers consider it important. German consumers have identified renewable materials much more often, rarely mentioning recycled materials, unlike French and US consumers. Each culture can have its own environmental value system (Herbes et al., 2018).

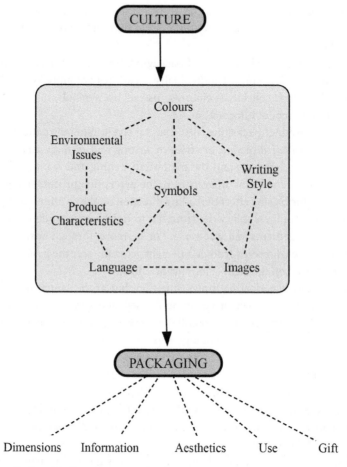

**Figure 11.3**　　Cultural influence on packaging

There are cross-cultural differences in consumers' interpretation of packaging signals. French consumers place the highest value on the materials that make up a package, compared to German or American consumers. The colours signal environmental merit (Herbes et al., 2020). This may be due to the fact that France scores higher in distance of power, and those cultures prefer to have clear, 'hierarchical' symbols to refer to.

Cues such as symbols, colours, logos and labels are effective in making packaging noticeable and influencing consumer purchase decisions, particularly across different cultures. For instance, a study shows that the differential effectiveness of colour, size and shape of packaging (of a German deodorant) modified for sale in different countries (Japan, the UK, the Netherlands) may be explained by cultural differences (Van den Berg-Weitzel and Van de Laar, 2001). The analysis shows that there is, in fact, a relationship between culture and packaging design, even though the relationship differs for each product category. Some product categories have packaging that quite clearly speaks a more international language than others. Some products are indeed more internationally accepted than others, for example luxury and fashion products.

Indiscriminately localizing the packaging of any products as they enter foreign markets may not be the most effective strategy for international marketers. For example, hedonic products, especially for well-known Western brands such as Coca-Cola and L'Oréal, do not benefit and may even suffer from localization.

The effectiveness of packaging localization depends on the nature of a product, particularly on whether the product serves utilitarian or hedonic needs. Hedonic products (such as spirits and perfumes) generate affective responses and experiences in consumers, and hedonic consumption is underpinned by emotional sensations, such as deriving fun from consumption. The use of a foreign language in brand names can also enhance the foreignness, thereby increasing the hedonic value, of products. If foreignness is used as a brand attribute in overseas markets, it may have a strong effect on the purchase intentions of consumers because of the high-quality perception associated with these brands.

By contrast, consumers fulfil functional needs from utilitarian products (such as laundry detergent) based on the functions performed by a product. In this sense, the evaluation and purchase of utilitarian products are often accompanied by rationalizing that may even involve localization of packaging (Khan et al., 2017).

There should be a separate discussion for gift packaging, typical of oriental cultures such as Chinese and Japanese, which are considered to be the countries where there is a true culture of giving gifts. Supermarkets in China allocate large spaces and long shelves to gift boxes of food products, which is much rarer in Europe and linked only to special holidays such as Christmas or Easter. It is therefore important to enrich the offer of special packaging for many products that can be gift items, for example a case of Ferrero Rocher and Nescafé in China.

In Japan, a country of culture with a high context, the care of packaging follows a specific ritual; it has the same value as the gift and therefore assumes a fundamental importance in the choice of products, sometimes greater than that of the gift itself.

In conclusion, there are several factors influencing product perception. Some of these are personal, some are extrinsic, and others are cultural (see Figure 11.1). In particular *Personal Involvement* depends both on personal and cultural conditions. Personal aspects concern the characteristics of the person, while cultural ones concern the cultural importance of the product. *Symbolic Value* of the product is a cultural factor that can differ in different societies. For example, coffee's symbolic value for the Italian culture is totally different from the Chinese, but also from the British. The *Use Mode* depends on the environment in which the product is used, concerning the enabling conditions and the expertise of the person involved. The *Cultural Context* affects the perception defining the criteria that the individual uses to judge the product. The *Social Value* of the product is created by the role of the product in creating relationships with people, for example in affecting their social status. The *Information* is an extrinsic factor that can take several forms: (a) official, absolutely important in low-context cultures; (b) personal, absolutely important in high-context cultures; (c) experiential, relating to the consumer's experience of a specific product; (d) mixed, including more forms.

The company acting internationally should carefully analyse the way the products proposed to the market are perceived, in order to promote them or adapt them.

## 11.4   NEW PRODUCT ACCEPTANCE IN DIFFERENT CULTURES

The concept of a 'new product' can be absolute or relative to the context of where the product has been introduced. Sometimes new products are the outcome of innovations that did not exist before, sometimes the products can be totally new for a specific market, and therefore for the consumers of that market, but they still existed in another market or they may even have been traditional. The concept of a new product from a cross-cultural point of view is relative to the specific culture of a certain market where it is introduced.

Food is a clear example. Normally food is traditional for a culture, perhaps for centuries, and then it is offered in a country with a totally different food culture, so it's a 'new product'. Many culturally distant cuisines have been proposed in Europe, from North Africa, the Middle East, China, Japan, Sub-Saharan Africa, and South America. Conversely, traditional Italian and French foods have been introduced in many countries on other continents. However, accepting food from different cultures is not that easy. Often it adapts to the local taste in order to be accepted more easily. For many cultures food is an identity product. Even inside Europe, the acceptance of food coming from other European countries is not so simple, considering the different European cultures. French and Belgian consumers seemed to be more open to innovation in foods than Polish consumers, where tradition (especially in rural areas) plays an important role in the life and personal relations of people. Norwegian consumers tended to be closer to the Polish point of view than to the French and Belgians, being quite critical of the idea of innovation. For Italian consumers innovations emerged as something they have to live with and accept because of the modern way of living. French consumers also admitted that innovations are unavoidable due to the modern way of life. Spanish consumers had a propensity to be more neutral, keeping in mind both the advantages and disadvantages that food innovations might introduce (Guerrero et al., 2009).

Edible insects, for example, have attracted much Western interest in recent years due to their nutritional and environmental advantages. Consumers, however, remain aversive towards a class of items that are not traditionally considered to be food. While the focus is often on Western disgust, looking at consumer perceptions in a culture that considers insects to be delicious could provide new insights into the psychological and cultural mechanisms that underpin these evaluations. Research (Tan et al., 2015) considering two different cultural attitudes, Dutch (not used to insects as food) and Thai (used to them), demonstrated how it can be difficult to accept what is common and liked in another culture. Moreover, the motivation to accept insects as food is different in the two cultures: the Dutch were considering insects as food because they were motivated by the idea of sustainable food consumption, while the Thais considered insects more in terms of their taste and familiarity. Individuals perceived stimuli differently according to their knowledge and made judgements according to expectations that differed according to their cultural background and individual experiences. The way to propose and promote the same product in other cultures can be really different.

In today's global marketplace, many firms are seeking standardized marketing strategies to take advantage of world-scale economies. Some have argued that mass media has played a role in the emergence of a global consumer culture and that firms have begun to pursue global positioning strategies as a result. There is, however, little evidence to suggest that world cultures are becoming more homogeneous, and quite possibly there is increasing divergence among industrialized countries.

Yeniyurt and Townsend (2003) put forward four hypotheses relating these cultural dimensions to acceptance rates of new products: power distance and uncertainty avoidance are hypothesized to have negative effects on acceptance, while the others are hypothesized to have positive effects. They also state several hypotheses concerning how socioeconomic factors such as gross domestic product, urbanization, literacy rate, and openness of the economy would moderate the effect of the cultural dimensions on new product acceptance rates. Of the four main effect hypotheses concerning culture, three were supported: individualism positively affected acceptance rates, while power distance and uncertainty avoidance negatively affected it (though the effect of uncertainty avoidance on acceptance rates was not significant across all three products studied). Only the masculinity trait had no significant effects on acceptance rates. The moderating effects were more complex. The results suggested that for countries with better economic conditions, uncertainty avoidance is related negatively to acceptance rates, but in countries with poorer economic conditions, the reverse is true. The aforementioned urbanization and economic well-being variables positively moderate acceptance rates, suggesting that cultural differences are more pronounced in customers' purchasing behaviour. A strong educational infrastructure (as measured by literacy rate) and economic openness were negative moderators, suggesting that these variables acted to suppress the cultural differences among countries.

The results are useful to new product managers in that they suggest that firms with new products and technologies should first target countries high in individualism but low in power distance and uncertainty avoidance at the time of launch. As a corollary, the results suggest that firms must find a balance between standardization and adaptation. Even in today's marketplace, culture still significantly impacts new product acceptance. Furthermore, the effect of socioeconomic variables must also be considered. Literacy and economic openness appear to restrict cultural effects on acceptance rates, so in relatively closed economies or in countries with poorer educational levels, greater adaptation will be more successful. Standardization is more likely to be successful in countries that score higher in openness or literacy level.

Hofstede's national culture model can be an appropriate tool for analysing cultural differences regarding the orientation to accept innovation and new products in intercultural environments. Considering each cultural factor, it is possible to define the different cultural approach to new products, therefore identifying the difficulty or ease for an international company to introduce new products to the international market (Hsu et al., 2010).

Members of large power-distance groups are found to have a lower level of acceptance toward innovativeness (Van Everdingen and Waarts, 2003). Members of high power-distance index groups also get a feeling that they seldom receive corresponding feedback while they try to adopt new things or ideas and, hence, they do not take innovativeness very well. Individuals belonging to this type of group also have a sense that they lack the resources or opportunities to make decisions on innovativeness, which lowers their interest in solving problems through innovation. As they do not actively consider the advantages of accepting new things, it is difficult to expect them to take on innovativeness. Therefore, it is possible to consider that the larger the power distance of a national culture is, the lower the consumer's level of acceptance of innovative marketing proposals will be.

In a society with a culture of high uncertainty avoidance, individuals may view new things as risky; conversely, individuals with low uncertainty avoidance are always interested and curious about new things (Hofstede, 1991). On the premise of avoiding risks, individuals do not like to accept innovativeness and they are unenthusiastic about novel concepts; thus, they cannot tolerate change. The stronger the uncertainty avoidance of a national culture is, the lower the consumers' level of acceptance toward innovative marketing or new products will be.

Where individualism is very high, people tend not to follow the social norm strictly and they tend to act independently, so the level of acceptance toward innovativeness is relatively higher. Besides, consumers' level of acceptance of innovativeness characterizes an individual's tendency to active behaviour, which also refers to his/her independence regarding other people. The stronger the individualism of a national culture is, the higher the consumers' level of acceptance of new products will be.

People with a high masculinity index are confident, positive, and willing to take on a challenge. They are attentive to their performance and development and they can demonstrate their wealth and success by showing off their acquisition of new products (Steenkamp et al., 1999). Furthermore, with masculinity, people are characterized by making decisions independently. The stronger the masculinity of a national culture is, the higher the consumers' level of acceptance of new products will be.

Individuals in a culture with short-term orientation respect tradition highly and this attitude may impede consumers' acceptance of new products. If consumers' attitude is more past-oriented, they prefer purchasing products that they are accustomed to than innovative ones. The stronger the long-term orientation of a national culture is, the higher the consumers' level of acceptance toward innovative marketing will be.

Cultures of indulgence, being interested in the 'pursuit of happiness', are positively related to the acceptance of new products, being focused on the perception of control over their personal life and the greater importance of leisure, while cultures of restraint, on the contrary, are not open to something new, people are less active, less likely to remember positive emotions, and quite traditional. Obviously, cultural factors can have both a positive and a negative effect on the attitude to new product acceptance (Figures 11.4 and 11.5).

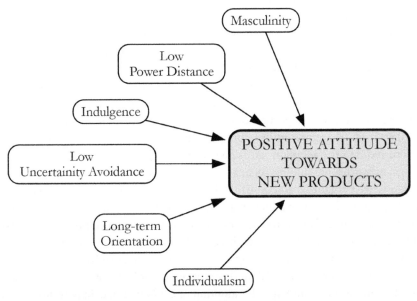

**Figure 11.4** Hofstede's cultural factors to positive attitudes towards new products

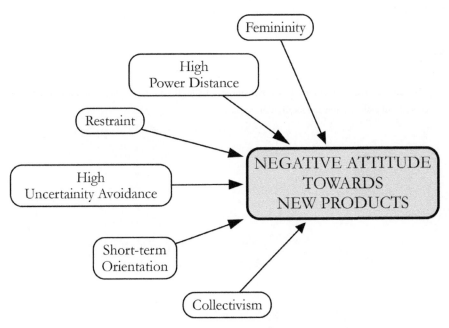

**Figure 11.5** Hofstede's cultural factors to negative attitudes towards new products

Concerning the high–low context culture model of Hall (Morden, 1999), people from high-context cultures try to become well-informed about facts by obtaining information from personal information networks. Alternatively, people in low-context cultures seek information about decisions from a research base and use information sources such as reports, databases, information highways, and the internet. These seem to be the type of information sources companies use to find information when making innovation adoption decisions. Personal network influences, which are important drivers in high-context cultures, may become more relevant when a considerable portion of consumers have already adopted the innovation or are deciding on it. Therefore, in low-context countries, people are more likely to adopt an innovation, and thus the adoption rate is higher than in high-context countries.

People in monochronic cultures act in a focused manner, concentrate on one thing at a time, and tend to be well organized and punctual. People in polychronic cultures can be considered to be less organized, being less punctual and doing many things at once, in an opportunistic way. In general, monochronic time cultures are often low-context cultures, while polychronic time cultures can be associated with high-context cultures. A decision to implement a new information system, for example, fits appropriately with well-organized and punctual organization styles. Consequently, in a B2B market of monochronic countries, companies are more likely to adopt innovations, and thus the adoption rate is higher than in polychronic countries.

In order to promote a new product or a marketing innovation internationally, the company should analyse the local culture to choose the correct way to do it. Concerning low-context culture and monochronic countries, the communication using official channels (media, web, press, etc.) can be a good solution, while for high-context culture and polychronic countries, personal communication channels should be used, such as social media, word of mouth, PR, events, sales force etc.

## NOTE

1.  Zygmunt Bauman (1998) introduced the concept of Glocalization, a mixed solution of the two opposite concepts of globalization and localization.

# 12
## Importers, retailers and sales force in different cultures

## 12.1 IMPORTERS, DISTRIBUTORS, RETAILERS

Local operators collaborate with MMNEs in a specific market. In particular, this concerns importers and distributors. Since operating in emerging countries usually presents significant differences compared to national markets, due to specific cultural norms and ways of consuming, distributors are key actors in helping companies to understand the market they are entering.

Small and medium-sized enterprises (SMEs) usually use exporting as an entry mode before fully operating in foreign markets, and often this represent a long-term entry strategy, because the financial resources required and the risks are lower. So, the role of importers or foreign distributors has become more and more important for the internationalization of companies, most of all in the case of products sold in local retail chains and department stores where the brand cannot be controlled.

Based on the Uppsala model (Johanson and Vahlne, 1977, 1990), exporting in mature markets may be less difficult since practices developed in one market can be used in another one, but when firms face emerging markets they have to cope with new and unexpected problems in order to distribute their products. For example, in recent research about Italian companies operating in the Chinese market, Vianelli et al. (2012) highlight that choosing the right partner to distribute the products represents the main problem to be solved.

So entering new and emerging markets may require a new marketing approach and the development of new business models, because these markets often follow completely different business rules, due to the high psychic distance, as well as a different cultural context, and to the different market expertise from both consumers and intermediaries who are not normally able to judge and evaluate the new products that are entering the market (Arnold and Quelch, 1998; Vescovi and Pontiggia, 2013). Since indirect export is one of the main ways of entering and continuing to operate in these markets, it is necessary to understand the role of distributors from incoming companies and the new approach that companies should adopt to enter these markets.

As discussed in Chapter 6, one of the most relevant theories on internationalization is the Uppsala model of the internationalization process, developed by Johanson and Vahlne (1977, 1990). According to this framework, companies gradually increase their international involvement and engagement in foreign markets using a process in which the development of knowledge is fundamental. Given the importance of experiential knowledge (i.e. the accumulation of knowledge from operating in foreign markets), the Uppsala model assumes that companies usually begin to internationalize through exporting, establishing agreements with intermediaries or agents in order to collect the information necessary to penetrate the market, and only at a later stage do some of them decide to build their own sales organization on foreign markets. Companies tend to internationalize through exports and/or foreign investment (Reynolds, 1997); however, the former seems to be particularly applicable to the internationalization of SMEs because there is often a lack of resources for FDI (Zahra et al., 1997). In fact, compared to alternative ways of accessing the foreign market, exporting is generally a less demanding approach to resources since it requires minimal risk, limited resources and offers high flexibility of movement (Al-Hyari et al., 2012).

One of the first decisions in the internationalization process is the choice between the company's distribution channels and independent foreign distributors (Alon and Jaffe, 2012; Cavusgil et al., 1995). The former allows you to control marketing activities, while the latter represents a low-cost way to enter the market. But even if indirect export is a low-cost and more flexible entry mode, finding suitable intermediaries is a significant problem faced by companies (Neupert et al., 2006). To operate effectively on foreign markets, it is important to choose distributors who produce and/or trade the same product line; however, sometimes manufacturers believe that their distributor may represent a competitor (Cavusgil et al., 1995). The lack of resources and the need for cost savings push SMEs towards a replication of the choices they apply in traditional markets, that is, they follow the *mirroring* strategy. But to cope with the differences between the destination market and the internal market, a company is often forced to modify the strategies that have previously been implemented in the domestic context (McDougall and Oviatt, 1996). This conflict often leads to half-decisions, resulting in failure.

Emerging markets, normally having a different cultural context, are characterized by a high level of uncertainty and 'institutional voids', defined as a lack of market information, efficient intermediary institutions, predictable government actions, and an efficient bureaucracy (Khanna and Palepu, 2000). In new markets there is little or no market data, poorly developed distribution systems, widespread product counterfeiting, and opaque power in local business and political players (Arnold and Quelch, 1998).

Not only is it necessary for these features to be considered by firms that want to expand their activities, but also the cultural aspects in doing business are relevant. First of all, one major difference is the need for relationships, based on which, in Confucian cultural areas, businesspeople prefer to deal with people they know and trust (Jiang and Prater, 2002), and the failure to follow the rules of reciprocity and equity results in a loss of face and being labelled as untrustworthy (Luo and Chen, 1996).

In new markets, consumers and customers' knowledge has not reached a sufficient level to understand and correctly evaluate the quality differences in the offerings proposed by competitors, where customers' behaviours (and choices) are not affected by previous experiences, being non-acquainted (Vescovi and Pontiggia, 2013). This has an impact on firms' marketing strategy because consumer behaviour is not fully known and competitors are often other foreign companies instead of local ones, so the positioning of the product cannot be based on the superiority or differences with competitors' goods. Entering those markets could require a new market approach and the development of new business models, because these markets often have completely different business rules. Therefore, new approaches should be developed in order to fit this specific environment (Hoskisson et al., 2005).

First, foreign firms that want to internationalize in new markets need to learn about the culture and how to operate in an institutionally constrained environment (Luo and Peng, 1999). New markets are usually markets with a high psychic distance, so companies need to accumulate knowledge before being fully involved. For this reason, because of the lack of market knowledge, SME companies tend to delegate important functions to their distributors: from physical distribution of products to customer service, from promotion to warranties, from selecting retailers to communication. The more functions are delegated, the more is the loss of control over brands and products.

A basic assumption in internationalization process models, as the Uppsala model describes, is that the next step after indirect exports should be operating in the foreign market with a more involved presence, thanks to the rise of experiential knowledge, that is, all types of knowledge that firms accumulate by being active in foreign markets and implying the ability to search, analyse and act on international business issues in local markets (Blomstermo et al., 2004). For big companies, like MNEs, establishing subsidiaries in foreign new markets, it has been accepted that knowledge may derive from sources that are internal – that is, transferred from a subsidiary to other MNE units – or external – which means that firms may acquire knowledge from interaction with external parties (Asmussen et al., 2011).

We can argue that, for SMEs, the latter is often the only way to get to know the foreign markets, since frequently they do not have sufficient subsidiaries to refer to, so the learning process is mediated by distributors that help firms understand the local market (Checchinato, 2011). However, in new markets this source could be more difficult to use because the transfer of knowledge between parties is hard due to the great social and cultural distance and high uncertainty (Jansson and Sandberg, 2008). This large distance could enhance the cost of knowledge transfer since the effort of encoding and decoding information is greater. A weak relationship between parties (i.e. seller and distributor/agent) and tacit knowledge are the main problems.

Problems relating to internationalization can be split between initial and ongoing problems. Usually, lack of experience and knowledge or lack of adequate training for customers are typical of initial problems (Neupert et al., 2006), but they could also become typical ongoing problems if firms do not develop their own experience. This problem is particularly crucial for SMEs because of their internationalization process, usually based on indirect exports, even in the advanced phase of internationalization.

The problem of the 'non-acquainted market', usually referring to consumers, could also be applied to the distributor–firm relationship, since also distributors do not have enough market knowledge to sell the products properly to consumers. Moreover, the accumulation of knowledge is important in order to understand and penetrate the market, but in new markets firms have to cope with a type of knowledge that is mainly tacit. This knowledge is not codified, structured or accessible to people other than the individuals originating it (Leonard and

Sensiper, 1998), and it is hard to transfer between parties. Activities and initiatives aimed at cooperating and establishing a dialogue with intermediaries are of major importance, especially in new markets having a high-context culture (Hall, 1976).

So firms are faced with a double problem of knowledge: on one hand, intermediaries do not have experiential knowledge to sell foreign products properly, and on the other hand, due to the actors' expertise, economic uncertainty, cultural distance and fast moving conditions, the context of new markets does not allow firms to accumulate knowledge under the same conditions (time, effort, resources) as in traditional markets.

The first step in internationalization is selecting the country to enter. Sometimes, even if a country seems to have a lot of potential, companies fail and exit the market. Two main alternative approaches are followed when companies do not reach their objectives: (a) exiting the market; or (b) changing distributors or distribution system. Usually, companies that select a particular country after market research continue to operate in the market, supporting the distributor(s) or changing them if there is a lack of trust. As an alternative, they develop their own direct chain of stores.

The Chinese market, for example, represents a new opportunity for MNEs and SMEs that implement internationalization strategies. However, its penetration requires more time compared to other markets, due to a different business approach and consumer behaviour patterns, therefore success may come years after the initial market entry. One of the reasons is related to the culture; in fact doing business requires a lot of meetings and negotiation, and sometimes managers state that 'it is not easy to understand if they are interested in our products', which is typical of a high-context culture. Moreover, 'we have to create a to-do list in order to cooperate with them'. Choosing the right distributors in China is also important because of the *guanxi*, that is, the personal relationships of the distributor. Describing its business in the Chinese market, a pressure washer company's manager highlighted the importance of their distributor's relations, since in this market working with a distributor that has good *guanxi* can 'open a lot of customers' doors'.

Since operating in new, culturally distant markets is usually different from doing business in the domestic market, due to specific cultural norms and consumption habits, distributors are expected to help companies to understand the market. Even if the distributor is a leading firm in the market, it does not mean that it has the necessary knowledge to push a specific foreign product in the market because of the new market characteristics.

Even if the distributor is a key partner in the diffusion of products, this does not mean that they have the necessary knowledge to promote a specific article properly that is new to that specific market. Often distributors in new markets have the following characteristics: (a) they do not have sufficient knowledge of consumer expectations and behaviour with respect to new categories of products from abroad, as the offer is unknown for that market and they have not accumulated sufficient specific skills; (b) they often have a long waiting list of foreign brands wishing to enter their market, and they are therefore focused on short-term results (if a brand/product does not enjoy quick success, they replace it by 'fishing' from the waiting list, looking for a producer that leads to greater results) rather than on the creation of possible results in the medium–long term, which would require investment in knowledge of the market and an increase in the value of the brand; (c) their marketing capabilities are under development and are not yet sophisticated enough for complex products and usage behaviours.

Often the distributor is not sufficiently informed on the specific market niche at which the offer of the SME (or MMNE) is aimed, it is often not even interested in creating a brand image in the foreign company, and it does not follow a long-term perspective. Its business is based on a shelf strategy, that is, it tends to accurately place the product on the shelves and wait for it to demonstrate its ability to sell out. That is, it implements an opportunistic strategy of low investment on the one hand, and on the other hand to manage only the sales and not the marketing aspects; in other words, it focuses on the themes that dominate the most. The management of the shelf is, in fact, their main competence, not the management of marketing. This requires a thorough knowledge of market mechanisms, the analysis and understanding of consumer behaviour, the study of competitors' strategies, as well as brand value development actions in a strategic partnership with the manufacturer.

This situation can create a big divide between the orientations, expectations and strategies of the producer and the importer. While the producer company is focused on constantly improving its offer following a medium–long time horizon, the importer is focused on finding the 'right' product among the huge number of offers they can access, following a short time horizon. The importer is not interested in knowing *why* the product is bought, but only *how many* products can be easily sold, reducing costs and increasing short-term profit. Therefore, the distributor asks the producer to provide all the marketing tools needed to increase the sales level. But the best the producer can do, if it is an SME having no knowledge of the market, is to replicate marketing strategies used in other countries, hoping to be effective in an unknown situation.

Often we even get the paradox of seeking the 'competence of the incompetent', that is, the request by the importer to be advised on which marketing policies to adopt on the market by the incoming company, leveraging its knowledge of the product and on experience in other markets, hoping that a process of replicating previous experience will solve the problem. This is clearly paradoxical, since the local market, being culturally and historically distant, has completely different specific characteristics, extraneous to the knowledge of the incoming company. In a reciprocal way, the company asks the importer, who is structurally inexperienced, for advice on the marketing policies to be adopted, as it normally does in its traditional export markets. Each side expects from the other a competence that it does not possess.

Despite the fact that the Uppsala model can explain the behaviour of MNEs in their internationalization process, the distribution strategy in a new market that is culturally different and non-acquainted cannot be the same for MNEs and MMNEs. Big companies such as MNEs, having enough resources to implement direct distribution, and increasing their presence in the market through direct investments, and MMNEs, facing a constant lack of resources in the internationalization process, are not playing the same game. They need to apply a different approach. The conditions of the new markets force SMEs to enter their internationalization age, moving from the traditional export approach in a different way. This means that the traditional strategy, focused on indirect exports as a first step, is transformed by many MMNEs into a permanent approach to international markets. It cannot work in new markets without adaptation. This is due to the sum of the different distances (cultural, geographical, structural, historical, experiential, etc.) between the origin and the destination markets. Actually, the importers are not able to play the expected role of cultural mediators, because of lack of knowledge and experience.

The solution that MMNEs implement is the following: (a) they keep the importer with the key role of distribution as a relationship maker, contacting and supplying the distributors and retailers throughout the country, managing the shelves and the product availability in the shops; (b) they create a local small direct marketing structure (1–2 managers) in charge of understanding the market, the consumer behaviour, the use of the product, and the potential opportunities for the company. This new structure also contributes to the strategy of collaboration between company and importer, suggesting market solutions, product improvement and adaptation, communication strategies, and new actions both to the company headquarters and to the importers. Therefore, the decision they take is to create a parallel small structure in charge of analysing the market, based on simultaneous direct (marketing manager) and indirect (exporter) presence, assigning different and complementary roles to the two parts.

## 12.2    HOW TO CHOOSE DISTRIBUTORS IN DIFFERENT CULTURAL CONTEXTS

One method that is proposed by some scholars (Cateora and Graham, 1993; Usunier and Lee, 2013) is to check a list of characteristics to be taken in account when making distribution choices on entering a new foreign market. The list of ten criteria can be the following:

- *Consumers and their characteristics.* Some segments of customers can be more attracted by a foreign product for several reasons, such as image, innovation, safeness, country of origin and so on. They can be different compared to the traditional customers, so they can be reached using specific distribution channels.
- *Purchase Culture.* The way people buy is deeply rooted in the culture of a country. In some cultures, people prefer to buy in street markets, in other online, in others in big supermarkets or small neighbourhood shops. People may be wary of new distribution formats or, conversely, they are attracted by innovation.
- *Product Image.* There should be coherence between the image of the product and the image of the distributor or retailer. In some situations direct investment is required. This is the case, for example, of luxury products. In other situations, customers may prefer a local distributor for their reputation for choosing and selecting quality products.
- *Investment.* This concerns the financial resources that are necessary to start and maintain a channel, or to relate to an existing one in a distant market.
- *Cost.* This concerns the trade margins and the overhead costs. It depends on the bargaining power of the company in relation to the distributor, the wholesalers, and the retailer chains.
- *Competition.* Competition can influence the choice of the company on two sides: if the company's offer has obvious advantages for the consumer that are easily understood by comparison with competitors (for example the price), the company can choose to be on the same shelf, in order to facilitate comparison. If the company's product has more

complex benefits that should be explained by the retailer, it can choose an exclusive channel, avoiding price comparison.

- *Coverage.* Some distributors, such as retail chains, can cover the entire market, having outlets in all cities and in all regions or provinces of the country. Other chains may only partially cover the market and the company would have to use several distributors. In some large countries like China, coverage could be achieved by using many distributors. Obviously a large number of distributors creates complexity in the distribution system. In some cases the company should offer different trading margin conditions, in some areas there may be overlapping of distributors, and so on.
- *Control.* The ideal situation for the best control of distribution is one in which the company creates its own distribution network. For MMNEs this is not easy, because this solution is the most expensive. Control can rely on rigorous and carefully drafted contracts, but this is only possible when contracts are fully respected; this is not always the case in new emerging markets with different business cultures, based on relationships rather than on paper. Another way is to create a team of sales inspectors, local or expatriate, who constantly monitor the commercial behaviour of distributors. In other cases, a hybrid solution can be developed between local distributors (for sales) and direct managers (for sales promotion and marketing actions).
- *Knowledge.* This concerns the knowledge of the distributor about the brand, the products, the story of the company and so on. It can be really important in choosing the retailers, especially for complex products that should be explained and narrated to the consumers.
- *Collaborative attitude.* A collaborative attitude is extremely important for a long-term relationship between a company and its distributors, especially in a different cultural context, because new solutions and adaptations should be continuously developed by both sides. The company and distributors should actively participate in the distribution strategy, finding and implementing creative innovation in distribution formats, services, assortments, customer relationships, and so on.

In some countries, opportunities for international retail expansion may be directly related to identifying an appropriate target market whose receptiveness to foreign retailers may be based upon tastes and preferences for apparel as defined by demographic characteristics, such as age or employment status (Eckman et al., 2015).

Frequent and bi-directional communication between companies and distributors of different countries can develop trust and satisfaction, which in turn facilitate joint action between them. It must be understood that joint action between cross-border buyers and sellers is not a direct result of communication between them but is rather fully mediated through trust and satisfaction. However, high psychic distance between buyers and sellers negatively moderates the relationship between communication facets and trust and satisfaction.

MMNE firms engaged in more joint action with their sellers than MNEs. It is likely that smaller firms may be able to make decisions on issues such as joint action faster and more efficiently given the small number of managers or key decision makers in such firms. It is also plausible that smaller firms will engage in more joint action than larger firms because, given their limited resources, smaller firms should gain more from joint action than acting alone on important marketing issues (Johnston et al., 2012).

With regard to leadership styles and international channel management practices, it can be asserted that cultures are seemingly resistant to change and that cultural differences require adaptation of management practices. Cultural variations across nations may well require adaptation of channel leadership styles in different countries. The problem of successfully managing international distribution channel partners in a cross-cultural context can be discussed using the Hofstede model.

In an individualistic and male-oriented society, channel partners are likely to emphasize their own self-interest, individual achievement, success and power; a major concern for other channel partners and the entire channel's success is not particularly paramount. These characteristics may well induce intense disagreements and conflict, particularly if there is discordance among channel partners' goals, policies and programmes. Under such conditions, a directive leadership style from the channel leader could clarify for channel partners what they need to do to be successful.

If a society exhibits weak uncertainty avoidance, a comfortable, friendly, collaborative environment (participative leadership) may seemingly afford channel partners the opportunity to deal with potential conflict through interpersonal, relational efforts. In collectivist societies, the focus is generally on group interests, group decision making, and group loyalty. There is an expectation of having the group determine what, how and when a task is accomplished. Thus, individuals in such a culture conceivably expect that group members (channel partners in this case) work together (Mehta et al., 2010).

Furthermore, if the society is also relatively low in power distance, participation in decision making is likely to be encouraged, which is consistent with a participative leadership style. Moreover, support, caring and concern, friendliness, and respect are likely to emerge in such instances, which are redolent of supportive leadership styles. Moreover, cultures that score clearly on the feminine side place emphasis on equity and people's welfare – issues compatible with both participative and supportive leadership styles. According to different cultural contexts, the impact of participative and supportive leadership vis-à-vis directive leadership when there is conflict among international distribution channel partners should be carefully monitored.

Despite the existence of formal contracts in the company–distributor relationships, unexpected litigated relationship dissolution occurs. This indicates that formal contracts may be limited in their capacity to regulate international distribution relationships. More importantly, this indicates that formal contracts may provide an incomplete safeguard against unexpected litigated relationship dissolution, thus necessitating the development of informal contract elements, such as socialization, relational norms, cultural understanding and so forth, in an international distribution relationship (Zhang et al., 2006).

## 12.3     MANAGING THE SALES FORCE IN DIFFERENT CULTURAL CONTEXTS

The sales force is strongly influenced by cultural diversity, as it must develop positive relationships with local distributors and consumers, who can have very different attitudes from those normally involved in the company's traditional markets.

Based on cross-cultural research, it is clear that multinational corporations (MNEs) are more likely to achieve success when expanding operations to new global markets by adjusting business strategies to fit the cultural norms of other countries (Klein, 2004). By extension, these cultural differences should be considered as an MNE builds a global sales force. If an MNE is recruiting, training and motivating a sales force to operate in markets separate from their country-of-origin, it needs to recognize that the salesperson attributes that are positively related to job performance may differ by country based on cross-cultural differences. More specifically, the impact of motivation on salesperson performance may differ by culture.

People from similar cultures tend to make decisions similarly but are likely to be surprised when people from another culture come to a completely different decision even when presented with the same information. Mismatched views with individuals from other cultures can create workplace ambiguity, confusion and conflict.

Klein (2004) proposed a cultural lens model with eight dimensions. The eight dimensions include: time horizon; achievement vs. relationship; mastery vs. fatalism; tolerance for uncertainty; power distance; hypothetical vs. concrete reasoning; attribution; and differentiation vs. dialectical reasoning. Some of those are really similar to Hofstede's cultural factors, particularly tolerance for uncertainty, power distance, and achievement vs. relationship, which can be considered very close to individualism–collectivism.

In particular, the dimension of *achievement vs. relationship* focuses on differences in orientation and cognitive framework (Klein, 2004). Success-oriented cultures are driven by the goal of completing a task at hand and individuals are judged on their merits (Markus and Kitayama, 1991). In these cultures, tasks are the central focus of interactions. These cultures push for change at a faster pace and aim to fulfil the required tasks above all else (Klein, 2004). Results-oriented salespeople compete with each other to achieve the best performance in a virtual, and several times even real, race. Better performances lead to career advancement.

*Relationship-oriented* cultures, however, focus on developing relationships, networks and/or affiliations with others, and individuals from these cultures are judged by their connections. In these cultures, cultivating relationships with others is the focus of interactions. These cultures allow change to happen at its own pace and focus on helping other people as a primary goal. Salespeople develop many relationships with customers and other salespeople. Achieving better group results is a common goal, and collaboration is an important value. Career advancement depends on the joint decision of the group. Sometimes this attitude favours the most empathetic person, not the best leader.

Salespeople from relationship-oriented locations (i.e. Asia) will be more motivated by the need for affiliation than those from achievement-oriented locations (i.e. Europe, Australia, South Africa and North America). Salespeople in countries with lower *power distance* are more likely to find positions of power and authority much more attainable than in locations with high-power distance. As such, we believe that individuals in low-power distance countries are more likely to be driven by power as a motivator, as it is something achievable.

Results from some research (Moberg and Leasher, 2011) found significantly higher levels of need for achievement and power in Western salespeople than Eastern salespeople. However, the results found significantly higher levels of need for relationships in Western salespeople, too, which is contrary to the findings in previous cross-cultural research. While it is instructive to confirm that a typical salesperson in a Western culture exhibits high levels of need for achievement and power, finding that Western salespeople also exhibit a higher need for relationships merits closer attention, as it is an interesting new trend for low context culture people such as North American and Australian salespeople.

Marketing has maybe entered a new era in which we have evolved from a traditional, product-centric, transaction-based marketing approach to a service-oriented and relationship-based approach where buyers and sellers work together to co-create value (Vargo and Lusch, 2004, 2008). It is a trend that leads to behaviours typical of a high context culture.

When a Western-based MNE or MMNE decides to enter a new market, there are two basic choices available in the development of the sales force. One is to send 'expatriate' salespeople from the home country to the new market and the other is to hire local salespeople to call on buyers from the same culture. When the culture of the new market is clearly different from the host country, a lack of sensitivity to the cultural differences during the selling process often leads to failure (Fang, 1999; Horwitz et al., 2008). While a sales manager should clearly consider the cultural similarities and differences that exist in a new market, it is important to remember that individual differences in motivation exist within every culture.

It would be a mistake for a 'Western' sales manager building a sales force in an 'Eastern' market to ignore the possibility of hiring salespeople from the 'Eastern' market for a business development position. Finding an 'Eastern' salesperson with motivations more typical of a 'Western' salesperson but who also possesses a profound understanding of the 'Eastern' culture could be a sales force development strategy that differentiates one firm from another.

A sales manager faced with the task of developing a global sales force is more likely to succeed in new markets if those salespeople assigned to a new market possess motivation similar to the buyers they will be negotiating with during the sales process. The need to match the motivation of salespeople to the buyers' home country motivational norms, or at least to demonstrate an awareness and cultural sensitivity of those differences, should hold true whether expatriate or local salespeople are hired. In any case, it is easier for a salesperson to understand and acquire the values of the corporate culture, rather than to understand and behave consistently with a local culture that is very different from that of his/her country of origin. This means that in international sales force recruitment, local people should be preferred over expats.

Furthermore, cultural differences influence the typical aspects of sales management (Collesei and Vescovi, 1999) which concern:

- *Recruitment, selection and training.* As already pointed out, the greater the cultural distance, the more recruiting should favour the local sales force. In the selection, in addition to the traditional aspects relating to the characteristics of the seller and the company's sales objectives, the ability of candidates to interact with the company and share its values must be taken into account, especially if they come from culturally distant countries. Training must be carried out according to a process that also takes into account the cultural context of the new sellers and not just the corporate objectives.

- *Territory*. The ethnocentric tendency to consider the country of destination uniformly must be avoided. There are almost always regional subcultures that require attention and adaptation to build positive sales relationships. In some large countries, the language may also be different. These aspects are evident for example in China, in the United States and in India, but also in Europe, such as in Belgium, Spain and Switzerland. The sales territory must therefore be studied not only on a quantitative (e.g. number of customers) or geographic (distances, difficulty in moving, etc.) basis, but also on the basis of cultural coherence.

- *Motivation and management*. Previously, cultural differences in sales force motivation were discussed based on power distance and achievement vs. relationship. It should be remembered that the aspects of motivation and relationship in personnel management must always be compared with the cultural values of the people involved. An international company cannot standardize these aspects.

- *Control*. Control of the sales force systems varies according to individual or collective cultures. While in the former, tools relating to the efficiency of the resources employed and the effectiveness of individual performance are generally used, in the latter social control is also implemented on the behaviour of individual sellers, since the entire sales force, as a group, considers itself responsible for results obtained and individual opportunistic behaviours will not be acceptable.

- *Salary*. The salary of the sales force traditionally has a different structure from other company salaries. In fact, it is always composed of a fixed part and a variable part commensurate with the results obtained. The weight of each of the two parts changes with respect to the type of market, the duration of the sales time, the type of approach required by the company, and the conditions in which the competition operates. To these aspects must be added the logic of fiscal, competitive and cultural diversity in international markets. If the remuneration structure is different for the same company in Italy, Germany and France, where the cultural aspects are very similar, even if different, it is conceivable that the differences will increase as cultural diversity increases. For the company, this poses a question of correctness in the treatment of personnel that is not easy to solve.

In conclusion, the management of the sales force must be analysed from the point of view of cultural diversity, seeking a balance that does not create excessive disparities in the international context of the company, which would end up creating internal conflict. Once again, it is a question of combining the corporate culture and the cultures of the markets in which the company operates.

# 13
# Cross-cultural marketing communication

One of the most difficult choices that multinational corporations face is deciding whether to run the same marketing campaign globally or to customize it to the local taste in different countries. In many cases, companies develop their marketing strategy in one country and then they 'mirror' the campaign in other countries. After that they are frequently forced to check the disaster created by globalizing the same strategy in other countries, instead of trying to discover what would work best in each market (Banerjee et al., 2009). This often leads to ineffective marketing campaigns and damaged reputations. As new global markets emerge, and existing markets become increasingly segmented along ethnic or subcultural lines, the need to market effectively to consumers who have different cultural values has never been more important. Thus, it is no surprise that in the last decade or so, culture has rapidly emerged as a central focus of research in consumer behaviour (Shavitt et al., 2009).

Analysing the cross-cultural content of advertisements can provide valuable evidence of distinctions in cultural values. For example, American advertisers often assume that consumer brand learning precedes other marketing effects, such as brand liking and buying. Therefore, advertisements that attempt to teach the consumer about the brand are typical in the United States. Conversely, the typical goal of advertising in Japan looks very different. There, the ads tend to focus on 'making friends' with the audience and showing that the company understands their feelings. The assumption is that consumers will shop once they become familiar with the company and have a sense of trust. Since Japan, Korea and other Pacific countries are collectivist cultures that tend to have implicit and indirect communication practices (Triandis, 1995), the mood and tone of advertisements in these countries will be especially important in establishing good feelings towards the advertiser. Ads in Japan and Korea rely more on symbolism, humour and aesthetics and less on direct approaches such as brand comparisons (Shavitt et al., 2009). Ads can be just as informative about the brand across cultures. It is the type of appeal that will vary. For example, an analysis of magazine ad content revealed that ads in Korea are more focused on family well-being, interdependence, group goals and harmony, while being less focused on self-improvement, ambition, personal goals, independence and individuality. However, the cross-cultural emphasis on communication strategy cannot ignore the type of product. For example, some scholars have compared high and low context cultures. Their results indicated that consumers from low-context cultures preferred commercials with high levels of information. Others have examined cross-cultural differences in advertising effectiveness along the individualistic/collectivistic dimension. Their findings suggest that advertisements that describe norms and roles consistent with local cultural values are more effective than advertisements that don't (Luna and Forquer Gupta, 2001).

Finally, it is important to note that, in countries experiencing rapid economic growth, advertising content does not necessarily reflect existing cultural values, instead promoting new, aspirational values such as individuality and modernity. For instance, in China, in recent years, Westernized ad appeals are increasingly common. Appeals to youth/modernity, individuality/independence, and technology are especially salient in Chinese advertisements that target the younger generation (Zhang and Shavitt, 2003).

## 13.1    COMMUNICATION TOOLS AND LOCAL CULTURE

The communication tools, media and vehicles most used in different countries are different. The media used in the USA, Europe, China and Japan are very different, and this certainly affects the characteristics and strategies of marketing communication. Furthermore, for example, in Europe the situation is quite homogeneous compared to other non-European countries, but it remains diversified due to the different habits, technological availability, cultural attitudes and laws in the different countries (see Table 13.1).

For example, television advertising is more widespread in some countries such as Italy and Spain, due to the history of television development in those countries, while in others, such as Germany, there are laws restricting the use of advertising in newspapers, in France use of the web outdoors is more widespread than elsewhere, and in the UK web advertising is used more frequently. In general, the trend is towards an increasingly accentuated use of social media and web communication, accelerated by the passage on web platforms of all newspapers and magazines, as well as TV on demand (Table 13.1).

Table 13.1  Media expenditure in Europe 2017 (Big 5 countries)

| Country | TV | Radio | Press | Web | Out of Home | Cinema |
|---------|------|-------|-------|------|-------------|--------|
| France  | 27.5% | 5.8% | 17.7% | 38.4% | 9.9% | 0.8% |
| Germany | 23.5% | 4.0% | 32.1% | 33.9% | 5.9% | 0.5% |
| Italy   | 46.9% | 5.0% | 13.2% | 31.8% | 2.9% | 0.3% |
| Spain   | 38.8% | 8.4% | 15.2% | 31.0% | 5.9% | 0.6% |
| UK      | 23.1% | 3.0% | 9.1% | 58.2% | 5.4% | 1.2% |

LaBarbera et al. (1998) document memory recall to be higher if it is associated with more intensive visual imagery activity rather than under conditions that are believed to be less imagery stimulating. Visual imagery creates multiple cues in human memory, and multiple retrieval processes associated with these cues increase the probability of recall. The results of some studies (Dobni and Zinkhan, 1990; Burns et al., 1993) demonstrate positive relationships between various dimensions of imagery (vividness, concrete vs. abstract wording, instructions vs. no instructions to imagine, etc.) and the subsequent advertising effects (attitude toward the ad, attitude toward the brand, intention to buy, etc.). Cultural environment has a significant influence on international marketing communications strategy and corresponding choice of brand claim recall evoking communication tools.

The need for image processing appears to be a cultural phenomenon influenced by the country's traditions, its media habits and the dominant lifestyle. Strong cultural predisposition to reading books and newspapers creates less need for viewing, while media habits oriented to watching TV and reading colourful magazines create image-based information processing models. The links evoked by the images result in higher product attribute recall capabilities for consumers from image-intensive multimedia environments. Conversely, consumers from reading-intensive environments, such as Russia, are more likely to process textual informa-tion rather than images contained in the ad. From a managerial point of view, investment in image-intensive advertising will not produce the same return for several international markets (Mikhailitchenko et al., 2009).

Another aspect that differs in many countries in the way of communication concerns the possibility or not of using comparative advertising. In some countries this is prohibited, while in others it is not customary as it is considered non-positive, especially if it is direct. Actually, there are different levels of comparative advertisements. For example, some ads compare competing brands and make comparisons on more than one attribute (direct comparative advertising) while others choose to implement a 'leading brand' approach without naming the compared brand (indirect comparative advertising). These comparisons are often framed in a negative way to portray the inferiority of a competitor rather than only the superiority of the sponsor (Sorescu and Gelb, 2000). Comparative ads are more effective in low-context communication cultures than in high-context communication cultures, in higher persuasion effect. Indirect comparative ads are more effective than direct comparative ads in high-context communication cultures (Shao et al., 2004).

## 13.2 ADAPTING COMMUNICATION APPEALS TO CULTURAL VALUES

Advertising has developed into particular systems of meaning transfers. The meaning transfers are culturally defined and vary frequently from country to country or even from area to area within a (large) country. Any advertising that does not tap into language differences or that contains a different set of symbolic references, such as myths, history, humour and arts, cannot finally utilize the designed meaning transfer.

The cultural concept of high- versus low-context cultures as well as the cultural dimension of individualism/collectivism, which are used to characterize the various nations, prove to be useful in explaining cultural differences in the perception and evaluation of the advertise-ments. Therefore, advertisers targeting Chinese consumers, for example, should pay special attention to the context of the ad as it plays a more important role in the acceptance of the ad and the brand than in Germany, being a low-context culture. If advertisers want an advertise-ment to be considered informative in Germany, it should contain objective, straightforward information (Chan et al., 2007).

International advertisers should note the differences between communications styles in high-context cultures and low-context cultures. Messages constructed by writers from low-context cultures may be difficult to understand in high-context cultures because they omit essential contextual materials. According to Muller (2011), low-context cultures (e.g., Switzerland, Germany, Scandinavia and UK) place high value on words, and communications are encouraged to be direct, unambiguous and exact, while high-context cultures (e.g., Japan, China, and Arab countries) prefer subtle and implicit messages. Consistently, the direct or hard sell approach, so common in American advertising, seems to leave the Japanese cold.

Advertising, therefore, can follow multiple ways of communicating depending on the content it wants to convey, in a manner consistent with the cultural values of the community to which it is addressed.

## Sex Appeal

As a major technique in advertising, *sex appeal* (the appearance of nudity and the use of sexual attractiveness or suggestiveness) has been widely used in mainstream consumer advertising in most European countries. As a major advertising technique, sex appeal has often featured in a brand's international advertising campaign. However, several key questions regarding the use of sex appeal in international advertising remain unclear. For example, can sex appeal be adopted in different cultures? Does sex appeal affect different types of advertising measures (e.g. brand or ad attitude) to the same degree in different cultures? To answer these questions, it is necessary to compare consumer responses to sex appeal advertising in the cross-cultural context (Liu et al., 2009).

First, the main purpose of using sex appeal is to attract attention. Second, using sex appeal in an ad may also help the audience remember the ad better. Third, sex appeal may serve in advertising to evoke emotional responses, such as arousal, excitement or even lust, which in turn can create stimulation and desire for the product.

However, there are some problems associated with the use of sex appeal (Judd and Alexander, 1983). First, sexual content may be eye-catching and entertaining, but it may distract the viewer from the main message and hence result in a reduction of recognition and recall. Second, the effectiveness of sex appeal also depends on its appropriateness to the advertised product. Third, sex appeal can be perceived as unacceptable in some cultures. For example, people from high-context cultures often find direct and explicit ads pushy and aggressive, whereas those from low-context cultures often find these ads informative and persuasive (Rossman, 1994).

Sex appeal ads these days are often illustrative and stimulating; thus, consumers in an individualistic society may respond more favourably to a sex appeal ad than consumers in a collectivistic society. Furthermore, in a high-context culture, people prefer implicit communication rather than explicit communication. Since sex appeal ads are becoming increasingly more explicit, consumers in a high-context culture may have less favourable attitudes towards a sex appeal ad than consumers in a low-context culture. However, this assumption was challenged by some studies, in which they found that the high-context French audience is more receptive to the use of sex appeal in advertising, whereas the more direct, low-context US audience is more likely to interpret the use of sex appeal in advertising as risqué (Biswas et al., 1992). In fact, cross-cultural analysis should be done carefully, because any simplistic explanation could be wrong. The crossing and interference of many different values is the main condition. Generalization is dangerous.

## Message Position

The *locations* of messages can increase the effectiveness of advertising alongside advertising strategies, themes or execution. Therefore, the order of content within a unit of advertising needs to be considered to further increase efficiency and effectiveness in balancing global integration and local responsiveness. Advertising effectiveness (i.e., attitude toward the product) is enhanced when the content order and culture match.

Noguchi et al. (2014) tested the existence/absence of the primacy effect across cultures in the formation of impressions. They argued that cultural differences in social cognition such as thinking styles (analytic versus holistic) caused a stronger primacy effect in information processing among Americans, while neither a primacy effect nor a recency effect was found among the Japanese. Indeed, American respondents were found to weigh initial information more heavily and to be less likely to change their first impression, whereas Japanese participants were found to be more sensitive to subsequent information. Specifically, Japanese participants paid attention to the field as a whole (holistic thinking), and to the interactions between the communication objects evenly and uniformly. Then, they further analysed these spread-out data comprehensively.

Holistic thinking is defined as 'involving an orientation to the context or field as a whole, including attention to relationships between a focal object and the field, and a preference for explaining and predicting events on the basis of such relationships'. Analytic thinking 'involves a detachment of the object from its context, a tendency to focus on attributes of the object to assign it to categories, and a preference for using rules about the categories to explain and predict the object's behaviour' (Nisbett et al., 2001). According to Hall (1976), low-context communication reflects an analytic thinking style and is used predominantly in individualistic cultures. Meanwhile, high-context communication reflects a holistic thinking style and is used predominantly in collectivistic cultures.

Thus, direct and up-front messages about the product in advertising can be considered an effective communication approach for low-context cultures, whereas they tend to be blind to relationships among the presented objects. Correspondingly, they may see the pictorial sequence of the final product (for example, orange juice) presented first and the major ingredient (e.g., oranges) later in advertising as appropriate, desirable, and thus convincing. This particular order should cultivate more favourable responses toward the advertising as well as the product because it matches their cognitive thinking style. In contrast, high-context cultures, who are holistic thinker people, will try to connect and integrate content – both visual information and verbal cues – and tend to perceive the entire advertisement as a part–whole relationship among elements. Therefore, high-context cultures may more easily integrate two pieces of information and understand the presented ingredient as materials and thus part of the product when elements are presented chronologically in product production (i.e., an ingredient first and the product made with it later). This particular order may be perceived as more natural, logical and satisfying by holistic thinkers.

The results of some studies (Jang and Shin, 2019) showed that the fit effect between content order and the high context culture led to a more favourable product attitude when the ingredient was presented earlier than the final product within a unit of advertising. This particular layout of advertising content in a unit mirrored how this culture typically displays meaningful phrases in cognition and communications, and thus was readily acceptable and liked. How to design the content in a unit of advertising should be researched seriously, in addition to the selections of advertising themes and appeals, before airing or publishing advertising in an international context. Content order may increase acceptance of the stories that advertisers are trying to convey. Culturally congruent and thus local-market-serving advertising can be designed and implemented to further increase advertising effectiveness cross-nationally. For example, in a country with a more holistic orientation, an advertising layout featuring high-quality materials shown first, clean and automated production facilities next, and finally the product being advertised would be most effective as the sequential flow of a commercial. In contrast, showing an image of the product with its functionalities emphasized would be more effective in markets with analytic-oriented consumers.

In collectivistic countries advertising audiences favour indirect communication approaches that are at the same time creative and informative, such as information-dominant humorous ads. For instance, Korean collectivistic advertisers initially try to build friendly relationships with potential customers through entertaining creative devices. Only when consumers feel that the enterprise is reliable do Korean advertisers provide information about the advertised brand. Furthermore, in Japanese TV ad executions, brand names are mentioned at a later stage than in US ads. The first part of the advertisement tries to gain the audience's trust, while the second part highlights brand benefits (Hatzithomas et al., 2011).

## Message Likeability

There are different *likeability* responses to standardized advertisements across the cultures, even in Europe. For example, three countries have been studied representing a Northern (Norway), Central (Germany), and Southern (Italy) European culture. People have judged two of Benetton's standardized provocative advertisements (Angel and Devil, HIV positive). Despite the fact that all three cultures showed likeability to both the advertisements, the reasons were different. In some cases, the likeability was based on the situation, in others on colours, and in other cases it was based on the people/models of the advertisement (Polegato and Bjerke, 2009).

Cross-cultural differences were found in overall likeability and likeability of three of four ad elements, particularly between respondents in Germany and Italy. There were also cross-cultural differences in ad elements that explained liking for each advertisement and in the strength of their explanatory power. The variable that had by far the most explanatory power was the likeability of the situation, followed by likeability of the colours, and lastly by likeability of the people/models. The logo had no explanatory power for overall likeability of any of the advertisements. The findings of the study indicate that there are different perceptions across cultures when it comes to liking for print advertisements for a global brand targeted towards young people and communicating about important societal issues (such as racism) and values (such as social justice), which are the core of advertising messages. Indeed, the findings call into question the existence of a homogeneous global youth segment for this product category and/or brand considering the common judgement, even if not exactly for the same reasons. A plausible explanation seems to lie in differences in cultural values. Different cultural contexts base the acceptability and the likeability of a message on the society values, styles of communication, local meaning of the symbols used and so on. Standardized communication represents an economic solution, and reduces costs and complexity, but does not fit perfectly with local sentiment, even in neighbouring cultures.

## Style of Advertising

Europe has long been suggested to be a possible theatre for a standardized *style of advertising*, since levels of economic development are similar, advertising industry infrastructures are relatively homogeneous, and the development of the European Union is facilitating a harmonization of laws and regulations. However, important differences still exist.

The comparison of advertising style between France and the UK presents low similarity. In France, the most common advertising style is 'egotistical', then comes 'funny' and 'catalogue', describing the features of the products using unadorned facts. In the UK, on the other hand, 'funny' is the prevailing advertising style, followed by 'catalogue'. 'Practical' (with straightforward information) is in third position. British viewers expect not only honest but also entertaining advertising. The French also expect to be entertained by advertisers, thus justifying the rank of 'funny', but value the beauty and dreamlike dimensions of advertisements above all, which explains the importance of the 'egotistical' advertising spirit in the French sample. They emphasize the luxurious aspect of the product, its social benefits or even its 'love affair' with customers. The less commonly standardized elements are obviously the text and the slogan. This is not surprising since these can easily be altered in order to respond to local expectations and in quite a cost-effective way. Text and slogan can be modified even more easily due to the fact that most international commercials use a voice-over (Whitelock and Rey, 1998).

## TV Commercials

People from low-context and high-context countries responded differently to *television commercials* with varied levels of information content, a phenomenon that could be attributed to cultural differences. Advertising messages should be congruent with values of a local culture because advertising reflects local cultural values. McCracken (2005) considered that advertising is a means of transferring meanings from a cultural context to a consumer good. Therefore, a favourable consumer attitude towards advertising is contingent upon congruence between advertising values and consumer values. People from collectivistic, high-context cultures have more positive attitudes towards TV advertising than people from individualistic, low-context cultures. Furthermore, consumers in collectivist cultures are less sceptical of advertising (Guo et al., 2012).

## Perception of Beauty

Each culture has a set of general beliefs about what constitutes *femininity and beauty*. According to Wood (1999), to be feminine in the United States is to be attractive, deferential, unaggressive, emotional, nurturing, and concerned with people and relationships. According to Hofstede (1997), in Confucian cultures femininity is associated with virtue and modesty. The script for femininity is written into a culture and is transmitted over time through family, peers, teachers and the media.

Many of the Western advertising conventions and poses for women were being transferred cross-culturally in conjunction with concepts like 'professionalism' by Western multinational advertising agencies. In an analysis of how Caucasian women are used in Japanese advertising, William O'Barr (1994) pointed out that Western models pose doing things that Japanese women would never do. He says that Caucasian women are often shown being 'sensual and willing' in Japanese advertising, and that this is merely mirroring the way women are portrayed in advertising in the West.

In a perfect world, we might expect that advertisements would be created by members of a particular society and consumed by members of the same society. However, globalization alters this process. Standardized campaigns can be created in the head offices of advertising agencies in Europe and run in foreign countries with only simple modifications, such as translated headlines. Foreign branch offices of the big multinational agencies often follow Western styles when creating campaigns. In addition, the creative people in these branch offices have often received their training in European universities or have interned in Western advertising agencies. The result is that the forms of representation, particularly of women, can take on a globalized or transnational look.

In Western societies, women may think it is mainly their bodies that get noticed by men, whereas in Asia, women may think it is their faces that are most important. Product categories differ significantly between advertising in the Western and Eastern magazines, supporting this contention. Beauty products that are aimed at improving women's hair, skin and face occupied the greatest proportion of ads in Singapore (40 per cent) and Taiwan (49 per cent), while clothing ads occupied the largest proportion of ads in the U.S. (54 per cent). Clothing is related to the body (Frith et al., 2005).

## Assertiveness

For the GLOBE model, cultural *assertiveness* reflects beliefs as to whether people are or should be encouraged to be assertive, aggressive and tough, or non-assertive, non-aggressive and tender in social relationships. Considering the Hofstede cultural factors, assertiveness can be associated to masculinity/femininity values.

The GLOBE framework identified *assertiveness* as one of nine cultural dimensions capable of describing cultural variation among a large number of countries (House et al., 2004), therefore it can be interesting in analysing how this dimension is used in advertisement.

Nike's former 'Just do it' slogan, which commanded the audience to be assertive and take control of their fitness regimen, is arguably one of the most prominent examples of an international campaign employing this appeal. With regard to advertising, provided that the assertive message is not perceived negatively (e.g. demonstrating exaggerated aggressiveness), employing assertive appeals may be an effective means of enhancing the success of a commercial. It is thus expected that advertisements perceived as assertive will be more positively evaluated than those perceived as non-assertive, regardless of the country (Terlutter et al., 2010).

In terms of advertising, the perception of assertiveness in commercial communications may be dependent upon the level of assertiveness surrounding the individual, which serves as a comparison standard for the perception of a given commercial. If the cultural environment (i.e. the society to which an individual belongs) is highly assertive and places importance on assertiveness, this level of assertiveness is likely to serve as the frame of reference. This means that in a culture with a high comparison standard regarding assertiveness, an ad designed to incorporate assertive appeal may be viewed as only mildly assertive. Conversely, in a cultural environment that is less assertive in nature, individuals have a lower reference value regarding assertiveness. In other words, a consumer socialized in an assertive environment might perceive a given advertisement as significantly less assertive than a consumer socialized in a relatively less assertive environment would evaluate that very same ad. The effectiveness of a message depends on the cultural environment in which the message is diffused. In Table 13.2, the assertiveness level of a group of countries is shown, considering how it is a real practice and a social value. The difference in score between practice and values shows how distant social values are from real practice. This means that a culture with a high assertiveness value score and a lower practice shows that social value assertiveness is too high for people's will, so it can be considered negative or useless. As shown in Table 13.2, in China and Japan people consider the assertiveness value of the company to be too high, while in Austria, Germany and the United Kingdom they believe that assertiveness is more important than the level of actual social sharing. This means that advertising assertiveness in Austria, Germany and the UK can be perceived positively, while it is negative in China and Japan. In other countries, with a smaller gap, it is less important, albeit to a different extent in every country.

**Table 13.2** Assertiveness score and gap between value and practice (GLOBE)

| Country Society | Practice | Society Values | Gap |
| --- | --- | --- | --- |
| Argentina | 4.22 | 3.25 | 0.97 |
| Austria | 4.62 | 2.81 | 1.81 |
| China | 3.76 | 5.44 | −2.18 |
| France | 4.13 | 3.38 | 0.75 |
| Germany | 4.64 | 3.16 | 1.48 |
| Italy | 4.07 | 3.82 | 0.25 |
| Japan | 3.59 | 5.56 | −1.97 |
| Spain | 4.42 | 4.00 | 0.42 |
| UK | 4.15 | 3.70 | 1.81 |
| USA | 4.55 | 4.32 | 0.23 |

Advertisers employing a standardized approach in their international efforts must be aware that an ad reflecting assertive appeals may well be perceived differently from one country to the next, dependent upon the role that assertiveness plays in that particular market.

## Gender Roles

In European countries there is a different perception about *gender roles*, depending on masculinity or femininity cultures, even if the situation in the last few years has significantly progressed to a more obvious femininity culture, particularly in West Europe. Tian (2017) introduces the concept of vertical independent (masculinity) and horizontal independent (femininity) cultures in Europe, considering Great Britain in the first case and Sweden in the latter. Advertising is affected by these cultures. Tian's research suggests that men may be more likely to be in 'dominant' positions in vertical nations. Conversely, given the strong emphasis of egalitarianism in horizontal nations, gender roles may be less pronounced in a horizontal society. Although men are present in 'housework' roles within advertising from each country, men are more commonly decoded as 'leaders' in Great Britain as compared to Sweden. It appears that horizontal nations also commonly depicted fathers in the standard head-to-chest placement, while vertical nation ads reserved this solely to indicate motherhood.

When presenting fathers only in the vertical nation, fathers were always situated as breadwinners, leaders and active, which maintains the conventional notions of gender inequality. In the horizontal nation, when fathers were in single shots with a child, they were decoded as nurturing, providing a gender-reversal frame which featured a mother as leader and father as passive.

Gender roles in advertising follow the cultural values diffused in a society, therefore they should be adapted to the local shared values in order to be easily accepted, even in European countries. Obviously, a company can decide whether to propose a counterintuitive positioning, considering the target, or not. Sometimes the values shared by the target are not the same as the entire company, especially for niche segments.

## Tailored Advertising

Tailoring is an advertising strategy that is used to target consumers individually by matching messages to their personal information or preferences. Made possible by technological developments, tailoring has been broadly adopted as a component of the online advertising strategies used in different domains, including email marketing, online shopping and health recommendations.

Countries differ with respect to different cultural dimensions, even in Europe, not only in distant cultures such as Western and Eastern ones. Concerning *tailored advertising*, collectivist and masculine cultures, as well as high power distance and high uncertainty avoidance cultures may play a role in the way in which individuals perceive advertisements. Among the participants in the tailored condition, both message relevance and the favourability of the respondents' thoughts about the messages were greater than in any of the other groups. They recognized the tailored messages as such and thus perceived them as more relevant, and became more involved with and less sceptical towards them. This led them to have more positive attitudes towards the advertisements and the brand compared to more feminine, individualistic, low power distance and low uncertainty avoidance cultures. People who valued competition, achievement and success may find this aspect of the tailored advertisement appealing. Such values are embraced in masculine societies as such but not in feminine societies (Maslowska et al., 2013).

In conclusion, the goal of advertising is to persuade consumers by appealing to the values held by the target group. If advertising is not aligned with the values of the target segment, it may alienate that group by reducing consumer identification with the brand. Thus, advertising is often said to be a reflection of the dominant cultural values in a society because culturally congruent representations in advertising are expected to be more effective than non-congruent appeals. Advertising is therefore a tool for transferring cultural meaning from advertisers to consumers (Czarnecka et al., 2018).

Advertising is particularly reflective of, and dependent on, the culture in which it exists for meanings of images and words and is one of the elements of the marketing mix most influenced by cultural differences. If it is to be persuasive, advertising must be culturally congruent; that is, it should reflect cultural values held by the target group.

The fact that advertising can be standardized or localized is also a question of the product and not just of culture. The product can have a different meaning in different countries since it can also carry a symbolic value and therefore communicate it. Its perception is not alien to the values shared by a society; its role can be identified with greater difficulty, because it is complex. On the other hand, images, colours, sounds and messages are more understandably related to cultural perception.

Unfortunately, advertisers do not often have competence and knowledge of cultural diversity and tend to prefer the proposal of global solutions.

## 13.3    ONLINE AND SOCIAL MEDIA COMMUNICATION IN DIFFERENT COUNTRIES

Despite the fact that social media diffusion seems to be a global phenomenon, in different countries and cultures different social media are diffused. Sometimes it appears as a geopolitical choice; anyway, the companies should monitor the situation, which is fast moving, in order to choose the right media to communicate to the market target they want to reach.

Even more, the various social media are structurally different in their functioning and the way they are used, and the tone of voice as well as the communication complexity are very different. For example, WeChat, defused in China, is a sort of all-purpose media, including messaging, payment facility, websites, video and so on, while in Europe specialized apps are preferred for each purpose (Tables 13.3, 13.4 and 13.5).

**Table 13.3** Diffusion of instant messaging apps in Europe 2019 (Big 5 countries)

| Country | #1 | #2 | #3 |
|---|---|---|---|
| France | WhatsApp | Messenger | Instagram |
| Germany | WhatsApp | Messenger | Instagram |
| Italy | WhatsApp | Instagram | Messenger |
| Spain | WhatsApp | Instagram | Messenger |
| UK | WhatsApp | Instagram | TikTok |

**Table 13.4** Diffusion of instant messaging apps in the world, 2019

| Country | Instant messaging app |
|---|---|
| China | WeChat |
| USA | Facebook Messenger |
| India | WhatsApp |
| Brazil | WhatsApp |
| Russia | WhatsApp |

**Table 13.5** Diffusion of social networks in the world 2020 (#1 by country)

| Country | Social Network |
|---|---|
| Central Asia | Odnoklassniki |
| China | QZone |
| Iran | Instagram |
| Russia | V Kontakte |
| Rest of the World | Facebook |

Cultural differences are as relevant to online advertising as to traditional advertising. Beliefs toward advertising vary across cultures in general. There are significant differences in beliefs in attitudes towards online advertising between Chinese and European cultures. Compared with the Chinese, Europeans tend to view online advertising as more informative, credible, and less value corrupting. In general, Chinese consumers tend to have a low level of trust in the internet and online advertising. According to a survey conducted by CNNIC, only one-third of Chinese internet users expressed trust in the internet. Additionally, fraud and the lack of legal regulation of advertising in China may contribute to the low credibility of online advertising among Chinese consumers. Moreover, one's evaluation of the credibility of information and its informativeness are closely linked. Hence, less credible information is more likely to be viewed as less informative (Wang and Sun, 2010). However, the Chinese are more likely to purchase online than are Europeans. Therefore, there is a gap between attitudes and actual purchasing behaviour. This is due to infrastructural conditions making it easier or less easy to buy online (distribution system, delivery system, payments habit, etc.).

Cultural differences are important contributors to differences in consumers' attitudes and behaviours towards mobile commerce. However, the degree to which culture influences mobile advertising may be different across different cultures.

Entertainment perception impacted high-context cultures' attitudes toward mobile advertising while informativeness perception is stronger for low-context cultures. So the question now is: in the mobile advertising context, is functional value more important than emotional value, or are they equally important? In an individualistic culture as well in a low-context one, people prefer to receive explicit and direct information while in a collectivistic culture, as well as in a high-context one, people prefer to receive implicit and indirect information. Therefore, people from collectivist cultures often find direct advertisements with explicit information pushy and aggressive, whereas those from individualistic cultures often find these advertisements informative and persuasive (Shimp and Andrews, 2013). Moreover, power distance has a positive relationship with the use of status advertising appeal, but a negative relationship with the use of humility appeal (Albers-Miller and Gelb, 1996).

Consumers from high, as compared to low, uncertainty avoidance cultures are more likely to engage in information sharing or searching behaviour. A number of studies have found that uncertainty avoidance influences consumer responses to advertising strategies; for example, De Mooij and Hofstede (2011) claimed that consumers in a high uncertainty avoidance culture are more influenced by health and nutrition appeals than those in a low uncertainty avoidance culture. Based on these studies, the dimension of uncertainty avoidance would be expected to influence mobile advertising. Based on such understanding, it can be inferred that in a high uncertainty avoidance culture the perceived advertising credibility value should have a stronger influence and a better mobile advertising acceptance on consumer responses than in a low uncertainty avoidance culture (Liu et al., 2019). In Liu's research the Chinese sample (low uncertainty avoidance) had a significantly higher level of mobile advertising acceptance than their Australian (higher uncertainty avoidance) counterparts. The Chinese sample had significantly more favourable perceptions on mobile advertising's functional and emotional values than the Australian sample. However, the Australian sample perceived mobile advertising to be more credible than did the Chinese sample.

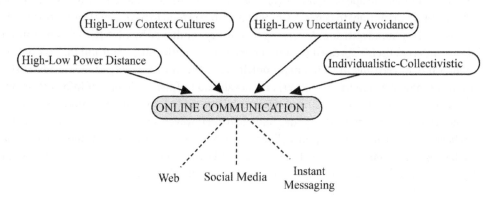

**Figure 13.1**    Online communication and culture influence

Significant differences about online advertising exist between US and some European countries. The findings of research on online magazines in France and in US (Lascu et al., 2016) suggest that, for the most part, the presence of need appeals is mostly in line with national character assumptions; for the highly individualistic US market, online advertisers are more likely to appeal to the need for prominence, attention and autonomy of this consumer, as compared to the French online magazine advertisements. Similarly, for the somewhat less individualist French consumer, online magazine advertisements are more likely to appeal to the need for guidance and safety of this consumer, as opposed to US online magazine advertisements. Also, in line with the national cultural character, French online magazine advertisements are more likely to have emotional appeal than US advertisements, although this difference is not significant. When developing advertisements for consumers in these two target markets, advertising managers would benefit if they designed their marketing communications in line with the cultural characteristics.

Actually, it would be wrong to give value to every single factor of Hofstede's model in terms of evaluating online communication, but it is necessary to evaluate a culture as a whole and the preponderance or not of some factors over others. Otherwise, we end up having a continuous contradiction because often, in different cultures, some values push towards the emotional, others towards the functional and so on. Moreover, online communication, overall through social media, is affected by a generation gap, which is reducing but to some extent is structural. New social media are a young people's phenomenon, rapidly moving, cross-cultural and constantly including many other communication tools. Young people are driving the wave and adults are following, and this is totally new in the business environment.

## 13.4 THE USE OF STEREOTYPES

Stereotypes are fixed impressions defined as 'a socially shared set of beliefs about traits that are characteristic of members of a social category' (Greenwald and Banaji, 1995) or – applied in the present context – stored beliefs about characteristics of a specific country which are socially shared. Based on this definition, a country stereotype refers to a set of 'stored beliefs about characteristics of a specific country which are socially shared' (Herz and Diamantopoulos, 2013). A country stereotype can be perceived straightforwardly by visiting the country, communicating with people from the country, and using the products made in the country, or based on some second-hand experience, such as learning about the country via mass media.

As a cognitive process, stereotyping works as a shortcut which simplifies an individual's perception of a complex environment; thus, country stereotypes help a consumer to make judgements about quality, particularly when other information cues are inaccessible or too complex to assess or when consumer expertise is low. Brand ratings and brand-related behaviour are improved when the underlying country stereotype matches the advertising execution format.

Based on the Social Adaptation Theory (Kahle, 1984) and the Theory of Cognitive Dissonance (Festinger, 1957), it is expected that a match-up between COO facets and country stereotypes will benefit advertising effectiveness. Also, product type should be taken into account in order to evaluate whether such match-up effects vary depending on different types of products. Product type is considered due to the fact that consumers tend to process information about utilitarian products more cognitively, while they process information about hedonic products more affectively.

Therefore, we can consider that there are two main categories of country stereotype: functional and emotional. The perception of functional countries is associated with utilitarian production, being famous for the precision and utility of their products, while emotional countries are associated with romantic and hedonic productions. Empirical evidence indicates that some countries tend to be more associated with a functional country stereotype, while others are associated with an emotional country stereotype (Verlegh and Steenkamp, 1999). The image of the countries of France, Italy and Brazil, for example, strongly communicates hedonism, thus mainly reflecting a stereotype of an emotional country (Leclerc et al., 1994). Germany, Switzerland and Japan, on the other hand, mainly have a stereotype of a functional country and are traditionally associated with utilitarianism (Jaffe and Nebenzahl, 2006). When presented with product-related information, a functional country tends to be processed cognitively by consumers, whereas an emotional country is more likely to be processed affectively.

Once stereotypes are spontaneously activated, their exact impact on consumer evaluations very much depends on the kind of stereotype evoked by the COO (Country of Origin) cue. When the advertising execution format and the country stereotype are consonant to each other, that is, functional (emotional) country stereotype accompanied by informational (emotional) advertising execution format, brand evaluations are expected to be more positive than when the country stereotype and the advertising execution format are dissonant (e.g., a functional country stereotype coupled with an emotional advertising execution format).

When a country stereotype matches the way that a COO facet is processed in an advertisement, the advertisement is rated more favourably. Interestingly, a mismatch between the country stereotype and the advertising execution format (e.g., Germany combined with an emotional advertisement) does not impair cognitive brand evaluations yet negatively impacts affective brand evaluations. Only when the country stereotype matches the brand communication are consumers' purchase intention and positive word-of-mouth significantly improved. Thus, consonance between the stereotype evoked by the COO cue and the associated advertising execution format is necessary for generating positive behavioural responses (Herz and Diamantopoulos, 2013).

When consumers are exposed to an advertisement with a match-up between COO facets and country stereotypes (COA (Country of Assembly) with a functional country or COD (Country of Design) with an emotional country), they express a more favourable attitude toward the ad, and toward the brand, and stronger purchase intention than those exposed to an advertisement with non-match-up between COO facet and country stereotype. Moreover, as shown in Figure 13.2, such a match-up effect is unaffected by product types. Consumers express consistent preference for COA with a functional country or COD with an emotional country in an advertisement, regardless of whether the product is utilitarian or hedonic (Wu and Dodoo, 2016).

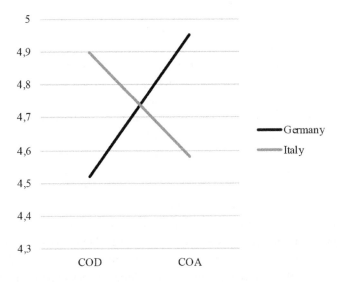

**Figure 13.2**     Perception of country stereotype on COD and COA

Moreover, marketing managers can also get involved with some nation branding campaigns which attempt to reinforce or change country images. This definitely requires more investment, but is worthwhile where the product's country of origin is extremely important and the desired match-up between the COO facet and country stereotypes does not exist. By doing so, a product brand can also become more closely related to a nation's brand.

Sometimes this is the result of the unplanned cooperative behaviour of many companies acting in the same direction without an official agreement, but all being worried about the effect of the current COO image on their products/brands.

## 13.5    COLOURS, NUMBERS, SENSE OF HUMOUR

Symbolic attributes refer to the way consumers interpret actions and react to them. They are usually associated with intrinsic qualities of the product as the idea of national product images, brand names, country of manufacture and the company itself. They play a key role in the product strategy's formulation since divergent symbolic interpretations affect the brand and product perception, requiring in some cases the modification of some features such as packaging or the outward appearance. Consequently, affecting the social meaning that consumers attribute to products, their interpretations are conveyed by attributes presenting hidden meanings and references such as the colour, shape, the numerical indication and the consistency itself. In this regard, researchers have proved that colours create inner symbolic productions associated with specific themes, countries, product categories and brands differing from culture to culture.

Colours and products have connotative meanings and are characterized by a strong congruity: the greater the similarity between them, the greater the colour perception of appropriateness to a specific product will be (Bottomley and Doyle, 2006).

Likewise, numbers are a significant driver in cultures characterized by religion and spirituality predominance such as high-context cultures. For instance, certain numbers are not used in phone numbers or even in floors in buildings. In China, Japan and Korea, the number 4 is considered to be unlucky because of its relationship with death; in the United States the number 13 is unlucky; in Japan the number 9 is unlucky as it is associated with torture or suffering; in Afghanistan the number 39 translates as 'dead cow'.

The meaning of symbolic attributes and in particular of colour, strongly impacts consumer behaviour and in turn affects which marketing applications to adopt and which positioning strategy to implement. Companies have to carefully investigate the possible mental association and select the best-related colour or visual appearance to display.

Colour is an integral element of corporate and marketing communications. It induces moods and emotions, influences consumers' perceptions and behaviour and helps companies position or differentiate themselves from the competition. A cross-cultural perspective of colour research and application is imperative for developing effective cross-cultural marketing strategies. Colour is a vital part of products, services, packaging, logos, displays and collateral. It is a potent cue for product and brand differentiation and for creating and sustaining corporate identities and consumer perceptions. Colours are known to possess emotional and psychological properties. The meanings associated with different colours are important to marketers because the tools used to communicate brand image are mechanisms of meaning transfer.

For example, colour ranks among the top three considerations, along with price and quality, in the purchase of an automobile. Colour is also an important component of many corporate and brand-building cues, such as logos, packaging and displays. The effects of culture on the meaning associated with marketing cues (such as colour) are critical for international marketing managers. If the meaning associated with a colour or combination of colours is different across cultures, marketers may benefit from pursuing a customized strategy with respect to the colour associated with the brand, packaging, and so on. Actually, people of different cultures have various preferences for colour. In contrast, when colour meanings are similar across markets, a standardized strategy is more viable (Madden et al., 2000).

Even when a few colours are found to be favourable in advertisements or retail environments, it is still important to realize that most of the colour research mentioned above should only be applied to Western culture. Colours do have distinctly different meanings across cultures. Such consideration of colour must be taken into account when entering foreign markets. A cross-cultural perspective is consequently vital in developing global marketing strategies that will be effective and also non-controversial (Shi, 2013).

Colour signals a product's attributes for merchandise, thereby influencing perceptions about price and quality. For instance, in the UK white is perceived as 'crap' and below average, while neutral or beige is perceived as 'boring and dull' but expensive and 'for a mature person', whereas pink, perceived as 'look young' and red, perceived as 'garish and tacky', are both considered as average priced (Kerfoot et al., 2003). In Italy light blue and pink are perceived as inexpensive, while dark blue and red can be associated with luxury. In most Asian countries, white skin is associated with beauty and class, whereas dark skin is related to hard labour. The annual growth rate of approximately 20 per cent in the Indian skin whitener market also indicates colour association with the consumer self.

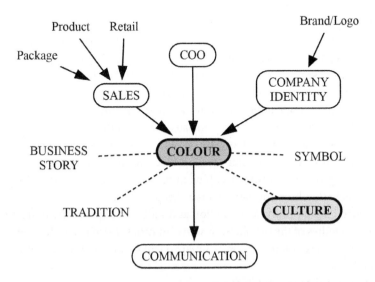

**Figure 13.3**   Colour choice components in cross-cultural marketing

Colour preferences are not identical across countries. Red is one of the most preferred colours by Americans, green by the Lebanese and blue–green by Iranians and Kuwaitis. Red is strongly related to China, purple to France, and blue to both France and Italy. Similarly, orange is the favourite colour in the Netherlands, since their monarchy is the House of Orange. Blue is the corporate colour in the USA, and red is the winning business colour in East Asia. Therefore the perception of country of origin can be associated with a specific colour. A dynamic culture-sensitive approach in colour research and its strategic use will enhance the corporate image, predict purchasing behaviour and reinforce customer relationships, allowing foreign businesses to establish value-based marketing systems and develop a competitive advantage in the emerging markets.

Therefore, Aslam (2006) suggests:

- A cross-cultural perspective of colour research and application is vital for developing global marketing strategies.
- The cultural values, marketing objectives and desired customer relationship levels in the target market determine the choice of colour in making global or local marketing decisions.
- Both culturally and structurally stable branding and packaging models maximize the marketing goals of the firm.

There are many different perceptions and meanings of colours across the world. In Western culture, *red* indicates passion and love; in the East, however, it is associated with joy and marriage. In China it is the colour of brides, it is used in celebrations and greeting cards and is associated with money; in India it indicates purity, in Japan life. In South Africa, however, it is the colour of mourning. In the Jewish religion it indicates both sacrifice and sin. In general, it identifies with sensuality and positive energy. It is an unfortunate colour in Chad and Nigeria. Red is transgressive in the West, traditional in China.

With the exception of Egypt, where it is associated with mourning, *yellow* usually has a positive connotation. In Buddhism it indicates wisdom and, in general, in Asia it is linked to sacredness; in India it is associated with commerce, knowledge and happiness. In the West it is also associated with disease, as the flag on quarantined ships is yellow. In China it is associated with royalty (it was the colour of the emperor), while in Japan it suggests courage. Also, in Japanese culture, gold is used alongside red for anniversaries and holidays. The golden yellow hue is generally everywhere positive and associated with wealth.

In many cultures, *blue* is associated with sadness, passivity and depression. It is no coincidence that in English the expression 'feeling blue' means 'feeling sad'. In the West it is associated with elegance and confidence. Blue in the East is feminine, while in the West it is masculine. In the East (China and Japan) it is a cheap colour.

*Green* in general has a positive connotation as it indicates hope; in the Islamic religion it is the colour of the clothes of the prophets. In some countries it also takes on other meanings: in the United States it is the colour of money, in Japan that of life, in Europe as well as in the East that of the environment.

*Orange* is the sacred colour of Hinduism.

*Purple* in Catholicism indicates death, mourning and crucifixion, but it also has the same meaning in many Eastern cultures, such as Thailand. In China it is connected to luxury, to harmony with the universe.

*White*, in Europe and in the West in general, is the colour of peace, of marriage. In the East it is the colour that most of all is linked to death: in India it indicates sadness, in China and Japan mourning, but also purity.

In Western culture, *black* is associated with death; in fact, it is a colour that has this connotation on a universal level, and even in many Eastern countries it is associated with bad luck, unhappiness, evil and mourning. However, it is also associated with elegance. It is a masculine colour.

*Grey* suffers from a lack of assertiveness so it suggests confusion, as in 'grey area'. But it is also associated with intelligence, futurism, modesty, boredom, coolness, sadness, safety, conservatism, security, practicality, dependability, elegance and decay.

In the West, as far as the adult population is concerned, blue is by far the preferred colour (about 50 per cent of the population), followed by green (20 per cent) and further back white and red (8 per cent). In Japan, the preferred colour is white (40 per cent), followed by black (20 per cent) and yellow (10 per cent). For the Japanese sensibility it is more important whether a colour is dull or bright, so there are many types of black and white. In many African cultures no importance is given to the border that separates reds from browns, nor from that of greens. Instead, it is essential to know whether a given colour is dry or wet, soft or hard, smooth or rough, dull or sonorous, cheerful or sad. This, as you can easily understand, has many different meanings in the colours of the products.

Religions also have a colour: for Catholic Christians the white and yellow of the Pope, for Calvinists it is black. Green is the colour of the Islamic religion, orange of the Hindu religion.

As for children, the scale of values is different; it varies a lot with age and countries and does not show the stability of adults. In general, red is preferred to yellow and white. There is no gender difference in preferences: being a cultural learning, gender differences in colour preference are acquired later. Warm colours are preferred by children, cold ones by adults.

Many products are associated with specific colours (Shi, 2013). Breakfast foods and soap (functional products) were best received in green and yellow, the colour combination most strongly associated with economy and cleanliness (functional benefits). Similarly, dignity and luxury (sensory-social benefits) were most strongly associated with silver and black, the combination ranked second for perfume (sensory-social product). There are functional colours and emotional colours. Blue is preferred for functional products, whereas red is preferred for emotional products (Bottomley and Doyle, 2006).

Based on the idea that associative patterns are formed through repetition, it can be argued that consumers create their colour associations in different contexts based on how colours have previously been disseminated. The benefits of colour associations may therefore be easier to achieve in contexts where colours occur regularly, that is, through the consistent and complete distribution of a colour with product associations. Such associations may be the result of the colours used on established competing products and brands. That is, it appears that context-specific associations may over time and eventually become general (universal) associations (Amsteus et al., 2015).

For example, green is associated with coffee in China due to Starbucks' widespread presence as the largest coffee distributor. On the other hand, that is absolutely not the colour of coffee in Italy, where tradition goes to red, black and gold. The meaning of colours and their combination with products therefore depends on the history and tradition of a culture, but also on the most recent success that a company has had in offering its products (especially if new to the market), creating a colour standard. In certain industries such as footwear, colour preferences are also affected by ethnic characteristics like skin colour. Indeed, some ethnic groups refuse or accept to buy a product juxtaposing their skin to the good itself.

Colouring of products can also be associated with historical conditions, from how these products were coloured in the past. For example, the colouring of mint sweets, from green (sweet mint) to ice white (strong mint), passing through different degrees of blue and grey-blue is the remnant of an ancient white–black axis from the year 1000 in Europe in which colours were distinguished, which was a scale that rejected all warm colours (Pastoreau, 1987).

In conclusion, four points can be proposed to summarize the issue of colour in intercultural marketing:

- People of different cultures perceive colours differently.
- The importance of colour choice for the same products varies from country to country.
- Colour is more important for self-expressive products than for functional products.
- There are some similarities between different cultures on the choice of colour of products in utilitarian products, less so in symbolic products.

*Numbers* are perceived differently across cultures, because they are associated with different stories, pronunciations, religions and traditions (Table 13.6).

The number 8 is the most favoured number in modern China due to its association with wealth and luck. The Chinese love this number, both in trivial matters and in big moments. The number 8 is given the highest priority when buying a number plate or buying a house. In India, 8 is considered the line between good and evil, or heaven and hell, so is avoided. The number 2, pronounced *er* or *liang*, is considered to be lucky as the Chinese believe that all good things come in pairs. This is observed in repeated characters in some brand names or gifts. The number 3, pronounced *san*, is considered lucky due to its similarity in sound to the word that means birth. Additionally, this number represents the three stages in the life of humans – birth, marriage, death – which adds to its importance in Chinese culture. The number 5 has more of a historic significance. In Chinese history, the number 5 is used in many classifications, such as five flavours (pungent, sweet, sour, salty, bitter), five sacred mountains (Huashan, Hengshan in Hunan, Hengshan in Shanxi, Songshan and Taishan) and so on. The number 7 has a similar meaning in Western culture. The number 6, pronounced *liu*, is considered lucky as it sounds like the word that means 'to flow', and can indicate smooth progress in life. It also means well-off. Similar to 8, 6 is preferred in number plates and phone numbers. When a couple gets engaged, the man customarily offers a gift to the girl's family, which is usually money (RMB 6666 and such), and this gift signifies a harmonious life for the couple. If a person is to celebrate their 66th birthday, that is a grand occasion. In business, 6 is considered lucky. New ventures or contracts are signed on dates that have a 6 in them.

It is quite common to give the name '666' to a shopping centre or to a business activity. In Western Christian culture 666 is 'the number of the beast'. This 'beast' is often interpreted as being the Antichrist, and thus the number is a sign of the devil.

**Table 13.6** Lucky and unlucky numbers

| Number | Lucky | Reason | Unlucky | Reason |
|---|---|---|---|---|
| 7 | USA, most of Europe | Bible sacred number 7 means many | China, Vietnam, Thailand | 7 July month of the ghosts |
| 4 | Germany, Italy | 4 leaf clover | China, Japan, Vietnam | Sounds similar to word 'death' |
| 8 | China, Japan | Sounds similar to word 'money' and 'prosperity' | India (South) | Represent a fine line between good and evil |
| 13 | Italy and China | In Italy it is the jackpot, in China it means 'growth' | Most of the world | Linked to dark events (Last Supper…) |
| 666 | China | Sounds similar to the word 'smooth' | Christian countries | The number of the Antichrist |
| 3 | China, most of Europe | Number of perfection | Japan, Vietnam | Photo with 3 people, the one in the middle will die |

The pronunciation of the number 4 in China is similar to that of the Chinese word for death. Many buildings in China skip the fourth floor, or in planes row number 4, just as US builders sometimes omit floor 13 and airlines omit row 13. Conversely, number 13 is considered lucky in Italy. Number 4 in Western countries is considered to be a lucky charm, associated with a four-leaf clover.

Some Italians are superstitious about Friday the 17th (the day of Christ's death) because rearranging the Roman numeral XVII can create the word 'VIXI', translated from Latin to mean 'my life is over'.

Therefore, in creating and proposing brand names companies should pay attention to the number they use considering the country where they promote the product.

*Humour* is one of the most commonly used emotional appeals in global advertising. Each humour mechanism accumulates some advantages as well as some disadvantages that can either enhance or diminish the effectiveness of advertisements. It seems that the humorous disparagement process (interpersonal mechanism) is the riskiest form of humour as it may irritate and annoy consumers when it crosses the line from tolerance to offensiveness (Meyer, 2000). If the target audience does not share the opinion being communicated, it may identify with the victimized advertising character and consider the ad insulting or offensive. Offensive humour is considered funnier in low uncertainty avoidance than in high uncertainty avoidance cultures (Kalliny et al., 2007). Also, collectivists are less favourable to offensive advertisements than individualists.

The arousal safety process (affective mechanism) may be perceived as offensive by the advertising audience. It is possible that the initial discomforting stimulus causes strong negative emotional responses such as irritation, fear and anger, inhibiting the safe judgement and appreciation of humour. Collectivistic cultures with higher uncertainty avoidance react consistently more favourably to humorous advertisements when the arousal safety process uses a safe judgement than when it does not. When there is no safe judgement, they have difficulty in understanding the joke and they are more critical about these ads compared to individualist consumers from low uncertainty avoidance cultures (Lee and Lim, 2008).

The incongruity resolution process (cognitive mechanism) is the simplest humour process and the best to clarify a brand's positioning. According to Freud, comic wit, which is based only on the incongruity resolution process, seems to have a lower emotional impact than sexual (involves arousal safety process) and aggressive humour (requires the humorous disparagement process), decreasing negative emotional reactions. Thus, a risk aversion strategy in advertising would favour the incongruity resolution process over the other two humour processes, since it seems a more neutral and less offensive way to create jokes. For instance, a risk-avoiding attitude in Germany directs advertisers to prefer incongruity and surprise to other more offensive humour processes. In Russia (a collectivistic society with high uncertainty avoidance), gag humour, a type of farce, is an unpopular humour device, since Russian consumers cannot understand it, whereas, in the USA, advertisements that incorporate gags are considered extremely hilarious (Six, 2005). Furthermore, in Japan, a collectivistic, high uncertainty-avoiding culture, advertisers use offensive humorous appeals less frequently compared with their Western counterparts.

In an individualistic culture, which ranks low on the uncertainty avoidance dimension, more risky, aggressive and affective humorous advertisements are used. In particular, ads seem to incorporate humorous appeals more frequently compared to the collectivistic culture ads. Advertisers in the individualistic society favour the arousal safety process, sentimental humour and full comedy and give emphasis to humour dominance. In collectivistic, strong uncertainty avoidance cultures, more neutral humorous advertisements whose appeal is not perceived as very offensive are considered more suitable. In those countries, there is a lower percentage of print ads that use humour. The simplest forms of humour, namely incongruity resolution and comic wit, constitute the core of the majority of the humorous ads (Hatzithomas et al., 2011).

Advertisers in the UK, an individualistic country, prefer to entertain consumers through the use of humour-dominant advertisements, rather to inform them through the use of information-dominant humorous ads. British advertisers often use sentimental humour when they try to build a brand image (image-dominant ads). Advertising practitioners in collectivistic countries approach humorous ads as creative devices that can engender a positive mood in order to gain consumers' trust. Their actual aim to provide information for the brand is disguised with the help of a humorous message. Conversely, advertisers have to harmonize the uncertainty aversion attitudes of the consumers that increase the need for concrete information and their collectivistic values that are in favour of indirect messages. Information dominant humorous illustrations seem to be able to convey accurate information in an indirect way.

International advertisers should adapt their humorous advertising strategies to the cultural characteristics of collectivistic and uncertainty avoidance cultures in order to target consumers effectively in these markets. When international advertisers aim to entertain collectivistic consumers with high uncertainty aversion attitudes, they can, also, use satire and full comedy. However, a more cautious use of these types of humour is suggested as they may insult or irritate collectivists. In collectivistic countries, citizens distinguish between in-groups and out-groups, and dislike those ads that humiliate the members of the group (Chan et al., 2007). Thus, international advertisers could reduce the possibility that collectivistic consumers identify with the victimized characters of the ad.

The individual-level culture on the dimension of individualism/collectivism has a positive impact on perceived humour in an ad, moderated by the level of aggression of the humour. Highly individualistic individuals perceive more intense humour when aggression levels are high. This provides further evidence for the self-orientation that derives pleasure from the pain or misfortune of others, or schadenfreude (Crawford and Gregory, 2011).

However, humour is always built on the meaning of ambiguity. There is an ambiguous and double-meaning passage between what is said and what is meant. So, it can be risky when the culture and symbolic meaning are different from those of the country where they were produced. Therefore, humour should be carefully considered in cross-cultural communication – it should be localized and very rarely globalized.

## 13.6    OFFENSIVE COMMUNICATION IN DIFFERENT CULTURES

Offensive advertising is context sensitive. The word 'offensive' is highly associated with the subtleties of relational and situational context. Whether a word or an image is perceived to be offensive depends on the relationship between the parties involved and the occasion/situation where it is exposed. Offensive advertising is also culture specific, because it is perceived and judged by different criteria across cultures.

The opening up of countries to foreign advertisements has meant that people across the world have a greater opportunity to be exposed to potentially offensive advertising. This includes advertising of products such as alcohol, contraception, underwear, and feminine hygiene products, and the use of indecent language and anti-social behaviour. Various types of products, both goods and services, have been suggested by past studies as being controversial when advertised. These include cigarettes, alcohol, contraceptives, underwear, and political advertising. In each culture there may be a different judgement about what is offensive or not and about the degree of offensiveness each product or message provokes. For example, one study (Waller et al., 2005) compared four countries from different cultural areas: Malaysia, New Zealand, Turkey and the UK.

Western images were used to determine whether they were perceived to be offensive, particularly to the Asian respondents. The list of reasons included: (1) anti-social behaviour; (2) indecent language; (3) nudity; (4) racist images; (5) sexist images; (6) subject too personal; (7) Western/US images.

In each country was listed a ranking of offensive type images describing cultural sensitivity to the theme (Table 13.7).

**Table 13.7** Example of different sensitivity to offensive themes

| Sample | Offensive Ranking |
|---|---|
| Malaysia | (1) racially extremist groups<br>(2) gambling<br>(3) cigarettes |
| New Zealand | (1) racially extremist groups<br>(2) guns and armaments<br>(3) religious denominations |
| Turkey | (1) gambling<br>(2) racially extremist groups<br>(3) funeral services |
| UK | (1) racially extremist groups<br>(2) guns and armaments<br>(3) religious denominations |

The countries that did have similar views are New Zealand and the UK (English-speaking, historically Christian-based members of the Commonwealth) and Malaysia and Turkey (secular democracies populated by mostly Muslims). Evidently, religion is a very important factor in shaping cultural values and shaping what can be offensive or not.

Anyway, there are other factors influencing the offensive perception of advertising, not only religious precepts. For example, McDonald's broadcasted a television commercial featuring a Chinese man kneeling down to beg for a discount and they were charged with insulting Chinese consumers. The answer lies in the cultural meaning of 'kneeling down'. The advertisement was perceived to present unequal power distribution between Chinese consumers and the advertiser. It hints at American imperialism. Nike's 'Chamber of Fear' advertising campaign featured the American basketball star LeBron James in a battle with Chinese-styled allegorical cartoon figures, including a Kung Fu master, some ancient fairies and two dragons. The ad was accused by the Chinese people of seriously hurting their feelings, denigrating Chinese culture and blatantly insulting China (Chan et al., 2007). The Benetton campaign showed varying offending visuals, for instance, blood-covered dirty clothes, an overcrowded boat with refugees jumping into the sea in despair, people with tattoos reading 'HIV positive', and dying people. The Benetton campaign was perceived offensive by many Germans and led to much debate. A recent example of offensive advertisement (an ad used by Freenet, an internet provider) showed a group of elderly men sitting at an open grave, and a boy who, though standing in the middle of mourners, is laughing and celebrating because he has won an iPod. Recently, an advertisement by Dolce & Gabbana received massive protests in Europe. The ad showed a woman, surrounded by four men, barely clothed, one of them bending over her and forcing her down. The action could be suggestive of gang rape. All the examples highlight the fact that the shared values of a culture (i.e. nationalism, social sensitivity, respect, etc.) are really important in the perception of any communication, and what in one cultural context may be acceptable, in another it is not.

In general, female consumers had a lower tolerance level toward advertisements illustrating nudity than male consumers (Prendergast et al., 2002). Despite education playing a role in the perception of offensive advertising, this is not the same for different cultures. While sex appeal has been widely used in most Western countries, in Korea, Japan and China it might be considered offensive. However, partial nudity and sexual suggestiveness are two commonly adopted strategies of sex appeal advertising in China due to the strict regulations on what visuals can be exposed. The sexual suggestiveness is often expressed through language because Mandarin, the official language in China, is a tonal language. Under the Chinese language system, the same pronunciation can mean different characters because many characters share the same vowels, same consonants and the same intonation. Many sex appeal ads exploit this characteristic of the language. For example, in a recent TV spot for a detergent brand, the man asks, 'Ni Piao Le Ma?', whose direct meaning is 'Have you bleached [the clothes]?'. This ad was stopped after being shown a few times on TV because many consumers believed that the ad was unethical. The character 'Piao', which means 'bleach' in the original ad, sounds the same as another Chinese character that means 'sleeping with prostitutes' (Liu et al., 2009).

In comparing offensive nude advertising in China and Germany, it was expected that the Chinese respondents would perceive the advertisements more negatively than the German respondents, but this was only partly the case. They often considered the ads to be more offensive, uncomfortable, disgusting and impolite than the German consumers, but the Germans judged them to be more irritating and ridiculous. It was also only partly true that German respondents will perceive the ads more positively than the Chinese respondents, as the Germans considered the advertisements as more creative, interesting and clever than the Chinese consumers, but less convincing and informative. This seems to suggest that German consumers are more likely to appreciate the creative elements in the potentially offensive advertisements than Chinese consumers. On the other hand, Chinese consumers are more likely to appreciate the informative elements in the potentially offensive advertisements than Germans consumers.

Shao and Hill (1994) argue that high-context societies rely more on social norms in restricting marketing communications than explicit laws and regulations. The analysis of regulations of advertisements of socially sensitive products highlights that sexually oriented products are more strictly controlled by regulations in high-context countries than in low-context countries. Sexually oriented and addictive (for example alcohol) products were found to be more offensive among Korean consumers than among Western consumers. The reason can be that high-context societies tend to be more strait-laced about sexually intimate matters. As sexually oriented products are less acceptable in high-context societies, sexually oriented appeals and executions are less acceptable in high-context societies. Low-context societies tend to be more liberal towards sex and pornography. It is probably because these products are perceived as social ills with negative impacts on collective society, and because of the importance of harmony. So, consumers from collective societies will find them less acceptable (An and Kim, 2006). Consumers in collective societies may be less accepting of advertising executions that violate societal norms. In individualistic cultures, products such as political products, addictive products, sex-related products and healthcare products are considered less offensive if compared to the perception in collectivistic cultures (Fam and Waller, 2003).

There appear to be significant differences in attitudes toward advertisements with violent image appeal across international sample groups, particularly along the lines of gender, country, intensity of religious belief, economic inclination, and offensiveness of social/political groups. Women and those with strong religious beliefs tend to be more offended by violent images, particularly those related to social/political groups. This may be because all religions preach 'peace' to their followers, and thus violent images would contradict these teachings and therefore be perceived as offensive. Also, specific religions may not be as important as people's intensity of belief, so stereotypes have to be reconsidered when advertising globally to countries with different religious majorities (Waller et al., 2013).

# 14
# Pricing across cultures – a framework

*Andreas Hinterhuber*

## 14.1 PRICING – AN IMPORTANT, YET NEGLECTED RESPONSIBILITY

Pricing is a fundamental part of the marketing mix. Pricing is the activity that has the largest impact on short-term profitability: small changes in selling prices have a far larger impact on profitability than similar changes in revenues or cost (Baker et al., 2010). Pricing is thus an extremely important element of the marketing mix. It is also, surprisingly, neglected: in its annual survey of chief marketing officers (CMOs) the American Marketing Association polls marketers on activities where marketing leads (Moorman, 2020). The results of the 2020 survey are in Figure 14.1.

Marketing typically does not lead pricing: in only 20 per cent of companies is marketing responsible for pricing. In 80 per cent of companies the responsibility for pricing is either dispersed – between sales, finance, controlling and marketing with no clear accountabilities – or other functional units have responsibility over pricing. A recent study (Liozu, 2019) tends to lend support to the former explanation: in the vast majority of companies there is no centralized, formalized and specialized organizational unit with responsibility for pricing. Taken together, these studies suggest that

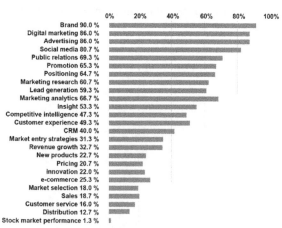

*Source*: Moorman (2020).

**Figure 14.1**    Domains of influence of the marketing function (

pricing, today, is not well managed. In most companies pricing falls between the cracks: everyone is responsible for pricing which means that, in the end, nobody is.

On the other hand, there are several studies that suggest that companies that actively manage pricing exhibit higher profitability: studies by consulting companies indicate that pricing initiatives contribute to increased firm performance (Meehan et al., 2012; Tohamy and Keltz, 2008). More importantly, a recent academic study has found that the adoption of pricing – measured via the use of pricing tools, organizational pricing knowledge, and use of innovation in pricing – is positively correlated with relative firm performance (Liozu, 2021). In summary: pricing is very important, not well managed, but managing pricing increases firm performance.

Managing prices in an international context presents its own challenges. For a start, prices for most products are far from being harmonized on a global basis. Table 14.1 provides an indication of price dispersion for some commonly purchased products and services (The Economist Intelligence Unit, 2020).

**Table 14.1** Cross-country price differences globally

| | | Singapore | Hong Kong | Osaka | New York | Paris | Zurich | Tel Aviv | Los Angeles | Tokyo | Geneva |
|---|---|---|---|---|---|---|---|---|---|---|---|
| **Average US$ price 1kg loaf of bread** | Current | $3.35 | $3.60 | $5.63 | $8.62 | $5.20 | $4.69 | $4.70 | $6.82 | $7.41 | $5.62 |
| | Last year | $3.40 | $3.91 | $5.20 | $8.33 | $5.66 | $4.78 | $5.09 | $6.26 | $7.12 | $6.06 |
| | 5 years | $3.54 | $4.31 | $5.77 | $8.62 | $8.83 | $5.96 | $4.94 | $6.02 | $6.88 | $7.48 |
| | 10 years | $2.88 | $4.48 | $6.78 | $6.85 | $9.23 | $5.48 | $3.49 | $5.57 | $8.75 | $5.22 |
| **Average US$ price 1 beer bottle (330 ml)** | Current | $2.25 | $1.57 | $2.49 | $3.50 | $1.86 | $2.55 | $3.27 | $1.91 | $2.47 | $1.37 |
| | Last year | $2.37 | $1.77 | $2.30 | $3.33 | $2.10 | $3.25 | $2.94 | $1.91 | $2.45 | $1.54 |
| | 5 years | $2.53 | $1.91 | $2.22 | $3.18 | $2.75 | $2.78 | $3.06 | $1.80 | $2.63 | $2.06 |
| | 10 years | $2.14 | $1.46 | $2.51 | $2.87 | $2.07 | $2.04 | $2.50 | $1.63 | $3.02 | $1.51 |
| **Average US$ price men's two-piece business suit** | Current | $1,167.14 | $1,639.41 | $1,483.82 | $3,073.09 | $1,724.23 | $689.12 | $1,979.17 | $1,607.67 | $960.85 | $506.69 |
| | Last year | $1,161.14 | $1,874.65 | $1,359.85 | $2,729.77 | $2,000.65 | $651.89 | $1,940.58 | $1,463.78 | $946.00 | $573.20 |
| | 5 years | $1,266.88 | $1,599.91 | $995.26 | $1,770.21 | $2,056.28 | $615.41 | $1,962.96 | $1,323.41 | $949.62 | $654.84 |
| | 10 years | $1,087.5 | $861.94 | $1,118.82 | $1,051.16 | $1,761.90 | $700.00 | $1,325.33 | $1,288.25 | $1,193.78 | $750.16 |
| **Average US$ price women's haircut** | Current | $96.01 | $112.88 | $55.63 | $210.00 | $124.03 | $72.47 | $102.55 | $199.88 | $65.74 | $93.30 |
| | Last year | $96.01 | $112.10 | $53.46 | $210.00 | $119.04 | $73.97 | $93.59 | $197.50 | $63.17 | $90.21 |
| | 5 years | $105.16 | $58.06 | $57.86 | $198.00 | $98.70 | $73.12 | $86.11 | $185.00 | $66.61 | $83.33 |
| | 10 years | $81.94 | $64.52 | $53.80 | $155.00 | $96.43 | $79.44 | $80.00 | $97.50 | $73.70 | $70.09 |

*Source*: The Economist Intelligence Unit (2020).

Even prices for easily tradeable products, such as smartphones, differ widely across narrow geographic markets, such as the European Union. Tables 14.2a and 14.2b provide data collected in 2018 on mobile phone prices in Europe (Koblbauer et al., 2018). The percentage difference between the highest and lowest price for any mobile phone is, on average 22 per cent, ranging from 12 per cent (Apple) to 42 per cent (Samsung). Prices in some countries (UK, Sweden) are consistently higher than in other countries (Germany, the Netherlands).

**Table 14.2a** Cross-country price differences in Europe: price

| | | Italy | Spain | Germany | Netherlands | UK | Sweden | Finland |
|---|---|---|---|---|---|---|---|---|
| 1 | G A3 2017 (16 GB) | 155.36 | 172.75 | 164.58 | 164.46 | 188.50 | **210.90** | **139.35** |
| 2 | G A5 2017 (32 GB) | 219.83 | **189.95** | 215.08 | 205.79 | 221.51 | **249.78** | 227.26 |
| 3 | G J3 2017 (16 GB) | 137.18 | 135.24 | **126.76** | 131.40 | **164.95** | 148.18 | 136.57 |
| 4 | G J5 2017 J530 (16 GB) | 160.32 | **149.59** | 157.02 | 156.20 | **216.80** | 189.69 | 150.73 |
| 5 | G S8 (64 GB) | 499.99 | 451.22 | 447.06 | **428.10** | 461.89 | 547.94 | **566.77** |
| 6 | G S9 (64 GB) | 691.73 | 656.55 | **548.70** | 685.12 | 696.67 | 696.98 | **727.34** |
| 7 | G S9 PLUS (64 GB) | **829.74** | 731.96 | **673.07** | 767.77 | – | 775.34 | 807.98 |
| 8 | ANNE (P20 Lite 64 GB) | 276.02 | 284.43 | **299.16** | **255.37** | 263.47 | 297.14 | 283.79 |
| 9 | EMILY (P20 128 GB) | **565.28** | 530.01 | 545.38 | **514.05** | 564.69 | 516.66 | 525.73 |
| 10 | FIGO (P Smart 32 GB) | 178.30 | 190.16 | **190.34** | 164.46 | 169.64 | **156.02** | 162.82 |
| 11 | PRAGUE 2017 (P8 Lite 16 GB) | 138.43 | 148.35 | 142.02 | **131.40** | 131.95 | – | **155.48** |
| 12 | IPhone 6 (32 GB) | 289.66 | 305.73 | 279.81 | 275.21 | **310.16** | 289.22 | **260.32** |
| 13 | IPhone 7 (32 GB) | **519.83** | 501.64 | 504.16 | 490.91 | 517.56 | **461.70** | 470.00 |
| 14 | IPhone 8 (64 GB) | **659.09** | 623.76 | 626.45 | 619.01 | 602.40 | **587.22** | 615.24 |

**Table 14.2b**     Cross-country price differences in Europe: percentage price difference

|   |   | Italy | Spain | Germany | Netherlands | UK | Sweden | Finland | Max/Min |
|---|---|-------|-------|---------|-------------|-----|--------|---------|---------|
| 1 | G A3 2017 (16 GB) | 91% | 101% | 96% | 96% | 110% | **123%** | **82%** | 42% |
| 2 | G A5 2017 (32 GB) | 101% | **87%** | 98% | 94% | 101% | **114%** | 104% | 27% |
| 3 | G J3 2017 (16 GB) | 98% | 97% | **91%** | 94% | **118%** | 106% | 98% | 27% |
| 4 | G J5 2017 J530 (16 GB) | 95% | **89%** | 93% | 93% | **129%** | 112% | 89% | 40% |
| 5 | G S8 (64 GB) | 103% | 93% | 92% | **88%** | 95% | 113% | **117%** | 29% |
| 6 | G S9 (64 GB) | 103% | 98% | **82%** | 102% | 104% | 104% | **108%** | 27% |
| 7 | G S9 PLUS (64 GB) | **109%** | 96% | **88%** | 100% | – | 101% | 106% | 20% |
| 8 | ANNE (P20 Lite 64 GB) | 99% | 102% | **107%** | **91%** | 94% | 106% | 101% | 16% |
| 9 | EMILY (P20 128 GB) | **105%** | 99% | 101% | **96%** | 105% | 96% | 98% | 10% |
| 10 | FIGO (P Smart 32 GB) | 103% | 110% | **110%** | 95% | 98% | **90%** | 94% | 20% |
| 11 | PRAGUE 2017 (P8 Lite 16 GB) | 98% | 105% | 101% | **93%** | 93% | – | **110%** | 17% |
| 12 | IPhone 6 (32 GB) | 101% | 106% | 97% | 96% | **108%** | 101% | **91%** | 17% |
| 13 | IPhone 7 (32 GB) | **105%** | 101% | 102% | 99% | 105% | **93%** | 95% | 12% |
| 14 | IPhone 8 (64 GB) | **106%** | 101% | 101% | 100% | 97% | **95%** | 99% | 12% |
|   | **AVERAGE** | **101%** | 99% | 97% | **96%** | 104% | 104% | 99% | 22% |

*Source*: Koblbauer et al. (2018).

In conclusion: markets globalize, but pricing still takes place on a country by country level. Simply put: pricing strategies are context-specific (Sousa and Bradley, 2008; Theodosiou and Katsikeas, 2001). The objective of this chapter is to provide a framework for pricing strategy development and implementation that considers relevant cultural factors.

## 14.2     A FRAMEWORK FOR PRICING ACROSS CULTURES

A widespread, but flawed, approach to pricing is cost-based pricing. Cost-based pricing starts the process of determining prices by analysing information from cost accounting. Value-based pricing turns the process on its head: value-based pricing starts the process of determining prices by understanding and increasing customer willingness to pay (Figure 14.2).

Researchers agree that pricing decisions, both for existing as well as for new products, must be based on a firm understanding of customer value, that is, of customer willingness to pay (Nagle and Müller, 2018). The framework for pricing across cultures therefore takes the shape outlined in Figure 14.3 (Hinterhuber, 2004).

**COST-BASED PRICING**

PRODUCT > COST > PRICE > VALUE > CUSTOMERS

**VALUE-BASED PRICING**

CUSTOMERS > VALUE > PRICE > COST > PRODUCT

*Source*: Nagle and Holden (2002).

**Figure 14.2**     Cost-based versus value-based pricing

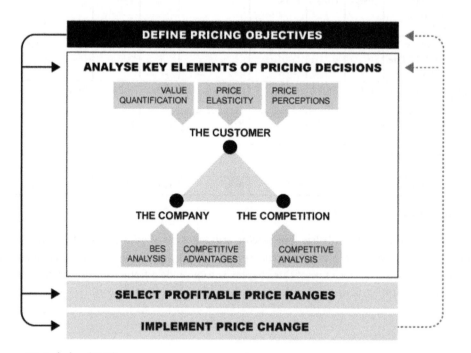

*Source*: Hinterhuber (2004).

**Figure 14.3**     A framework for international pricing

## 14.2.1   Define Pricing Objectives

A first important step in establishing international prices is the determination of objectives. Avlonitis et al. (2005) report the findings on pricing objectives from a study in the service industry and find that companies typically pursue a variety of objectives via pricing: goals related to market share, profitability, price image, price war avoidance and price differentiation are most prevalent. Simplifying, goals can be split between goals related to market share and goals related to profitability. The PIMS project (Buzzell et al., 1975) had a huge influence in encouraging managers to pursue goals related to market share. The belief was that a large market share, ideally the number one position, would translate into high profitability. This view is outdated: 'The use of market share as a measure of corporate or executive performance is at best a waste of time; at worst, it is totally misleading. We recommend that you never make the market share calculation' (Anterasian et al., 1996, pp. 74–5). The PIMS project is, by now, effectively dead (Buzzell, 2004). Rather than pursuing goals related to market share, recent research advises managers to pursue goals related to profitability (Hinterhuber, 2016).

A study on pricing strategy objectives among firms in the US, India and Singapore (Rao and Kartono, 2009) finds, as the study cited above, that pricing objectives can be sensibly split into market share and profitability goals. The study does not find significant differences in objectives across countries. Across countries, managers seem to aim at similar objectives via pricing. How to achieve objectives across countries, however, is another matter.

Setting goals effectively requires an understanding of the cultural context in which individuals operate: in a study among sales managers, in the US the relationship between goal difficulty and sales effort has the shape of an inverted U (Fang et al., 2004). American managers seem to evaluate goal difficulty and then calibrate efforts based on the estimated likelihood of achieving outcomes. When goals are easy, sales managers have confidence in their ability to meet goals with little effort; in this case, they are not motivated to work hard. When goals are very difficult, managers have little expectation in their ability to meet goals; they are, again, not motivated to work hard. US sales managers exercise maximum effort at intermediate levels of goal difficulty. Not so in China: goal difficulty has a positive linear relationship with effort. This may be the result of a prevailing attitude in China that one can succeed at anything if one tries really hard (Fang et al., 2004). In addition, goal specificity has a positive effect on sales effort in the US, but a negative effect on sales effort in China, possibly a result of the low-context communication culture in the US and the high-context communication culture in China (Hall, 1976). The implication is straightforward: in the US, moderately difficult, but highly specific goals lead to the greatest effort, whereas in China, very difficult, but non-specific goals lead to the greatest effort.

## 14.3   ANALYSE KEY ELEMENTS OF PRICING DECISIONS

Pricing strategies should be developed based on the 3Cs model (Hinterhuber, 2004), analysing customers, the company, and competition.

### 14.3.1 The Customer Perspective

The key dimension in international pricing decisions is the customer. As outlined in Figure 14.3, three aspects need to be examined in order to develop effective pricing strategies on the dimension related to customers.

- Customer value quantification: the most important starting point for developing any pricing strategy is quantification of customer value. Customer value 'is the price of the customer's best alternative (called the reference value) plus the value of whatever differentiates the offering from the alternative (called the differentiation value). Differentiation value may have both positive and negative elements ... Economic value is the maximum price that a "smart shopper", fully informed about the market and seeking the best value, would pay' (Nagle and Holden, 2002, p. 75). Examples of economic value analysis are discussed in other studies (Hinterhuber, 2004; Hinterhuber and Snelgrove, 2017; Nagle and Müller, 2018). Value quantification essentially means translating competitive advantages – Nagle's differentiating features – into quantified value. This is demanding and requires a set of skills: 'The value quantification capability refers to the ability to translate a firm's competitive advantages into quantified, monetary customer benefits. The value quantification capability requires that the sales manager translates both quantitative customer benefits—revenue/gross margin increases, cost reductions, risk reductions, and capital expense savings—and qualitative customer benefits—such as ease of doing business, customer relationships, industry experience, brand value, emotional benefits or other process benefits—into one monetary value equating total customer benefits received' (Hinterhuber, 2017, p. 164). A substantial amount of literature suggests that value quantification capabilities are critically important capabilities at the level of the sales force that set high-performing organizations apart (Hinterhuber, 2017; Luotola et al., 2017; Mullins et al., 2020; Terho et al., 2017; Terho et al., 2012; Töytäri and Rajala, 2015).
- Price elasticity: value quantification is required to determine the upper bound of prices, information on price elasticity is required to determine specific price points. Price elasticity is typically countercyclical – highest during weak growth and lowest during periods of economic expansion (Gordon et al., 2013). Price elasticity is not given – managers can influence customer price elasticity by marketing actions. Nagle and Holden (2002) and Hinterhuber (2004) provide a series of effects that managers can use to lower customer price elasticity and customer price sensitivity: by way of example, an understanding of the substitution effect, the unique value effect, the switching cost effect or the difficult comparison effect can be used to position the product relative to more expensive alternatives, to highlight the product's unique attributes, to increase switching costs or to decrease comparability with alternative offers.
- Price perceptions: customer perceptions of value and price are not given, they take place inside a context. The literature on psychological and behavioural pricing (Dowling et al., 2020; Hinterhuber, 2015; Kienzler, 2017, 2018; Monroe et al., 2015) shows that managers can favourably influence customer perceptions of value and price without actually lowering the price. Figure 14.4 provides an overview of some salient effects (Hinterhuber, 2015).

**Price-quality effect**
High price signals high quality. For differentiated products, a price increase can lead to a sales increase.

**Irrelevant attributes**
An irrelevant attribute combined with a price premium creates relevant differentiation.

**Framing**
Framing influences perceptions: e.g. framing savings as free bonus leads to greater sales than framing as discount. Reference prices are powerful.

**Discount presentation format**
For low-price products percentage discounts ('% off'), for high-price products absolute discounts ('€ off') increase perceived attractiveness.

**Scarcity effect**
Customers will purchase substantially larger quantities if the offer is limited or if the product is perceived as scarce.

**Color, cents & font size**
Prices in red font are perceived as more attractive. Large prices are perceived as less attractive. Sale prices should be presented in smaller font size.

**Price precision effect**
Precise prices are perceived to be smaller than round prices. Increasing a round price to a precise number increases purchase likelihood for high price items.

**Sale signs**
Adding a "sale" sign to a product increases sales.

**Price partitioning**
Customers underestimate partitioned prices; price partitioning leads to more favorable price perceptions and increased purchase likelihood.

**Preference reversals**
If a product scores low on an attribute that is difficult to evaluate, separate evaluation increases willingness to pay. Joint evaluation decreases WTP.

**Denominator neglect**
Customers underestimate likelihoods when probabilistic events are expressed in percentage terms rather than in absolute terms.

**Unit effect**
Customers treat product attributes as dimensionless quantities: Attributes expressed on a scale with higher numbers of units appear larger.

**9-endings**
Customers underestimate the prices of products ending in 9. Products with prices ending in 9 have larger sales than other products.

**Justifications for discounts**
Perceptual responses to discounts depend on rationale that retailers provide: plausible discount explanations increase perceived attractiveness.

**Decoy effect**
The introduction of an irrelevant option provides a strong justification for the choice of an initially unappealing option.

**Deal obsession**
Customers purchase larger quantities or pay higher prices just to experience the benefits of having obtained a deal.

**Paying more & being happy about it**
Flat fee bias: Customers prefer higher, but predictable fees. Conditional discounts: Customer satisfaction is higher for lower conditional discounts.

**Compromise effect**
When faced with a range of non-dominant options that vary along price and quality, consumers will opt for the intermediate option.

**Anchoring**
Arbitrary anchors (e.g. prices of unrelated products) increase willingness to pay and prices actually paid.

**Advertised reference prices (ARPs)**
ARPs influence customer behavior, even when customers know these ARPs to be untrue.

**Willful overpricing**
Setting prices moderately higher than what consumers expect to pay increases their willingness to pay.

*Source:* Hinterhuber (2015).

**Figure 14.4** Behavioural biases in pricing

Culture creates the cognitive map of beliefs, values, meaning and attitudes that drive perceptions, thoughts and actions (Hoppe, 2004). Hofstede (2001) characterizes culture with five dimensions: power distance refers to the degree that the less powerful expect unequal power distribution; uncertainty avoidance to tolerance for the unknown; masculinity/femininity to the degree to which values like assertiveness, success and competition prevail over warmth, quality of life and solidarity; individualism/collectivism to the degree to which people perceive their identity as distinct or as part of a group; and long-term orientation to the degree to which people delay gratification for their material, social or emotional needs. The dimensions are distinct and statistically independent, but some combinations are more prevalent than others (Hofstede, 2001). A meta-analytic review of close to 600 published studies finds a high predictive power for the four classical dimensions at the country level, with an ability to predict also individual behaviour (e.g. innovation conflict management, ethical behaviour) at least as well as other commonly used traits, such as the Big Five (Taras et al., 2010).

Culture influences perceptions and preferences: when asked a simple question – $3400 now or $3800 in one month – 85 per cent of respondents in Germanic/Nordic countries chose to wait, as do about 70 per cent of Asians, but only about 30 per cent of Africans (Wang et al., 2016). The cultural values of individualism and long-term orientation strongly predict this tendency to wait for higher future rewards (Wang et al., 2016).

Researchers have started to examine the influence of Hofstede's five dimensions on price sensitivity only very recently. Lee et al. (2020) analyse scanner data and conduct a series of studies in the US to examine the influence of the five dimensions on price sensitivity. The authors do not compare country scores on a national level, choosing instead to compare scores across individuals. Hofstede states: 'dimensions are meaningless as descriptors of individuals', 'warning that his dimensions do not make sense at the individual or organizational level' (Minkov and Hofstede, 2011, p. 12). The study finds that of Hofstede's five dimensions, only one dimension is related to price sensitivity: power distance. Consumers that have a high power distance belief are significantly less price sensitive than consumers that have a low power distance belief (Lee et al., 2020). These individuals are likely to be conservative and religious. The authors suggest that a high power distance belief can also be activated by brand communication – for example, 'You deserve to reach the top!' – in order to reduce customer price sensitivity (Lee et al., 2020, p. 113). The paper concludes with the speculation that customers in countries with a high power distance (China), should be less price sensitive than customers in countries with a low power distance (USA). This clearly is a far stretch. The data for sure are very robust in their local context – the US – but we will need further data, collected at a cross-country level, to better understand the influence of national cultural values on customer price sensitivity. This certainly is a promising area for future research.

Culture of course influences customer perceptions of value and price across cultures. The question is thus: is it possible to measure customer perceptions of value with one construct across cultures? The answer to this question is 'yes'.

A study with managers from the US, UK, India, Singapore and Sweden finds that B2B customer value measurement can be standardized across cultures and that the notion of customer value as a multidimensional trade-off between benefits and sacrifices holds up well across cultures (Blocker, 2011).

On to price: based on the seminal paper by Lichtenstein et al. (1993), we know now that price perception is a not a unidimensional, monolithic concept, but a construct with seven dimensions, positive and negative (see below). The key question is therefore, again: is the multidimensional stimulus of price measurement invariant across countries? Several studies conducted in Germany, Poland, China, Japan, Korea and the US (Jin and Sternquist, 2003; Meng, 2011; Meng and Nasco, 2009; Watchravesringkan et al., 2008; Zhou and Nakamoto, 2001; Zielke and Komor, 2015) suggest that the multidimensional construct of price perception is quite robust, has high external validity and can be generalized across cultures. Thus, customer perceptions of value as well as customer perceptions of price can be reliably measured with one construct across cultures.

Now, Lichtenstein et al. (1993) conceptualizes price perception as a multidimensional construct with seven dimensions, two positive and five negative. Two constructs positively influence price perception: price-quality schema and prestige perception. Five constructs negatively influence price perception: value consciousness, price consciousness, coupon proneness, sale proneness, and price mavenism (Lichtenstein et al., 1993).

Price-quality schema refers to the buyer's internal belief that high prices normally correspond to high quality. Prestige sensitivity, by contrast, refers to the desire to signal to other people prominence and status associated with high prices. Price-quality schema and prestige sensitivity are dimensions where high prices positively influence overall price perception. This, of course, is the exception. For the other five dimensions, high prices lead to unfavourable overall price perception.

Value consciousness refers to the concern about the ratio of quality received to price paid with the objective of obtaining the most favourable, albeit undefined, quality/price relation. Price consciousness refers the degree to which the consumer focuses exclusively on paying low prices. Coupon proneness refers to the propensity to respond favourably to offers because of coupons. Sale proneness refers to an increased propensity to buy because products are on sale. Price mavenism refers to the extent to which an individual is a source for price information for others (Lichtenstein et al., 1993). In a marketplace setting, these seven constructs show a high predictive validity in predicting customer purchase behaviour, price recall and sales responsiveness (Lichtenstein et al., 1993).

Across cultures, the relative importance of these dimensions differs: a study with Chinese, Japanese and US students (Meng and Nasco, 2009) finds that Chinese students are significantly more sensitive to price and prestige, while US students have a higher sales proneness, with no difference in price quality schema. A study with Chinese and Korean students (Sternquist et al., 2004) finds that, in the Chinese sample, neither of the positive price constructs are significant. In that study, in China, all price perceptions are negative, indicating a very high price consciousness.

A study with East Asian, including Chinese, students, by contrast, finds that across cultures price has, as expected, both a positive and negative role, with respondents rating value consciousness and sale proneness more highly than prestige sensitivity, price mavenism and price-quality schema, reflecting an overall high frugality and price consciousness (Watchravesringkan et al., 2008). In this study, Chinese students have a higher price-quality schema than other East Asian students. A study with US and Korean students finds that US students have higher levels of prestige sensitivity, price mavenism and value consciousness than Korean students, and that Korean consumers have higher levels of sale proneness and price consciousness, with no difference in price-quality schema (Jin and Sternquist, 2003).

Finally, a study of Chinese and US college students finds that the Chinese perceive a weaker price–quality relationship, are more prestige sensitive, less price conscious, less coupon prone, but as value conscious as their US counterparts (Zhou and Nakamoto, 2001). In this study, Chinese students are less price conscious than American students.

The problem inherent to all these studies on price perceptions across cultures is the sample: students. Using student samples is problematic: 'This is not to say that findings based on students are always wrong. It is only to say that findings based on students are always suspect' (Wells, 1993, p. 492). Consumer researchers note that they 'should not build universal theories on student-based results' (Wells, 1993, p. 494). In a recent study, researchers compare the results of a simple survey across dozens of similar student populations and find disconcerting differences in terms of scale means, scale variances and structural relationships (Peterson and Merunka, 2014). The researchers conclude: 'statistical inferences drawn from convenience samples of business students do not even generalize to a business student population' (Peterson and Merunka, 2014, p. 1040). This means that the studies examining the multiple dimensions of price perceptions across countries must be replicated with consumers, in B2C as well as in B2B, to yield truly meaningful relationships.

A field study conducted in the US finds meaningful relationships on price sensitivity among Chinese consumers: prices in Chinese supermarkets are substantially lower than prices targeting mainstream American customers (Ackerman and Tellis, 2001). Chinese buyers thus exhibit a higher price sensitivity than American buyers. A social norm of frugality in China may contribute to high price sensitivity among Chinese consumers (Weidenbaum, 1996). The price sensitivity of Chinese consumers is thus certainly higher than price sensitivity of Western consumers.

Finally, a series of studies in the US and China shows that consumers with a local identity have lower price sensitivity and are more tolerant of price increases than consumers with a global identity: perceived local identity affects price sensitivity and the willingness to pay higher prices for all products, not just local products (Gao et al., 2017). These studies thus suggest that firms launching premium products or planning to increase prices in China or the US should target consumers with a strong local identity first.

Furthermore, the role of superstitious beliefs requires attention. Superstitious beliefs are beliefs that are inconsistent with the laws of science. Superstitious behaviour arises when individuals want to create an illusion of control over events they perceive as being unable to control (Malinowski, 1948). In fact, high scores on a superstitious beliefs scale correlate with a high external locus of control (Huang and Teng, 2009). Western thinking, scholars argue, is based on the ability of humans to control nature, whereas Eastern thinking stresses the unity of humans and nature and has non-rationalistic tendencies (Nakamura, 1991). Thus, superstitious beliefs are more prevalent in the East than in the West.

Superstitious beliefs influence price perceptions. In China, two numbers stand out: 4 and 8. The number 4, associated with death, is perceived as unlucky, whereas the number 8, associated with prosperity, is considered lucky. An analysis of price endings in 500 newspaper ads in

China shows in fact that the number 4 as rightmost salient ending is underrepresented (1 per cent) and that the number 8 as rightmost salient ending is overrepresented, with a frequency of about 40 per cent of all price endings (Simmons and Schindler, 2003). A subsequent study of prices in ads in Singapore confirms that the number 8 as rightmost salient ending is over-represented, 4 is underrepresented, but so are many other numbers (Westjohn et al., 2017). A study with hotel managers confirms that cultural beliefs lead managers to set prices that end in 8 (Ngan et al., 2018). In a similar vein, about 90 per cent of hotels in China do not name the fourth floor as such (Pratt and Kwan, 2019).

Experimental research finds that lucky prices lead to more favourable price responses when customers hold superstitious beliefs and for high involvement products; as expected, prices ending in 8 are perceived more favourably than prices ending in 9 (Westjohn et al., 2017). Superstitious beliefs influence willingness to pay: Taiwanese consumers with superstitious beliefs are willing to pay substantially more for a package that contains a lower, but lucky (8), number of units than for a package with a higher, but not lucky (10), number of units (Block and Kramer, 2009). In conclusion: lucky numbers clearly influence customer choice and cus-tomer willingness to pay, in strong violation of rational choice principles.

Superstitious beliefs are also widespread in Western cultures: surprisingly, superstitious beliefs do not depend on education, but seem to be associated with situational factors, such as strong interest in sport and environmental influences (Mowen and Carlson, 2003). In Western cultures, there are also two numbers that stand out: 7 and 13: 7 is perceived as lucky, 13 as unlucky. In a study of US newspaper ads, the numbers 9, 5 and 0 are overrepresented – with no indication of an overrepresentation of the number 7 or an underrepresentation of the number 3 (Schindler, 2009). Another study of 500 prices on internet shopping portals, by contrast, finds that, in the US, prices ending in 3 are infrequent (Nguyen et al., 2007). All this points to the need for further research aimed at understanding if prices ending in lucky or unlucky numbers influence customer perceptions and price setting as much in Western cultures as they undoubtedly do in Asia.

Finally: an important question concerns the extent to which individuals in different cultures respond to psychological and behavioural pricing biases (see Figure 14.4). Surprisingly, except for the study documenting the influence of superstitious beliefs on willingness to pay (Block and Kramer, 2009), there are few studies that explore this fascinating research question.

For example, results on the price–quality effect in the price perception studies discussed previously are inconclusive: one study finds that the price–quality effect in China is weaker than in the US (Zhou and Nakamoto, 2001); two studies, one with Chinese, one with Korean students, find no difference between US and Asian students (Jin and Sternquist, 2003; Meng and Nasco, 2009); one study finds a non-significant price–quality effect in China (Sternquist et al., 2004); a study among only East Asians finds that the price–quality effect is higher in China than in other Asian countries (Watchravesringkan et al., 2008). A study among tourists finds a strong price–quality effect among the Japanese, but no effect among Australians (Jo and Sarigollu, 2007). Finally, a meta-analysis suggests that the price–quality effect is higher in China and India than in the US (Völckner and Hofmann, 2007).

Researchers increasingly call for studies conducted at the individual level (Hinterhuber and Liozu, 2017). A nascent stream of research takes the concept of global versus local identity as a starting point to understand customer price perceptions and price sensitivity (Gao et al., 2020; Gao et al., 2017; Yang et al., 2019): a series of studies in China and the US suggests that the price–quality effect is stronger for customers with a local identity than for customers with a global identity (Yang et al., 2019). The concept of a locally anchored self – individuals viewing themselves as local citizens first – leads to greater susceptibility to the price–quality effect. This study thus suggests that managers should activate consumers' local identity when promoting high-price products, whereas when promoting low-price products, managers should situationally activate consumers' global identity, thus reducing the perceived price–quality relationship (Yang et al., 2019).

In sum, we understand how psychological biases affect perceptions of value and price (Hinterhuber, 2015), but we do not understand how psychological biases affect perceptions of value and price in different cultures. This for sure is a research area that is bound to attract further attention.

## 14.3.2   The Company Perspective

The next dimension is the company. Two types of analysis are relevant: the analysis of competitive advantages and break-even sales analysis.

Understanding a company's competitive advantages: competitive advantage is 'the result of an enduring value differential between the products and services of one organization and those of its competitors in the minds of customers' (Duncan et al., 1998, p. 7). Understanding of competitive advantages is essential to determine the differentiation value in customer value quantification. Frameworks for understanding competitive advantages are discussed in other publications (Hinterhuber, 2015).

Break-even sales analysis: break-even sales analysis calculates the volume implications of price changes and is thus an internal benchmark of the minimum required volume increase or the maximum affordable volume loss that managers need to compare against available or estimates rates of price elasticity in order to decide on the opportunity and magnitude of price changes.

It is surprising how few executives are able to answer the following question: 'If prices are raised by 10 per cent, how much turnover can the company afford to lose, if overall profits are at least to be maintained?' The answer to this question depends exclusively on a product's profitability, that is, on its contribution or gross margin (net sales revenues less variable expenses). Break-even sales analysis is the tool designed to perform this analysis (Nagle and Holden, 2002). The formula is (Smith and Nagle, 1994):

$$BES\left(\%\right)=\frac{-\Delta P\left(\%\right)}{CM\left(\%\right)+\Delta P\left(\%\right)}$$

where: BES(%) = break-even sales volume (i.e., minimum required volume increase for price reductions or maximum affordable volume loss for price increases);

$\Delta P(\%)$ = % change in price;

CM(%) = % contribution margin (i.e., price minus variable costs divided by price).

For products with 20 per cent contribution margins, for example – which manufacturing companies generally consider to be low margin products – a price reduction of 10 per cent would have to translate into a 100 per cent increase in sales in order to be profitable. On the other hand, for products with contribution margins of 70 per cent, a price increase of 10 per cent is profitable if sales decline by 13 per cent or less.

Break-even sales analysis is a simple, yet powerful tool to assess whether contemplated price changes have any chance of being profitable for the company. Low margin products usually require fairly large volume increases for price reductions to be profitable; it should thus be considered either to increase/maintain the price or to exit. For high margin products, on the other hand, price increases can be quite profitable if volumes are expected to decline less than the amount calculated with the formula.

Chinese companies differ from Western companies in many ways: in China the creative use of utilitarian networks to obtain personal favours and to build organizational relationships is widespread and a distinctive feature of local business practices (Park and Luo, 2001). In addition, an emphasis on harmony seems to characterize company culture in both privately owned as well as in state-owned enterprises (SOEs) in China (Tsui et al., 2006). These and other aspects are discussed elsewhere in this book.

Chinese companies differ from Western companies also in one important aspect related to pricing: a near complete absence of pricing managers. In a recent study, Liozu (2019) finds that, among the 19 Chinese firms present in the top 100 of the Fortune 500 firms, not a single firm has a dedicated pricing manager: 77 per cent of the top 100 Fortune 500 companies, however, have at least one. The practice of pricing is thus severely underdeveloped in China.

### 14.3.3   The Competition Perspective

In the context of analysing competitors, the following data are relevant and should be collected: threat of new entrants, price trends in existing markets, strategies of main competitors, likely competitive reactions to own price changes (Hinterhuber, 2008).

China is a fiercely competitive market that is, at the same time, characterized by periods of collusion among firms engaged in price wars (Zhang and Round, 2011). Collusion is a characterizing feature of competition in China: for a long time scholars have characterized the attitude of Chinese policy-makers on antitrust laws as 'ambivalent at best' (Owen et al., 2005, p. 131), torn between the desire to break up administrative monopolies and doubts on whether or not antitrust laws for small and medium-sized enterprises are needed or should be enforced at all. This clearly is in stark contrast to attitudes in the EU and the US: price fixing, a violation of antitrust laws, is a criminal offence in the US, where convicted executives are jailed, and a civil offence in the EU, where convicted executives face civil damage claims, in addition to heavy fines imposed on companies.

The Anti-Monopoly Law (AML), which also contains provisions sanctioning price fixing, was finally enacted in China in 2008. As of recently, prohibitions against price fixing are also enforced against local Chinese companies, but cases are few and enforcement is patchy. Legal scholars argue that the AML acts as a shield 'protecting SOEs from foreign competition' while at the same time allowing SOEs to wilfully 'disregard the new law' (Zhang, 2011, p. 651).

The legal environment in China is hostile and favours local firms, regardless of just cause (Al-Khatib et al., 2007).

In terms of relevant competitive set, the Chinese market was traditionally split into the low-end and mainstream market dominated by local competitors and the high-end market in which Western companies competed. As a full member of the WTO, many multinational companies now produce in China and compete head-to-head in the mainstream market against Chinese competitors (Chang and Park, 2012). All this points to increased competition in China among Western companies and globally, increasingly involving Chinese companies.

## 14.4   SELECT PROFITABLE PRICE RANGES

In this step, the analysis performed previously is aggregated to determine prices that meet specific objectives such as profit optimization. Value quantification, price elasticity analysis, break-even sales analysis and competitor analysis (i.e. assumptions on likely reactions to own price changes) lead to prices that optimize profits.

If, for example, customer value quantification suggests that the product be repositioned and the prices increased by 30 per cent, break-even sales analysis can be used to determine the maximum amount of affordable volume loss. For a product with a 70 per cent margin, this price increase is profitable if volumes decline by less than 30 per cent.

Price elasticity analysis – historical market data, expert estimates or conjoint analysis – indicates whether the actual volume loss is likely to be larger or smaller than this number. If this research suggests that the actual customer price elasticity is lower and that the predicted volume loss, after taking competitive reactions into account, is 15–20 per cent, managers have a strong case for implementing the contemplated price increase.

### 14.4.1   Cross-cultural Differences: Setting Prices

There are three approaches to setting prices: cost-based, competition-based and customer value-based pricing. Across all studies, less than 20 per cent of companies practise value-based pricing and the predominant approach to pricing is competition-based pricing (44 per cent), followed by cost-based pricing (Hinterhuber, 2008). In the US and Europe, the number of companies setting prices based on value is increasing in any event (Hinterhuber and Liozu, 2012; Liozu and Hinterhuber, 2013). Price-setting practices in Asia differ: value-based pricing is, unsurprisingly, even less widespread than in other parts of the globe and competition-based pricing is even more widely practised (Chia and Noble, 1999; Rao and Kartono, 2009).

## 14.5   IMPLEMENTING PRICE CHANGE

Implementing price changes has two dimensions: price implementation within the firm, that is, securing the collaboration of other departments and of sales managers; and price implementation vis-à-vis customers, that is, convincing customers (Dutta et al., 2003).

Implementing pricing strategies internally touches upon different aspects related to organization, capabilities and incentives (Frenzen et al., 2010; Homburg et al., 2012; Terho et al., 2015). The literature provides several generic frameworks which can be helpful in implementing pricing strategies within the firm (Hinterhuber and Liozu, 2020). One such framework, specific to pricing, is the 5Cs model highlighting key aspects in implementing lasting and effective pricing strategies: champions, capabilities, centre-led organizational design, confidence and change management (Liozu, 2015). Several studies in fact show that these five factors explain superior firm performance (Liozu et al., 2014). Internal alignment is important. Lancioni et al. (2005) document the difficulties pricing managers face in implementing their strategies vis-à-vis different internal departments given the plethora of internal and external economic political influences that shape a firm's pricing decisions: in industrial companies the finance department and senior management are the largest obstacles in pricing strategy execution (Lancioni et al., 2005). Getting buy-in from senior management and the finance department is thus key.

Implementing pricing vis-à-vis customers is about value quantification, pricing discipline and price negotiation. Several studies provide guidelines (Alavi et al., 2018; Chapnick et al., 2014; Hinterhuber, 2017; Hinterhuber and Snelgrove, 2020; Lawrence et al., 2021; Loschelder et al., 2016).

### 14.5.1   Cross-cultural Differences: Implementing Pricing

With respect to the two dimensions of price implementation, scholars have studied cross-cultural differences especially with respect to price implementation vis-à-vis customers. What is considered acceptable negotiation behaviour differs across cultures: several studies confirm that Chinese negotiators rate ethically ambiguous negotiation tactics as more appropriate than do Western negotiators, which can be seen as the Chinese view that Western negotiation counterparts do not belong to their in-group, giving Chinese negotiators latitude to use questionable negotiation practices to achieve desired outcomes (Rivers and Volkema, 2013; Yang et al., 2017). Price negotiations with Chinese managers thus require a tolerance for ethical behaviour that Western cultures consider unacceptable.

## 14.6   CONCLUSION

This chapter presents a series of elements that should be considered in order to develop and implement pricing strategies effectively. Cultural factors influence this process along every step. Where available, this chapter reports relevant findings. Much is still to be learnt, to be clear, and in many ways some of the available studies barely scratch the surface on what we should know in order to implement pricing strategies across cultures.

# 15
# Case studies part III

## INTRODUCTION

Coffee is a drink that occupies a very important place in Italian culture. Drinking coffee is a daily habit, but it is also and above all an opportunity for socializing, an excellent excuse to discuss work, have a chat with a friend or invite someone to go out for a break. The Italian coffee culture, with its variety of drinks, is not a phenomenon confined to national borders, but has known a great diffusion abroad, bringing with it many names such as 'espresso', 'cappuccino', 'latte' and 'macchiato', which remain untranslated and yet are spoken daily by many consumers around the world.

The world can be divided into two parts: the coffee part and the tea part. Italy is in the coffee part, China in the tea part. It is ascertained that at least until the sixth century in China the drink of tea was used as medicine and prepared as a decoction rather than an infusion, while its date of origin as a drink is uncertain, probably because the plant was not cultivated, but the leaves of wild shrubs were used. There is no real coffee culture in China. The national drink is tea, compared to which coffee is a very recent product. The first attempts to cultivate the plant date back only to the second half of the nineteenth century, by a French missionary who tried to start a small-scale production in Yunnan, the area of the country whose climate is more favourable. Coffee began to become more popular only in the early decades of the twentieth century, through the entry of Europeans into China with foreign concessions. In the Shanghai of the 1920s and 1930s, the first coffee shops began to be opened, managed, and frequented mainly by Westerners and some upper-class Chinese. With the founding of the People's Republic of China in 1949, those premises were closed, and coffee only reappeared in the 1980s.

Travelling around China, one realizes that one of the many definitions of a country, undoubtedly prosaic but frequent in behaviour, is how China is the land of hot water. It is not only the amount of tea drunk, it is also the preference in avoiding drinking anything cold, from beer to wine, to fruit juices, to water; the definition also lies in the availability of hundreds of pre-cooked foods to which hot water is added. When tea is served in porcelain cups with lids in which the leaves float during business meetings, it turns out that it never ends. There is always someone who fills up the cup with hot water. Observing this attitude and preferring the simplicity of hot water, gives us a key to understanding the coffee issue in China.

# COFFEE CULTURE IN ITALY

Let's take a step back and go back to the coffee culture in Italy. The national identity includes coffee, the Bialetti moka (the coffee machine), the preparation of coffee, of which every Italian family keeps its secret, which arises from the composition of some simple variables, but considered fundamental: the quantity of water in the tank, the amount of powder to put in the filter, the intensity of the flame, the moment to take it off the heat, according to an art handed down in families. In other words, coffee is not a drink, it is an individual and social identity ritual.

The fact that coffee is not considered a drink demonstrates the misfortune of instant coffee in Italy. Italian coffee is born from this premise, which requires a prepared product

(roasted, powdered coffee), a set of hardware (one or more Bialetti moka), specific production conditions (low flame) and high preparation skills. Well, to understand this story we must remember that Chinese families do not have a Bialetti moka, they do not have a low flame on the stove, they do not know how to prepare coffee. So, in China, coffee remains a hot drink that must be easy to prepare with the tools normally available, preferably ready-made. From the fable of Italian coffee, we then move on to the Chinese history of coffee. In China, coffee is a drink and not a complex ritual. Therefore, the characteristics of a successful drink are: (a) ease of preparation; (b) large quantities for the price paid; (c) taste pleasing to the consumer. These are three things that Italian coffee, as it is, cannot offer the Chinese consumer.

**Figure 15.1**    The Bialetti Moka

# CULTURAL DIFFERENCES TO BE ADDRESSED

For an Italian coffee company there are therefore numerous differences in the perception of the product and significant obstacles to overcome. There is also a further cultural aspect concerning the relationship between quality and quantity. In the Italian imagination, the concept of quantity collides with that of quality in a proportionally inverse relationship, answering with the assumption that high quality is difficult to achieve, so its quantity should be low. Coffee is also subject to this law. In China, in particular, the cultural concept of quality is directly proportional to that of quantity, responding to the assumption that if there is an abundance of it, it is because it is of good quality, otherwise it would not stand the test of consumers. The offer of coffee or cappuccino (24 cl, 36 cl, 72 cl) in coffee shop chains such as Starbucks, Costa Coffee or Coffee Bean, for example, is therefore perfectly consistent with this idea and the concept of the ratio of quantity to price; paying 30 RMB for a drop of drink would be unwarranted, but for 36 cl it is acceptable for a Chinese customer.

Considering what is told in this story in China, coffee was consumed in bars before it was drunk at home, instant coffee is more easily usable than capsules, and to use ground coffee it is necessary to buy a coffee maker, which Chinese consumers are not used to. These conditions involve some very difficult feats, and others that are impossible. Let's start with the difficult ones.

To make coffee known to Chinese consumers, they must be given the opportunity to taste it under the best conditions, with the correct preparation, and in a suitable environment. The diffusion and growing success in China of the current version of the coffee shop, Starbucks in primis, but also of other international chains that use similar formats, is a necessary first step to spreading the product. There are direct sales points of Italian producers, but their number is too small, and, without the presence of US and US–British chains which developed the mass market, no diffusion of coffee would be possible. For a young Chinese citizen, entering these places means spending a few hours in the West, in a desired place, which makes them feel part of the global world. Coffee is therefore the magic potion that transports them through time and space.

Instant coffee does not belong to the Italian tradition, so Italian companies do not have much experience in marketing it. In reality, the instant product has an extraordinary advantage in a new coffee market: it does not require special equipment or extraordinary skills to be prepared. Only hot water. If you want to spread the product in non-biblical times, you have to reduce the learning costs for using it.

If there is no Bialetti moka in the house, no one will be able to make a coffee and therefore no one will buy ground coffee. Bringing an Italian coffee pot to Chinese homes is the last impossible task to complete if you want to sell traditional Italian coffee. Capsules have recently been a very successful alternative in traditional markets. But the capsules require a specific, expensive coffee maker, the doses are designed for what is internationally called 'espresso', that is a cup, where the value for money can only be understood correctly by a consumer educated in coffee, able to evaluate its quality according to European standards. This is definitely not the Chinese situation. Even this alternative product is therefore difficult and slow to spread. Mercilessly, China's market share data says it all:

- 0.4 per cent ground coffee powder (packs + capsules);
- 73 per cent instant coffee;
- 27 per cent ready-to-drink coffee.

A new and growing product is ready-to-use bottled coffee drinks, but that's yet another story. In China, a person consumes an average of 30 grams of coffee per year. Compared to the average of Western countries, these quantities appear almost negligible; for example in Italy about 6 kg per person are consumed in a year. However, there are some things that might shed a different light on this data. First of all, 90 per cent of coffee consumption in China is attributable to the urban population of the country, to young people, to the high bourgeoisie that is becoming international. Coffee is therefore a trendy drink, representing the modern, urban, professional and international lifestyle.

Coffee therefore represents a different idea of life from the traditional Chinese one; it is its flag. The offering of products and brand images cannot ignore this vision.

The 'therapeutic' factor is currently negligible, as the drink is not yet so well known that it is usually sought as a remedy for fatigue. Its interesting antioxidant and cardiovascular disease prevention properties are also topics of great potential interest for the Chinese consumer.

**Figure 15.2** Illy coffee shop entrance

Currently, the success of an international coffee brand in the Chinese market does not fundamentally depend on quality and taste, as happens in Italy. Many customers find the experience of going to a particular coffee shop to be important, if not the most satisfying. And many shops are often decorated even more richly than they are in their country of origin. As many Chinese like to stop at cafés, many offer comfortable seating and a large selection of pastries and cookies. To become established in a country where the dominant culture is that of tea, coffee, as an imported product, still has a long way to go. Cafés in China are crowded in the afternoons after work, while in the West people go for breakfast in the morning. In five years, premises have doubled, from 16 000 to 32 000. While Starbucks tries to create a 'third space' in its cafés that is different from home and work, Costa Coffee wants to convey to consumers a sense of familiarity as if, after the fatigue of work, they were returning home for a pleasant cup of steaming coffee. Coffee shops and instant blend manufacturers are experimenting with new aromatic formulas and medical properties to offer to Chinese consumers, getting closer to their desires, accepted and favourite tastes: sugary flavours, reduced caffeine content, low fat creams. Starbucks is launching new ad hoc products in China or re-proposing the most famous products (such as Frappuccino), but with blends of different ingredients and flavours, to better meet the tastes of local consumers.

## ILLY STRATEGY

The Espressamente Illy coffee shop is a different case. It is aimed at a sophisticated, coffee-educated customer. First of all, great attention is paid to the red interior design, which helps to reflect the colours of the brand and the idea of elegance and refinement

that Illy wants to convey. We must not forget that in China red is the favourite colour. On the walls there are photos that evoke the culture of coffee and on some television screens there are images relating to the coffee production chain, from photos of crops, to roasting, to the drink, with the aim of relating the coffee process to consumers not accustomed to the product. Products chosen for coffee shops in China include a wide range of coffee-based beverages. Among the food,

**Figure 15.3** Illy coffee shop atmosphere

some typically Italian specialities have been chosen, such as filled ciabatta and focaccia and snacks. Prosecco has also been included in the assortment of products available to customers, even if it is not a choice entirely consistent with Chinese culture.

Coffee was initially communicated as an exotic, precious and expensive drink, which lent itself well to being given as a gift on special occasions, visits to friends and family, or holidays. In this way it was also intended to leverage the culture of giving that characterizes China, used as a sign of gratitude and respect, but also as a demonstration of status, according to the price and refinement of the gift. In this sense, a well-known foreign brand of a product constitutes a guarantee of quality, since there is a widespread belief that products from abroad are more valuable. Instant coffee was initially marketed in gift packs, containing a real kit for the preparation of the drink, complete with cups, spoons and instructions for use. Going to supermarkets, one is surprised to see how much space is dedicated to coffee gift boxes.

## QUESTIONS FOR DISCUSSION

1. What are the conditions for the success of coffee in China?
2. What should the contents of the communication campaign be?

## CASE STUDY 15.2    NATUZZI GROUP IN TURKEY: THE BEARABLE CLASSICISM OF ITALIAN SOFAS
COMMERCIAL STRATEGIES

*Vera Costantini*

# INTRODUCTION

Is there a more iconic and enduring symbol of nineteenth-century bourgeoisie life than the sofa? As soon as people could afford them, sofas started to appear in the world's family portraits as status-proving favourites, with the parental couple sitting and other members – mostly children – placed around them in different postures and positions according to age and sex (Figure 15.4). Perhaps due to its peculiar function of representing a family's access to modern comfort, this quintessentially European piece of furniture boasts a wide spectrum of names.

The English word 'sofa' and the Italian *divano* both derive from Arabic words most probably smuggled into European languages via Ottoman mediation. *Suffa* defined 'a recess in a hall, with a sofa on

*Source*:    Claude Sciaky-Menasché Private Archives.

**Figure 15.4**    Istanbul-born cut-diamond dealer Leon Menasché and family, all Ottoman subjects, around 1910

its sides raised about six inches above that of the hall',[1] while *dîvân* indicated 'a public seat of a governor, counsel or judge, for the transaction of business of state, or for the hearing and settlement of cases'.[2] Surprisingly, these two words refer to open and even public spaces, while in Europe sofas are more commonly considered items representative of an exquisitely private dimension.

While in English and Italian these two words were experiencing a radical semantic re-settlement, the late Ottoman urban élite had become acquainted with *Marquise* and Chesterfield-type sofas, which they defined as *qânâpe*, from the French *canapé* (which in turn derives from the Medieval Latin *canapeum*). Undoubtedly due to its Western origin, this word was spared by the 1932 Turkish Language Reform. Hence, Turks still define sofas with the term *kanape*, although occasionally palatalized as *kanepe*.[3] To add a further argument to these remarkable phenomena of cross-cultural lexical exchange, the Italians call the bed-like rectangular sofa with movable cushions an *ottomana* (which in France is known as a *sommier*). The reference to the Ottoman-Turkish world could not be more explicit.

Since the end of the eighteenth century, French culture has always laid down the law among the Ottoman and then Turkish urban classes as far as taste and social behaviours are concerned. Therefore, I was not surprised when Mr Francesco Amendola, Country Manager for Turkey of the Natuzzi Group, told me that in spite of their open-minded and cosmopolitan consumerism, the Turks still stick to the magazine *La Maison Française* as though it were the bible of interior design and home furnishing. 'Italian design is appreciated worldwide, and we sell our sofas in Sicily as well as in Tokyo', Mr Amendola states with thinly concealed pride, 'but it is true that the Turks have cultivated a deeply rooted propensity for classical, more rounded shapes'. Before taking a closer look at this propensity and its sociological and historical premises, allow me to give a brief presentation of the Natuzzi Group and its Turkish commercial network.

*Source*:   Natuzzi Private Archives.

**Figure 15.5**    Pasquale Natuzzi (second from left) in his workshop in 1959

## NATUZZI COMPANY

One of the world's leading companies producing sofas, the Natuzzi Group was founded in 1959 in Puglia by Pasquale Natuzzi (Figure 15.5). The once small workshop now boasts eight plants and 558 stores employing 4346 employees (Figure 15.6). This success story has not prevented the Natuzzi Group from keeping its family-based structure: the founder's children are all working within the company.

Once luxury items, since the second half of the twentieth century sofas have become a must-have of any Italian private abode, requiring the Natuzzi Group to adapt to a varied demand. In spite of heavy pressure to lower production costs, the firm has maintained its plants in Puglia and nearby Basilicata, honouring the flag of south-Italian entrepreneurship and the true spirit of Italian quality brands. Rather than externalizing its production, the Natuzzi Group has chosen to internationalize its offer, establishing long-term partnerships with foreign firms.

## THE TURKISH MARKET

Present on the Turkish market for over twenty years, the Natuzzi Group has collaborated with Fatih Kiral since 2016. 'Mr Kiral is the Turkish version of Pasquale Natuzzi. The partnership could not occur with a more appropriate partner', says Mr Amendola. In his smile, I immediately recognize the relief felt by Italians when experiencing the sophisticated Turkish taste for relationships and passionate engagement in business. Used as we are to taking for granted the insane connection between efficacy and cold-tempered behaviour, we Italians cannot but feel less alone when dealing with trading partners such as the Turkish entrepreneurial bourgeoisie, who share our work ethic as well as numerous aspects of our lifestyle. Moreover, mutual partnership is further encouraged by the two countries' common structure of small and medium-sized family businesses, as demonstrated by the successful encounter between the Natuzzi Group and Fatih Kiral.

This partnership has led to seven single-brand stores opening in Turkey. Obviously, the COVID-19 pandemic has led to a contraction of a market that had already been put under stress due to the devaluation of the Turkish lira. Nevertheless, and Mr Amendola has no doubt about it, the Turkish market will soon thrive again and there are all the signs for a sharp recovery and stronger cooperation in the near future.

When I ask him to list them, Mr Amendola immediately refers to Turkey's potential in the communications sector. Apparently, Turks are among the most enthusiastic consumers of digital advertising in Europe. Extremely active on social media, Turks seem particularly sensitive to commercial communication, especially when it stimulates their fascination for glamorous foreign-branded products.

Certainly, we live in a globalized world and tastes have become internationalized. Mr Amendola mentions the existence of common threads connecting the tastes of consumers from all over the world. For example, metal-footed, square-shaped sofas are undoubtedly today's favourites. Nevertheless, local or national peculiarities still exist and taking them into consideration may determine the fate of a foreign firm's venture.

In fact, in spite of their cosmopolitan orientation, Turks are still attached to certain traditional values, in particular their affectionate devotion towards previous generations. Visiting parents, grandparents and

**Figure 15.6**    The Natuzzi firm in 2021

relatives in their homes is a recurrent phenomenon in Turkish society, which the COVID-19 emergency might have only temporarily interrupted.

According to Anatolian and Central-Asian tradition, visitors were conveyed to a large room called the *selamlık*. This defined a public space within the house, radically separated from the inner part. The floor was generally covered by carpets and a bench surmounted by cushions facing the entrance. As can be noted in famous examples such as Topkapı Palace, respect for symmetries was a central factor in these rooms. Since the mid-nineteenth century, the Ottoman urban élite had grown fond of French *salons* and English living rooms, where essential items of Oriental tradition, such as handmade carpets imported from the Ottoman Empire or Persia, were particularly popular.

In the 1930s, Kemalist Westernization accelerated the general modernization of Turkish society. The traditional Anatolian *selamlık* slowly started to evolve into the Turkish *oturma odası*, basically a European living room. Nevertheless, several decades had to pass before this urban pattern spread to the provinces and eventually to rural areas. Moreover, in spite of the ultimate success of the Kemalist assimilation process, the memory of public seating within a private house is still alive in heterogeneous Turkish culture, and receiving guests in living rooms somehow echoes the old *selamlık* tradition. This is perhaps the reason why formalism is still an issue and classical shapes are preferred to more modern, fashionable models. In this framework, the attachment to French taste may also find explanation.

# CONCLUSION

Turkey's accession to the French sofa civilization may be comparable to Italy's, since both countries experienced a gradual top-down dissemination of this product during the twentieth century, which in both cases required a structural diversification of supply. Nevertheless, as I have tried to explain above, Turkey's historical traditions displayed characteristics that the Natuzzi Group faced by offering classical solutions. It is no coincidence that one of the newest and most successful sofa models sold by this company on the Turkish market is called the 'New Classic' (Figure 15.7). Designed by Italian stylist Fabio Novembre, it revisits the Chesterfield model and is available in fabric as well as in leather. Its description in the advertising leaflet states that this model 'is the perfect balance between classic and contemporary that adapts to any lifestyle'. Are there more appropriate words to define Turkish consumers?

**Figure 15.7**    The 'New Classic' sofa, designed by Fabio Novembre for the Natuzzi Group

**CASE STUDY 15.3     ITALIAN SCOOTERS IN VIETNAM**
PIAGGIO MOTORCYCLES IN VIETNAM

# INTRODUCTION

Piaggio & C SpA is the largest Italian motor vehicle manufacturer, established in 1884, famous for the two-wheeled motor scooter and compact commercial vehicles. With over 50
per cent of market share, Piaggio is the leader in Europe and is ranked third in the world.
The products of Piaggio, including scooters, motorcycles and mopeds from 50 cc to 1400
cc under Piaggio, Vespa, Gilera, Derbi, Moto Guzzi and Scarabeo brands, are distributed
in more than 60 countries.

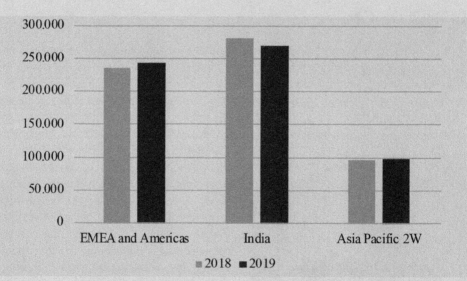

**Figure 15.8** Piaggio sales worldwide (number of products)

Thanks to his idea and the excellent design of Corradino D'Ascanio, the Vespa was first
introduced in 1946, and quickly became a legend in history. Piaggio's business continued to expand internationally, with over 40 per cent of its sales coming from the foreign
market. Currently, Piaggio Group's headquarters are in Pontedera (Pisa, Italy) and other
production plants all around the world such as Noale (Venice), Scorzè (Venice), Madello

del Lario (Lecco, Italy), Baramati (India), and Vinh Phuc (Vietnam). In the 1990s Piaggio Group took control of a historical Spanish marque, Derbi-Nacional Motor SA, one of the leaders in the small-capacity motorcycles segment. An agreement between Piaggio and a Chinese group named Zongshen was reached in 2004 concerning the manufacturing and sale of the engines and vehicles. In the same year, Piaggio finally completed the acquisition of the Aprilia-Moto Guzzi Group, creating the largest group of two-wheeled vehicles in Italian industry.

The Asia Pacific 2 Wheeler has been responsible for establishing the companies Piaggio Vietnam, Piaggio Asia Pacific, Piaggio Group Japan Corporation, Foshan Piaggio Vehicles Technology Research & Development and Piaggio Indonesia.

In 2019, the Piaggio Group sold over 611 000 vehicles worldwide, reporting net sales of the group of 1521.1 million euros (see Figures 15.8 and 15.9).

The sales of the Asia Pacific region had the highest growth rate, by 14.6 per cent, from 85 700 to 98 200 units.

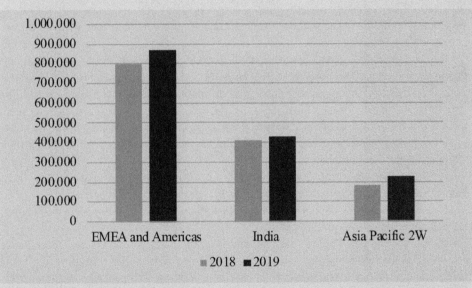

**Figure 15.9** Piaggio sales worldwide (turnover in euros)

The first Piaggio factory in Vinh Phuc, Vietnam went into operation in the second half of 2009, producing two-wheelers such as Vespa, Fly and Piaggio Liberty. Due to demand and market expansion, two production plants are active, the total capacity of those plants being approximately 300 000 units per year. It is also the first Research and Development unit centre for the two-wheeler sector in Asia. With that, Piaggio Vietnam became the third largest production facility, after Pondera in Pisa, Italy, and Baramati in India. The objective of the Piaggio Group in the Asia Pacific region is to continue to expand sales and to explore opportunities for medium and large engine motorcycles.

# CULTURAL BACKGROUND

In Vietnam, the family and clan are valued more than individualism. The clan is the most important social unit in the country and each clan has a patriarch at the head of the clan and a clan altar. Even today, in some parts of the country, the tradition of clan members living together in long houses is quite widespread. It is not uncommon to see three or four generations of a family living under the same roof. Clan members are blood-related and often call their villages by the name of their clan. All clan members usually attend the commemoration of the death of other clan members.

There are a few shared cultural norms that deeply influence behaviour and communication across the general population of Vietnam. The first is the concept of face. This is the quality embedded in most Asian cultures that indicates a person's reputation, influence, dignity and honour. By complimenting people, showing them respect or doing something to increase their self-esteem, you give them face. Similarly, people can lose face by being criticized or by behaving in a way that is considered socially inappropriate. Therefore, individuals in Vietnam generally act deliberately to protect their self-worth and peer perception.

The Vietnamese do not like to stratify their people into 'classes' and prefer to feel unified in their society. The government's communist orientation particularly supports this view. Nevertheless, in reality, there are quite distinguished stratifications in society. The differences in wealth between those living in rural and urban areas are increasing. As such, there is not much of a recognized middle class; people are mostly distinguished as either 'rich' or 'poor'. Brand items are admired and those who are wealthy tend to exhibit their affluence to differentiate themselves.

There is a general cultural acceptance of hierarchies in society regarding one's age, gender, status and education (relating to Buddhist, Confucian and Taoist concepts).

There is a noticeable nationalism in the culture as the retention of the Vietnamese identity has been such a long-enduring feat.

According to the Lewis model, the Vietnamese cultural classification is basically reactive and the Confucian influence is still strong. They are, however, dialogue-orientated, this being partly due to the French influence and, in the south, prolonged contact with the Americans.

The following are the values and core beliefs: Confucian: work ethic, duty, morality; Respect for learning; Filial Piety (pre-Chinese); Theme of sacrifice; Resistance to foreigners; Resilience, Tenacity; Nationalism; Forbearance; Sense of proportion; Collectivist (society over individual); Women play important role; Pro-Westernism; Pride, Self-respect (esp. North); Entrepreneurialism (esp. South).

The tradition is of a collective leadership according to Confucian tenets.

The Vietnamese are a group-orientated society used to living and working in close proximity to each other. The Red River Delta, with almost 19 million inhabitants, is one of the most densely populated areas on earth. The Vietnamese are not, however, tactile. Their sense of time, basically Asian and cyclical, has been affected by French and American influences, so that mañana tendencies observable in the Philippines and Indonesia are less of a problem in Vietnam. The bureaucracy is, however, stifling, particularly in the North.

The traditional enmity for and resistance to China is the central theme of Vietnamese society.

The Chinese cultural influence in Vietnam is, however, pervasive, just as it is in Japan. This is evident in art, architecture, religion, music, literature, poetry, theatre and language (script, governmental, literacy, philosophical and technical vocabulary).

Currently the Vietnamese are trying to solve their problems by following the Chinese model – that is, to liberalize the economy as quickly as possible and encourage investment, while at the same time maintaining strict political control.

# PIAGGIO IN VIETNAM

To survive and separate itself from the competitive market, every brand must possess strong characteristics and unique features; Piaggio is no exception.

Vietnamese urban consumers are very open to foreign brands. American, French and Italian names are the most attractive and are preferred to Chinese or Korean brands. Hence, Italy enjoys a very high reputation, and its image is very positive. Piaggio has a historical brand recognition, and is now very famous in the world. When the name Piaggio is mentioned, the

most iconic and symbolic model is the Vespa. On the 2013 World Industrial Design Day, CNN listed Vespa as one of the twelve best designs from the past 100 years. The design of Vespa is linked to Italian looks and lifestyle, and has been recognized as a moving artwork for many years. Due to its worldwide reputation, Piaggio's entrance into the motorcycle industry in Vietnam was much easier than it was for other brands, and it also quickly drew great attention from customers on the market.

Furthermore, people in Vietnam are now more and more concerned about quality when making a purchase decision. Therefore, Piaggio attracts many customers with its great quality products. The produc-

**Figure 15.10    Vespa in Vietnam**

tion site in Vietnam has held certifications for Quality management systems since 2009, Environmental management system in 2011, Occupational Health and Safety Management System since 2013, a guarantee for the qualified systems.

To improve performance and reduce fuel consumption and pollution, Piaggio has created a 3-valve engine generation performing smoothly and also in an environmentally-friendly way. Another advanced technology is the hybrid technology, a combination of a low environmental impact conventional internal combustion engine and a zero-emissions electric motor, both reducing fuel consumption and carbon dioxide emissions.

Piaggio has several drawbacks that need to be improved to gain market share in Vietnam.

First, the average income per person in the big cities of Vietnam is approximately US$150 per month, equivalent to US$1800 per year. However, Piaggio's lowest available product price in Vietnam is the Piaggio Zip, with a selling price of $1300, which means a worker would have to spend 9 months' earnings to purchase this product. The Piaggio Beverly model, with 3-valve engine technology, has the highest listed price, at nearly $6500. Only the middle to high-income class can afford this price range, which prevents Piaggio from gaining a larger market share.

Additionally, there are only six Piaggio product lines available in Vietnam, including Vespa, Liberty, Beverly, Fly, Medley and Zip. Compared to other brands such as Honda and Suzuki, Piaggio has a limited diversification. For instance, Honda has a range of product lines for the needs of every kind of customer, from low-income to high-income groups. With the same amount of money needed to purchase a Piaggio Zip, customers can choose from over 20 different models from Honda at reasonable prices.

With a population of 90 million people, demand for the motorcycle is growing rapidly in this industry. Moreover, due to the poor infrastructure in Vietnam, other public means of transportation such as buses and the metro are not well developed. This is a great opportunity for Piaggio to extend their production.

Moreover, with the Piaggio plant in Vinh Phuc, the approaches and distribution to other potential Asian markets such as Thailand and Indonesia are easier. Recently, the burden of import tax has been lowered. Also, the lower labour cost in Vietnam reduces the manufacturing cost, improving profitability.

Although the demand for the motorcycle is growing, the economists have predicted that Vietnam's market will soon reach saturation point. Instead of gaining a greater market share in Vietnam, Piaggio could accelerate its exporting to other Asian countries to create more profitability.

Competition within the motorcycle industry is fierce. Piaggio must compete with many reliable brands such as Honda, Suzuki and Yamaha. Hence, the switching cost in this industry is low, customers being able to choose among many alternatives, so there is rarely customer loyalty here. Due to the economic crisis in 2008, customers' price elasticity increased, lead to lower margins because of price competition.

To gain market share in developing countries including Vietnam, Piaggio's strategy is to expand production lines, and especially to launch low-medium cost scooters; also it is shifting from a premiumization strategy to a price strategy. Otherwise, Piaggio is unable to compete with its rivals.

# MARKET SEGMENTATION – TARGETING

Being one of the largest motorcycle manufacturers in the world, the Piaggio Group focuses on the segmentation, targeting and positioning process to serve the greatest number of potential customers rather than spreading its resources and capacities.

First, the price range of Piaggio's product varies from $1400 to $6500, which is considered a very high price. Hence, Piaggio Vietnam is focusing on the potential customers who have high purchasing power, particularly the middle and upper-middle-income class. Regarding age and gender, young people, especially women, can be another potential customer group.

Advanced technology is one of Piaggio's competitive advantages in Vietnam's motorcycle industry. Hence, a potential group is people who are interested in technological innovation. They are the customers who are willing to pay a significant amount of money to explore the latest technology.

On the basis of lifestyle, people who love classic Italian looks and design will be Piaggio's potential customers.

Therefore, Piaggio Vietnam is focusing on customers who live in urban areas.

Summarizing, although there are many potential groups, Piaggio Vietnam is focusing on only two main target markets. The first target market is the middle or upper-middle income class who want to explore advanced technology. The other target is young people, especially women, who tend to love Italian design.

# MARKET POSITIONING OF PIAGGIO VIETNAM

Currently, Piaggio provides Vietnamese customers with five product lines including Beverly, Liberty, Medley, Fly and Zip, as well as the subsidiary Vespa.

All the four ranges of Vespa, Medley, Beverly and Liberty have different designs and characteristics. However, those ranges are sold at a high price and innovated with the latest technology, so they meet the demands of the middle to upper-income class customer who wish to explore advanced technology.

The young who love Italian style, however, may not be able to afford those ranges due to their price. For this reason, Piaggio Vietnam has introduced Piaggio Zip and Fly to meet their demand. Piaggio Fly is a classic Italian design model equipped with the super efficient 3-valve 125 cc engine, with large tubeless tyres for easy handling and safety. It is a more economical model, sold at only $1800.

With the dense intensity of the distribution channel, Piaggio products can reach customers throughout the whole country, from rural to urban areas (Figure 15.11).

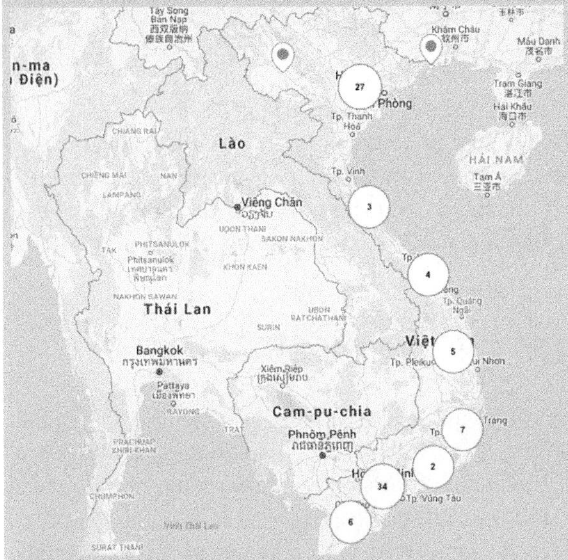

Taken as a whole, the two main factors that affect Piaggio's business are offered products and price. Piaggio has done an excellent job by providing a range of products with Italian style and great quality. In particular, products such as Vespa and Liberty have become a new trend among customers. It can be seen that Piaggio and has a firm foothold and favourable reputation. However, Piaggio's market share in the motorcycle industry is still small. The price of its products is considered to be high compared to the average income of the Vietnamese.

**Figure 15.11**  Distribution network of Piaggio Vietnam

Air pollution has been an area of concern in Vietnam in recent years. Caused by coal-fired power plants, industrial activity, transport vehicles and construction activities, the PM2.5 index in Hanoi is five times higher than the World Health Organization's (WHO) standard level, as shown in a report by GreenID. As a consequence, many customers are looking for a motorbike with new advanced technology to reduce emissions. Piaggio should take this into account and develop innovative products with this technology. It is a way to attract attention and trigger the desire for Piaggio's products.

Electric vehicles, including electric bicycles and electric cars, have become common and widespread in recent years. If Piaggio can develop a new electricity-based product, it will draw a great deal of attention from customers. The electricity-based product could take advantage of the favourable iconic design of Piaggio, not only environmentally friendly by cutting emissions, but also reducing the production cost and price, making the pricing strategy more effective.

Actually, the Piaggio Group is developing another innovative product in electric mobility designed for the Asia Pacific market, the most important in the world for the volume of electric scooters.

## QUESTION FOR DISCUSSION

1. Suggest to Piaggio an improved marketing strategy and communication campaign in order to increase sales and brand reputation, justifying the premium price.

## CASE STUDY 15.4    CHINESE CONSUMERS IN EUROPEAN LUXURY SHOPS
### CHINESE GLOBETROTTERS AND DIOR LUXURY SHOPS

# SUMMARY

Luxury shoppers have been considered a sort of global segment. As they travel more, indeed, the Chinese are making a rapidly increasing share of their luxury purchases outside the Mainland. 'Mystery' research has been conducted in order to analyse Chinese consumer behaviour inside the luxury Dior shops. Chinese consumers act very differently compared to traditional clients.

# INTRODUCTION: LUXURY AND CHINESE CLIENTS

For years, luxury shoppers have been considered a sort of global segment, acting in the same way in different cultures and places. As a matter of fact, luxury flagship stores are almost the same for a brand all over the world, consistently following the brand image strategy, the brand/store experience, and the customer care service.

The market for luxury goods continues to demonstrate huge potential growth, especially with the Chinese consumer market. The demand for luxury goods in China continues to increase, driven by a number of positive factors such as the growing number of affluent and middle class, rising household disposable income and higher luxury spending, the affirmation of women as business leaders, as well as the increasing number of people travelling.

In buying luxury products Chinese buyers are more differentiated and unique, ranging from experienced consumers with a high degree of sophistication, to luxury novices. In addition, Chinese consumers are the most generous, allocating about 50 per cent of their spending to luxury gifts (against a global average of 40 per cent).

China continues to play a fundamental role in global luxury brands. As consumers travel at an increasing rate, their tastes and knowledge of products continues to widen.

It is therefore increasingly important for luxury players to maintain a strong brand image and synergies in their marketing and product selection, both in China and overseas.

Chinese consumers also make a selective choice among countries and associate specific products with each one. It is easy to guess that Switzerland comes top for luxury watches, France for cosmetics, Italy for clothes and leather goods, while Germany comes top for the automotive industry. This phenomenon is increasing in the Chinese mentality, since it represents a direct link with the product itself and the corresponding heritage associated with it. Heritage is, indeed, one of the strongest values added to a product, since it embodies the craftsmanship and history carried out over a long time.

As they travel more, indeed, the Chinese are making a rapidly-growing share of their luxury purchases outside the Mainland; in 2015, 10 per cent more compared to 2014 (Bain & Co., 2016). Much of this overseas shopping takes place in Hong Kong and Macau, but Europe is growing in appeal among Chinese luxury consumers. That is more than double the European share two years ago. According to the China Tourism Research Institute, China had 127 million outbound visitors in 2017 and they spent 126 billion US dollars, increases of 4 per cent and 5 per cent compared with 2016. Among overseas travellers, nearly one out of four reported that they bought a luxury good while travelling, expressing positive feelings. The first five, out of ten, destinations were in East Asia, while the sixth and the seventh were France and Italy, as the first European destinations. Looking closely at the Italian situation, according to ENIT (Italian National Agency for Tourism), in 2018, 3 785 000 Chinese tourists visited Italy, since visas are valid for the whole Schengen area.

If the number of Chinese travelling abroad for personal reasons has increased tenfold in ten years, the use of the Web has helped them to find out about brands and prices of their favourite European products. According to the declaration made by the managers of several luxury brands, in the main tourist destination cities in France and Italy, more than 70 per cent of the retail stores sales can be attributed to Chinese overseas tourists. Therefore, the buying behaviour of the Chinese globetrotters concerning luxury products is an important phenomenon that should be studied in order to understand if their wants and expectations fit in with the traditional retail mix strategies of the luxury European retail stores.

## REASONS TO BUY ABROAD

There are several reasons that drive Chinese luxury consumers to make their purchases outside their home country, which are economic, cultural and social. The following are the motives that prompt them toward this choice.

The price discrepancy between luxury products sold in China and overseas is one of the main drivers of economic advantage that encourages wealthy Chinese consumers to shop outside their Mainland. Based on data estimated by the Chinese Ministry of Commerce, the average price of luxury goods in China is 45 per cent higher than in Hong Kong, 51 per cent higher than in the United States, and 72 per cent higher than in France.

Luxury products are not delivered in the same quantities and collections everywhere. One basic reason why the Chinese are more apt to travel for buying is that often there is a limited product selection, imposed by government and brands, on what they receive in their home country. On the brands' side, the relative offer is intentionally limited in China, as it is due to different import policies regarding materials and goods. More than that, it is mainly basic items that are found in the Chinese market, whereas limited editions and special editions are only sold in the main European shopping hubs.

Chinese consumers are aware and know that having a luxury product where it has been made adds prestige and honour per se. They are even aware that, even if identical in China, buying abroad adds value, because of the risk of counterfeit products. Even though they are not well-educated consumers, they can understand the meaning of Made in Italy or Made in France, and show it off to friends and family. Shopping in countries where products are effectively made increases the preciousness of the product itself, since many Chinese consumers, either for economic reasons or working constraints, do not have much time to travel to Europe.

Social gifting is particularly entrenched in Chinese culture; those having the chance to travel are used to always buying presents for their relatives, friends or business partners, as it is considered a must for them, having had the chance of being in Europe or the United States.

Since China's worldwide reputation in handcrafted products is often, if not always, associated with counterfeits of luxury products, the Chinese are more apt to make their purchases where they are 100 per cent sure that what they are choosing is genuine. Since Chinese consumers are extremely aware of their counterfeit culture, they have become more conscious of the quality of products than their counterparts elsewhere in the world. They are much more aware of the difference between an authentic bag and a fake one. For this reason, Chinese luxury consumers buy a large percentage of their luxury goods while travelling abroad.

In order to analyse the impact of the growing wave of Chinese globetrotters on European luxury shops, a qualitative research was made.

Luxury shops are quite different compared to the rest of the retail outlets, because of the client expectations, customer service, atmosphere and the experience, but it seems that the literature considers these characteristics as normal, maybe because of the traditional and consolidated approach. So, the retail mix of a luxury store is expected to be characterized by good customer service, a luxury atmosphere, relative permanence, customization, and privacy. The research tried to verify if these traditional beliefs are still consistent with the new Chinese globetrotter luxury consumers.

# MYSTERY RESEARCH

The research methodology adopted was observation of the behaviours followed by Chinese shoppers. In doing this, without directly affecting any brand–customer relationship, the mystery shopper method has been used in two different approaches: (1) a mystery shopper role, entering the store twice a week, on different days and at different times, staying in the store for at least one hour observing the behaviour of Chinese customers; (2) a mystery salesperson role, acting as a salesperson for four months, serving Chinese customers with the help of a salesperson in the store.

The luxury flagship store chosen for the research was the Christian Dior shop, and the location was Venice. Christian Dior was chosen because is a globally known luxury French brand having a great number of products in its Made in Italy lines. So the country of origin of the brand in many cases is different from the country of origin of the products, even if both are European. In Dior's case the country-of-origin perception was analysed in a complex context, French, Italian, European, from a Chinese point of perception. Moreover, in buying a French brand in Italy, the consumer is making an interesting shortcut to the perception of European goods.

Venice was chosen as the location because it is one of the most visited cities in Italy by tourists (more than 9 million tourists in 2019, for 34 million nights). Venice is also the second most visited Italian city by Chinese tourists (87 per cent of tours made by Chinese tourists include Venice). The Chinese consumers' behaviour related to the purchase of luxury goods was directly observed, while the sales personnel were constrained to tailor the shopping experience directly to meet their preferences. The observations (346) were made on all days of the week, weekends included, in the afternoon (being the most popular time that the targets shopped). In order to avoid disturbing the buying behaviour within a luxury store, no questionnaire was submitted or interview done (also language and cultural barriers were considered).

The main observations can be summed up in the following points.

a.   Targets: the Chinese consumers interested in luxury goods are extremely heterogeneous: there are consumers belonging to very high social classes, as well as some from medium-high ones. The latter, though, have been the main focus for luxury brands in recent years, since they are expanding their level of wealth and are moving towards a more Western lifestyle.

b.   Product preferences: the Chinese consumers' attention is mainly aimed at everything that might show a brand logo, opting for bright colours and gold details rather than any other more sober versions. It can be stated that the consumers rely much more on the overall brand country-of-origin effect rather than the specific technical features, the manufacturing techniques and the country where the products are made. On the other hand, in most cases they come into the store with information already acquired through the web; nevertheless they are quite easily persuaded to look at other products. Usually, they come with photos of what they are looking for, being either a direct choice or requests sent by friends or relatives. More than that, what most attracts their attention are the products advertised in their country, mainly by stars and celebrities; these are a very strong influence on their choice. Jointly, the same attitude occurs for all those products targeted specifically for their country. One example of this is the animal shape bracelet, sold in January and February, to celebrate the Chinese New Year, which is identified every year with a symbolic animal.

c.   Shopping interaction: conducting a sale with a Chinese consumer is not easy, because very often they look for someone who is able to communicate in their own language. In fact, even though several of them have studied the English language, their knowledge is widespread but limited. Venice is one of the most important poles of attraction for Chinese consumers, and most of them travel in visiting groups, which helps with the language and cultural barriers. The time that Chinese groups have available for their shopping tours is extremely important. The majority of Chinese consumers travel abroad through organized group tours, where excursions and sightseeing opportunities are precisely planned in the whole day. That's why the time factor is another important element to be taken into consideration, since it can often represent a barrier to achieving a final sale. Another interesting aspect is that Chinese consumers often do not have a clear idea about the brand country-of-origin. Indeed, a misunderstanding often occurs between the country of origin and the country where the products are physically made.

d.  Other incentives: another element of great relevance is the reliance on the tax-free refund. The Chinese are the number one nationality among the top 10 spenders, spending abroad over three times what they spend locally. They accounted for 35 per cent of the world's tax-free refund in 2019, since for 82 per cent shopping represents a vital part of their travelling experience. Christian Dior fixed the tax-free refund at 12 per cent, resulting in a consistent portion of saving.

e.  Timeline: as they travel in a group most of the time, Chinese shoppers have a limited amount of time to spend in the store and a strict deadline. This means that purchases are often made in a frantic hurry, and shoppers often have to put down their purchases and leave the point of sale. Therefore, time management become a strategic issue.

The evidence from the observation of Chinese consumers' behaviour underlines some aspects that should be analysed and considered in facing the Chinese consumer going global. First of all, their buying behaviour is strictly influenced by the 'recipe' the shopper has prepared before leaving the country and that has been given to them by the friends and relatives they are buying for. So, the number of decisions and choices taken inside the shop is far lower than usual, if compared with a non-Chinese customer. Luxury goods companies should therefore advertise their brands and products in China in order to sell them in European stores, even products that are not sold in China, but normally part of European collections. This is important for the new trend for Chinese consumers who wish to have products that are not normally available in their country so they can appear socially different and more sophisticated. Together with these kinds of products not sold in China, European shops should sell typically Chinese oriented products, such as for the Chinese New Year tradition, which are totally devoted to globetrotter Chinese travellers and not to European customers.

A second aspect concerns the tourist behaviour of the luxury goods shoppers. As we discovered during the research and observation period, the greatest number of Chinese customers travel in groups, and this condition should be taken in account when defining the sales strategies of retail stores in the touristic cities of Europe. This means that the luxury brand companies should develop agreements with the incoming tour operators in order to include their stores in the travel itinerary. This is positive both for the luxury brands, increasing their sales opportunities, and for the tour operators, because Chinese tourists are really interested in shopping. Nevertheless, this strategy represents a new challenge for the luxury brands, because they are not used to such a relationship, which is normally considered inconsistent with the image and prestige of the brand. Actually, these agreements with the tour operators, even informal ones, are normally promoted by medium-low-cost local ethnic stores. Obviously, a relationship between tour operators and luxury brands should lead to a rich service and exclusive offer, which would be coherent with the image of the brand.

A third point is time management in the buying and sales behaviour. The customers don't manage their personal time because they are travelling in a group. This means that when the group leader announces that the time is up everyone leaves the store immediately, because they have a strict timetable. In welcoming the Chinese customers, all the salespeople should know the precise time the shoppers can spend in the shop, because they are the only ones who can manage the available time and avoid being unable to close the sale in time. In fact many observations showed that the customer left the product they were buying because their time was up. So, time management should become a new important skill of the salesperson in luxury sales.

A fourth aspect concerns the perception of country of origin. As the Chinese consumer is not completely acquainted with brands, country of origin, and Made-in differences, this should be explained clearly to the customers and not considered as given, as in case of an European customer. A strong motivation for Chinese consumers making purchases in Europe is the reputation of authenticity of the products, which they consider more reliable than the ones available in China. This is obviously a perception due to the story of the Chinese market. However, emphasizing information on the country of origin should be considered in order to enforce the value of the purchase in European retail stores.

The fifth point is connected with customer service. As the observations illustrate, salespeople serving Chinese customers must speak the Chinese language; moreover they should be Chinese in order to facilitate the relationship and understand the buying culture of the customers. Also, at the point of sale a communication in Chinese should be displayed, together with the local language, and the customer service should be tailored to consider Chinese standards and expectations (for example shipment to Hong Kong in order to avoid import taxes).

The luxury brands retail stores should assume a dual image, both Chinese and European; Chinese for customer service, European for atmosphere. It is clear that this is a difficult choice to make, because following this approach the stores would be managing one of two totally different strategies according to whether or not the customer is Chinese, considering service, time management, payments (due to tax refunds) and product presentation. If at the same time there are the two different profiles of customer in the shop, it would be reasonably expected that every day the shop attendants would have to manage a totally different set of expectations that are often not easily combined.

As a matter of fact, the Chinese luxury shoppers, who represent a high percentage of sales in European stores, are changing the rules of the game. The traditional customer service theory, based on a long and careful relationship, exclusive space and atmosphere, timeless and experiential experiences inside the point of sale, do not fit in with the needs of Chinese luxury shoppers. The idea of a luxury flagship store must be reconsidered and firms need to innovate to cope with the paradox represented by traditional European customer desires and new Chinese ones: the same location for two totally different approaches.

**CASE STUDY 15.5      WESTERN COSMETICS IN THE FAR EAST**
THE CULTURE AND THE IDEAL BEAUTY CONCEPT

# SUMMARY

The Chinese, Korean and Japanese beauty ideal has traditionally differed in large measure from the Western one. This is possibly because the impact of Chinese culture on purchasing habits is behind the preference or low diffusion of certain categories. Western beauty companies have had an important role in shaping beauty standards around the world and after decades of promotion of Caucasian ideals, a shift is happening, with increasingly higher degrees of diversity in terms of the models employed and products offered. They have chosen different strategies.

# INTRODUCTION

The cosmetics sector is one of the fastest growing and belongs to the top five sectors of consumer goods in China, in thirty years developing from being non-existent to becoming the second largest market in the world. The influence of Chinese culture on companies' strategies is potentially strong. The most influential factor is the fact that the Chinese beauty ideal has traditionally differed in large measure from the Western one. Despite Western influence, Eastern beauty criteria could represent an obstacle to a standardized marketing approach. Nevertheless, the Chinese cosmetics market is dominated by Western multinational companies and the luxury segment of the market is the one where there is the fastest growth. In China there was no market tradition in luxury cosmetics. This has allowed companies to have a different positioning compared to their home markets and to sell their brands as 'luxury', gaining competitive advantage, since luxury usually comprises uniqueness and differentiation from competitors. Also, the concept of accessible luxury is important in China. The brands belonging to accessible luxury have been extremely successful in recent years. A characteristic of luxury brands is to rely on a standardized strategy because they respond to universal needs and the segmentation of the market is natural. Due to brand value, an adaptive approach has been avoided. This case study investigates whether this approach has changed in the Chinese market.

In China self-beautification practices were prohibited during Mao's regime and the equality of genres was pursued in a collectivist society. The non-existence of a domestic industry represented an opportunity for Western companies, who were attracted by the potential of the market. Today they dominate 80 per cent of the market. However, the different beauty ideal, cultural barriers, and the rise of competition from domestic and regional players that can offer products aimed specifically at East-Asian women are putting pressure on Western companies.

**Figure 15.12**   Far East ideal beauty types: Korean, Chinese, Japanese

## THE BEAUTY IDEAL

However, the Chinese traditional ideal of beauty differs to a high degree (Figure 15.12). Not only does the ideal differ, but adaptation to the Western stereotype, because of people's natural features, is impossible to obtain. Despite the rise of plastic surgery operations, the result has been a mixture, a composite of traditional criteria and Western ones. For example, wide open eyes came to be considered extremely beautiful, but the adoration of white skin persisted. The main Western companies, historically so reluctant to adapt their luxury cosmetic brands, had to go in a new direction and offer products that are suited to the different skin tone and texture of Asian women and to their hair. However, an analysis exclusively focused on the Chinese market, without including consideration of Japan and South Korea, would not provide a complete picture or the necessary tools to comprehend the Chinese market as a single market inserted in the East Asian region or the reasons behind certain strategies adopted by Western firms.

While Western beauty ideals have exerted great influence on Eastern beauty ideals, a new awareness and pride in East Asian ideals is happening. The appreciation of a different ideal came from the diffusion of exposure to famous and beautiful Chinese actresses. Japan has been the first country to develop a strong industry and to become the second market in the world. However, its development has been dictated by the influence of Western ideals and fashions. Brand names and their allure are connected with Europe. Despite the low market share of Japanese brands in Western markets, they have established a status of high innovative and quality products.

China is the main driver of the actual change, supported by the rise of Korea. The emergence of China and Korea as powerful economies legitimates the praise of the Asian beauty ideal. Because its understanding has been so crucial for Western companies in China, it is influencing Western women too.

In all three countries ideal beauty is identified with the following characteristics:

- White skin: not only does the skin have to be as white as possible, but it should also be smooth and free from wrinkles and blemishes.
- High-bridged nose: noses that are not too flat and wide are preferred.
- Black hair: long black shiny hair is still preferred.
- V-shaped face: long and slim oval shape with a pointy chin is ideal.
- Double eyelids: wide-open eyes are undoubtedly the most desired feature.
- Petite figure: there is a great accent on thinness and most women are victims of extreme dieting from an early age.
- Long legs: Women wear short skirts to show off their legs.

Having depicted the Chinese beauty ideal, it is possible to derive the impact of Chinese culture on purchasing habits and the reasons behind the preference or low diffusion of certain categories. From what has been said so far, consumption is driven by the desire to reach the described ideal which relies on skincare for obtaining a jade-coloured complexion, while adopting low use of makeup and fragrance, which are not perceived to be natural. Skincare is the dominant category, followed by hair care, while makeup and fragrance offer many opportunities for market development strategies by Western companies. However, since the use of beauty products is filtered through Chinese culture, the consumer is still not accustomed to using certain product categories.

The education of the consumer it is an important factor in the quality of the shopping experience. Even if beauty culture has increased significantly among certain parts of the population, millions of people year by year become new users of some categories of beauty and cosmetic products and there is still a lack of knowledge, especially in rural areas. Highly trained sellers are also a way of gaining a good reputation and brand recognition.

Even if beauty products are also highly popular in the Western countries, in China it assumes a cultural importance. Gifting is a distinctive trait of Chinese culture and beauty companies are aware of that. People like to buy beauty products as a present, and sets are best suited for this purpose.

The big multinational cosmetics companies that started to enter the market were well known around the world, but not in China. The first step towards promoting the brand successfully is to find a good corresponding brand name in Chinese. However, this is a difficult task due to language barriers and differences. A successful brand translation should consider the language, sound and meaning. However, a preference for the original brand name was increasing, particularly having both the original and the translated name, an approach that the multinationals are following.

The question to be addressed is: does the East-Asian beauty ideal influence Western companies' strategies?

Beauty companies have had an important role in shaping beauty standards around the world, and after decades of promotion of Caucasian ideals, a shift is happening, with increasingly higher degrees of diversity in terms of the models employed and products offered.

# L'ORÉAL

L'Oréal, the most global brand, follows a peculiar globalization strategy: universalization. This means globalizing but respecting diversity around the world in terms of beauty ideals, routines and traditions. 'The more global your company becomes, the more local your strategy has to be' is the strategy followed.

L'Oréal chose to create a Chinese name that means 'Elegance coming from Europe'. Lancôme's Chinese name means 'Girls in the bloom of youth'.

L'Oréal entered the market later than some other competitors, in 1996, by establishing a partnership with an important Chinese Medical University, the Suzhou Medical College, from which it founded the Suzhou L'Oréal Beauty Products company. It also started to build a new factory in response to the forecasted development of the industry. At that time

Chinese consumers were more used to Europe in general than to Paris itself (while today French brands are really appreciated). L'Oréal decided to focus more on skincare, in accordance with the Chinese beauty ideal. Another choice that differed from the strategies adopted in other countries was selling the L'Oréal brand as an affordable luxury. It was sold at around half the price of a real luxury brand, in department stores of the biggest cities. The consumer was educated using trained shop assistants at the stands, since a culture regarding cosmetics was totally absent.

In 2005, as a sign of commitment to the market, the group opened a research centre in Pudong, outside Shanghai. Its goal is to gain in-depth knowledge of Asian skin and hair and to develop products suitable for all Asians around the world.

In a market like China where preference for local ingredients is so strong, the acquisition of national brands has been a good strategy to strengthen their position. The company decided to acquire the national skin care brand Mininurse in 2003. In 2004 another skin care brand was acquired: Yue Sai. In 2014, the Magic brand, the Chinese leader in the face mask segment, was acquired.

A major role in strengthening the brand over the years has been played by massive advertising campaigns. L'Oréal makes extensive use of famous models and celebrities for its advertising campaigns, and this was the strategy adopted in China too, endorsing its first ever Chinese ambassador, the actress Gong Li. Celebrities had the dual role of presenting L'Oréal to Chinese women and 'encouraging them to pursue beauty', while at the same time attracting a Western audience and diffusing the ideal of Eastern women.

# ESTÉE LAUDER COMPANIES

Skincare brands offer different solutions and price ranges, starting from Clinique to Estée Lauder and La Mer. Since Estée Lauder is a premium brand it is targeted at the globetrotters and indeed the website proposes selections of products to carry onto the plane, different sets and boxes already packaged as gifts. Whitening products and some targeted creams and serums, with the packaging suited to Chinese preferences, have been added to the range. However, the aim is to sell all products on a global level. Estée Lauder did not acquire a domestic brand.

Local production has not been established but due to the strategic importance of the market, in 2005 a research centre was opened in Shanghai. The China Innovation Institute, later called the Estée Lauder Companies Asia Innovation Centre, was founded in order to 'help the company understand Chinese consumers' preferences, needs and interests in new trends'. In 2014 a historic brand launch was made by the company: the Osiao Asia Skin Institute. It is the first ever brand specifically developed for a particular region. Instead of acquiring a local brand, the group engaged its New York-based researchers and the Shanghai-based ones worked for five years on a comprehensive study of more than 1000 Asian women to understand the secrets of glowing skin. The products that resulted are a combination of Chinese medicine and its traditional ingredients and Western technology and science.

In 2010 the model Liu Wen become the first Chinese woman to be signed by the brand, in the role of global brand ambassador. Later that year a model with dark skin and a Polish model with fair skin, blue eyes and blonde hair formed a trio. Choosing a local model and proposing localized campaigns was not an option but having a trio of models who could represent all the women around the world was a move that was favourably received. Liu Wen represented the company around the world but was particularly present in all the campaigns for China and represented the brand in new shop openings and events.

# LVMH LOUIS VUITTON MOET HENNESSY SE

The Guerlain brand entered the market in 1993, while the exact year of Dior's entry is uncertain but it can be assumed that it may be similar to Guerlain's. The other brands have entered the market in recent years.

Vertical integration is pursued in all the divisions of LVMH in order to have more control over the operations and assure the quality standards that distinguish a luxury brand. The Chinese affiliate is a manufacturing and distributing facility. The company reports extensive collaborations around the world with various centres and universities, but the official research centres are located in France.

In terms of product adaptation, Dior and Guerlain offer a whitening line, respectively Diorsnow and Blanc Perle, in order to meet the Chinese preference for fair skin. By comparing the Dior products available at the Chinese and French Sephora outlets, the following figures emerge: the perfume segment includes 30 products for China and nearly 90 for France; there are 65 makeup products in China compared to 95 in France; and 51 skincare products in China compared to 47 in France. It can be concluded that the offer is adapted in the sense that is reduced according to Chinese preferences. Guerlain's offer shows the same picture: perfumes and makeup are downsized and with a changed mix, while skincare prevails. It can be concluded that overall the adaptation of the products is limited.

The Dior TV campaigns are in the typical Chinese style, considering the colours, the music, and the accent on the way the products work inside the skin. Indeed, the company signed with a local agency in Shanghai to handle Dior's online campaigns in order to make them more appealing to the Asian public. A revolutionary step concerning the models was also made by the brand. Both the campaigns featured Asian models, who only appeared in Asia.

The evidence and the findings concerning the three case studies highlight different solutions and strategic approaches to the distant culture markets, in particular East Asia. Nevertheless, there is a common basic strategy concerning the alternative between standardization and adaptation in the cosmetics industry: adaptation. The focus on skincare, the lighter makeup products, the different assortments connected with the different beauty ideal, the development of new specific products with the ingredients of the Chinese cosmetics tradition, and the communication strategy focused on Asian models, are all clear evidence of the influence of the East-Asian beauty ideal on cosmetics companies.

## QUESTIONS FOR DISCUSSION

1.　What can be considered the most effective strategy/strategies?
2.　Why?

**CASE STUDY 15.6    VALUE CREATION FROM FRANCE TO JAPAN**
**LOUIS VUITTON JAPAN[4]**

*Mitsuyo Itonaga-Delcourt*

## SUMMARY

Japan is one of the most important luxury markets in the world. Cultural factors affect the influence of Japanese customers regarding quality of both products and customer service. Retail plays an important role in delivering the right service and quality experience expected by the Japanese client during the purchase process.

## INTRODUCTION

The Japanese luxury market is ranked third in the world, at 18 billion euros in 2020 (–24 per cent vs. 2019). Japan is a strategic country for the French luxury brands, members of the *Comité Colbert*.[5] Among them, Louis Vuitton (hereafter LV) remains one of the most popular brands. After its launch in the Japanese market in 1978 with five stores, LV has made great strides. According to a survey, 44 per cent of Japanese women aged 15 to 59 owned a LV-brand bag in 2013 (Hata, 2004). In 2015, LV had 1800 employees and sales of over 100 billion yen (800 million euros). In the global development of the brand business in post-war Japan, it may be worth tracing LV's retail-management interaction with department stores who have contributed to building the Japanese consumer society and lifestyle. Culturally speaking, different aesthetics throughout history are important as their embedded values may influence Japanese customer idiosyncrasies with regard to quality of both products and customer service. Also noteworthy is LV's customer relationship management, inspired by Japanese customer-centricity hospitality *omotenashi*.

## SOCIO-ECONOMIC CHANGES AND BRAND BUSINESS IN JAPAN

After the opening of the country in the middle of the nineteenth century, most women still wore the traditional kimono.[6] It was only after World War II as modernity accelerated that they adopted Western-style clothing together with accessories.

The history of retail in Japan is strongly linked to the development of consumer purchasing power in the post-war Japanese economy. Economic growth was driven by a sharp increase in population (from 72 to 93 million between 1945 and 1960) and the government's 'Income doubling plan' initiated in 1960 and achieved by 1967 boosted an 'economic miracle' (1954–1973), resulting in Japan's becoming the world's second-largest economy in terms of GDP as of 1968 (until 2009). In the meantime, entry into the Japanese market by foreign retailers had legal barriers due to the Foreign Capital Law (1950), enacted to create a framework for foreign investment. Although the capital controls were progressively lifted, leading a rapid expansion of capital flows in the 1970s, foreign retailers were limited to 10 stores up until 1975.[7]

Improved standards of living are reflected in a population's perceived social status; according to annual survey from the Japanese Cabinet Office, over 80 per cent of Japanese people considered themselves middle class from 1970. The colloquial expression *'itten gôka shugi'* (one-luxury principle) coined by poet Shuji Terayama in 1967 means making a monotonous daily life stimulating or transformational with a single luxury beyond one's economic means, be that by buying a luxury item, occasionally consuming expensive food, or attending a high-priced cultural event. This thinking could correspond to today's marketing concept of 'Ordinary and Extraordinary experiences'.[8]

In the 1970s, a strange phenomenon was observed: parallel importers purchased quantities of LV products in Paris and sold them in Japan for three to five times their price. As an increasing number of Japanese travellers tried to acquire LV products in Paris at the local price, the LV headquarters commissioned research on the Japanese market.[9] The LV brand launched in 1978, which was timely as the end of the 1970s saw a boom in the consumption of luxury goods.

In 1981, Yasuo Tanaka, then a business school student, published a best-selling book *Nantonaku Crystal*, which depicted the strong consumerist tendencies of young, urban populations. The main protagonist, a female college student and model, was driven to 'feel somewhat crystal' in her brand-oriented consumerism. About 450 annotations were added explaining each of the brands, music and trendy stores featured in the book. In fact, the author intended a parody of catalogue-like magazines full of attractive products of luxury brands targeting young adults. He also predicted a change in consumption patterns due to a shrinking population. The Japanese economy largely depends on domestic demand. Although Japan is ranked fourth in the world in terms of export volume, its ratio of GDP is 16.1 per cent (2019 CIA data).

## *SHINISE* – TRUST AS KEY WORD IN BUSINESS

Japan is home to more than 33 000 so-called *shinise*, or companies that have at least 100 years of history (41 per cent of the world's total), according to a study conducted by the research institute Teikoku Databank in 2019. These are highly respected companies in Japanese society. Apart from global companies such as Sumitomo (1590), Shiseido (1872), Nintendo (1889) or Panasonic (1918), the majority of *shinise* are family-run small to medium businesses, such as: carpentry, ryokan (traditional hotels – the oldest one was established in 705), paper manufacturing, pastry making, sake brewing, and so on. The common characteristics of these long-lasting companies are: a clear mission and philosophies with a long-term vision; a client-oriented business based on quality and trust earned through daily interaction with their customers, flexibility and innovation, especially in times of socioeconomic change; originality; respect for employees; and lean financial management.

Japan is said to be a learning country where return on investment is generally longer than anywhere else because it can be related to the time needed for building trust with business partners and stakeholders. Without exception, LV Japan had to adopt this principle while negotiating retail space or projects (Hofstede's 'uncertainty avoidance' is scored high) with department stores.

On the list of *shinise* there are major department stores, originally kimono retailers: Mitsukoshi (1673), Isetan (1886), Takashimaya (1831), Matsuya (1869), Matsuzakaya (1611) and Daimaru (1717). Mitsukoshi (formerly Echigoya) was particularly instrumental in popularizing fashion and consumerism. Established in the capital city of Edo (today Tokyo), its storefront shop proposed a cash-sales system of a no-haggle price and cash on delivery. The shop expanded its customer base to include ordinary citizens by selling kimono fabric by piece. Before then, kimono businesses would operate by bringing goods to wealthy customers' households.[10] This new business model would later be applied to the opening of the first department store in 1904.

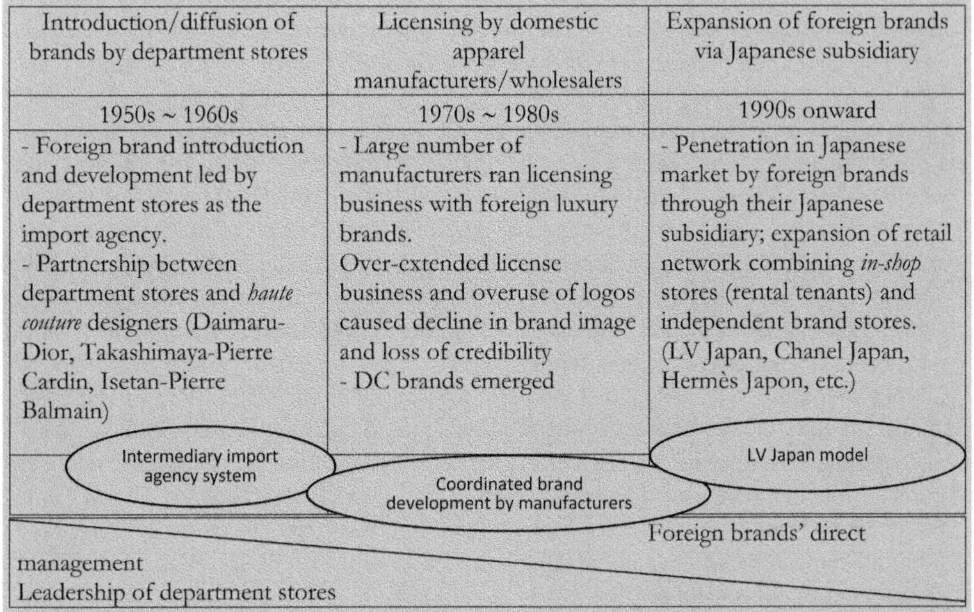

| Introduction/diffusion of brands by department stores | Licensing by domestic apparel manufacturers/wholesalers | Expansion of foreign brands via Japanese subsidiary |
|---|---|---|
| 1950s ~ 1960s | 1970s ~ 1980s | 1990s onward |
| - Foreign brand introduction and development led by department stores as the import agency.<br>- Partnership between department stores and *haute couture* designers (Daimaru-Dior, Takashimaya-Pierre Cardin, Isetan-Pierre Balmain) | - Large number of manufacturers ran licensing business with foreign luxury brands.<br>Over-extended license business and overuse of logos caused decline in brand image and loss of credibility<br>- DC brands emerged | - Penetration in Japanese market by foreign brands through their Japanese subsidiary; expansion of retail network combining *in-shop* stores (rental tenants) and independent brand stores. (LV Japan, Chanel Japan, Hermès Japon, etc.) |

Intermediary import agency system

Coordinated brand development by manufacturers

LV Japan model

Foreign brands' direct management

Leadership of department stores

**Figure 15.13** Evolution of fashion brand business in Japan

Department stores had been at the centre of the brand business at least until the collapse of the bubble economy (1991). Figure 15.13[11] shows how they popularized brands in general and how brand businesses evolved. In the 1950s and 1960s, at the time of a boom around Dior's *New look*, they established a partnership with French *haute-couture* brands to reproduce products. Although this business was not financially successful, it served to learn dressmaking techniques and to enhance each store's brand image (Bouissou et al., 2014). During a second phase in the 1970s and 1980s, buyers of department stores hunted talented, even unknown designers and introduced them to Japanese consumers.[12] In parallel, small start-up fashion brands emerged and created trendy clothing by quickly adopting the latest fashion trends from Paris, London and New York. They presented and sold their collections in an apartment in Harajuku, a popular area for fashionable young people in Tokyo. Facing this phenomenon, large, established Japanese apparel companies opted to develop licensing partnerships with foreign brands for short-term profit instead of nurturing their own designers and brands. Seventy-five French licences were thus registered in the 'textile and textile products' category in 1977.[13] As a reaction, DC brands (Designer Brands) such as Comme des Garçons began to crop up. From the 1990s onward, a large shift can be seen, from department store-led intermediary businesses to fully managed brand businesses led by foreign companies: LV, Chanel and Hermès through their local subsidiaries.

# LV RETAIL STRATEGY

In the LV retail network nationwide (57 stores in 2015), over 40 stores are shop-in-shop (*in-shop*), located in department stores as rental tenants although they are directly managed by LV. The company has a well-balanced distribution strategy between their own stores and *in-shop* stores by combining the advantages of both. Their own stores are a real showcase for the brand with a high degree of freedom in designing interiors and exteriors with original architecture, while well-known department stores (particularly in the middle-sized cities) at good locations offer high probabilities of attracting customers. From the point of view of (potential) customers, *in-shop* stores are more accessible physically and psychologically, whereas own stores offer a more thrilling experience with a large range of products and discovery of a brand universe through temporary events such as art exhibits and interior settings.

While preparing to launch on the Japanese market, LV Japan concluded two important contracts (Hata, 2004). One covers distribution, signed between LV Paris and Japanese partner department stores. Through their subsidiary in Paris (opened to support Japanese tourists), merchandise was transferred from the LV storage (the contract covered until this stage) and sent to Japan. For a company that operated only two stores in France and didn't have much experience in handling customs-clearance procedures and logistics, it was certainly a convenient solution.

The other contract concerns brand-images protection between LV Japan and local department stores. This covers corporate identity (uniforms of salespeople, wrapping paper) and advertising, to be created by LV. No discount. Problems related to product quality were handled directly by LV Japan. Finally, all the salespeople were to be employees of the department stores whereby LV Japan had to provide company-specific training. LV Japan registered sales of 1220 million yen (about 9.7 million euros) in 1978, which increased to 2460 million yen in 1980. These results show that the collaboration between the two parties functioned well, partly thanks to the contribution of salespeople of partner department stores.

Department stores used to preserve the heritage of training new employees as a traditional apprenticeship. All of the new employees, including four-year university graduates, started their careers as salespeople so that they could understand individual customers' needs and aspirations. Each of them was accompanied by an experienced mentor, generally for one year. A wide range of training was provided, from correct bowing, using polite language, to how to handle customer claims. The primary objective was customer loyalty. As per the expression '*ron yori shôko*' (facts rather than theory), this experience was beneficial in particular for marketing and merchandising. A similar system was also implemented at LV.

In the mid-1990s, LV Japan concluded its policy of sending their own salespeople to their *in-shop* stores. Shigehiko Yarita, who served as the general manager of the human resources division of LVMH for 21 years, commented that the cornerstone of LV Japan's success has been its direct management, given that the sales efficiency increased as well as the level of devotion to the LV brand.[14]

## TOTAL QUALITY, BOTH VISUALLY AND SUBSTANTIALLY

Japanese consumers are known as the most demanding in the world, as commented on by B. Ganne (2009).[15] Like other luxury brands such as Hermès, in the beginning LV Japan received frequent claims about defects such as tiny spots or irregularities on the surfaces of products or stitching around fasteners. These were seen as a result of careless manufacturing and lack of respect for end users. It was necessary for LV to resolve these problems through numerous exchanges with the Paris office and adaptations to specific quality requirements from Japan. To convey the brand value and philosophy, LV Japan obtained an agreement from the Paris headquarters that 50 per cent of the communication budget could be used by the Japanese subsidiary for locally specific advertising. For example, the print advertisement featuring all the parts of a LV rigid suitcase reads:

> **Louis Vuitton is repairable**. Please rest assured [the word *anshin* is used]. From the small rivet to the entire frame, all parts can be replaced [...] We use the same parts and employ the same techniques as Paris, the quality is guaranteed by our dedicated craftspeople. They will make your piece look just like new. When repairing tanned leather, our concern is for the overall harmony of the product and we match color tones of leather of your piece [...]

## SPECIFIC PERCEPTIONS OF QUALITY AND AESTHETIC VALUES

The linguist Susumu Ono notes that the Japanese adjective *utsukushii* (beautiful) originally meant 'affectionate feeling toward the family'. During the Heian period (794–1185), aristocratic classes developed a sophisticated culture with a sensibility to the four seasons that was expressed in poetry, novels, paintings, food and clothing. Particular attention was given to fine, graceful, small things.[16]

At the crossroads of different aesthetic notions is a history linked to shoguns and samurai. Elaborate protocols of gift wrapping were invented and developed during the Muromachi shogunate period (1336–1573). Depending on the purpose, the recipient's social rank, the season, the quality and colours of the wrapping paper used, the ways of folding and their shapes were carefully selected. All had to be performed in a very precise and neat way. The adjective *orime-tadashii* (properly folded) describes persons of good manner and behaviour who are highly appreciated in customer service.

In a Japan almost completely shut off from foreign contact during the Edo period (1604–1867), the shogunate established a caste society based on a Confucian value system with privileged rights exclusively given to samurai. The authorities penalized *zeitaku* (luxury consumption) by common people. In the face of sumptuary laws that restricted them to wearing sober colours, they playfully invented 48 variations of browns and 100 greys, some of which are named after popular actors of the *kabuki* theatre, their favourite pastime. They also developed small patterns called *komon* with extremely sophisticated dyeing techniques to make them appear plain when viewed from a distance. The aesthetic notion of *iki* (chic, stylish)[17] reflects people's interest in alluring fashion. During the Edo period, refined crafts requiring meticulous care and rigor flourished, even in common household items. Exhibited at the Universal Expositions of 1867 and 1889 in Paris, Japanese crafts and art contributed to the artistic movements of *Impressionism* and *Japonism*.

Overall, Japanese consumers are attentive to the details as well as the harmony of a product as a whole.

## *OMOTENASHI* – JAPANESE-STYLE HOSPITALITY

Symbolical, and largely used in the hospitality sectors and by brands such as Shiseido as an important concept in customer service, *omotenashi* is a word that originated in the Heian period.[18] It was later developed in relation to the tea ceremony, founded by Sen no Rikyû (1522–1591). In the philosophy of *omotenashi*, hospitality is meant to make guests feel comfortable. What is important is the memory of a good time spent together. In this sense, *omotenashi* is an equal and 'mutually beneficial' approach. In the retail and hospitality industries, it means creating agreeable experience with customers that leads to customer loyalty.

Emmanuel Prat, former CEO at LVMH Japan, states: 'Japan has great customer service, care-focused omotenashi, so salespeople need to improve soft skills … It's not just selling products, they need to build a relationship with customers and develop it'.[19]

## EXCEPTIONAL SKILLS AND PASSION ARE NEEDED TO SELL LUXURY GOODS

The Japan Professional Salesperson's Association (JASPA) was founded in 2016 by the initiative of Prat, Yarita and Collasse (then CEO of Chanel Japan), aiming to improve the status and professional skills of salespeople and to promote their long-term career development. It brings three types of companies together: foreign-luxury brands, department stores and major Japanese apparel companies. All of them express concern about the difficulties in recruiting talented salespeople when customer service is the 'core' of the fashion business and the most important touchpoint with customers. Through programmes including visual merchandising (VMD), customer relationship management (CRM) and cultural courses, they also train women with retail experience who wish to return to the workforce after having left it to raise children. They offer a certificate to those who succeed in exams (both written and practical in-store exams by mystery shoppers). By wearing the certificate badge, JASPA hopes that they will be a model for other salespeople.

# CONCLUSION

In the process of establishing itself in the Japanese market and adapting through inter-actions and learning with local business partners and customers, a tactically designed strategy supported by solid foreign capital had a significant impact on the Japanese brand business environment. In this respect, LV Japan's brand value creation is an exemplar case study.

The skilfully designed strategy and value creation of the LV brand was appropriate for the fertile soil of the Japanese market with positive resonance to Japanese people's psy-che. Several factors contribute to its popularity:

1. For Japanese consumers, a luxury product represents quality and *anshin* (peace of mind). Psychological security - *anshin* - is of primary importance as aesthetically satisfying and solidly crafted articles are reliable and reassuring. As bags and purs-es are for daily use, Japanese customers are drawn in by the functional aspect of the LV products.
2. LV is a French brand, a country synonymous with culture and sophistication.
3. Established in 1854 in Paris, LV is a *shinise*, representing a guarantee of quality and prestige.
4. The company is founded on the quality of its craftsmanship, something greatly val-ued in Japan where skilled, creative craftspeople enjoy high esteem.
5. By owing a LV product, a certain customer will maintain harmony in his or her social group whose members also own LV items. Other values appreciated are long-lasting products supported by repair services (since 1993) and the timeless design of the iconic model with the *damier* pattern and the interlocking LV monogram, fitting for almost any occasions.

In 2020, during the pandemic crisis, LV opened two flagship stores: one in Osaka with a restaurant and café and another in Tokyo, the world's first LV flagship of men's collec-tions, as the Japanese market is considered to be a laboratory for the brand in view of its further development in other countries.

## QUESTIONS FOR DISCUSSION

1. Which are the pillars of value for Japanese customers in luxury products?
2. Which are the main differences comparing Japanese and European customers in value evaluation in luxury fashion products?

**CASE STUDY 15.7    FERNET AND COLA IN ARGENTINA**
THE ITALIAN *AMARO* AND THE AMERICAN ICON GIVE RISE TO A CONSUMER PHENOMENON NEVER SEEN BEFORE: FERNANDITO

*Rosana Beatriz Fabbiani*

## SUMMARY

Fernet Branca and other liqueurs launched in the early twentieth century were intended for Europe and American countries where Italian emigrants brought their customs. The Fernet boom in Argentina is due to an exciting and semantically perfect combination: an *amaro* with a hard personality is mixed with Coca-Cola, in a national adaptation that has become cultural rooted. Branca is trying to export its success to other countries, but this is not easy.

## INTRODUCTION

Fernet Branca's successful formula in Argentina may look a lot like the cocktail recipe that turned it into a myth. Its main ingredients are cultural roots, the value of friendship and the pleasure from intense flavours. Another ingredient is the mental freedom that underlies every innovation: in this case, the combination with the American drink, a secret recipe too.

Results exceed every marketing strategy: the traditional Fratelli Branca *amaro*, a secret receipt – even today – created by its founder in the mid-nineteenth century as an ancient cure against cholera, malaria and digestive problems, has developed in the country of the tango a consumption per capita of 1.8 litres per year, an absolute record. How? Keep reading.

## FRATELLI BRANCA, THE ENTERPRISE OF A MILANESE APOTHECARY AND HIS HEIRS

Bernardino Branca was a master speziale (apothecary) from Milan. In 1845 he developed a recipe based on medicinal herbs to produce a formula that helped fight fever and aid digestion.

A secret infusion of 27 herbs coming from four continents, that after a long process of infusion and decoctions and a long storage in oak barrels, finally emerges in its unique form as a dark liquid with a bitter, slightly aromatic flavour. Even today, the Fernet recipe remains a secret closely guarded by fifth-generation family members and the president, Niccolò Branca.

He called it Fernet, a name whose meaning is still a legend. A few years later, Bernardino founded Fratelli Branca Distillerie together with his sons. He moved production to a laboratory in the Porta Nuova area where it remained until 1911, when the Branca found its final destination in via Resegone, in Milan, where Bernardino's great grandson still preserves the original recipe.

The company went through the most turbulent decades in European history and passed the torch from one generation to another. Stefano Branca, Bernardino's son, was to develop the company, launching new products and introducing them in important international exhibitions. After Stefano's untimely death, Maria Scala, his wife, felt compelled to take over the company until his first child became an adult.

How this woman, in the very first years of the twentieth century, had been able to lead the company into the future, following the vision of its founder, remains a very interesting content of Branca's history.

Bernardino's management after the end of the war boosted the company in a remarkable way, opening other production sites across Europe and America.

Fernet changed from being a remedy for Milan-based customers to a product spread throughout Europe and known at international exhibitions for its innovative characteristics, obtaining distinctions in the London Exhibitions (1862), Paris (1867) and Vienna (1873).

From 1999, Niccolò Branca, the fifth generation, has led the company and under his guidance Fratelli Branca has developed all over the world, with a large range of new brands and products: Brancamenta, Vermouth Carpano, Punt e Mes, Caffè Borghetti, Grappa Candolini, Vodka Sermenova, and Sambuca Borghetti.

## FERNET BRANCA, AN ITALIAN *AMARO* THAT IDENTIFIES ITALIANS IN THE WORLD

Fernet and other liqueurs launched in the early twentieth century were intended for Europe and American countries where Italian emigrants were bringing their own customs.

Its internationalization strategies consisted of a relocation of production at an early stage and then a concentration of production in Italy after the Second World War.

Today, Fratelli Branca's exports make up 80 per cent of its revenue, of which Fernet is the best seller. Other products with a softer and more versatile taste, both as aperitifs and digestifs, joined the legendary bitter liqueur.

A market in which Fratelli Branca has always wanted to implement strong strategies to answer the local demand is Argentina, where a challenging mix of sociocultural factors has led to an unparalleled consumer phenomenon that Niccolò Branca knows well, since he led the South American branch for many years.

### ARGENTINA: A SECOND HOMELAND FOR BRANCA AND THE FIRST FOR FERNET

Italian immigrants arrived at Buenos Aires port for the first time in the mid-nineteenth century. But the biggest wave of migration from Europe occurred between the 1880s and 1930s, four decades during which entire families, escaping poverty and war, populated Argentina, looking for a job and attracted

**Figure 15.14**    Fernet Branca 1 litre bottle

by the granting of public land where they could develop their agricultural activities.

More than two million Italians took part in work programmes from agriculture to other craft activities: labourers, tailors, carpenters, textile workers, tireless workers who dreamed of a project in the promised land.

Many of them always brought along an unfailing medicine for digestion: Fernet Branca, a bitter tonic with eupeptic properties, which was essential as an after-dinner drink in meetings between fellow citizens and at parties held by the Italian regional communities in Argentina.

Fernet's organized distribution in the Argentine market began in 1926 thanks to Hofer & Co, which was authorized by Fratelli Branca to produce its Fernet in Argentina, starting from the concentrated extract sent from Italy. In a few years the consumption of Fernet in Argentina was greater than in Italy.

In 1941, Fratelli Branca repurchased its production plant, investing directly in the territory that would give its product the epic of a second legend.

The author of this case study is the daughter of Venetian emigrants and clearly remembers the preparation of Brancamenta with ice and soda water, waiting for Sunday lunch with the extended family in the 1970s.

The seed of success in the third millennium was a mix of conviviality, nostalgia and a masculine lexicon: Fernet was a very bitter drink that only men appreciated, almost as a test of bravery. On the other hand, for Argentine people with Spanish origins, the aperitif consisted of Vermouth or bitter martinis.

Between the 1970s and the 1990s, sales of Branca's *amaro* stalled in Argentina too: old immigrants changed their habits and the after-meal drink was drunk much less. Local distillates based on juniper or sugar cane had an important role in rural consumption. Fernet had become a '*tanos viejos*' (old Italians) drink.

From the 1990s onwards, Fernet Branca has been enjoying a second season, with sales growing by 200 per cent in ten years and 40 million litres of the product being drunk by a total population of 44 million inhabitants.

The local federation, which includes liqueurs and spirits producers, confirms that they accounted for 5 per cent of total alcohol consumption by volume in 2020, including wines and beers. It is, maybe, one of the world's highest market shares, of which Fernet accounts for as much as 34 per cent ahead of other classic aperitifs or spirits such as whisky and vodka.

The Fratelli Branca Argentine branch has expanded its plant every year, growing to almost 50 000 square meters where not only Fernet, but also other distillates such as Brancamenta, Punt e Mes and Caffé Borghetti, intended for the entire production market, are produced.

## HOW A TRADITIONAL *AMARO* BECAME THE STAR INGREDIENT OF THE ICONIC ARGENTINE COCKTAIL

The Fernet boom in Argentina is due to an exciting and semantically perfect combination: an *amaro* with a hard and masculine personality is mixed with the legendary and sparkling Coca-Cola in a fresh, immediate and inspiring cocktail, suitable for several occasions.

When and who invented this drink is the main subject of many market studies on local consumption sociology, but it is also the subject of rivalries between regions and artists who hold its intellectual property.

Several sources, including the company itself, are convinced that this consumption pattern began in the Mediterranean province of Cordoba, located in the centre of the country, characterized by a strong identity that combines values of its university students, football fans and local musicians. Cordoba, as a rival of Buenos Aires, has always been a place of young people, with their emerging thoughts and behaviours.

Bars around Cordoba's football stadiums sold litres and litres of mixed drinks: classic combinations were beer and cola and beer and orange soda. According to legend, a small suburban bar had run out of other alcoholic drinks and took an old bottle of Fernet and created the thirst-quenching and euphoric magic: sweet-bitter, fresh, effervescent ... perfect.

Mixing Fernet with cola in variable proportions has become a national tradition before barbecues with friends or family, as well as football games on Sundays and, finally, it has also become a pre-disco drink. Therefore, it is a night and day drink, combined with other alcoholic drinks during the meal, such as wine and beer.

Nowadays, it is a must on any celebration menu, such as during happy hour and also at restaurants while waiting for food, resulting in an annual consumption of 40 million litres.

Branca's original recipe, with 45 per cent alcohol, was later revised for international alignment.

Fernet-Cola aims to reach the status of a national soft drink and it has been named Fernando or Fernandito, recognized as an IBA official cocktail from 2020 (International Bartender Association).

## MEANINGS, CODES AND COMMUNITY CONTENT ON SOCIAL NETWORKS

Fernet's cocktail has supported and enriched a very well-established experience in popular culture that has reached the status not only of brand phenomenon, but also of

category phenomenon. The Fernet-Cola cocktail belongs to consumers; it is not a strategic marketing creation. The strategy of Branca and other operators has reached the pinnacle of success, giving voice through social media and traditional communication to those who are central to this system: the consumers themselves.

We can say that the Fernet Argentinian case is one of the most successful cases of the 'prosumer', in which the producing company acts as guarantor and spokesperson of values: friendship, trust, fidelity, collective rituals, and national identity.

**Figure 15.15**   Fernandito (Fernet Branca and Coca-Cola) cocktail

Today, an unstoppable flow of social media content produced by the brand's own followers is added to the dense communicative brand history that since the post-war period has created one of the richest and most interesting stories, giving birth to a mosaic of stories and images strongly featured on digital channels.

Moreover, the combination of Coca-Cola and Fernet inspired creative co-marketing campaigns, where the two ingredients meet and create a passionate couple, with Fernet being the male and Coke the female.

## NOT ONLY BRANCA: ARGENTINE FERNET MARKET EXPANDS TO LOCAL PLAYERS

When a single brand holds 100 per cent of such a significant market share, the product becomes an attractive category for new players. Other local companies of the liqueur segment have targeted the Fernet share of the market, but the recipe is secret, and imitations are recognizable. The real Fernet is Branca, even if since 2002 the economic crisis and the expansion of low-cost brands have offered local small producers interesting opportunities to enter the market with 'me too products'.

Today the consumption of Fernet is divided between an indisputable leader, Branca, with 70 per cent value market share, and some followers: 'Vittone' and 'Veneto' by Fratelli Branca; '1882' by Porta Hermanos; 'Cinzano' and 'Lusera' by Cepas de Argentina; 'Capri' and 'Ramazzotti' by Pernod Ricard; 'Pini' and 'Imperio' by Licores Argentinos; 'El Abuelo' by Saenz Briones; 'Cazalis' by Cinba and 'Bari' by Servamsur SA.

## FROM ARGENTINE PAMPAS TO MILAN-BASED BARTENDERS? PERHAPS SAN FRANCISCO IS BETTER

Fratelli Branca has tried to recreate the Argentine phenomenon in Italy too. In 2012, they planned a guerrilla and digital marketing strategy to introduce the new cocktail to young people. People were invited to taste the cocktail, presented with a multilingual lexicon. Fernandito Mezcla hasn't won over Italian palates in the same way as Argentines, possibly because of the vertiginous rise of Aperol or Campari spritz

The fact is that behind the Argentine phenomenon there is domestic conviviality among friends, stimulating the consumption of Fernet at home, not only in bars. Too bitter, too sweet, too strong … Fernandito is only for early adopters and it will struggle to overtake other Italian cocktails based on prosecco or sparkling wine.

Maybe California and San Francisco are the new lands where Fernet will succeed among millennial innovators and their social media sharing experience about the coolest cocktail of the west coast. Will they beat the land of the tango? See you in the next season.

## QUESTION FOR DISCUSSION

1. How should the cultural Italo-Argentinian drink be exported back to Italy and enter the European and American markets?

# NOTES

1.  The information required to write this case study was gathered thanks to the kind help of Mr Luciano Romanello (ICE-Istanbul) and to the assistance of Mrs Ece Kutay (Natuzzi Group).

2.  J.W. Redhouse (2001), *A Turkish and English Lexicon*, 2nd edn, Çağrı Yayınları, Istanbul, pp. 1179–80.

3.  J.W. Redhouse (1999), *Türkçe/Osmanlıca-İngilizce Sözlük*, Istanbul, pp. 593–4.

4.  My sincere gratitude to Mr E. Prat, former CEO of LVMH Japan for the interview he granted me, his sharing of experience with deep insights on the business culture in Japan. Many thanks also to Ms H. Dauzie, Merchandising Manager at Chanel who had worked at LV stores in Tokyo and Mr Y. Obatake, former chief coordinator at Kenzo licence division in Paris, who gave me valuable information through their experience.

5.  Association founded in 1954 to promote the French luxury industry and art of living whose members include 83 luxury brands and 16 cultural institutions such as the Louvre museum.

6.  Kimonos are sewn from rolls of fabric 35 cm wide by 12 m long. Due to the constraints (limited shape), large variations of fabrics (weaving, dyeing, patterns, colours, embroidery…) exist for differentiation and individuality.

7.  Okabe, M. [in Japanese], accessed at https://core.ac.uk/download/pdf/230529796.pdf.

8.  Schmitt, B. (2011), *Experience Marketing: Concepts, Frameworks and Consumer Insights*, Columbia University.

9.  Mr Kyojiro Hata, who later became the first president of LV Japan, was in charge of this research.

10. This system, called 'gaisho', refers to today's personal shopping services that are proposed to wealthy loyal customers at department stores.

11. Adapted from the figure of Ikezawa, T. (2009), 'Brand portfolio and transaction system on Japanese department store: selective appliance to suppliers in the process of branding on foods and meals', p. 8 [in Japanese], accessed at https://www.jstage.jst.go.jp/article/jsds/2009/24/2009_3/_pdf/-char/ja.

12. These products underwent strict quality checks (colour fading, stains, fakes, etc.) carried out by specialists with a scientific background at an in-house quality control division.

13. Ministère de l'Industrie, *Les Relations Industrielles entre la France et le Japon*, vol.1 *Analyses et Propositions d'action*, Paris, La Documentation Française, 1980, pp. 96–8, 223–4, in Bouissou et al. (2014), *Esthétiques du Quotidien au Japon*, pp. 96–7.

14. The love of salespeople generates 100 billion yen: 'The Direct Management Strategy, the Cornerstone of Louis Vuitton's Success' [in Japanese], December 2015, WWD Japan Fashion College, accessed at https://logmi.jp/business/articles/118692.

15. Ganne, B. (2009), 'Target Japan – total quality, case of Merial' (CD-ROM), CNRS Publishing. The case study of Merial (Boehringer Ingelheim Animal Health) in Lyon specialized in vaccines for domestic pets and farm animals. The packaging process takes in general 5 hours as against 30 hours for the Japanese market. The Japanese undertake full inspection of vials one by one, such as clean labels, no scratch marks on the vials, etc. as complaints from Japan mainly relate to visual aspects.

16. Sei Shônagon (966–1017), Whatever small is charming. In *The Pillow Book* (2007), Penguin Classics.

17. Shûzô Kuki, *La Structure d'Iki* (2004), PUF, France (translated from 'Iki no kôzô', 1930).

18. Definition of 'o-motenashi' according to the Kôjien dictionary: 1. handling things or events; 2. attitude, gesture, or manner; 3. a thoughtful way in which someone/something is treated; 4. welcoming guests with good meal.

19. 'Exceptional skills, passion needed to sell luxury goods' (Interview with Mr Emmanuel Prat), 24 December 2017, *The Japan Times*, accessed at https://www.japantimes.co.jp/life/2017/12/24/people/exceptional-skills-passion-needed-sell-luxury-goods/. According to Euromonitor (January 2021), the digital platform was used in 2020 more as a place to engage with customers rather than actually to sell luxury goods.

# References – Part III

Ackerman, D. and Tellis, G. (2001). Can culture affect prices? A cross-cultural study of shopping and retail prices. *Journal of Retailing, 77*(1), 57–82.

Ahmed, Z.U., Johnson, J.P., Ling, C.P., Fang, T.W. and Hui, A.K. (2002). Country-of-origin and brand effects on consumers' evaluations of cruise lines. *International Marketing Review, 19*(3), 279–302.

Aiello, G., Donvito, R., Godey, B., Pederzoli, D., Wiedmann, K.P., Hennigs, N. and Singh, R. (2009). An international perspective on luxury brand and country-of-origin effect. *Journal of Brand Management, 16*(5), 323–37.

Ajzen, I. (1991). The theory of planned behaviour. *Organizational Behavior and Human Decision Processes, 50*(2), 179–211.

Al-Hyari, K., Al-Weshah, G. and Alnsour, M. (2012). Barriers to internationalisation in SMEs: Evidence from Jordan. *Marketing Intelligence & Planning, 30*(2), 188–211.

Al-Khatib, J.A., Vollmers, S.M. and Liu, Y. (2007). Business-to-business negotiating in China: The role of morality. *Journal of Business & Industrial Marketing, 22*(2), 84–96.

Alavi, S., Habel, J., Guenzi, P. and Wieseke, J. (2018). The role of leadership in salespeople's price negotiation behavior. *Journal of the Academy of Marketing Science, 46*(4), 703–24.

Albers-Miller, N. and Gelb, B. (1996). Business advertising appeals as a mirror of cultural dimensions: A study of eleven countries. *Journal of Advertising, 25*(4), 50–70.

Alon, I. and Jaffe, E. (2012). *Global Marketing: Contemporary Theory, Practice, and Cases*. New York: McGraw-Hill Education.

Alon, I., Littrell, R.F. and Chan, A.K.K. (2009). Branding in China: Global product strategy alternatives. *Multinational Business Review, 17*(4), 123–42.

Amsteus, M., Al-Shaaban, S., Wallin, E. and Sjöqvist, S. (2015). Colors in marketing: A study of color associations and context (in) dependence. *International Journal of Business and Social Science, 6*(3).

Amuso, M. and Montagna, M. (2009). Branding intelligente: Trasferire il marchio in Cina. *Economia e Management, (3), 31–41.

An, D.C. and Kim, S.H. (2006). Attitudes toward offensive advertising: A cross-cultural comparison between Korea and the United States, paper presented at the *2006 Annual Conference of the American Academy of Advertising*, Reno, NV, 30 March–2 April.

Anterasian, C., Graham, J. and Money, B. (1996). Are US managers superstitious about market share? *MIT Sloan Management Review, 37*(4), 66–77.

Arnold, D.J. and Quelch, J.A. (1998). New strategies in emerging markets. *Sloan Management, 40*(1), 1–20.

Aslam, M.M. (2006). Are you selling the right colour? A cross-cultural review of colour as a marketing cue. *Journal of Marketing Communications, 12*(1), 15–30.

Asmussen, C.G., Foss, N.J. and Pedersen, T. (2011). Knowledge transfer and accommodation effects in multinational corporations: Evidence from European subsidiaries. *Journal of Management, 39*(6), 1397–429.

Aulakh, P.S. (2003). International product strategies: An integrative framework. In J. Subhash (ed.), *Handbook of Research in International Marketing*. Cheltenham, UK and Northampton, MA, USA: Edward Elgar Publishing.

Avlonitis, G., Indounas, K. and Gounaris, S. (2005). Pricing objectives over the service life cycle: Some empirical evidence. *European Journal of Marketing, 39*(5/6), 696–714.

Bain & Co. (2016). Luxury Good China Market Study. Accessed at http://www.bain.com/publications/articles/luxury-goods-china-market-study-2016.aspx.

Baker, M.J. and Ballington, L. (2002). Country of origin as a source of competitive advantage. *Journal of Strategic Marketing, 10*(2), 157–68.

Baker, W.L., Marn, M.V. and Zawada, C.C. (2010). *The Price Advantage* (2nd edn). Hoboken, NJ: John Wiley & Sons.

Balabanis, G. and Diamantopoulos, A. (2008). Brand origin identification by consumers: A classification perspective. *Journal of International Marketing, 16*(1), 39–71.

Balabanis, G. and Diamantopoulos, A. (2011). Gains and losses from the misperception of brand origin: The role of brand strength and country-of-origin image. *Journal of International Marketing, 19*(2), 95–116.

Banerjee, S.B., Carter, C. and Clegg, S. (2009). Managing globalization. In M. Alvesson, T. Bridgman and H. Willmott (eds), *The Oxford Handbook of Critical Management Studies.* Oxford: Oxford University Press, pp. 186–212.

Bauman, Z. (1998). *Globalization: The Human Consequences.* New York: Columbia University Press.

Bengtsson, A. and Venkatraman, M. (2008). The global brand's meaning melange: Seeking home abroad through global brands. In Angela Y. Lee and Dilip Soman (eds), *NA – Advances in Consumer Research* Vol. 35. Duluth, MN: Association for Consumer Research, p. 822.

Biggs, Chris, Chande, A., Chen, L., Mathews, E., Mercier, P., Wang, A. et al. (2017). The Chinese consumer's online journey from discovery to purchase. *BCG Perspectives,* Boston Consulting Group.

Biswas, A., Olsen, J.E. and Carlet, V. (1992). A comparison of print advertisements from the United States and France. *Journal of Advertising, 21*(4), 73–82.

Blanckaert, C. (1996). *Les Chemins du Luxe.* Paris: Grasset.

Block, L. and Kramer, T. (2009). The effect of superstitious beliefs on performance expectations. *Journal of the Academy of Marketing Science, 37*(2), 161–9.

Blocker, C.P. (2011). Modeling customer value perceptions in cross-cultural business markets. *Journal of Business Research, 64*(5), 533–40.

Bottomley, P.A. and Doyle, J.R. (2006). The interactive effects of colors and products on perceptions of brand logo appropriateness. *Marketing Theory, 6*(1), 63–83.

Bouissou, J-M., Siboni, J. and Zins, M.-J. (2013). *Argent, Fortunes et Luxe en Asie: Japon, Chine, Inde.* Arles: Philippe Picquier.

Bouissou, J-M. (2014). *Esthétiques du Quotidien au Japon.* Paris: IFM (Institut Français de la Mode) & Édition du Regard, pp. 83–104.

Bradley, F. (1999). *International Marketing Strategy.* London: Prentice Hall Europe.

Burns, A.C., Biswas, A. and Babin, L.A. (1993). The operation of visual imagery as a mediator of advertising effects. *Journal of Advertising, 22*(2), 71–85.

Buzzell, R.D. (2004). The PIMS program of strategy research: A retrospective appraisal. *Journal of Business Research, 57*(5), 478–83.

Buzzell, R.D., Gale, B.T. and Sultan, R.G. (1975). Market share: A key to profitability. *Harvard Business Review, 53*(1), 97–106.

Cateora, P.R. and Graham, J.L. (1993). *International Marketing,* 8th edn. RR Donnelley & Sons.

Cateora, P.R. and Graham, J.L. (2007). *Marketing Internazionale: Imprese Italiane e Mercati Mondiali.* Milan: Hoepli.

Ceglia, D., de Oliveira Lima, S.H. and Leocádio, Á.L. (2015). An alternative theoretical discussion on cross-cultural sustainable consumption. *Sustainable Development, 23*(6), 414–24.

Chan, H., Wan, L.C. and Sin, L.Y. (2009). The contrasting effects of culture on consumer tolerance: Interpersonal face and impersonal fate. *Journal of Consumer Research, 36*(2), 292–304.

Chan, K., Li, L., Diehl, S. and Terlutter, R. (2007). Consumers' response to offensive advertising: A cross cultural study. *International Marketing Review, 24*(5), 606–28.

Chan, R.Y. (1999). Environmental attitudes and behavior of consumers in China: Survey findings and implications. *Journal of International Consumer Marketing, 11*(4), 25–52.

Chang, S.-J. and Park, S.H. (2012). Winning strategies in China: Competitive dynamics between MNCs and local firms. *Long Range Planning, 45*(1), 1–15.

Chang, W.L. and Lii, P. (2008). Luck of the draw: Creating Chinese brand names. *Journal of Advertising Research, 48*(4), 523–30.

Chapnick, D., Glatz, K., and Gordon, M. (2014). *The Value of Pricing Discipline - A Vantage Partners Sales Study on the Impact of Pricing Exceptions.* Boston, MA.: Vantage Partners.

Checchinato, F. (2011). Tre imprese italiane nel mercato cinese: Le esperienze di Illycaffè, Irsap e Faam. *Micro & Macro Marketing, 20*(3), 605–14.

Checchinato, F., Disegna, M. and Vescovi, T. (2013). Does country of origin affect brand associations? The case of Italian brands in China. *Journal of Global Scholars of Marketing Science, 23*(4), 409–21.

Chia, J. and Noble, P. (1999). Industrial pricing strategies in Singapore and the US: Same or different? *Asia Pacific Journal of Management, 16*(2), 293–303.

Chow, C.S., Tang, E.P. and Fu, I.S. (2007). Global marketers' dilemma: Whether to translate the brand name into local language. *Journal of Global Marketing, 20*(4), 25–38.

Chryssochoidis, G.M. and Wong, V. (2000). Customization of product technology and international new product success: Mediating effects of new product development and rollout timeliness. *Journal of Product Innovation Management, 17*(4), 268–85.

Collesei, U. and Vescovi, T. (1999). *Sales Management.* Padua: Cedam.

Craig, C.S. and Douglas, S.P. (2005). *International Marketing Research.* Chichester: John Wiley & Sons.

Crawford, H.J. and Gregory, G.D. (2011). Cross cultural responses to humorous advertising: An individual difference perspective. In Z. Yi, J.J. Xiao, J. Cotte and L. Price (eds), *AP – Asia-Pacific Advances in Consumer Research*, Vol. 9. Duluth, MN: Association for Consumer Research, pp. 239–45.

Czarnecka, B., Brennan, R. and Keles, S. (2018). Cultural meaning, advertising, and national culture: A four-country study. *Journal of Global Marketing, 31*(1), 4–17.

De Mooij, M. (2015). Cross-cultural research in international marketing: Clearing up some of the confusion. *International Marketing Review, 32*(6).

De Mooij, M. and Hofstede, G. (2011). Cross-cultural consumer behavior: A review of research findings. *Journal of International Consumer Marketing, 23*(3–4), 181–92.

Dobni, D. and Zinkhan, G.M. (1990). In search of brand image: A foundation analysis. In M.E. Goldberg, G. Gorn and R.W. Pollay (eds), *NA: Advances in Consumer Research*, Vol. 17, Provo, UT: Association for Consumer Research.

Doran, K. (2002). Lessons learned in cross-cultural research of Chinese and North American consumers. *Journal of Business Research, 55*(10), 823–9.

Douglas, S.P. and Craig, C.S. (1983). Examining performance of US multinationals in foreign markets. *Journal of International Business Studies, 14*(3), 51–62.

Douglas, S.P. and Craig, C.S. (2006). On improving the conceptual foundations of international marketing research. *Journal of International Marketing, 14*(1), 1–22.

Dowling, K., Guhl, D., Klapper, D., Spann, M., Stich, L. and Yegoryan, N. (2020). Behavioral biases in marketing. *Journal of the Academy of Marketing Science, 48*(3), 449–77.

Duncan, W.J., Ginter, P.M. and Swayne, L.E. (1998). Competitive advantage and internal organizational assessment. *Academy of Management Perspectives, 12*(3), 6–16.

Dutta, S., Zbaracki, M.J. and Bergen, M. (2003). Pricing process as a capability: A resource based perspective. *Strategic Management Journal, 24*(7), 615–30.

Eckman, M., Sakarya, S., Hyllegard, K., Borja, M.A.G. and Descals, A.M. (2015). Consumer receptiveness to international retail expansion: A cross-cultural study of perceptions of social and economic influence of foreign retailers. *The International Review of Retail, Distribution and Consumer Research, 25*(3), 260–75.

Elhoushy, S. and Lanzini, P. (2020). Factors affecting sustainable consumer behavior in the MENA region: A systematic review. *Journal of International Consumer Marketing*, 1–24.

Elliott, G.R. and Cameron, R.C. (1994). Consumer perception of product quality and the country-of-origin effect. *Journal of International Marketing, 2*(2), 49–62.

Evanschitzky, H., Emrich, O., Sangtani, V., Ackfeldt, A.-L., Reynolds, K.E. and Arnold, M.J. (2014). Hedonic shopping motivations in collectivist and individualistic consumer cultures. *International Journal of Research in Marketing, 31*(3), 335–8.

Faiers, J. and Bell-Price, S. (2015), *Luxury: History, Culture, Consumption*, Vol. 2. London: Bloomsbury.

Fam, K.S. and Waller, D.S. (2003). Advertising controversial products in the Asia Pacific: What makes them offensive? *Journal of Business Ethics, 48*(3), 237–50.

Fan, Y. (2002). Questioning guanxi: Definition, classification and implications. *International Business Review, 11*(5), 543–61.

Fang, E., Palmatier, R.W. and Evans, K.R. (2004). Goal-setting paradoxes? Trade-offs between working hard and working smart: The United States versus China. *Journal of the Academy of Marketing Science, 32*(2), 188–202.

Fang, T. (1999). *Chinese Business Negotiating Style.* Thousand Oaks, CA: Sage Publications.

Festinger, L. (1957). *A Theory of Cognitive Dissonance.* Evanston, IL: Row, Peterson.

Fox, S. (2008). China's changing culture and etiquette. *China Business Review*, July–August.

Franzen, A. (2003). Environmental attitudes in international comparison: An analysis of the ISSP surveys 1993 and 2000. *Social Science Quarterly, 84*(2), 297–308.

Frenzen, H., Hansen, A.K., Krafft, M., Mantrala, M.K. and Schmidt, S. (2010). Delegation of pricing authority to the sales force: An agency-theoretic perspective of its determinants and impact on performance. *International Journal of Research in Marketing, 27*(1), 58–68.

Frith, K., Shaw, P. and Cheng, H. (2005). The construction of beauty: A cross-cultural analysis of women's magazine advertising. *Journal of Communication, 55*(1), 56–70.

Gao, G.Y., Pan, Y., Tse, D.K. and Yim, C.K. (2006). Market share performance of foreign and domestic brands in China. *Journal of International Marketing, 14*(2), 32–51.

Gao, H., Mittal, V. and Zhang, Y. (2020). The differential effect of local–global identity among males and females: The case of price sensitivity. *Journal of Marketing Research, 57*(1), 173–91.

Gao, H., Zhang, Y. and Mittal, V. (2017). How does local–global identity affect price sensitivity? *Journal of Marketing, 81*(3), 62–79.

Ghemawat, P. (2001). Distance still matters. *Harvard Business Review, 79*(8), 137–47.

Godey, B., Pederzoli, D., Aiello, G., Donvito, R., Wiedmann, K.P. and Hennigs, N. (2013). A cross-cultural exploratory content analysis of the perception of luxury from six countries. *Journal of Product & Brand Management, 22*(3).

Gordon, B.R., Goldfarb, A. and Li, Y. (2013). Does price elasticity vary with economic growth? A cross-category analysis. *Journal of Marketing Research, 50*(1), 4–23.

Greenwald, A.G. and Banaji, M.R. (1995). Implicit social cognition: Attitudes, self-esteem, and stereotypes. *Psychological Review, 102*(1), 4.

Grunert, K.G. (1997). What's in a steak? A cross-cultural study on the quality perception of beef. *Food Quality and Preference, 8*(3), 157–74.

Guerrero, L., Guàrdia, M.D., Xicola, J., Verbeke, W., Vanhonacker, F., Zakowska-Biemans, S., Sajdakowska, M. et al. (2009). Consumer-driven definition of traditional food products and innovation in traditional foods. A qualitative cross-cultural study. *Appetite, 52*(2), 345–54.

Guo, G., Cheung, F.S.L. and Leung, W.F. (2012). Cross-cultural differences in attitude towards TV advertising among Beijing, Hong Kong and Warwick viewers. *International Journal of Integrated Marketing Communications, 4*(1), 43–60.

Gupta, A. and Wang, H. (2011), Why Barbie flopped in Shanghai. *Business Week*, April.

Hall, E.T. (1976). *Beyond Culture*. New York: Anchor Books.

Hall, E.T. and Hall, M.R. (2001). Key concepts: Underlying structures of culture. In M.A. Albrecht (ed.), *International HRM: Managing Diversity in the Workplace*. Oxford: Blackwell, pp. 24–40.

Han, T-I. and Stoel, L. (2017). Explaining socially responsible consumer behavior: A meta-analytic review of theory of planned behavior. *Journal of International Consumer Marketing, 29*(2), 91–103.

Hata, K. (2004). *Louis Vuitton Japon : L'Invention du Luxe*. Paris: Assouline Publishing.

Hatzithomas, L., Zotos, Y. and Boutsouki, C. (2011). Humor and cultural values in print advertising: A cross-cultural study. *International Marketing Review, 28*(1), 57–80.

Haubl, G. and Elrod, T. (1999). The impact of congruity between brand name and country of production on consumers' product quality judgements. *International Journal of Research in Marketing, 16*(3), 199–215.

Herbes, C., Beuthner, C., & Ramme, I. (2018). Consumer attitudes towards biobased packaging–A cross-cultural comparative study. *Journal of cleaner production, 194*, 203–218.

Herbes, C., Beuthner, C. and Ramme, I. (2020). How green is your packaging: A comparative international study of cues consumers use to recognize environmentally friendly packaging. *International Journal of Consumer Studies, 44*(3), 258–71.

Herbig, P.A. (2000). *Handbook of Cross-Cultural Marketing*. Binghamton, NY: The Haworth Press.

Hernandez, M.D., Wang, Y., Sheng, H., Kalliny, M. and Minor, M. (2017). Escaping the corner of death? An eye-tracking study of reading direction influence on attention and memory. *Journal of Consumer Marketing, 34*(1), 1–10.

Herz, M.F. and Diamantopoulos, A. (2013). Activation of country stereotypes: Automaticity, consonance, and impact. *Journal of the Academy of Marketing Science, 41*(4), 400–17.

Hibbert, E.P. (1990). *The Principles and Practice of Export Marketing*. Heinemann Professional Publishing.

Hinterhuber, A. (2004). Towards value-based pricing: An integrative framework for decision making. *Industrial Marketing Management, 33*(8), 765–78.

Hinterhuber, A. (2008). Value delivery and value-based pricing in industrial markets. *Advances in Business Marketing and Purchasing, 14,* 381–448.

Hinterhuber, A. (2015). Violations of rational choice principles in pricing decisions. *Industrial Marketing Management, 47,* 65–74.

Hinterhuber, A. (2016). The six pricing myths that kill profits. *Business Horizons, 59*(1), 71–83.

Hinterhuber, A. (2017). Value quantification capabilities in industrial markets. *Journal of Business Research, 76,* 163–78.

Hinterhuber, A. and Liozu, S. (2012). Is it time to rethink your pricing strategy? *MIT Sloan Management Review, 53*(4), 69–77.

Hinterhuber, A. and Liozu, S.M. (2017). The micro-foundations of pricing. *Journal of Business Research, 76,* 159–62.

Hinterhuber, A. and Liozu, S. (eds) (2020). *Pricing Strategy Implementation: Translating Pricing Strategy into Results.* Abingdon: Routledge.

Hinterhuber, A. and Snelgrove, T. (eds) (2017). *Value First, then Price: Quantifying Value in Business Markets from the Perspective of Both Buyers and Sellers.* Abingdon: Routledge.

Hinterhuber, A. and Snelgrove, T.C. (2020). The present and future of value quantification. *Journal of Creating Value, 6*(2), 295–303.

Hinterhuber, H.H. (2015). *Strategische Unternehmungsführung: Das Gesamtmodell für Nachhaltige Wertsteigerung.* 9th edn. Erich Schmidt Verlag.

Hofstede, G. (1991). Empirical models of cultural differences. In N. Bleichrodt and P.J.D. Drenth (eds), Contemporary Issues in Cross-cultural Psychology. Lisse: Swets & Zeitlinger Publishers, pp. 4–20.

Hofstede, G. (1997). *Cultures and Organizations: Software of the Mind.* New York: McGraw-Hill.

Hofstede, G. (2001), *Culture's Consequences: Comparing Values, Behaviors, Institutions and Organizations Across Nations.* Thousand Oaks, CA: Sage.

Hofstede, G. (2006). What did GLOBE really measure? Researchers' minds versus respondents' minds. *Journal of International Business Studies, 37*(6), 882–96.

Homburg, C., Jensen, O. and Hahn, A. (2012). How to organize pricing? Vertical delegation and horizontal dispersion of pricing authority. *Journal of Marketing, 76*(5), 49–69.

Hong, F.C., Pecotich, A. and Shultz, C.J. (2002). Brand name translation: Language constraints, product attributes, and consumer perceptions in East and Southeast Asia. *Journal of International Marketing, 10*(2), 29–45.

Hoppe, M.H. (2004). Introduction: Geert Hofstede's *Culture's Consequences: International Differences in Work-Related Values. Academy of Management Perspectives, 18*(1), 73–4.

Horwitz, F., Hemmant, R. and Rademeyer, C. (2008). Chinese business negotiations: South African firm experiences and perspectives. *South African Journal of Business Management, 39,* 1–13.

Hoskisson, R.E., Johnson, R.A., Tihanyi, L. and White, R.E. (2005). Diversified business groups and corporate refocusing in emerging economies. *Journal of Management, 31*(6), 941–65.

House, R.J., Hanges, P.J., Javidan, M., Dorfman, P.W. and Gupta, V. (eds) (2004). *Culture, Leadership, and Organizations: The GLOBE Study of 62 Societies.* Thousand Oaks, CA: Sage Publications.

Hsu, Y., Hsu, L. and Yeh, C.W. (2010). A cross-cultural study on consumers' level of acceptance toward marketing innovativeness. *African Journal of Business Management, 4*(6), 1215–28.

Huang, L.-S. and Teng, C.-I. (2009). Development of a Chinese superstitious belief scale. *Psychological Reports, 104*(3), 807–19.

Huang, X. (2009). The influence of national culture, history and institution on strategic management in Chinese firms: A complexity based perspective. *International Journal of Business Studies, 17*(1).

Hultman, M., Robson, M.J. and Katsikeas, C.S. (2009). Export product strategy fit and performance: An empirical investigation. *Journal of International Marketing, 17*(4), 1–23.

Ieva, M. and Ziliani, C. (2018). Mapping touchpoint exposure in retailing. *International Journal of Retail & Distribution Management, 46*(3), 304–22.

Ignatow, G. (2006). Cultural models of nature and society reconsidering environmental attitudes and concern. *Environment and Behavior, 38,* 441–61.

Jaffe, E.D. and Nebenzahl, I.D. (2006). *National Image and Competitive Advantage: The Theory and Practice of Place Branding* (2nd edn). Copenhagen: Copenhagen Business School Press.

James, W. (2004). *The Varieties of Religious Experience.* New York: Touchstone.

Jang, J.M. and Shin, S. (2019). Content order in advertising and thinking styles: A cross-cultural study of the United States and South Korea. *Journal of Advertising, 48*(5), 457–72.

Jansson, H. and Sandberg, S. (2008). Internationalization of small and medium sized enterprises in the Baltic Sea region. *Journal of International Management, 14*(1), 65–77.

Jeannet, J.P. and Hennessey D.H. (2001). *Global Marketing Strategies.* Boston, MA: Houghton Mifflin Company.

Jiang, B. and Prater, E. (2002). Distribution and logistics development in China: The revolution has begun. *International Journal of Physical Distribution & Logistics Management, 32*(9).

Jin, B. and Sternquist, B. (2003). The influence of retail environment on price perceptions. *International Marketing Review, 20*(6), 643–60.

Jo, M.-S. and Sarigollu, E. (2007). Cross-cultural differences of price-perceived quality relationships. *Journal of International Consumer Marketing, 19*(4), 59–74.

Johanson, J. and Vahlne, J.-E. (1977). The internationalization process of the firm: A model of knowledge development and increasing foreign market commitments. *Journal of International Business Studies, 8*(1), 23–32.

Johanson, J. and Vahlne, J.-E. (1990). The mechanism of internationalization. *International Marketing Review, 7*(4).

Johnston, W.J., Khalil, S., Jain, M. and Cheng, J.M.S. (2012). Determinants of joint action in international channels of distribution: The moderating role of psychic distance. *Journal of International Marketing, 20*(3), 34–49.

Judd, B.J. and Alexander, M.W. (1983). On the reduced effectiveness of some sexually suggestive ads. *Journal of the Academy of Marketing Science, 11*(2), 156–68.

Kahle, L.R. (1984). *Attitudes and Social Adaptation: A Person–Situation Interaction Approach.* Oxford: Pergamon.

Kalafatis, S.P., Pollard, M., East, R. and Tsogas, M.H. (1999). Green marketing and Ajzen's theory of planned behaviour: A cross-market examination. *Journal of Consumer Marketing, 16*(5), 441–60.

Kalliny, M., Cruthirds, K.W. and Minor, M.S. (2007). Differences between American, Egyptian and Lebanese humor styles: Implications for international management. *International Journal of Cross Cultural Management, 6*(1), 121–34.

Kang, M. and Moscardo, G. (2006). Exploring cross-cultural differences in attitudes towards responsible tourist behaviour: A comparison of Korean, British and Australian tourists. *Asia Pacific Journal of Tourism Research, 11*(4), 303–20.

Kaynak, E. and Herbig, P. (2014). *Handbook of Cross-Cultural Marketing.* Abingdon: Routledge.

Keen, A. (2007). The cult of the amateur. In H. Doneland, K. Kear and M. Ramage (eds), *Online Communication and Collaboration.* New York: Routledge.

Keller, K.L. (2008). *Strategic Branding Management: Building, Measuring, and Managing Brand Equity* (3rd edn). Upper Saddle River, NJ: Prentice Hall.

Kerfoot, S., Davies, B. and Ward, P. (2003). Visual merchandising and the creation of discernible retail brands. *International Journal of Distribution and Retail Management, 31*(3), 143–52.

Khan, H., Lockshin, L., Lee, R. and Corsi, A. (2017). When is it necessary to localise product packaging?. *Journal of Consumer Marketing, 34*(5), 373–83.

Khanna, T. and Palepu, K. (2000). The future of business groups in emerging markets: Long-run evidence from Chile. *Academy of Management Journal, 43*(3), 268–85.

Kienzler, M. (2017). Does managerial personality influence pricing practices under uncertainty? *Journal of Product & Brand Management, 26*(7), 771–84.

Kienzler, M. (2018). Value-based pricing and cognitive biases: An overview for business markets. *Industrial Marketing Management, 68*, 86–94.

Klein, H.A. (2004). Cognition in natural settings: The cultural lens model. In M. Kaplan (ed.), *Cultural Ergonomics: Volume 4, Advances in Human Performance and Cognitive Engineering,* Boston, MA: Elsevier, pp. 249–80.

Kleppe, I.A., Iversen, N.M. and Stensaker, I.G. (2002). Country images in marketing strategies: Conceptual issues and an empirical Asian illustration. *Journal of Brand Management, 10*(1), 61–74.

Koblbauer, A., Hoffmann, R. and Tietze, D. (2018). European price curve for mobile phones. H&Z. Accessed at https://huz.de/wp-content/uploads/2018/06/hz-European-price-curve-Mobile-Phones_JUNE-2018.pdf.

Koschate-Fischer, N., Diamantopoulos, A. and Oldenkotte, K. (2012). Are consumers really willing to pay more for a favorable country image? A study of country-of-origin effects on willingness to pay. *Journal of International Marketing, 20*(1), 19–41.

Koubaa, Y. (2008). Country of origin, brand image perception, and brand image structure. *Asia Pacific Journal of Marketing and Logistics, 20*(2), 139–55.

Krutulyte, R., Costa, A.I. and Grunert, K.G. (2009). A cross-cultural study of cereal food quality perception. *Journal of Food Products Marketing, 15*(3), 304–23.

Kumara, P.S. and Canhua, K. (2010). Perceptions of country of origin: An approach to identifying expectations of foreign products. *Journal of Brand Management, 17*(5), 343–53.

LaBarbera, P.A., Weingard, P. and Yorkston, E.A. (1998). Matching the message to the mind: Advertising imagery and consumer processing styles. *Journal of Advertising Research, 38*(5), 29–30.

Lalwani, A.K., Shavitt, S. and Johnson, T. (2006). What is the relation between cultural orientation and socially desirable responding?. *Journal of Personality and Social Psychology, 90*(1), 165.

Lancioni, R., Schau, H.J. and Smith, M.F. (2005). Intraorganizational influences on business-to-business pricing strategies: A political economy perspective. *Industrial Marketing Management, 34*(2), 123–31.

Lascu, D.N., Marcheva, M. and Thieringer, K. (2016). Magazine online advertising in France and the United States. *Journal of Fashion Marketing and Management, 20*(1), 120–35.

Lawrence, J., Scheer, L., Crecelius, A. and Lam, S. (2021). Salesperson dual agency in price negotiations. *Journal of Marketing, 85*(2), 89–109.

Leclerc, F., Schmitt, B.H. and Dub, L. (1994). Foreign branding and its effects on product perceptions and attitudes. *Journal of Marketing Research, 31*(2), 263–71.

Lee, H., Lalwani, A.K. and Wang, J.J. (2020). Price no object!: The impact of power distance belief on consumers' price sensitivity. *Journal of Marketing, 84*(6), 113–29.

Lee, Y.H. and Lim, E.A.C. (2008). What's funny and what's not: The moderating role of cultural orientation in ad humor. *Journal of Advertising, 37*(2), 71–84.

Lemon, K.N. and Verhoef, P.C. (2016). Understanding customer experience throughout the customer journey. *Journal of Marketing, 80*(6), 69–96.

Leonard, D. and Sensiper, S. (1998). The role of tacit knowledge in group innovation. *California Management Review, 40*(3), 112–32.

Levitt, T. (1983). The globalization of markets. *Harvard Business Review,* May–June, 92–102.

Li, T., and Cavusgil, S. T. (1995). A classification and assessment of research streams in international marketing. *International Business Review, 4*(3), 251–277.

Lichtenstein, D.R., Ridgway, N.M. and Netemeyer, R.G. (1993). Price perceptions and consumer shopping behavior: A field study. *Journal of Marketing Research, 30*(2), 234–45.

Lin, Y. and Lai, C.Y. (2010). A study of the attitudes of Chinese consumers to aesthetic product designs. *International Journal of Management, 27*(1), 177.

Liozu, S. (2015). *The Pricing Journey: The Organizational Transformation Toward Pricing Excellence.* Stanford, CA: Stanford University Press.

Liozu, S. (2019). Penetration of the pricing function among global Fortune 500 firms. *Journal of Revenue and Pricing Management, 18*(6), 421–8.

Liozu, S. (2021). The adoption of pricing from an organizational perspective and its impact on relative firm performance. *Journal of Revenue and Pricing Management, 20*(4), 1–13.

Liozu, S. and Hinterhuber, A. (2013). Pricing orientation, pricing capabilities, and firm performance. *Management Decision, 51*(3), 594–614.

Liozu, S., Hinterhuber, A. and Somers, T. (2014). Organizational design and pricing capabilities for superior firm performance. *Management Decision, 52*(1), 54–78.

Liu, F., Cheng, H. and Li, J. (2009). Consumer responses to sex appeal advertising: A cross-cultural study. *International Marketing Review, 26*(4/5), 501–20.

Liu, F., Kanso, A., Zhang, Y. and Olaru, D. (2019). Culture, perceived value, and advertising acceptance: A cross-cultural study on mobile advertising. *Journal of Promotion Management, 25*(7), 1028–58.

Lodge, G.C. (1990). *Comparative Business–Government Relations.* Englewood Cliffs, NJ: Prentice Hall.

Loschelder, D., Friese, M., Schaerer, M. and Galinsky, A. (2016). The too-much-precision effect: When and why precise anchors backfire with experts. *Psychological Science, 27*(12), 1573–87.

Luna, D. and Forquer Gupta, S. (2001). An integrative framework for cross-cultural consumer behavior. *International Marketing Review, 18*(1), 45–69.

Luo, Y. and Chen, M. (1996). Managerial implications of guanxi-based business strategies. *Journal of International Management*, 2, 293–316.

Luo, Y. and Peng, M.W. (1999). Learning to compete in a transition economy: Experience, environment, and performance. *Journal of International Business Studies*, 30(2), 269–95.

Luotola, H., Hellström, M., Gustafsson, M. and Perminova-Harikoski, O. (2017). Embracing uncertainty in value-based selling by means of design thinking. *Industrial Marketing Management*, 65(August), 59–75.

Madden, T.J., Hewett, K. and Roth, M.S. (2000). Managing images in different cultures: A cross-national study of color meanings and preferences. *Journal of International Marketing*, 8(4), 90–107.

Magni, M. and Atsmon, Y. (2010). A better approach to China's market. *Harvard Business Review*, March.

Maignan, I. (2001). Consumers' perceptions of corporate social responsibilities: A cross-cultural comparison. *Journal of Business Ethics*, 30(1), 57–72.

Malhotra, N.K., Agarwal, J. and Peterson, M. (1996). Methodological issues in cross-cultural marketing research: A state-of-the-art review. *International Marketing Review*, 13(5), 7–43.

Malinowski, B. (1948). *Magic, Science, and Religion, and Other Essays*. Boston, MA: Beacon Press.

Marchetti, R. and Usunier, J.C. (1990). Les problèmes de l'étude de marché dans un contexte interculturel. *Revue Française du Marketing* (130), 5–17.

Markus, H.R. and Kitayama, S. (1991). Culture and the self: Implications for cognition, emotion, and motivation. *Psychological Review*, 98(2), 224.

Maslow, A.H. (1943). Dynamics of personality organization. I. *Psychological Review*, 50(5), 514–39.

Maslowska, E., Smit, E.G. and van den Putte, B. (2013). Assessing the cross-cultural applicability of tailored advertising: A comparative study between the Netherlands and Poland. *International Journal of Advertising*, 32(4), 487–511.

McCracken, G.D. (1990). *Culture and Consumption: New Approaches to the Symbolic Character of Consumer Goods and Activities* (Vol. 1). Bloomington, IN: Indiana University Press.

McCracken, G.D. (2005). *Culture and Consumption II: Markets, Meaning, and Brand Management* (Vol. 2). Bloomington, IN: Indiana University Press.

McDougall, P.P. and Oviatt, B.M. (1996). New venture internationalization, strategic change, and performance: A follow-up study. *Journal of Business Venturing*, 11(1), 23–40.

Meehan, J., Davenport, C. and Kahlon, S. (2012). The price of pricing effectiveness: Is the view worth the climb? *Deloitte Review*, 11, 18–29.

Mehta, R. and Belk, R.W. (1991). Artifacts, identity, and transition: Favorite possessions of Indians and Indian immigrants to the United States. *Journal of Consumer Research*, 17, March, 398–411.

Mehta, R., Anderson, R.E., Dubinsky, A.J., Polsa, P. and Mazur, J. (2010). Managing international distribution channel partners: A cross-cultural approach. *Journal of Marketing Channels*, 17(2), 89–117.

Meng, J.G. (2011). Understanding cultural influence on price perception: Empirical insights from a SEM application. *Journal of Product & Brand Management*, 20(7), 526–40.

Meng, J.G. and Nasco, S.A. (2009). Cross-cultural equivalence of price perceptions across American, Chinese, and Japanese consumers. *Journal of Product & Brand Management*, 18(7), 506–16.

Meyer, J.C. (2000). Humor as a double-edged sword: Four functions of humor in communication. *Communication Theory*, 10(3), 310–31.

Mikhailitchenko, A., Javalgi, R.R.G., Mikhailitchenko, G. and Laroche, M. (2009). Cross-cultural advertising communication: Visual imagery, brand familiarity, and brand recall. *Journal of Business Research*, 62(10), 931–8.

Millan, E., De Pelsmacker, P. and Wright, L.T. (2013). Clothing consumption in two recent EU Member States: A cross-cultural study. *Journal of Business Research*, 66(8), 975–82.

Minkov, M. and Hofstede, G. (2011). The evolution of Hofstede's doctrine. *Cross Cultural Management: An International Journal*, 18(1), 10–20.

Minton, E.A., Kahle, L.R. and Kim, C.H. (2015). Religion and motives for sustainable behaviors: A cross-cultural comparison and contrast. *Journal of Business Research*, 68(9), 1937–44.

Moberg, C.R. and Leasher, M. (2011). Examining the differences in salesperson motivation among different cultures. *American Journal of Business*, 26(2), 145–60.

Monroe, K.B., Rikala, V.-M. and Somervuori, O. (2015). Examining the application of behavioral price research in business-to-business markets. *Industrial Marketing Management*, 44(5).

Moorman, C. (2020). *The CMO Survey: Highlight and Insights Report*. American Marketing Association.

Morden, T. (1999). Models of national culture: A management review. *Cross Cultural Management*, 6(1), 19–44.

Mowen, J.C. and Carlson, B. (2003). Exploring the antecedents and consumer behavior consequences of the trait of superstition. *Psychology & Marketing*, 20(12), 1045–65.

Muller, B. (2011). *Dynamics of International Advertising*. New York: Peter Lang.

Mullins, R., Menguc, B. and Panagopoulos, N.G. (2020). Antecedents and performance outcomes of value-based selling in sales teams: A multilevel, systems theory of motivation perspective. *Journal of the Academy of Marketing Science*, 48(6), 1053–74.

Nagle, T. and Holden, R. (2002). *The Strategy and Tactics of Pricing: A Guide to Profitable Decision Making*. 3rd edn. Englewood Cliffs, NJ: Prentice Hall.

Nagle, T. and Müller, G. (2018). *The Strategy and Tactics of Pricing: A Guide to Growing More Profitably* (6th edn). Abingdon: Routledge.

Nair, S.R. and Little, V.J. (2016). Context, culture and green consumption: A new framework. *Journal of International Consumer Marketing*, 28(3), 169–84.

Nakamura, H. (1991). *Ways of Thinking of Eastern Peoples: India, China, Tibet, Japan*. P. Wiener (trans.). Honolulu: University of Hawaii Press.

Nam, H. and Kannan, P.K. (2020). Digital environment in global markets: Cross-cultural implications for evolving customer journeys. *Journal of International Marketing*, 28(1), 28–47.

Neupert, K.E., Baughn, C.C. and Dao, T.T.L. (2006). SME exporting challenges in transitional and developed economies. *Journal of Small Business and Enterprise Development*, 13(4), 535–45.

Ngan, H.F.B., Ren, L. and O'Bree, G. (2018). Lucky 8-ending: A case study on managerial price-ending beliefs in Macao. *Journal of Hospitality and Tourism Management*, 36(September), 22–30.

Nguyen, A., Heeler, R.M. and Taran, Z. (2007). High-low context cultures and price-ending practices. *Journal of Product & Brand Management*, 16(3), 206–14.

Nguyen, T.D., Dadzie, C.A., Chaudhuri, H.R. and Tanner, T. (2019). Self-control and sustainability consumption: Findings from a cross cultural study. *Journal of International Consumer Marketing*, 31(5), 380–94.

Nisbett, R.E., Kaiping, P., Choi, I. and Norenzayan, A. (2001). Culture and systems of thought: Holistic versus analytic cognition. *Psychological Review*, 108(2), 291–310.

Noguchi, K., Kamada, A. and Shrira, I. (2014). Cultural differences in the primacy effect for person perception. *International Journal of Psychology*, 49(3), 208–10.

O'Barr, W. (1994). *Culture and the Ad: Exploring Otherness in the World of Advertising*. Boulder, CO: Westview.

Onkvisit, S. and Shaw, J.J. (2004). *International Marketing: Analysis and Strategy*. New York: Routledge.

Owen, B.M., Sun, S. and Zheng, W. (2005). Antitrust in China: The problem of incentive compatibility. *Journal of Competition Law and Economics*, 1(1), 123–48.

Papadopoulos, N.G. and Heslop, L. (1993). *Product-country Images: Impact and Role in International Marketing*. Binghamton, NY: Psychology Press.

Park, S.H. and Luo, Y. (2001). Guanxi and organizational dynamics: Organizational networking in Chinese firms. *Strategic Management Journal*, 22(5), 455–77.

Pastoreau, M. (1987). L'uomo e il colore. *Storia e Dossier*, no. 5.

Pellicelli, G. (2007). *Il Marketing Internazionale: Fattori di Successo nei Mercati Esteri*. Milan: Etas Libri.

Peterson, R.A. and Merunka, D.R. (2014). Convenience samples of college students and research reproducibility. *Journal of Business Research*, 67(5), 1035–41.

Picot, L. (2020). *Les Secrets du Luxe: Histoire d'une Industrie Française*, Vanves: Édition EPA/ Arte Éditions.

Ploom, K., Pentus, K., Kuusik, A. and Varblane, U. (2020). The effect of culture on the perception of product packaging: A multimethod cross-cultural study. *Journal of International Consumer Marketing*, 32(3), 163–77.

Polegato, R. and Bjerke, R. (2009). Cross-cultural differences in ad likeability and ad element likeability: The case of Benetton. *Journal of Promotion Management*, 15(3), 382–99.

Pontiggia, A. and Vescovi, T. (2013). When size does matter. Trends of SMEs internationalization strategies in Chinese economy. Working Papers (2013/28), Department of Management, Università Ca'Foscari Venezia.

Pratt, S. and Kwan, P. (2019). Unlucky for some? Are some hotel rooms and floors really unluckier than others? *International Journal of Culture, Tourism and Hospitality Research*, 13(1), 70–83.

Prendergast, G., Ho, B. and Phau, I. (2002). A Hong Kong view of offensive advertising. *Journal of Marketing Communications, 8*(3), 165–77.

Rao, V. and Kartono, B. (2009). Pricing objectives and strategies: A cross-country survey. In V. Rao (ed.), *Handbook of Pricing Research in Marketing.* Cheltenham, UK and Northampton, MA, USA: Edward Elgar Publishing, pp. 9–36.

Rawson, A., Duncan, E. and Jones, C. (2013). The truth about customer experience. *Harvard Business Review, 91*(9), 90–98.

Reynolds, P.D. (1997). New and small firms in expanding markets. *Small Business Economics, 9*(1), 79–84.

Rivers, C. and Volkema, R. (2013). East–West differences in 'tricky' tactics: A comparison of the tactical preferences of Chinese and Australian negotiators. *Journal of Business Ethics, 115*(1), 17–31.

Roberts, J.A. (1993). Sex differences in socially responsible consumers' behavior. *Psychological Reports, 73*(1), 139–48.

Rogers, E.M. (1983). *Diffusion of Innovations,* New York: The Free Press.

Rokka, J. and Uusitalo, L. (2008). Preference for green packaging in consumer product choices: Do consumers care? *International Journal of Consumer Studies, 32,* 516–25.

Rossman, M.L. (1994). *Multicultural Marketing: Selling to a Diverse America.* New York: American Management Association.

Sarre, P. (1995). Towards global environmental values: Lessons from western and eastern experience. *Environmental Values, 4*(2), 115–27.

Schindler, R.M. (2009). Patterns of price endings used in US and Japanese price advertising. *International Marketing Review, 26*(1), 17–29.

Schulz, D.E. (2002). Another turn of the wheel. *Marketing Management,* March–April.

Shao, A.T. and Hill, J.S. (1994). Global television advertising restrictions: The case of socially sensitive products. *International Journal of Advertising, 13*(4), 347–66.

Shao, A.T., Bao, Y. and Gray, E. (2004). Comparative advertising effectiveness: A cross-cultural study. *Journal of Current Issues & Research in Advertising, 26*(2), 67–80.

Shao, X.F. and Ji, J.H. (2008). Evaluation of postponement strategies in mass customization with service guarantees. *International Journal of Production Research, 46*(1), 153–71.

Shavitt, S., Lee, A.Y. and Torelli, C.J. (2009). Cross-cultural issues in consumer behavior. In M. Wänke (ed.), *Frontiers of Social Psychology: Social Psychology of Consumer Behavior.* Psychology Press, pp. 227–50.

Shi, T. (2013). The use of color in marketing: Colors and their physiological and psychological implications. *Berkeley Scientific Journal, 17*(1).

Shimp, T.A. and Andrews, T. (2013). *Advertising, Promotion and Supplemental Aspects of Integrated Marketing Communications* (9th edn). Mason, OH: Thomson South-Western.

Simmons, L.C. and Schindler, R.M. (2003). Cultural superstitions and the price endings used in Chinese advertising. *Journal of International Marketing, 11*(2), 101–111.

Singh, S. (2006). Cultural differences in, and influences on, consumers' propensity to adopt innovations. *International Marketing Review, 23*(2), 173–91.

Six, I. (2005). What language sells: Western advertising in Russia. *The Journal of Language for International Business, 16*(2), 1–12.

Slater, S. and Yani-de-Soriano, M. (2010). Researching consumers in multicultural societies: Emerging methodological issues. *Journal of Marketing Management, 26*(11–12), 1143–60.

Smith, G.E. and Nagle, T.T. (1994). Financial analysis for profit-driven pricing. *MIT Sloan Management Review, 35*(3), 71–84.

Sorescu, A.B. and Gelb, B.D. (2000). Negative comparative advertising: Evidence favoring fine-tuning. *Journal of Advertising, 29*(4), 25–40.

Sousa, C. and Bradley, F. (2008). Antecedents of international pricing adaptation and export performance. *Journal of World Business, 43*(3), 307–320.

Soyez, K. (2012). How national cultural values affect pro-environmental consumer behaviour. *International Marketing Review, 29*(6), 623–46.

Statista (2017). *Consumer Survey: Made-In-Country-Index (MICI) 2017 Report,* Statista.com.

Steenkamp, J.B.E. and De Jong, M.G. (2010). A global investigation into the constellation of consumer attitudes toward global and local products. *Journal of Marketing, 74*(6), 18–40.

Steenkamp, J.B.E., Ter Hofstede, F. and Wedel, M. (1999). A cross-national investigation into the individual and national cultural antecedents of consumer innovativeness. *Journal of Marketing, 63*(2), 55–69.

Sternquist, B., Byun, S.-E. and Jin, B. (2004). The dimensionality of price perceptions: A cross-cultural comparison of Asian consumers. *International Review of Retail, Distribution and Consumer Research, 14*(1), 83–100.

Swoboda, B. and Elsner, S. (2013). Transferring the retail format successfully into foreign countries. *Journal of International Marketing, 21*(1), 81–109.

Tan, H.S.G., Fischer, A.R., Tinchan, P., Stieger, M., Steenbekkers, L.P.A. and van Trijp, H.C. (2015). Insects as food: Exploring cultural exposure and individual experience as determinants of acceptance. *Food Quality and Preference, 42*, 78–89.

Tantong, P., Karande, K., Nair, A. and Singhapakdi, A. (2010). The effect of product adaptation and market orientation on export performance: A survey of Thai managers. *Journal of Marketing Theory and Practice, 18*(2), 155–70.

Taras, V., Kirkman, B.L. and Steel, P. (2010). Examining the impact of culture's consequences: A three-decade, multilevel, meta-analytic review of Hofstede's cultural value dimensions. *Journal of Applied Psychology, 95*(3), 405–39.

Terho, H., Eggert, A., Haas, A. and Ulaga, W. (2015). How sales strategy translates into performance: The role of salesperson customer orientation and value-based selling. *Industrial Marketing Management, 45*, 12–21.

Terho, H., Haas, A., Eggert, A. and Ulaga, W. (2012). 'It's almost like taking the sales out of selling': Towards a conceptualization of value-based selling in business markets. *Industrial Marketing Management, 41*(1), 174–85.

Terho, H., Eggert, A., Ulaga, W., Haas, A. and Böhm, E. (2017). Selling value in business markets: Individual and organizational factors for turning the idea into action. *Industrial Marketing Management, 66*, 42–55.

Terlutter, R., Diehl, S. and Mueller, B. (2010). The cultural dimension of assertiveness in cross-cultural advertising: The perception and evaluation of assertive advertising appeals. *International Journal of Advertising, 29*(3), 369–99.

The Economist Intelligence Unit (2020). *Worldwide Cost of Living 2020: Which Global Cities have the Highest Cost of Living?*

Theodosiou, M. and Katsikeas, C.S. (2001). Factors influencing the degree of international pricing strategy standardization of multinational corporations. *Journal of International Marketing, 9*(3), 1–18.

Tian, K. (2017). The influence of cultural orientation on gender role representations: Horizontal-vertical values in cross-cultural advertising. *International Journal of Business Anthropology, 7*(1), 49–84.

Tohamy, N. and Keltz, H. (2008). *Building a Bulletproof Business Case for Pricing Improvement Initiatives.* AMR Research.

Töytäri, P. and Rajala, R. (2015). Value-based selling: An organizational capability perspective. *Industrial Marketing Management, 45*, 101–112.

Triandis, H.C. (1995). *The Importance of Contexts in Studies of Diversity.* In S.E. Jackson and M. N. Ruderman (eds), *Diversity in Work Teams: Research Paradigms for a Changing Workplace.* American Psychological Association, pp. 225–33.

Tsui, A.S., Wang, H. and Xin, K.R. (2006). Organizational culture in China: An analysis of culture dimensions and culture types. *Management and Organization Review, 2*(3), 345–76.

Usunier, J. and Lee, J.A. (2013). *Marketing across Cultures.* Harlow: Prentice Hall, Pearson Education.

Valdani, E. and Bertoli, G. (2006). *Mercati Internazionali e Marketing.* Milan: Egea.

Van De Vijver, F.J. and Poortinga, Y.H. (1982). Cross-cultural generalization and universality. *Journal of Cross-Cultural Psychology, 13*(4), 387–408.

Van den Berg-Weitzel, L. and Van de Laar, G. (2001). Relation between culture and communication in packaging design. *Journal of Brand Management, 8*(3), 171–84.

Van Everdingen, Y.M. and Waarts, E. (2003). The influence of national culture on the adoption status of innovation. *Marketing Letters, 14*(3), 217–32.

Varey, R.J. (2010). Marketing means and ends for a sustainable society: A welfare agenda for transformative change. *Journal of Macromarketing, 30*(2), 112–26.

Varey, R.J. (2013). Marketing in the flourishing society megatrend. *Journal of Macromarketing, 33*(4), 354–68.

Vargo, S.L. and Lusch, R.F. (2004). Evolving to a new dominant logic of marketing. *Journal of Marketing*, *68*, 1–17.

Vargo, S.L. and Lusch, R.F. (2008). Service-dominant logic: Continuing the evolution. *Journal of the Academy of Marketing Science*, *36*, 1–10.

Verlegh, P.W.J. and Steenkamp, J.-B.E.M. (1999). A review and meta-analysis of country-of-origin research. *Journal of Economic Psychology*, *20*(5), 521–46.

Vescovi, T. (2011). Strategie di marca per i prodotti italiani in Cina. *Micro & Macro Marketing*, *20*(1), 73–92.

Vescovi, T. (2013). L'Italian Sound Branding e gli effetti sull'immagine del Made in Italy. In G. Aiello (ed.), *Davanti agli Occhi del Cliente: Branding e Retailing del Made in Italy nel Mondo*. Rome: Aracne, pp. 97–110.

Vescovi, T. and Gazzola, P. (2007). Immagine territoriale e identità globale: L'utilizzo del legame con il territorio nello sviluppo della marca. *Micro & Macro Marketing*, *16*(3), 321–38.

Vescovi, T. and Pontiggia, A. (2013). Medium size multinational firms internationalization strategies: When size matters in Chinese markets. In *13th EURAM Conference Proceedings*, Istanbul.

Vescovi, T. and Trevisiol, R. (2011). L'adattamento di prodotto nel mercato cinese: Imprese italiane di minore dimensione e processi di internazionalizzazione. *Micro & Macro Marketing*, *20*(3), 503–526.

Vianelli, D. (2001). *Il Posizionamento del Prodotto nei Mercati Internazionali*. Milan: Franco Angeli.

Vianelli, D., De Luca, P. and Pegan, G. (2012). *Modalità d'entrata e Scelte Distributive del Made in Italy in Cina*. Milan: FrancoAngeli.

Völckner, F. and Hofmann, J. (2007). The price-perceived quality relationship: A meta-analytic review and assessment of its determinants. *Marketing Letters*, *18*(3), 181–96.

Waller, D.S., Deshpande, S. and Erdogan, B.Z. (2013). Offensiveness of advertising with violent image appeal: A cross-cultural study. *Journal of Promotion Management*, *19*(4), 400–417.

Waller, D.S., Fam, K.S. and Erdogan, B.Z. (2005). Advertising of controversial products: A cross-cultural study. *Journal of Consumer Marketing*, *22*(1), 6–13.

Wang, M., Rieger, M.O. and Hens, T. (2016). How time preferences differ: Evidence from 53 countries. *Journal of Economic Psychology*, *52*(February), 115–35.

Wang, Y. and Sun, S. (2010). Modeling online advertising: A cross-cultural comparison between China and Romania. *Journal of Marketing Communications*, *16*(5), 271–85.

Watchravesringkan, K.T., Yan, R.N. and Yurchisin, J. (2008). Cross-cultural invariance of consumers' price perception measures. *International Journal of Retail & Distribution Management*, *36*(10), 759–79.

Weber, E.U. and Hsee, C. (1998). Cross-cultural differences in risk perception, but cross-cultural similarities in attitudes towards perceived risk. *Management Science*, *44*(9), 1205–217.

Weidenbaum, M. (1996). The Chinese family business enterprise. *California Management Review*, *38*(4), 141–56.

Weiss, B. (2001). Coffee breaks and coffee connections: The lived experience of a commodity in Tanzanian and European worlds. In D. Miller (ed.), *Consumption: Critical Concepts in the Social Sciences*. Abingdon: Routledge, pp. 38–51.

Wells, W.D. (1993). Discovery-oriented consumer research. *Journal of Consumer Research*, *19*(4), 489–504.

Westjohn, S.A., Roschk, H. and Magnusson, P. (2017). Eastern versus western culture pricing strategy: Superstition, lucky numbers, and localization. *Journal of International Marketing*, *25*(1), 72–90.

Whitelock, J. and Rey, J.C. (1998). Cross-cultural advertising in Europe. *International Marketing Review*, *15*(4), 257–76.

Wood, J. (1999). Communication, gender and culture (3rd edn). Belmont, CA: Wadsworth.

Wu, L., Ju, I. and Dodoo, N.A. (2016). Understanding the impact of matchup between country-of-origin facets and country stereotypes on advertising effectiveness. *Journal of Global Marketing*, *29*(4), 203–17.

Yaghi, A. and Alibeli, M. (2017). Theoretical and empirical analysis of citizens' willingness to pay: Ethical and policy implications for the environment in the United Arab Emirates. *Public Integrity*, *19*(1), 41–57.

Yang, Y., De Cremer, D. and Wang, C. (2017). How ethically would Americans and Chinese negotiate? The effect of intra-cultural versus inter-cultural negotiations. *Journal of Business Ethics*, *145*(3), 659–70.

Yang, Z., Sun, S., Lalwani, A.K. and Janakiraman, N. (2019). How does consumers' local or global identity influence price–perceived quality associations? The role of perceived quality variance. *Journal of Marketing, 83*(3), 145–62.

Yaprak, A. (2008). Culture study in international marketing: A critical review and suggestions for future research. *International Marketing Review, 25*(2), 215–29.

Yeniyurt, S. and Townsend, J.D. (2003). Does culture explain acceptance of new products in a country? An empirical investigation. *International Marketing Review, 20*(4), 377–96.

Yorio, V.M. (1983). *Adapting Products for Export.* New York: The Conference Board.

Yu, C. and Bastin, M. (2017). Hedonic shopping value and impulse buying behavior in transitional economies: A symbiosis in the Mainland China marketplace. In J.M.T. Balmer and W. Chen (eds), *Advances in Chinese Brand Management.* London: Palgrave Macmillan, pp. 316–30.

Zahra, S.A., Neubaum, D.O. and Huse, M. (1997). The effect of the environment on export performance among telecommunications new ventures. *Entrepreneurship: Theory & Practice, 22,* 25–46.

Zhang, A. (2011). The enforcement of the anti-monopoly law in China: An institutional design perspective. *The Antitrust Bulletin, 56*(3), 631–63.Zhang, C., Griffith, D.A. and Cavusgil, S.T. (2006). The litigated dissolution of international distribution relationships: A process framework and propositions. *Journal of International Marketing, 14*(2), 85–115.

Zhang, J. and Shavitt, S. (2003). Cultural values in advertisements to the Chinese X-Generation: Promoting modernity and individualism. *Journal of Advertising, 32*(1), 23–33.

Zhang, S. and Schmitt, B.H. (2001). Creating local brands in multilingual international markets. *Journal of Marketing Research, 38*(3), 313–25.

Zhang, Y. and Round, D. (2011). Price wars and price collusion in China's airline markets. *International Journal of Industrial Organization, 29*(4), 361–72.

Zhou, N. and Belk, R.W. (2004). Chinese consumer readings of global and local advertising appeals. *Journal of Advertising, 33*(3), 63–76.

Zhou, Z. and Nakamoto, K. (2001). *Price perceptions: a cross-national study between American and Chinese young consumers.* In M.C. Gilly and J. Meyers-Levy (eds), *NA –Advances in Consumer Research*, Vol. 28, Valdosta, GA: Association for Consumer Research.

Zhuang, G., Wang, X., Zhou, L. and Zhou, N. (2008). Asymmetric effects of brand origin confusion. *International Marketing Review, 25*(4), 441.

Zielke, S. and Komor, M. (2015). Cross-national differences in price–role orientation and their impact on retail markets. *Journal of the Academy of Marketing Science, 43*(2), 159–80.

# PART IV
## CROSS-CULTURAL MARKETING CHALLENGES

# 16
## Differently acquainted markets

As societies become more globalized, cultural boundaries will become more blurred and new hybrids of cultural values will emerge, along with an increased need to understand these phenomena better (Shavitt et al., 2009). This means that the future of cross-cultural marketing should be the study of the evolution of cultures, which are connected and share values, goods and knowledge. The world is not transmitting a single common culture, but creating several new hybrids, challenging international marketing strategies.

**Figure 16.1** 'White and red' Chinese marriage

If in Chapter 6 the concept of knowing non-acquainted markets was introduced, assuming a constant evolution towards acquainted markets, this does not mean that the markets are moving towards convergence. Consumers and companies are increasing their competence on products, brands, and market conditions, making themselves 'acquainted', but they do so on the basis of the existing cultural values, thus basing the judgement criteria, behaviours and product choices on the cultural bases that characterize their community. Just as there are modern German, French, American, Japanese or Korean markets, different in their specific characteristics and common in others, so it is the case for Chinese, Vietnamese and African markets and consumers, which are generally acquiring skills and knowledge about international brands and products. The need for constant intercultural research does not end, as cultures are living entities in constant transformation. In particular, there are some situations that can be very evident examples of hybridization phenomena, which build new symbols and social ceremonies, and which nevertheless maintain a profound cultural value, influencing the purchase of the products connected to them. These ritual elements are strongly culturally and historically conditioned. One of these examples is undoubtedly marriage, for which many products of great symbolic and social value are purchased that are deeply immersed in an important cultural context that follows a prescribed procedure.

In the contemporary world, weddings are no longer perceived as a significant change in one's life stage, and a consuming one-upmanship has filled the vacuum of meaning left by this shift. This is especially true for the bride, who is usually the centre of attention at the wedding ceremony. The bride becomes an actress who plays a starring role in the creation of her 'fairy-tale' wedding. Her success depends on her ability to discipline her body and physical appearance (Boden, 2001) and to make the correct decisions concerning the presentation of the ceremony. Nelson and Deshpande (2003) mention that the white wedding, including an appropriate wedding dress and shoes, became a popular tradition after the much publicized cross-cultural wedding of England's Queen Victoria to her German cousin Albert. Together with the cake-cutting tradition, cards, the tossing of the bride's bouquet, honeymoons, engagements, and so on, the Western 'white' wedding evolved as a unique style and is today heralded by newspapers, magazines, films and websites in every part of the globe as the proper way to marry. The Chinese version of the wedding ceremony moved from the traditional version to the present new starring ceremony using both Western (white dress, cake-cutting, ring, bride bouquet, etc.) as well as Eastern symbols (dragons, fireworks, red colour, traditional music) (Figure 16.1). Although Western rituals have greatly influenced local customs, scholars have argued that homogenization is not a sufficient describer of globalization because it ignores the multiple ways in which a culture can be indigenized (Lo, 2018).

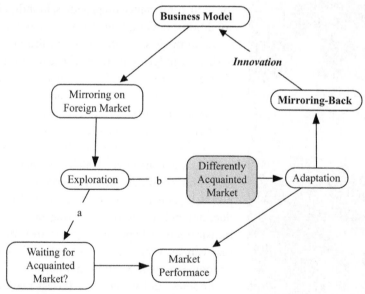

**Figure 16.2** Differently acquainted market entry process

The new context in the recently emerged markets is therefore based on the hybridization between cultural models imported through multiple exchange processes (economic, personal, cultural, migratory, etc.) and pre-existing traditional cultural models. This fact complicates the cross-cultural analysis of markets, as not only do companies need to know about local cultures, their symbols, rituals and values, but they also need to know how products, symbols and rituals of Western cultures (European and American) are used and adapted to local cultures. This operation becomes difficult because they are recognized as Western by companies and therefore interpreted according to Western cultures, which can turn out to be completely wrong, since, once assimilated to local cultures, they can take on very different roles and values. A superficial cross-cultural analysis may lead to gross marketing mistakes.

As shown in Figure 16.2, the entry process to differently acquainted markets should go through a phase of exploration, identification of market characteristics and adaptation as the only way to hopefully succeed. Conversely, European and American markets are affected by an opposite direction of hybridization, acquiring cultural symbols, rituals and values from Eastern cultures. The mirroring-back process introduces hybrid elements in the home markets, forcing a constant analysis of the consumer expectations, interpretations and behaviour. It is a rolling cultural process.

## 16.1 CHINESE CONSUMERS ARE *NOT* BECOMING MORE WESTERNIZED

*Francesca Hansstein[1]*

With tremendous economic growth in the last four decades and subsequent exposure to international trade and globalization, China has inevitably absorbed Western culture and habits. After China entered the World Trade Organization in 2001, Chinese consumers were increasingly exposed to the influence of Western products, brands, advertising and lifestyles. They became acquainted with and came to recognize the value of Western consumption behaviours and habits. Western food was perceived as being safer and of higher quality, Western clothes signalled social status, and Starbucks coffee or French gourmet food was perceived as a sign of worldliness. For most of the 2000s, the majority of business and consumer observers considered this to be an ineluctable trend and predicted that the distance between Chinese and Western preferences would shrink further in the future. Not only did Chinese consumers see the functional attributes of Western products, but they saw them as vessels for higher life satisfaction in their pursuit of new social values. During the booming economy of the 2000s, many Chinese consumers stopped looking just at the price and functionality of products and services and directed their attention almost exclusively towards 'aspirational brands', many of which were from the West.

Going forward, however, the Chinese consumer identity is likely to be embodied and represented by a growing middle-class seeing the future in its own tradition rather than a process of Westernization. We argue that a potentially sharp and even radical turn towards traditional Asian and Chinese values may occur, as expressed in brands and products, and that after the decades-long dominance of Western brands, the emerging Chinese middle class will 'go East'. What if China is converging towards a new consumer identity, choosing as a reference the trends already observed in Taiwan, Hong Kong, Japan and South Korea? Recent trends in specific product categories, such as makeup and furniture, suggest that this might be the case. What if we are witnessing a transition towards what we call an 'Asian blend' of tastes and preferences? If so, Western brands may find themselves unprepared to react to a 'new normal' of consumer preferences, and this may lead to counterproductive marketing and strategy. Chinese consumers are now rediscovering new forms of appreciation for their traditions and values, and this translates into alternative consumption choices, some of which are drawn from a sophisticated youth culture. In recent years, Chinese consumers have developed a different sense of self embedded in a specifically Chinese modernity and become more critical toward Western cultural models. This need not mean that Chinese consumers will be dismissive of or hostile towards the West, but that the simple statement that 'Western is good' will be less accepted in Chinese society more generally, and as a mark of quality, sophistication or aspiration in the Chinese consumer market more specifically.

## 16.1.1   Modernization, Westernization, and Status Signalling

The basic reason for the misconception that China must inevitably continue to Westernize is a confusion between the processes of modernization and Westernization, which are in fact distinct. As societies like China develop economically from relative poverty, to middle-income societies, to relative affluence, their values and consumption habits at first mimic the advanced West but later transform as they become more affluent. The political scientist Ronald Inglehart has founded an entire research paradigm arguing that the 'materialist' values of developing societies experience transitions and later turn to 'post-materialist' values once modernization has been achieved.[2] His core insights are that (1) values don't transform in lock-step with the level of economic development, but 'interact with the driving forces of modernization and the persisting influence of tradition', and that (2) modernization is not necessarily Westernization, and even less so a process of Americanization (Inglehart and Welzel, 2009). While the West has historically been on its own path of modernization, not all modernizations can be classified as paths to societies, cultures or values similar to the West. Crucial instead is an ongoing interaction and interdependence between traditional culture and economic development, which ultimately produces non-Western, yet 'modern' values of which consumption behaviour is one expression. Indeed, newly modernized societies usually take elements of their traditional cultures and put them in modern forms, for example, popular music from Taiwan or Japan, which to the untutored ear might seem 'Western' using the Western scale and influenced by decades of Western pop, yet expressing an emotional sensibility more characteristic of the East. The same came be said of fashion, food and the consumption of other durables such as cars, home furnishings, and even technology in developed East Asia and, increasingly, China.

Consumption is an eminently social phenomenon, especially when countries are developing from poverty to and middle- and high-income societies. When fast-changing societies become wealthier, newly available goods and services lose their connotation as mere necessities and progressively shift toward being useful for the expression of identity and the signalling of social status. Classic analyses of this social phenomenon include the nineteenth-century sociologist Thorstein Veblen's concept of 'conspicuous consumption' (Veblen, 2005) and the economist Fred Hirsch's concept of 'positional goods' (Hirsch, 2005 [1972]). Consumption is seen by both as a tool to signal the occupation of a place or status in a social hierarchy, more than the mere purchase of commodities for the satisfaction of individual needs and necessities on the basis of pre-existing individual preferences outside of any social context. When in the process of economic development, consumers become increasingly affluent, they become more sophisticated and devote a larger share of their consumption to status acquisition and signalling, but at the same time shift their attention to the 'intrinsic value' of what they buy. This process can now be observed among the urban and increasingly wealthy elites in the first-tier Chinese cities, whose focus on 'intrinsic value' contributes both to a more individualized and refined demand for goods and services and to increasingly sophisticated strategies to signal (and in some cases 'counter-signal') social status.[3]

## 16.1.2 Shifting Preferences in the Food and Beverage (F&B) Industry

Since the late 1990s, China has lifted itself out of poverty and experienced a shift in dietary habits typical of rapidly developing countries (Popkin, 2001). Such nutritional transitions consist of a progressive substitution of cereals, fibres and edible oils to sugar, meat-protein, and animal fats in some population segments, that is, a shift in dietary habits, observed at all income levels, that has been interpreted as a sign of Westernization. One important effect of this change in dietary habits was the explosion of the fast-food industry in China, especially KFC, McDonald's, and Pizza Hut, whose total revenue grew from $10.5 billion to $94.2 billion from 1999 to 2013 (Wang et al., 2016). This huge increase in fast food consumption need not, however, be interpreted chiefly as an effect of Westernization, but as an effect of this nutritional transition in combination with the availability of fast foods. Similar growth rates have for example been observed in other emerging markets after incomes have reached a threshold and fast foods have entered these markets.

Perhaps the best-known case of success in China's F&B industry is Starbucks, which is present in 141 cities and is now opening a new store in China every 15 hours, including their biggest store in the world in 2018.[4] Unlike the case of fast foods, however, this trend reflects more a lifestyle choice and the desire for diversified consumption and self-expression as affluent consumers (rather than, at least initially for the Chinese, a love of coffee). When asked what coffee they prefer at Starbucks, for example, they are much more likely to say they prefer lattes or cappuccinos rather than espressos or americanos. Chinese consumers are also well-known for their willingness to pay for famous or high-end brands compared to other countries, especially given an overall lower purchasing power than the West, and the Starbucks pricing strategy is evidence of this. While a 'tall flat white' costs $3.75 (about 25 RMB) in Manhattan, in Shanghai this coffee costs 37 RMB, a mark-up of nearly 50 per cent for the China market. Chinese willingness to pay this premium and the consequent success of Starbucks is not necessarily due to the Westernization of Chinese consumers, nor merely Starbucks' prime-mover advantage and lack of strong competitors, but it rather reflects the affluent Chinese consumer's interest in luxury brands, ultimately explained by a desire to signal social status in a fast-changing society.

The consumption of branded drinks in China has risen with the continued growth of middle-class incomes, and many modern tea franchises have opened in the last few years offering a wide variety of tea flavours. Companies like Yi Dian Dian, HEY TEA, Coco, Gong Cha,

Happy Lemon, and Dakas can now be found on many street corners in Shanghai. Starbucks itself offers 'iced shaken tea' and 'tea latte', which were launched to cater explicitly to Chinese tastes. The craze for bubble tea is also worth mentioning in this connection. Although bubble tea arrived in the mainland China market about 25 years ago, it has only become hugely popular in the last decade and is now sold in a wide variety of flavours and combinations. Young adults and professionals tend to enjoy bubble tea, not only buying it but also making it themselves, as shown on the popular app Xiaohongshu, where thousands of video tutorials explain how to make it. The popularity of bubble tea has even reached a point where Kung Fu Tea has proclaimed 30 April to be 'Bubble Tea Day'. Unlike Starbucks, these more Chinese drinks cater to more typically local tastes, but much like Starbucks, they too are an expression of emerging lifestyles, and while they are not premium brands, they reflect the larger trends within which Starbucks has found success. In the words of tea entrepreneur Jiang Jiadao, 'The popularity of Starbucks does not have anything to do with changing tastes for coffee instead of tea, or more love of Western culture. I think we love the lifestyle it stands for. If we can offer a similar lifestyle and experience over tea, this would work'.[5]

Five or more years ago, it was not uncommon to spot wealthy Chinese couples eating spaghetti, pizza, or burgers in popular Western food chains, their pictures taken and posted on social media to show all of their leftover food. This was one obvious sign that 'going Western' signalled social status rather than a love of Western foods, and that Western fast foods could not sustain indefinite growth in China. Indeed, according to a 2019 report from Euromonitor, the fast-food industry in Asia-Pacific will be driven by the growth of Asian fast food chains and the preferences of rising millennial and white-collar workers, who will tend to be more secure in their status compared to the newly rich. In contrast, after many years of rapid expansion, the major American fast-food chains all lost from 1 to 5 per cent of their market share from 2014 to 2018 and now face the challenges of a stagnant market.[6] Apart from the declining popularity of American fast food brands generally, part of this shift is due to more sophisticated consumer preferences among the rising middle classes. Asian fast-food chains usually provide consumers with healthier menu options and more quickly cater to new trends, such as for example how the Chinese hot pot chain Haidilao offers their customers the option of having their nails done or their shoulders massaged while waiting to be seated. The shifting preferences of Chinese consumers reflect their changing lifestyles, and while Western F&B has indeed had much success, this has been more a stage in their preferences and an expression of their taste for premium brands than a permanent shift toward Westernization.

## 16.1.3    Consumer Technology and Social Media

Like Starbucks, Apple is well-known for success in the China market, and in the last few years, having a MacBook reached a peak of popularity among university students and young professionals. Apple products were seen in China (as elsewhere) as easy to use and fancy to show, again undoubtedly a status symbol to show off a specific taste. At the start of 2019, however, Apple reported a loss in valuation of $446 billion attributed in part to poor sales of MacBooks, iPhones and iPads in China, for example, sales of only 7 million phones in China in the second quarter of 2018.[7] One part of the explanation for this has been the loss of market share to increasingly strong local brands such as Oppo, Vivo and Xiaomi, whose total share increased from 32 per cent to 46 per cent from 2015 to 2017, while iPhone's share decreased from 14 per cent to 9 per cent.[8] This reflects a more fundamental shift in perceptions of the iPhone, which according to MobData is increasingly seen as the aspiration of the 'invisible poor' who want to look more successful than they really are. Indeed, according to MobData, the income of the typical iPhone buyer is now only '3000 RMB per month', compared to '3000 RMB to 10,000 RMB per month' for Oppo and Vivo, and 'over 20,000 RMB per month' for higher-end Huawei and Xiaomi.[9]

Apart from mobile phones, China is also a world leader in other consumer-facing technologies. For example, China is currently the world leader in drone technology and production, due in part to massive government investment in artificial intelligence, as shown by how EHANG has now successfully tested a fully autonomous aerial vehicle able to carry one or two passengers (like a drone taxi).[10] As is now well-known from the recent American trade actions (and trade war) against China, Huawei is considered the world's leading producer of telecommunications equipment, its 5G technology currently considered second only to Samsung's for research activity and M&A of major players working on 5G technology.[11] Indeed, Huawei's success in the global market points to the issue of how the 'made in China' label is now evolving into a mark of quality for global consumers, and this includes not only Huawei but other globally successful made-in-China brands like Xiaomi, Lenovo, Haier and Hisense. For example, Lenovo's share of global markets increased markedly from 2013 to 2019, rising from 20 per cent to 24 per cent in the Mediterranean market and from 15 per cent to 32 per cent in the North America market.[12] Although in the early stages of global expansion, Chinese home appliance makers such as Haier and Hisense are also increasing their shares of the American and European markets, driven not just by lower cost by a growing appreciation of their designs and features among Western consumers. For example, Haier has succeeded in the American market with compact refrigerators with pizza-sized drawers to target millennials and university students. The growing success of these firms in global markets is likely consequently to reinforce their brand value among Chinese consumers in the domestic market.

Among the most commented-on aspects of China's consumer landscape is the ubiquity of social media and its centrality to the identity of its users. Mobile payments have revolutionized shopping in China, and the fact that a large proportion of consumers pay for everything with their phones distinguishes Chinese from Western consumers. Compared to their Western counterparts, Chinese consumers are not very concerned with privacy issues and are indeed often likely to see online shopping (by mobile or on the web) as safer than offline markets. The penetration of mobile payments has indeed reached such an extent that vendors of everything across the entire society can be paid by phone, including taxi drivers, small store owners, roadside fruit-sellers, and so on, so that cash is almost entirely unnecessary to pay for anything that Chinese consumers want.

WeChat is of course largely responsible for this revolution in the social media lifestyle in China, of which mobile payments and social networking are only two of the simplest aspects. In the 'discover' section of WeChat, users can access a news aggregator, a search browser, and some of the most popular online games, as well as mini-programmes, or applications developed specifically for the WeChat platform, many of which directly connect customers with online stores, takeouts, and discount coupons. In the 'WeChat pay' section, users can not only directly access a QR code to pay or be paid, but can also choose from a menu of options which include taxi-hailing, credit card payment, utilities payment, and even health management. WeChat pay also includes direct access to other third-party applications, the vast universe of which include those for booking an after-school activity for the kids, a same day in-home manicure service, buying or selling second-hand goods, finding flash sales discounts, and so on. The rapidity with which users can switch from one activity to another with just a click makes WeChat very convenient, and a high degree of trust and centralization are surely two other factors that explain the huge success of the platform. Indeed, Wechat is a paradigmatic example of a Chinese technological ecosystem that is extremely well adapted to the increasingly more sophisticated Chinese preferences in the user experience. Finally, apart from its core functionality, WeChat also facilitates specifically Chinese ways of communication, as exemplified by its rich universe of emojis, which express feelings that are typical of Chinese culture, such as the facepalm (捂脸), witty (机智), or frown (皱眉). Such WeChat emojis typically denote a greater complexity of attitudes than their Western counterparts and are a sign of increased sophistication and a desire to express feelings less directly and with more subtlety.

## 16.1.4　Luxury and More Personalized Style

The global luxury brands industry has been driven in large measure by Chinese consumers in their thirties and forties who want to signal social capital and success in a fast-changing society. According to McKinsey's 2019 China Luxury Report, Chinese consumers accounted for an entire 32 per cent of the global market for luxury goods in 2018 (defined as including 'ready to wear', accessories, watches and jewellery, and beauty), exploding from 19 per cent in 2012 and projected to increase to an entire 40 per cent in 2025. Global luxury brands like Chanel, Burberry and Louis Vuitton have capitalized on the China market to fuel their growth, and they continue to hold leading positions in their categories. At the same time, however, the report also states that one in ten consumers under the age of 30 would opt for a high-end Chinese brand, and that 'this likely will increase in the near future as Chinese brands gain greater prominence'.[13] This can be predicted with some confidence given the growing influence of a core of leading-edge, sophisticated consumers who prefer Chinese brands.

During the 2019 Fashion Week in Milan, Chinese design was in the spotlight for the first time in history, as seven talented young designers from China were showcased on one of the world's most famous catwalks. According to Zac Zeng, a Chinese designer from the brand F/FFFFFF, 'Young people in China are showing a growing interest in fashion and style. They always want to be special and attractive, and they like to find their style to be different'.[14] While expensive Western brands are still a common way to signal status, a newer 'light luxury' trend has emerged that is in many ways contrary to the spirit of Western luxury. Most popular among Chinese consumers under the age of 30, Chinese light luxury is both less expensive than Western luxury and perceived to be more subtly sophisticated. This space is currently dominated by young Chinese or South Korean designers, who make limited pieces for small circles of people who know the brand and recognize the style. Their creativity is a major driver of light luxury and the rising popularity of Asian fashion in China, as is the interaction they like to have with consumers who appreciate their combination of traditional and modern elements in their designs. Some examples of light luxury brands include Particle Fever, founded by three Chinese millennials mixing art, technology and fashion; Angel Chen, who was shortlisted on the China Forbes '30 under 30'; and Samuel Gui Yang, born in China and educated in the UK, who mixes traditional outfits with modern patterns. Recognizing this emerging trend, Alibaba has even announced a sharp increase in e-commerce support for these local brands.[15]

Apart from light luxury, local Chinese personal care brands have also experienced increasing success within the larger fast-moving consumer goods (FMCG) category (having grown three times faster than other FMCG products in the China market). Among the most successful of these are local skincare and makeup brands, such as Marie Dalgar (玛丽黛佳) and One Leaf (一叶子). Marie Dalgar's success, for example, stems from a deep understanding of Chinese consumer needs and preferences, resulting in the launch of specific products for Asian skin, for example mascara that thickens and lengthens eyelashes, as well as the capacity to fully embrace the concept of 'new retail', for example with augmented reality virtual stores. Another case is the facial-care brand Pechoin (百雀羚), which went from being tenth to number one in the skin care category in the period from 2013 to 2015 corresponding to a shift in its marketing and communication strategy.[16] While Pechoin's advertising had before 2013 focused on an innocent 'English rose' kind of beauty, with a Western lady immersed in a natural green environment, after 2013 it chose to portray a sensual Chinese lady wrapped in a tight Qipao with heavy makeup, sipping a drink in dim light, waiting in vain for a man to show up at a jazz club (thus invoking Republican era Shanghai). As should be clear, this change in branding mirrored a shift among Chinese consumers away from emulating the West and toward an invocation of their own beauty standards and rich traditions.

China is coming into its own as a confident and increasingly influential society, and Western brands must tread carefully in the China market, especially if they are to balance the appeal of their brands with increasingly localized preferences and pride. One outstanding and well-known example of failing to understand the changing China market was a hugely controversial television ad by D&G in November 2018.[17] The ad showed a traditionally dressed Chinese woman who had difficulty eating pizza and spaghetti with chopsticks and was accused of being racist and disrespectful of Chinese culture. Without dwelling on further details of the controversy, which caused the immediate cancellation of the upcoming D&G show in Shanghai and a massive boycott of the brand, this case is a clear example of how young Chinese consumers increasingly want to defend the dignity and respect of their country. Though nationalism is commonly thought to express itself in politics, it was in this case invoked in response to the dominance of Western brands in China, and especially their until-recent monopoly on the high-end and stylish. In their identities as consumers and market actors, these young Chinese expressed pride in their country and through their outrage wanted to tell the world that China deserves respect and has little reason to envy other countries and cultures. Another recent case was a photo campaign by Burberry for Chinese New Year.[18] Their ad depicted a traditional Chinese family, with the grandmother at the centre, but because of the severe look of the whole family, some netizens felt that it communicated a secret plan to kill the grandmother and inherit her money, while others felt that it depicted a sad and heartbroken family. This was far from the image Burberry had intended to associate its brand with, and far from depicting dependability, it instead put consumers off, who felt the ad was odd and stale. In the cases of both D&G and Burberry, Western marketing with too little local input and decision-making failed spectacularly to capture and interpret the Chinese consumer mindset and culture as it exists today in a fast-changing landscape, erring on the one hand by being 'too Western' or on the other by being 'too Chinese', without taking into account the tensions in China's dynamic shift from Western to more local tastes.

## 16.1.5   Conclusion

In the above, we have discussed the common misconception that Chinese consumers are becoming more Westernized in their consumption patterns. We see the misconception as a self-serving bias, because it is often supported by Westerners who see what they want to see in Chinese society. In contrast, we suggest that Chinese consumers are moving toward an 'Asian blend' of preferences which better mirror their real tastes and preferences. We have also tried to give some indications of what an 'Asian blend' would look like, whether in branded drinks, social media, or fashion design, and have stressed how the interactions between new and old, individual and social, and slow and fast, will potentially produce innovation and trends that are difficult to forecast. As stated earlier, this 'Asian blend' of new brands and products reflects a shift in values and lifestyles more typical of modern, yet non-Western societies, as indigenous culture and traditions play an increasing role in consumer tastes and preferences, unlike the simpler status-signalling that had resulted in the success of Western brands. Chinese society is not easy to understand, given its supercharged growth, fast-changing dynamics, and complex interaction between social and individual expression, as reflected in the evolving consumer landscape. An 'Asian blend' framework may, however, provide a lens to make sense of the messy reality of China today, especially the coexistence of successful Western brands with emerging Chinese brands, and the shift from the status signalling of the newly affluent to the focus on uniqueness and intrinsic value among a growing elite more confident in themselves, and far less likely to look to the West.

Western companies would be well advised to take up the challenge of China's newly blending market, since failing to do so could mean the loss of the world's largest group of middle-class consumers and a huge missed opportunity for their well-established brands. They should carefully research and test their current and future brand positioning and put extreme care into their marketing and communications, so as not to alienate Chinese consumers or present them with images of Western brands attractive in China five years ago, but not China five years from now. They should also be open to faster cycles of product innovation to cater to rapidly changing Chinese tastes, ideally through greater localization and decision-making by the Chinese themselves, thus mimicking the speed and flexibility of the best Chinese companies. Finally, Western companies would be well advised to show a degree of humility in claiming to understand China and seeing in China only a reflection of the West itself, or a thoroughly Westernized consumer market in the making. As observed by long-standing China marketing guru Tom Doctoroff, Westerners may have misinterpreted the outward reserve and humility of many Chinese, 'firmly rooted in the Chinese culture, with reverence and admiration. This is not the case. After years of silence, what is changing is their desire to speak up and show off (Doctoroff, 2012).

## 16.2    NEW MODERN CROSS-CULTURAL CONSUMERS

Changing patterns of socio-cultural communication, created by easier travel, satellite communication links, and the internet, for example, have generated an increasingly complex patterning of consumer behaviour and consequently of marketing approaches. Links between spatially dispersed groups are becoming established more readily. At the same time, members of different cultural and ethnic groupings are moving from one country or macro-culture to another, bringing with them their distinctive interests, values, and behaviour patterns and intermingling with each other, thus further clouding the spatial and social boundaries of countries and cultures.

By introducing new products, services and ideas into the global marketplace, firms gradually alter traditional patterns of behaviour. Thus, the very behaviours that consumer researchers seek to isolate and study are continually permeated by new and diverse influences.

A complex collage of culture and context is emerging in which no clear demarcation line identifies where one culture begins and another ends, and influences from one country or culture are constantly permeating others. At the same time, cultural influences are becoming all pervasive, further heightening the need to take into consideration and understand how they impact consumption.

New cultural units (group of people sharing the same culture) are being formed, which might purchase certain products as symbols of membership of the group, exchange information relating to products and brands and relevant purchase criteria, and exhibit similar lifestyles, consumption, usage and purchase behaviour (Douglas and Craig, 1997). Yet, while this unit shares a common ethnic core, members are not necessarily physically located in close geographical proximity. Integrated means of communication enable members located at geographically dispersed sites to communicate, interact, and establish a strong closely knit community of shared interest and identity. This does not, however, mean that the cultural unit is a transitory or ephemeral contact group. Rather, it is one which endures and evolves and whose values and identity are transmitted from one generation to another. The transmission of a collective cultural identity requires a sense of continuity, shared memories, and a sense of common destiny in order to endure.

Another aspect of importance to consider is the role of situation-specific variables. For example, Italian teenagers might adopt the values and preference patterns of the global teenage cultural unit when purchasing music, or in their choice of leisure activities or clothing, but in relation to food consumption they might exhibit preferences similar to those of their Italian families. Similarly, on formal occasions such as weddings, religious events or family dinners, they might conform more closely to the practices of the Catholic culture, while with friends they may behave and wear the clothes symbolic of other teenagers in the same macro culture. Consumers often belong to multiple cultural groupings, that is, ethnic, linguistic or religious groups, and hence have multiple identities. For example, a Catholic French Swiss teenager is a member of the French Swiss culture, the Catholic French culture, and the European teen culture.

The influx of immigrants into different parts of Europe from Turkey, Eastern Europe, North Africa, Sub-Saharan Africa and Asia has exposed consumers to lifestyles and behaviour patterns from a broad diversity of cultures. While on the one hand, immigrants begin to assimilate the values and behaviour patterns of their host culture, at the same time they introduce ideas and behaviour from their own culture, thus further blurring cultural boundaries and making it difficult to isolate the impact of external cultural influences. This is further reinforced by increased consumer mobility and travel, and exposure to global, intercultural media. As a result, cultural identities are continually changing and evolving over time.

A new cross-cultural consumer is emerging that we could define as 'modern', emerging from a phase of post-globalization, in which there are unstoppable aspects of globalization and others of local rooting, in a new mixture that includes both. It does not produce homogenization, but new diversity, in which some aspects (symbols, rites, values) are recognized as general, even if their interpretation is not always so, and others belong to different cultural roots. This new balance between global and local characterizes this beginning of the millennium era. It is neither a simple nor a stable equilibrium; on the contrary, it is constantly evolving and is undergoing variations in speed, following predictable and other unforeseen events. Among the first we can consider the economic developments of the various countries that can slow down or accelerate, and among the second the pandemic brought by COVID-19, which has changed the rules of the game for two years, creating situations of stasis and depression, changes in behaviour, closure of borders, and so on, completely unpredictable only a few days before they occurred.

The challenge for all marketers, not only those directly engaged in cross-cultural research, is to account for the evolving of cultures in their marketing strategies. These influences are pervasive and powerful, affecting not only how consumers respond to stimuli, but their values, aspirations, role models, acquisitions, and so on. Thus, the key imperative in an increasingly evolving world is to develop new paradigms that reach beyond national boundaries and encompass the complex collage of constantly changing cultural influences.

## NOTES

1.  I would like to thank Frank Tsai for his invaluable suggestions and editing.
2.  In terms of Inglehart's paradigm of materialist and post-materialist values, modernization is essentially to be interpreted as the emergence of self-expression values and secular-rational values, which gradually substitute self-preserving and survival values, which become less salient as development occurs. There are clearly problems with this claim, as it can be argued that what happens is not so much substitution as the very change of what we mean by survival and self-preservation. In the first case there is a transition from the preservation of biological life to social image, while in the second survival transitions from survival in young age to life-extension in old age, which is something that rich societies take great account of.

3. Countersignalling is the behaviour where agents with the highest level of a given property invest less into proving it than individuals with a medium level of the same property. In other words, it is showing off by not showing off.

4. This is now the second largest in the world as of the opening of the largest store in Tokyo in February 2019.

5. 'China's bubble tea boom: Top 10 of popular milk tea shops in the PRC', *What's on Weibo*, April 2018, accessed at: https://www.whatsonweibo.com/chinas-bubble-tea-boom-top-10-of-popular-pearl-milk-tea-shops-in-china/.

6. Fast food in Asia Pacific Markets, *Euromonitor International*, January 2019, accessed at: https://www.euromonitor.com/fast-food-in-asia-pacific/report.

7. 'Hashtag trending: China iPhone sales flop; Apple loses $446 billion; ready for CES', *itbusiness.ca*, accessed at: https://www.itbusiness.ca/news/hashtag-trending-china-iphone-sales-flop-apple-loses-446-billion-ready-for-ces/108083.

8. 2018 年中国智能手机销量现状及苹果iPhone手机在中国市场占有率走势分析, accessed at: https://m.chyxx.com/view/662323.html/#m/http://www.chyxx.com/industry/201807/662323.html.

9. 'Research highlights class divide between "poor" Apple iPhone and "rich" Huawei users in China', *South China Morning Post*, November 2018, accessed at: https://www.scmp.com/tech/article/2174310/research-highlights-class-divide-between-poor-apple-iphone-and-rich-huawei.

10. EHANG, accessed at: http://www.ehang.com/ehang184/index.

11. '5G market research: What are the top companies up to?', *GreyB*, accessed at: https://www.greyb.com/companies-working-on-5g-technology/.

12. Share of Lenovo's quarterly revenue by region from 2012/13 to 2018/19, *Statista*, January 2019, accessed at: https://www.statista.com/statistics/255256/share-of-product-sales-by-lenovo/.

13. *China Luxury Report 2019*, McKinsey & Company.

14. 'Chinese design in spotlight at Milan Fashion Week', *Xinhuanet*, February 2019, accessed at: http://www.xinhuanet.com/english/2019-02/22/c_137842359.htm.

15. '7 avant-garde Chinese fashion designers with a large millennial following', *South China Morning Post*, June 2018, accessed at: https://www.scmp.com/magazines/style/fashion-beauty/article/2150388/7-avant-garde-chinese-fashion-designers-large.

16. 'Local insurgents shake up China's two-speed market', Kantar World Panel and Bain & Co., *China Shopper Report 2018*, Vol. 2.

17. Dolce and Gabbana Commercial 2018, https://www.youtube.com/watch?v=TBFC5isQuYA.

18. 'Burberry's weird Chinese New Year tribute stirs controversy', *Jing Daily*, January 2019, accessed at: https://jingdaily.com/burberrys-chinese-new-year/.

# 17
# Marketing strategies for a multipolar market

Considering traditional strategies in international marketing, Wind et al. (1973) identifies four types of attitudes or orientations toward internationalization that are associated with successive stages in the evolution of international operations: *ethnocentrism* (home country orientation), *polycentrism* (host country orientation), *regiocentrism* (a regional orientation), and *geocentrism* (a world orientation). These attitudes reflect the goals and way of thinking of the company with respect to international operations and lead to different management strategies and planning procedures with regard to international operations. In the ethnocentric phase, top management views domestic techniques and personnel as superior to foreign ones and as the most effective in overseas markets. Therefore, home country procedures are followed and expatriate managers are sent to the new market. As the company begins to recognize the importance of inherent differences in overseas markets, a polycentric attitude emerges. The prevalent philosophy at this stage is that local personnel and techniques are best suited to deal with local market conditions. This frequently gives rise to problems of coordination and control, and to problems in cultural comprehension and in communication, resulting in the adoption of a regiocentric position. Regiocentrism recognizes regional commonalities and leads to the design of regional strategies, for example the Asia-Pacific Region. At the extreme, this orientation may lead to geocentrism, which is characterized by the attitude of 'the best man for the job' irrespective of national origin; the company becomes really international. After the introduction of the *globalization of markets* concept (Levitt, 1983), many global marketing strategy options were described. It seemed that the only way to access the international market was the substantial standardization of the strategy. It was argued that the worldwide marketplace had become so homogenized that multinational corporations could market standardized products and services all over the world using identical strategies, with resultant lower costs and higher margins. According to some scholars (Jain, 1989), the decision on standardization should be based on economic pay-off, which includes financial performance, competitive advantage, and what they consider minor 'other aspects'.

The proposed framework implied that business managers could influence certain variables to create a climate in which a greater degree of standardization would be possible. These variables included: (1) establishing a geocentric orientation in the organization (conducive to achieving standardization); (2) balancing the objectives of the headquarters and large affiliates (because the presence of the latter offered greater opportunities for standardization); (3) offering opportunities for continuous parent–subsidiary dialogue for greater harmony (to avoid conflict between the two groups); and (4) encouraging an international view in general.

At a different level, business managers could have reduced the damaging effects of cultural differences between corporate and subsidiary marketing managers through an adequate staff training system. Evidently, the cross-cultural issue could have been resolved through a training process, in order to teach local managers the 'right way' of thinking. Nothing has been said about consumers and how to get them to accept a globalized marketing offer. The alternatives of efficiency/effectiveness (standardization/adaptation) ever exist in the minds of businesspeople who are mainly focused on efficiency and cost reduction as the crucial aspects of company strategy.

The findings indicate that the effect of country-based interaction orientation and marketing strategy implementation on profit growth is more susceptible to local environmental influences when the implementation of the marketing strategy is less standardized across country markets (i.e., adaptation). For firms opting for an adapted marketing strategy implementation approach, country-based interaction orientation exerts a positive effect on profit growth when competitive intensity levels are high (Lee and Griffith, 2019).

As mentioned above, the most common characterization of international marketing strategy is along the *standardization–adaptation* dimension. A second way of characterizing international marketing strategy stems from the *concentration–dispersion* perspective (Roth, 1992). This perspective is concerned more with the geographic design of the international marketing organization. The underlying premise of this perspective is that a multinational firm should seek an optimal geographic spread of its value-chain activities such that synergies and comparative advantages across different locations can be maximally exploited.

A third characterization of international marketing strategy is concerned with how competitive marketing activities across country markets are orchestrated. This perspective, referred to here as the *integration–independence* perspective, is heavily influenced by the competitive 'warfare' description of Hamel and Prahalad (1985). The key question here is whether a multinational firm treats its subsidiary units as standalone profit centres (i.e., independently), or as parts of a grander strategic design (i.e., as integrated units). Zou and Cavusgil (2002) propose a second-order factor construct, termed the 'GMS', which overarches eight first-order dimensions of global marketing strategy spanning the three broad characterizations. They define the GMS as the degree to which a firm globalizes its marketing behaviours in various countries through standardization of the marketing-mix variables, concentration and coordination of marketing activities, and integration of competitive moves across the markets. Thus, any multinational firm's global marketing strategy, with given degrees of standardization, concentration and integration, can be captured by a single GMS score. Lim et al. (2006) proposed three archetypes of international marketing strategy referring to both standardization–adaptation and concentration–dispersion perspectives.

Archetype A follows a comparatively more standardized market offering policy. Companies grouped under this archetype display, on average, higher degrees of standardization in product design, advertising theme and pricing as compared with the other archetypes. On the dimensions of brand name and sales promotion tactics, this archetype is also arguably more standardized. Only on the dimension of channel design is this archetype not evidently the most standardized. In view of its greater degree of standardization, concentration and integration, they label this archetype the *Global Marketers*.

Archetype B, in contrast to the Global Marketers, pursues a rather mixed standardization policy for its market offering. While its brand name and channel design elements are arguably more standardized (similar to the Global Marketers), its advertising theme and sales promotion tactics are relatively more localized as compared with at least one other archetype. Its product design and pricing dimensions are also more localized than those of the Global Marketers. Similarly, its advertising and promotional planning function is more geographically dispersed. In view of its selective approach of standardizing only the brand name and channel design with corresponding concentration of product design/development and distribution/logistics functions, they label this archetype the *Infrastructural Minimalists*.

Archetype C, like the Infrastructural Minimalists, adopts a mixed standardization policy, but in a different way. Although it is moderately standardized in the area of sales promotion tactics, its product design, advertising theme, pricing policy, and especially channel design are more localized as compared with at least one other archetype. And, although its average brand name standardization rating is not low, this rating is comparatively lower than those of the other two archetypes. Its marketing value chain activities, especially the product design/development and distribution/logistics functions, are also more dispersed. Likewise, its advertising and promotional planning function is clearly more dispersed. Because the emphasis of its international marketing strategy is in the coordination of tactics rather than in the standardization of tangible elements such as product designs and channel design, or in the concentration of marketing functions, they label this archetype the *Tactical Coordinators*.

The cultural distance, so important in defining marketing strategies, can be measured in two ways: 'objective distance' and 'psychic distance'. Objective cultural distance has been measured using social analysis by mean of factors describing the average behaviours and opinions of a cultural (mainly national) group of people. The models of Hofstede, Hall, Schwartz, Lewis, and GLOBE are good examples of this approach. But the company strategy is not decided by a society, it is designed and applied by individuals. They can perceive cultural distance differently, being affected by their individual culture, experience, values, and so on. This is what we can call psychic distance, the subjective perception of cultural distance. Evans et al. (2008) redefined psychic distance as the 'distance between the home market and a foreign market, resulting from the perception of both cultural and business differences'. The fact that psychic distance is a composite of cultural and business differences means that it will have a greater effect on international marketing strategy. Moreover, psychic distance can be applied to the individual level since it derives from individual perceptions of cultural and business differences between the home country and the foreign country.

Objective cultural distance and psychic distance are conceptually different, so the methods used to measure them must necessarily be different. Cultural distance reflects a difference in cultural values among countries that should be assessed at the cultural or country level. Psychic distance is based on the individual's perception and should be assessed at the individual level. By assessing psychic distance at the individual level, it is possible to take appropriate steps to reduce the manager's psychic distance toward foreign markets. Although the firm may address the consequences of psychic distance, this is not the case with cultural distance, which is outside the firm's control (Sousa and Bradley, 2006).

Some scholars support the *contingency approach* of international marketing strategy. Rather than full standardization or adaptation, this perspective argues that the degree of standardization and adaptation is determined by organizational and external conditions (Cavusgil and Zou, 1994; Jain, 1989).

Culture has a significant effect on buyer behaviour, which in turn determines the nature of the firm's international marketing strategy, so it is important for international marketers to fully consider and comprehend the foreign culture of a target market. Consequently, of the two strategic options that marketers can adopt, adaptation of an international marketing strategy might be more desirable when a cultural gap exists across countries (Moon and Park, 2011).

In other words, the managerial perception of cultural distance may have the greater explanatory power on international marketing strategy adaptation than the objective measures of cultural distance. Managerial perception of cultural distance will be a better predictor for international marketing strategy adaptation than either of the two objectives measures of cultural distance, that is, the Hofstede (2011) model and the GLOBE model (House et al., 2004).

The *strategic fit* paradigm asserts the necessity of maintaining a close and consistent linkage between the firm's strategy and the context within which it is implemented (Venkatraman, 1989). The core proposition is that matching the marketing strategy with the environment leads to superior performance (Lukas et al., 2001). Strategic fit thus offers a relevant foundation for performance assessment of a given international marketing strategy. Therefore, the degree of international marketing strategy standardization leads to higher performance levels only to the extent that there is a fit between the environmental imperatives and the strategy being deployed (Katsikeas et al., 2006). Three macro-environmental factors (regulatory environment, technological intensity and velocity, customs and traditions) and three micro-environmental forces (customer characteristics, PLC stage, competitive intensity) are identified as simultaneously affecting strategic fit and, in turn, subsidiary performance among MNEs.

Given the analysis of the literature and the results of empirical research, as well as the experience accumulated in culturally distant markets over the last twelve years (Pontiggia and Vescovi, 2014), it is possible to identify six alternatives of international marketing strategies in the culturally distant markets approach:

- global marketing strategy;
- marketing adaptation strategy;
- marketing innovation strategy;
- waiting/presence marketing strategy;
- supporting marketing strategy;
- marketing rebound strategy (mirroring back).

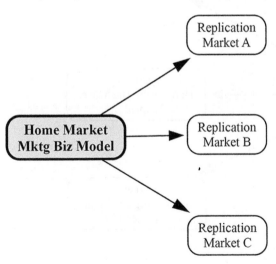

**Figure 17.1**    Global marketing strategy

The *global marketing strategy* (Figure 17.1) is simply to replicate the business model that has been chosen and developed in the home market and that is substantially applied (very small adaptations are possible) in the various international markets in which the company is present. This strategy is adopted in the presence of two fundamental conditions. The first is that there are no substantial differences in the use and symbolic meaning perception of the brands/ products by customers in the various cultural contexts, even in the presence of countries with an objective cultural distance. An example of this is consumer electronic products. The second is that price advantages are a key aspect of competitive behaviour, and therefore cost efficiency is essential to compete in international markets.

The global marketing strategy is conceptually simpler and less complex for the company from an organizational point of view, so it is often preferred even when there are not sufficient environmental conditions. In these cases, an organizational marketing strategy prevails over a market-oriented strategy. Managers prefer to think it will work because it costs less. Of course, it generally doesn't work.

The *marketing adaptation strategy* (Figure 17.2) is instead adopted if the company believes that the cultural differences existing in the different countries require a serious adaptation of the marketing strategy since the methods of use, the symbolic value, and the contextual situation of the various markets are very different and do not allow replications. In these cases, a common core strategy is generally maintained and aspects that need to be localized to be competitive in culturally distant markets are adapted.

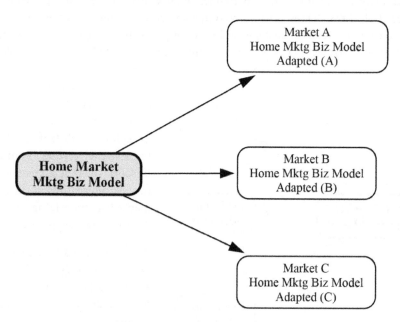

**Figure 17.2**    Marketing adaptation strategy

The *marketing innovation strategy* (Figure 17.3) represents a more radical version of the adaptation one, as it gives rise to a true innovation of the marketing business model in culturally distant markets, in which a new strategy is studied, clearly separated from the one implemented in the home market. This occurs when the market context is so different that it is necessary to rethink from the base to the offer and the consequent competitive strategy.

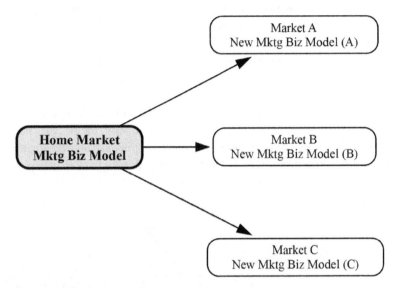

**Figure 17.3** New marketing international strategy

These three strategies follow the institutionalized standardization–adaptation binomial which represents a constant guideline throughout the managerial literature. However, the intercultural approach has highlighted other possible strategies.

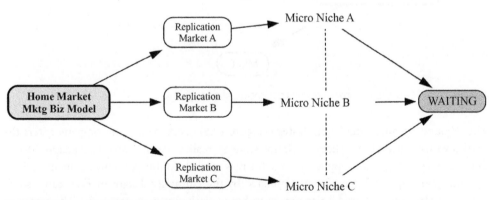

**Figure 17.4** Presence/waiting international marketing strategy

The *presence/waiting marketing strategy* (Figure 17.4) plans to substantially replicate the domestic market business model, but the company is aware that this strategy will not lead to significant success. On the other hand, it does not consider greater adaptation convenient due to the high costs that this would entail or because the value structure of its offer cannot allow changes in the offer and in the strategy worldwide. The company therefore tries to satisfy micro-niches of customers who have habits and values similar to those present in the domestic market, considering the opportunity to maintain a presence in the culturally distant market while waiting for this situation to evolve into greater opportunities. This is often the case with luxury or high-end products that cannot be globalized.

The *support marketing strategy* (Figure 17.5) is activated in the event of unexpected success (see Chapter 6) which completely changes the strategic marketing vision of the company. In this case the company enters the market with any of the strategies described above and discovers that it obtains unexpected success thanks to aspects of its offer that it had not considered, which therefore have not been emphasized in its strategy and which depend on the cultural particularity of the specific market. At this point the company 'follows the market', in the sense that it modifies its marketing strategy as quickly as possible, accompanying its success and emphasizing the characteristics of its offer that are at the origin of an unexpected success.

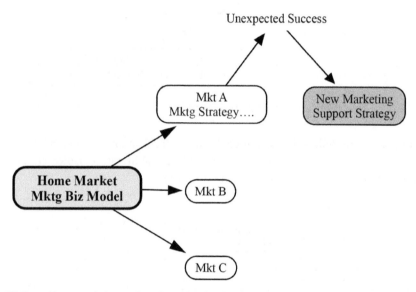

**Figure 17.5**     Support international marketing strategy

The rebound, or mirroring-back, strategy (Figure 17.6) occurs when the company enters the market with a substantial replica of its home strategy, realizes it can't work, so it adapts, identifies necessary changes, and applies them to the new market. At this point the company realizes that the changes, which have been stimulated by the culturally distant market, can also be applied in other contexts and it also renews its home marketing business model. The company learned from the new cultural distant market.

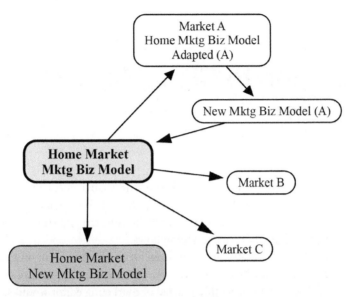

**Figure 17.6**   Rebound international marketing strategy

The proposed description concerns the archetypes of international marketing strategies. Obviously, hybrid solutions of these strategies are possible, depending on the context and business conditions. Just as cultures constantly evolve, so business strategies also constantly evolve.

# 18
## Conclusion to *Cross-Cultural Marketing*

The inevitable paradox of the science of marketing and management in general is its relationship to time. It is the impossible attempt to stop it, made by scholars, entrepreneurs and managers to describe and give stability to the results of research and strategies on companies and markets. Time passes, *pánta rheî*, everything flows.

Scholars, of course, do not consider the management and marketing literature of 20–30 years ago to be very important. If you were to write articles or books with references that are 30 years old, any reviewer of any scientific journal or marketing editor would say: 'update the literature on the subject!'. So, each scholar updates the literature in search of data and research possibly published a couple of years earlier, which had been written two more years earlier, so much is the time required for the publication process, which concern facts detected and emerged a couple of years before, in order to be observed and told: a total of at least six years earlier. Also, in the final part of the article, it is generally advised that the research is just beginning, and that future research should deepen it. All this hoping that what is written describes what is happening today and that it is hoped that it will happen for a while longer.

These are the foundations on which the discipline of marketing management is founded, which could have made sense 30–40 years ago, when the social, economic and market context was more stable, even if contemporaries considered those times terribly turbulent. Now they are much more so and who knows what they will be like in twenty years. The history of the management and marketing facts and choices that have been successful in the past is not useful in predicting the future, in suggesting the strategy to follow, but sometimes it helps to build interpretative models of the situation that could prove useful. They should be dynamic and non-deterministic models, as no normative approach makes sense.

What is needed in a dynamic world like the present is curiosity and respect, to explore and learn, and flexibility and creativity, to be able to change.

However, at the end of this book I would like to offer six instructions for a student, manager or entrepreneur preparing to face a culturally distant market. They are suggestions to understand, not what to do, and they concern art, history, markets, food, home and language.

*A look at art*: visiting museums, listening to music, and reading the most important literature should be the first steps as soon as you enter a country with a very different culture, to understand its fundamental cornerstones, to get an idea of the taste, the perception of beauty and its characteristics. When you enter a Chinese or Japanese museum, when you listen to traditional and contemporary music, when you read a novel that is the basis of the country's literature, you immediately feel that the European canons must be forgotten and that it is necessary to change them to understand.

*A look at history*: buying and reading a book that tells the history of the country is certainly very useful for understanding the genesis and the reason for so many cultural differences, behaviours, ways of thinking, and stereotypes widespread among people. It is a reading that could prove very useful to understand the context in which you will find yourself operating.

*Shopping at the market*: it is important to go to the markets of the country, be they traditional open-air markets or modern facilities such as supermarkets and shopping centres. This activity aims to observe the rituality of the purchase, how consumers buy, which aspects they consider important, how the price is reached, how the goods are arranged, how the departments are organized, and so on. Observing how people shop is very important to understand the purchasing processes, obstacles and touchpoints that the consumer goes through.

*Lunches and dinners at the restaurant*: it is advisable to go to ordinary restaurants, as well as to the more exclusive ones to understand everyday food as well as the food for special occasions, what are considered delicacies and what are common foods. It is necessary to understand how the ritual of the meal takes place, how the arrangement of the guests is organized, what are the drinks, and the logic of the courses. Food represents one of the cultural pillars of any culture. Therefore, international restaurants in luxury hotels, where you hardly learn anything new, should be avoided.

*Home visits*: as soon as the opportunity arises, it is necessary to visit people's homes, to understand their organization and the hierarchical order of the rooms. For example, in many European countries the kitchen is the main room of the house, the most frequented, where the family spirit resides. In China, on the other hand, the kitchen is a food production laboratory and plays a secondary role, while the dining room is the centre of the home. In Japan, rooms take on different roles depending on the time of day. All the products that a house contains are influenced by its cultural organization. The way the home is lived in says a lot about consumer behaviour and expectations.

*Learning the language*: you cannot understand a culture, a way of thinking, a way of communicating and relating between people, if you don't know the local language. This is certainly not something that is resolved like the previous points in a few weeks, or with a few books. It takes months and years. But if a manager thinks that they will stay for a long time in a culturally distant country speaking only the lingua franca of business, international English, they will remain a stranger to that country for a significant part of that time. It is an effort that will always pay off.

A lesson must be explained after it has taken place: to do this at the beginning would be useless as it would be listened to with distraction and the references that are cited would not be recognized, therefore it would remain in many respects obscure. I have often looked at the faces of students and executives as I tried to explain why I was going to say the things I had not yet talked about, convincing myself that I was doing something pointless and foolish. At the end of the lesson, however, the secret that built it and the purpose that guided it can be revealed. Paradoxically, the premise, the introduction, becomes clear at the end.

Therefore, at the end of this book, I can try to explain its purpose.

This book collects a series of intercultural points of view on the behaviour of market players in different cultures. It therefore analyses at least three components of our life that are not petrified in marble, but which possess a liquid nature (Bauman, 2005) and therefore change shape very easily. They are the social context, the cultural context and the economic context. The speed of change is not the same everywhere and for every country. There are areas of the world where changes are very rapid, others where they are slower, and the different areas are constantly changing speed. Geography belongs more to sky than to earth. It is the geography of the clouds and not that of the continents, constantly evolving according to the wind of human societies. One might therefore wonder why it is useful to describe constantly evolving situations and behaviours. In fact, by the time the reader has finished the book, there have already been unexpected and unforeseen changes.

This book, therefore, wants to represent a challenge for the reader: the challenge of having shown a complex and interrelated reality that must still, and continuously, be discovered. Models were suggested, visions were opened, it was recommended to pay attention not to maintain an easy ethnocentric attitude in looking at the world. The final suggestion that I feel I can give, and that I have learned from my students, coming from dozens of very different countries, is to make the curiosity that is in each of us survive and grow, to continuously change the point of observation from which we look at the world and not be afraid, consequently, of changing opinion about the things we see, trying to understand why there is another way to judge them. In this way, our marketing and management behaviour could also be successful.

We will have to understand the causes and reasons for the differences, but, above all, the similarities, the things and the values that unite us between different cultures, which always exist, with the aim of making them the basis on which to build common work. If the discovery and understanding of cultural differences enrich our social and professional life, the points in common reinforce them.

I think a book should be used to help us think, not to give us recipes for what should be done. Every past story and every book cannot predict the future, nor teach how to deal with it, since even if some facts can be repeated, the context in which they will unfold will be different. Therefore, a new solution will always have to be found, at least in part.

At the end of this book, therefore, after reading it, you should start writing yours.

# 19
# Case studies part IV

## INTRODUCTION

Made by the Fabbri 1905 company, Amarena Fabbri is an iconic product in Italy, due to its long story and to the success it has had over the years. It is a cherry fruit and syrup sweet product, packed in a ceramic jar, used as a topping on ice cream, cakes and pancakes. It has enjoyed remarkable success in Europe, Argentina and the USA and it is exported to 74 countries. Fabbri 1905 is also the biggest Italian company producing ice-cream ingredients and syrups.

In the confectionery market in China, Fabbri 1905 used the great experience of its business professionals in the B2B market for syrups and ice-cream ingredients. Fabbri 1905 aimed to discover Amarena's potential in a B2C context, analysing the consumer's perception of a traditional Italian product and discovering new potential consumers, as well as new uses of the product. In particular this was done for two main reasons: the first, the company wanted to analyse how the product could be perceived by Chinese consumers before launching it on the Chinese market. The second reason is its potential matching with some popular and widely used confectionary goods that are already present in the Chinese consumer's daily life, such as ice-cream, yogurt and pancakes.

## THE CROSS-CULTURAL ISSUE

Research has been conducted in order to verify the existence of cross-cultural issues in launching the new product on the Chinese market, developed in order to understand how a different cultural context can affect the perception of the product. A focus group methodology was chosen as the main tool to analyse consumer perception and purchasing behaviour in the confectionery market in China. Three focus groups have been conducted in Shanghai between April and May 2019:

- Group 1 innovators; generation Z people;
- Group 2 early adopters; young professionals;
- Group 3 early majority; young mothers.

Schwartz's theory of human value has been chosen as reference, since it is regarded as a cross-culturally validated classification system of personal values used in more than 60 countries, including China (Schwartz, 1992).[1]

# MAIN FINDINGS

## PACKAGING

For participants, the Amarena jar had a strong traditional valence, it reminded them of a traditional and classic product, and they thought it was aesthetically beautiful and attractive. All the participants agreed on the fact that the jar respects Chinese culture. More specifically, they stressed that the flower motif, the shape and the colours have a clear connection with traditional Chinese blue and white vases. However, the participants were confused about the nature of the product; in fact, because the jar was completely covered, it was nearly impossible for them to understand what its contents were.

This particular aspect should be given more thought when entering the Chinese market, as Chinese consumers are always more concerned about the quality and features of the products they are buying. If the product is hidden in completely opaque packaging, especially in a food market, it will be even more difficult to convince consumers to make a purchase. Moreover, the participants were guessing it could be a sweet product, such as yogurt, or even a savoury product, like a pickle jar. In China, the traditional packaging for pickles is very similar to Amarena Fabbri jars. Therefore, the shape and the design of the packaging make the participants think of pickles, which are considered as a food product that is not fresh, too salty, and not healthy.

One aspect that assures mothers about product safety is the glass packaging, which is considered safer than plastic or any other materials. They also consider the jar strange and somewhat inappropriate for a jam jar. In addition, they would prefer to have a clearer sight of the contents in order to feel more assured about the product.

## BRANDING AND COMMUNICATION

The country of origin, not revealed on the jar, together with the ice cream image used to demonstrate how Amarena could be served, led to unclear perceptions. None of the connections the jar raised in participants' minds about the product's origin were ever directly related to European countries, at least not to Italy.

Moreover, the image displayed on the jar was mainly about ice cream.

The product's description translated in Chinese on the lid of the jar is very vague. They explained that this is caused by the use of a confusing font and an unclear description of the ingredients. The repetition of the brand all over the jar is confusing

**Figure 19.1**    The Amarena Fabbri jar

for the participants. According to Chinese consumers, the brand should stand out from the packaging. That means it should have a distinctive colour, different from the colours used for the packaging itself, and it should have a proper space, in order to be clear and noticeable. Participants criticized the Chinese translation for *Guojiang* 'jam', because the product's contents is entire pieces of cherry fruit and cherry syrup, which means that the translation 'jam' is not appropriate. Also participants considered the expression *fruit and fruit syrup* on a jar strange for the Chinese market and difficult to understand. They thought the English version, 'Fruit and syrup', was more precise and accurate.

## PRODUCT

Mothers' attention is immediately focused on the product ingredients, especially if we are dealing with a sweet product. This means that in buying sweets for their children, mothers are concerned about the sugar content, and most of the time if it is too high they won't buy them. If the product is too sweet or too high in fat, it would be considered unhealthy and automatically unsuccessful for this target. For a Chinese consumer, there should first be a healthy reason for food to be eaten, while in Western countries taste is the first consideration. This is due to the cultural aspects connected with traditional medicine.

The ice cream image used to demonstrate the product causes a huge barrier in a potential purchase decision made by young mothers. In fact, mothers are very restrictive in giving iced and cold products to their children. This aspect stems from the Chinese culture and tradition to prefer warm and hot products to cold ones, which are considered unhealthy.

## TASTE DIMENSION

According to participants, the taste experience of Amarena was overall positive, even if the product's sweetness was too intense for the majority of them. Overall, their perception of Amarena was that the product should be matched with other flavours to reduce the sweetness and the intensity of the cherries, which they were unlikely to eat by themselves. The Chinese don't like very sweet products.

The participants spontaneously perceived yogurt to be a perfect match for Amarena, because it is a well-known product for Chinese consumers in general, and because they are used to preparing it at home. However, they still considered ice cream as a not directly appropriate food product for Chinese consumers. This is considered to be a typical and traditional use only in Italy.

According to *young mothers*, the flavour by itself reminds them of Chinese cough syrup medicine. They would directly consider the product to be unhealthy because the excessive sweetness is too strong, making it difficult for them to accept.

## SUGGESTED USE

The participants confirmed that they wouldn't buy a product whose main use would be in combination with ice cream because they would never have ice cream in the house. In China ice cream is bought in special shops and is eaten outside the home with family or friends. Also, ice cream flavours can be different, such as green bean, green tea, red bean, and so on.

Participants stated that they would like to try using Amarena in some traditional Chinese recipes, such as for example pork braised meat or any other dishes of Shanghai, Chengdu, Guangzhou cuisine that are typically recognized for their mixed sweet and sour flavours. Due to its perfect combination with yogurt, participants would also consider milk or milk custard as a possible match. They also related Amarena to Italian wine or cocktails, pancakes, smoothies, bitter flavour ice cream (to create a contrast with the cherries' sweetness), bitter fruits, spirits and sparkling water, or it could be used as a decoration on cakes and bakery products.

The participants' perception before and after tasting Amarena in combination with other products changed a great deal. They defined Amarena as a versatile product and it generally tastes better when used in combination with other sour products rather than alone. However, they perceived it to be a product for a niche market, whose consumers are updated about the latest imported food industry products.

They explained that, to reduce the sweetness, they would prefer to have Amarena with something colder or at least fresher. In fact, they enjoyed Amarena most in combination with smoothies and ice cream; they created an easy recipe that is becoming even more popular among *Generation Z* participants, called *bingfen*, which is a salad prepared with ice cubes and flavourings like sauces, milk or syrups. They explained that in relation to Chinese cuisine they would probably only use it in combination with fermented glutinous rice or yogurt. Chinese cuisine doesn't include any desserts, so Chinese people are not accustomed to enjoying this flavour.

Professional participants, in particular, referred to different recipes of Chinese cuisine that could embrace the cherry flavour. They include traditional savoury and sweet recipes, like *dousha tangyuan*, a special type of Chinese dumplings made of glutinous rice flour served in soup and filled with sweetened red bean paste, and *dousha zongzi*, a pyramid-shaped dumpling made of glutinous rice wrapped in bamboo or red leaves, filled with sweetened red bean paste. The participants thought that they could both be filled with Amarena cherry and syrup. Sweet and sour mandarin fish (deep-fried mandarin fish in sweet and sour sauce), double cooked pork slices, or spareribs braised in brown sauce, according to participants, could include Amarena as one of their ingredients and become part of new creative combinations.

## DISCUSSION

Collecting this kind of information helped the company understand under which values or influences consumers could feel more engaged in the purchase of this product.

**Table 19.1  Different perceptions of Amarena Fabbri in home and destination markets**

| Characteristics of the offer | Home Market (Italy) | Destination Market (China) |
|---|---|---|
| Country of origin effect | Very positive and valuable, generally considered a point of strength | Confused, perceived as 'Western' |
| Packaging | Very distinctive, identity, 4 sizes, clear information | Confusing, unclear, hiding the product, smaller sizes |
| Food expectations | 1 taste, 2 organic, 3 healthy | 1 healthy, 2 organic, 3 taste |
| Product definition | Clear | Confusing |
| Brand | Well known, traditional, high reputation | Unknown, not evident, no reputation |
| Perception of sweetness | Perfectly fitting with expectations, consistent with use, appreciated | Too intense, needs to be reduced |
| Suggested use | Ice cream, cakes, dessert | Sweet and sour dishes (pork, fish, rice), bitter food (yogurt) |
| Price | In line with jam | Premium, expected discount |
| Gift role | None, personal consumption | Perfect for a gift for a woman or kids |
| Shelf life | Correct | Suspicious |

Generally speaking, Chinese consumers feel more assured about the quality of an imported product rather than Chinese processed food products. *Young mothers* will consider buying a new product online only if they perceive a specific need, and they will mainly rely on votes and feedback from other consumers, which must be over 50 per cent positive. When a new product has a high sales rate, even if the knowledge and experience of it might be low, they may be curious about trying it. In their purchasing decisions, friends' opinions are considered more important than online feedback, and advice from colleagues or other mothers even more important than friends' opinions. In general, all the participants considered word of mouth as the fundamental tool to share information.

In introducing a new product in a different culture many cross-cultural issues emerge. The case of Amarena Fabbri is an evident example of this. The country of origin, Italy, and the country of destination, China, are embedded in really different cultures even if we are acting in a global economy. To this evidence should be added the characteristics of a non-acquainted market. In other words, there are two main factors that should be considered when entering a culturally distant market: (a) the low level of knowledge of the product; (b) the different product environment (use, perception, role, complementarity etc.).

Paradoxically, what is considered a strength in the home country and in traditional Western markets that are culturally similar to the home market (sweetness, packaging, brand, shelf life, country of origin, etc.), turn into a weakness in a destination country with a different culture, such as China, caused by different cultural references and no knowledge about the product. Some consumers' habits according to how they use some products (i.e. no one eats ice cream at home in China, while this is extremely common in Italy), as well as contextual elements (different traditional cuisine recipes), make the use of the product difficult or at least really different, and these may be unexpected by the company, which is ready to replicate a marketing strategy that was successful in its traditional foreign markets. Marketing strategies, such as communication, packaging, branding, pricing and distribution, should totally be rethought and adapted to the different cultural context. The company had to reconsider the marketing strategy that was designed for the product's launch in the Chinese market, changing the communication, the suggested use, and modifying the packaging and the product name.

# CONCLUSIONS

Therefore, different cultures greatly influence the development, perception, usage and appreciation of products. This means that the international marketing activities of Fabbri 1905 had to be redesigned in order to fit expectations and customs not considered by the company during the product development in the home market, where a different contextual culture suggested consistent solutions with that particular culture. In particular, the different cultural context suggested a new product name, modification of the design of the package and a different communication, suggesting uses of the product consistent with the local cuisine and the local taste. The information about the country of origin was increased in the package as well as in the communication.

Furthermore, the product has been suggested as a perfect gift for a woman.

The finding demonstrated that cultural context can greatly influence the product perception by the consumer in a different way in a distant culture market, and the international marketing strategy of the company should be modified to adapt to the local cultural situation.

Marketing managers should avoid the easy shortcut of replicating the strategies and action that have been successful in other markets. This would be really risky and ruinous business behaviour. They should study the cultural context seriously and adapt their marketing strategies as well as some product features to the destination market.

Cultural differences are sometime subtle and difficult to perceive, analyse and understand. For this reason, they are often really important and strategic. As the case of Amarena Fabbri demonstrates, sometimes the SWOT analysis should be completely changed and the marketing strategy of the company totally rethought.

## QUESTION FOR DISCUSSION

1. Which are the main adaptations Amarena Fabbri should make to be successful in the Chinese market?

## CASE STUDY 19.2    UK, EUROPE AND CHINA
### *THE CHRISTMAS PRESENT* BY ALEXANDER MCCABE

*Beverly Wagner and Juliette Wilson*

# INTRODUCTION

When considering export destinations, relationships with consumers in new markets need to build upon shared values so as to engage in culturally appropriate ways. This understanding ensures marketing decisions relating to distribution channels, messaging, promotion, marketing communications and merchandising are culturally aligned and exporting success more likely.

# BACKGROUND AND CONTEXT

Prior to *The Christmas Present*, Alexander McCabe had written and successfully published two books for adults but had little knowledge of the market and distribution networks for children's books and in particular Christmas story books. The book was written while Alexander and his family lived in Canada and to publicise his new book he attended a Toronto trade show in August 2016. The response to the book at the trade fair was overwhelmingly positive and he was disappointed to realize that any products to be sold for Christmas in December had to be in the retail pipeline by the previous March. Taking this information on board, he had to think about how to move the business forward. Alexander was born in Scotland and the family decided to return to Scotland for three reasons: first, the size of the European market was far greater than in Canada, second, they knew the publishing system better in Scotland, and third, he had access to local universities who could help him build the brand and assist him with the commercialization of the business. The move also allowed him freedom to embark on book signing tours throughout the UK.

 Due to his experience of studying for a Master's degree in Scotland he was aware that local universities provided support to micro businesses through student projects. Linking up with the University of Strathclyde's Department of Marketing, he worked with post-graduate students who helped him develop his brand and marketing plan. This was pivotal and Alexander said,

> The WH Smiths relationship would not have happened if it had not been for
> the initial marketing works project at Strathclyde. That first year I got the book
> signing tour in Scotland and the sales that I got were enough to make the book
> in the top five children's books in Scotland for WH Smith that year.

Alexander wrote the book for his eldest son Gabriel as a gift that no one else could give him. The idea came to him when he was sitting in church, the whole book, beginning, middle and end. He knew that the opening line would be 'I hate you' and the last line would be 'I love you'. He published a Kindle edition on 16 November and by 12 December it was 129 out of 8 million Kindle books and number 1 on four continents. This was the moment that Alexander realized his book had commercial value; some reviews referred to the book as a modern day *Christmas Carol*.

For any Christmas story, publishers and the public seek several key components: Santa, elves, snow and a Christmas tree with an angel on top. This means that it is difficult to bring something new to a Christmas story book as it must incorporate existing traditions. Alexander managed to do this with *A Christmas Present* by telling a simple story, which also resonates with adults, by referencing contemporary social norms, beliefs and practices.

## THE STORY IN THE BOOK

The main character Gabriel is a young ten-year-old boy struggling to believe in himself and his belief in Christmas. He lives with his mother who is a single parent with little income and he thinks that it is going to be a poor Christmas. All his Mum can really give him is her time and he does not appreciate this. He assumes that his Christmas morning will be disappointing, with 'a scrawny tree, a couple of bits of coal on the fire and few presents under the tree'. He wants to be with his father and his new family where he thinks everything will be so much better. Gabriel decides to run away to his father's new home and as he leaves the village to go to the town, a car comes in the opposite direction. He has to hide in a small wood as he knows that every car going to the village knows his Mum and they would stop and take him home. It is here that he meets with the reindeer and the elf. The elf was aghast that Gabriel did not believe in Santa and he told him a story that:

> the minute you are born Mrs Claus allocates every child with their very own elf, who has the same name as the child. So the implications being that you have your guardian angel with you. The minute you stop believing in Santa your elf is banished from the North Pole to the South Pole and will get back when you start believing.

The elf shows Gabriel a snow globe, which is a tele-transporting device, and it takes Gabriel on a journey to his father's new home, where he sees his step-siblings 'one at each side of the couch, with iPad and iPhone', and he begins to realize that he was wanting something he could not have. The teleporter takes him to his own home where he sees 'his Mum looking sad. This is Christmas day for your Mum when you are not here. She never asks for herself- because she is your mum'. The elf and reindeer take him back home and Gabriel wakes up on Christmas morning and has a wonderful Christmas.

Alexander said, 'That is why it is called *The Christmas Present* – the idea – life is a jigsaw and everyone is missing a piece. Enjoy what you have with who you have, when you have it'.

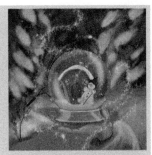

**Figure 19.2** Cover of the book and gift package

# TAKING PRODUCTS FROM ONE MARKET TO ANOTHER MARKET

A 'Make it to Market' grant allowed Alexander to have the book translated into French, Spanish and Italian and each one became an international best-seller. The book is now in every market with Kindle, with success in Mexico with the Spanish edition and in Japan with the French edition and also in Australia and New Zealand.

China is the most difficult market to enter and to help Alexander understand the Chinese market he reached out once again to university students to explore how the book could enter this large and difficult-to-access market. The project highlighted a number of key cultural differences between UK, European and Chinese markets. These are outlined as follows:

*Product attributes*: The book and box set are produced to a very high standard and beautifully illustrated. The book has been easily translated into many languages and for the Chinese market it has remained exactly the same as the book sold in the UK. The book is based upon three key concepts that are cross-culturally relatable:

1.   it is socially relevant and acceptable;
2.   wealth cannot buy time;
3.   parents always want the best for their children.

Notably, the book and presentation box is sold at the same price point as in the UK, despite the fact that transportation and logistics costs are lower in China. Price is an important signifier of status in China and this book would be classed as a luxury item.

*Consumer profile*: The main push for sales in the UK and Europe is for Christmas in December, only one month in the year, whereas in China it could be sold throughout the entire year for education purposes. This market is huge, with over 400 million people in China registered to learn English, more than the population of the USA. *The Christmas Present* is generally bought by parents and grandparents as a gift. However, in China the main demographics would be those people seeking to learn the English language, the majority of whom are the young and the elderly.

*Distribution and sales channels*: Entering the Chinese market is very difficult and an exporter must have a Chinese partner to facilitate payment and distribution. While in the UK book tours would be an important sales channel, in China social influencers would be key and the Chinese social media platform Weibo is particularly important.

*Consumption experience*: In the UK and Europe this book is seen as Christmas story book full of traditional representations of Christmas, such as Gladys the reindeer and Gabriel the elf. 'The Reindeer and Elf are the Holy Grail in terms of Christmas books and Gladys, she is the happiest of all the reindeer- she has glad in her name'. In China it is more commonly used as an educational tool to support English language learning as it is easy to read, and Gladys the reindeer provides a feel-good factor.

*Branding and communications*: The potential for merchandising is huge. Alexander McCabe stated: 'If the copyright is extended on Rudolph that tells you that there is a value in the IP of Rudolph. This can be mirrored with Gladys; we now own the trademarks of Gabriel, the elf and Gladys'. A full IP audit has been conducted to safeguard the ownership of the main characters in the book. The author added, 'We got a lot of help - we had a full IP audit and that was 80% paid for. The help we get from grant bodies and the universities has just been phenomenal'.

*Relationship management*: There is a national holiday every month in China with the exception of December. It is known that a national holiday in December would be popular in China and fit with their gifting culture. *The Christmas Present* reflects the Western holiday and celebration of Christmas as well as providing cultural understanding from an educational point of view.

## CHALLENGES

Alexander has had to overcome a number of setbacks and challenges on his journey to publishing and distributing *The Christmas Present*. The main motivation that has kept him on his path is the knowledge that the product is relevant to children and adults around the globe. Three challenges needed to be overcome: (1) to understand the UK publishing system; (2) to appreciate retail requirements' time-lines; and (3) copyright law.

The issues related to understanding the rules and systems around publishing were one of his first challenges; in particular he did not appreciate how far in advance books had to be ordered by retailers before December. Another hurdle was understanding copyright law and how important it was to secure the intellectual property (IP) for the characters in the book.

Finally, the most complex challenge was the need to find an agent in China who would facilitate export procedures, distribution and payment of the goods. This requires building relationships, which may take some time.

## DISCUSSION AND CONCLUSION

*The Christmas Present* is self-published by Alexander McCabe and although early indications are that the book has commercial potential it has been difficult to get a foothold in a highly competitive UK and European market. The Christmas market exceeds £90 billion for one month in the year. The Chinese market is very appealing as it would be all year round. Table 19.2 illustrates the main differences between the UK/ European and the Chinese markets.

**Table 19.2  The Christmas Present: Main differences between the UK/European and the Chinese markets**

| Product Dimensions | UK/Europe | China |
|---|---|---|
| Product Attributes | The product attributes are understood and associated with the traditions of Christmas. | The book is sold in exactly the same format in China as in UK and Europe. Consumers use the product as an educational tool to facilitate learning the English language. |
| Consumer Profile | The consumer profile is parents and grandparents. | Consumers are mainly young people and elderly people who are learning the English language. |
| Distribution and Sales Channels | For the hard copy, book tours and book retailers are the main distribution channels. E-books are important; Kindle has a fully illustrated version. | The hard copy is important for educational use. E-books are popular. Social media influencers are seen as key to communicating the brand. |
| Consumption Experience | A children's story about a little boy and Christmas day. It is consumed as a family social experience with parents and significant others relating the story to their children. It is cleverly illustrated with traditional characters. | A simple story written in simple language. Although used as an education tool, the story provides cultural insights into long-held Western traditions. |
| Brand Communication | The brand is still relatively unknown. Book reviews are always very positive and book tours are the main means of communicating the brand. | Communicating the brand in China requires support from agents in China and also social influencers on social media platforms such as Weibo. |
| Relationship Management | Personal relationships with Retailers are developing. | Local management of relationships in China are lacking. |

In order to grow his business, Alexander needs to be able to access the vast Chinese market. This is a challenge as the product is not sufficiently well known to be recognized as a trusted brand. Going forward he continues to build UK relationships with key retailers such as WH Smith. The product is very beautiful and all that is needed now is a little bit of magic and concentrated efforts to access the education sector in China.

## QUESTIONS FOR DISCUSSION

1.  Using Schwartz's (Chapter 2) theory of human values, analyse the dimensions of *The Christmas Story* in relation to UK/European and Chinese markets.
2.  What are the main cultural factors that help or hinder consumer buying behaviour in the UK/Europe and China?
3.  What advice would you give Alexander to help him to access the Chinese market?

**CASE STUDY 19.3    INDIAN SOFTWARE PROGRAMMERS IN ITALY**
THE BODY RENTAL TREND INCREASED CULTURAL CLASH? INDIAN
SOFTWARE PROGRAMMERS' PERSONAL TRADE-OFF BETWEEN A COOL
CLIENT IN THE FASHION SECTOR AND CULTURAL INTEGRATION
DIFFICULTIES IN A SMALL-MEDIUM-SIZED TOWN

*Anilkumar Dave*

# INTRODUCTION

What makes a Zegna or Loro Piana or Marzotto suit so great and valuable? Two things:
excellent raw materials and an extraordinary treatment process. Despite being competitors in the fashion arena, these three brands (we should say *griffe* nowadays) decided to
jointly preserve what makes them the most desired and admired ambassadors of Italian
fashion in the world. In 2012 they decided to buy the majority shares of Pettinatura di
Verrone (https://www.pettinaturadiverrone.com/), one of the oldest combing mills, located in Biella, the world-renowned wool district of Italy. Over the years the company has
specialized in the manufacturing of super and extra fine wools as well as cashmere and
speciality fibres such as vicuña, guanaco, alpaca and mohair, becoming leaders in the
first stage manufacturing process: the core of the product. The business is global and raw
materials can come from the other side of the world; Australia, New Zealand and Latin
America are some of the spots where materials are sourced. Over time, logistics became
the critical element driving the entire supply chain as sourcing, shipping and the first stage
manufacturing process were fundamental to starting fabric production. The IT department
of the company was barely 5 per cent of the total manpower and was also in charge of
enterprise resource planning (ERP) and customer relationship management (CRM) development, hardware and infrastructure maintenance, equipment purchase and so on, thus
they were overwhelmed by the daily routine and not able to focus on the new challenges of
such demanding customers: optimize logistics to allow them to be truly global and support
the transition from 'brand to *griffe*'. Some IT help was needed.

# BODY RENTAL BOOM

Since the mid-1970s India has bootstrapped its booming IT industry, leveraging both
on ad hoc policies (i.e. Software Technology Parks) and STEM-intensive education (i.e.
competitive engineering schools). The national GDP contribution from the ICT sector (IT,
BPO, software development) rose in less than two decades from barely 1.2 per cent to
almost two-digit figures thanks to incentives and state-level policies that favoured the
creation of first-tier IT hubs all over India such as Bengaluru, Hyderabad, Chennai, Pune
and Mumbai. The so-called second-tier cities/states followed on by designing attractive
schemes for FDI (mostly North America and UK) and building a proper infrastructure.
The 'golden state' of Gujarat, until then a commercial spot for the O&G group, pharma/
chemicals industry, agro-food and automotive (being the home state of the Tata family),
entered the Indian IT arena, promoting two main cities: Ahmedabad and Vadodara. The
fast growth of world-class education centres like IIM, IIT, and the lower cost of real estate

compared to first-tier cities, made Gujarat an interesting place to launch IT start-ups and software outsourcing companies. Over the years, southern European countries have not been favoured for Indian software services due to the language barrier and a different cultural approach. The first Indian software company, Tata Consultancy Services (TCS), set up branch offices in Paris, Milan and Madrid only to follow some global customers (e.g. GDF-Suez, Ferrari, Pega) with large projects and multi-million dollar contracts. On the other hand, medium-sized Indian software companies appeared to be more interested in local client acquisition, thus accepting low-budget projects such as website/portal development, GUIs, online CRM, different software vendors' integration modules. TCS, and later on Wipro, Infosys and Cognizant, have been forerunners in developing a first-of-its-kind service model: body rental. This involved mixed project teams, with mid-senior-level resources, physically located at a client's premises with a back-end development team based in HQs in India or in big Software Technology Parks. This worked well for the North American market apart from some frequent drawbacks such as personnel moving from the Indian company to the client's internal IT team (this was also happening to big consulting firms like Accenture, PWC, McKinsey etc.) or staff resigning once they obtained a permanent visa. Anyway, the body rental approach was a win–win situation as it was reducing the cost for the customer and allowing turnover of resources (e.g. non-key personnel) to the service provider and the flexibility of dynamic teams running joint selection (interviews) of staff.

## THE INDO-ITALIAN TIGER TEAM

Prakash Software Solutions (PSS) was one of the first software companies located in a second-tier city of Gujarat state (Vadodara), riding the wave of IT excitement in the region. Some customers from northern Europe were outsourcing their web portal development and online management of CRM to PSS. Pettinatura di Verrone was in a dilemma: the need to increase software development capacity vs. budget allocated to production and not to IT. Some months previously a young Indian-origin programmer, Ms Ila, (born and brought up in Italy) was added to the team. She created a link with an Indo-Italian Project Manager who after some meetings and exchange of documents with the company decided to test the capacity of PSS programmers by giving them a small project. It was a success, and the cost was definitely lower than expected. After a couple of months, the CEO of PSS met the Project Manager in India and expressed confidence in his team and plans for expansion in Europe, including Italy: 'Why don't we create an Indo-Italian tiger team to develop software for south Europe?'. The plan was indeed ambitious but everything seemed to be in the right place and even the horoscope was good: proven team, young entrepreneur, solid financial background, government support, local contact point, acquired references, potential joint venture opportunity, new country to discover and conquer!! Discovery was definitely there but there was one thing that, strangely, the horoscope didn't mention: culture diversity.

The easiest part of the 'Indo-Italian twinning in the name of software' was the contract and the selection of the team: Amit and Jigar were selected to be the two PSS argonauts to land in Italy and under the supervision of the Project Manager and the Indian programmer set up the first colony in Europe. The most difficult part was the bureaucracy and the visa procedure: climbing Everest could have been easier than obtaining a work permit for two Indian programmers for more than six months. The attitude and perseverance of Ila carried the process through. She also took care of finding a cosy apartment in downtown Biella (the closest large town to Pettinatura di Verrone). Ready, get set, go. Arrival, welcome party, first day on duty.

## B2B DOES NOT MEAN BUSINESS TO BUSINESS

That the devil is in the detail is valid for all cultures. Despite some language barriers, in one year the two programmers developed an entire logistic management software system following the direction of the Head of IT and created a complicated system between Australia and Italy. The payments were regular, the customers and the service providers were both happy and planning an extension of their contract as well as a possible joint venture to sell software together for the pure wool industry. The Project Manager was thinking of signing a long-term contract with PSS, and Ila was even planning to get married as she was offered a higher position as coordinator of the Indo-Italian team.

Everything seemed really good and even the PSS CEO's trip to Italy for a mid-term review was a success in establishing a personal relationship with the Pettinatura di Verrone IT Head. The last day of that visit, Ila's parents invited all the 'Indians' to their home for dinner. It was a get-together mixing two cuisines and wishing to celebrate the success of the team. Amit and Jigar had two helpings of every dish and enjoyed the company, singing and telling jokes till midnight. Ila remarked that this felt strange behaviour as in the office they were always silent, shy and 'distant'. Months later, it was discovered that the dinner was a glimpse of nostalgia for India and made both of them decide to leave. The process of B2B 'Back to Bombay' started by missing food, friends and culture.

## WHAT WENT WRONG

After the falling-in-love period where everything is new and interesting and the fascination of exploring new territory fades, the cultural gap appears. Amit and Jigar were smart enough to manage the apartment, cook the food they had crammed in their luggage from India, arrange weekend travel to Milan and Turin by train, handle the washing machine and interact with the cashier of the supermarket.

But the things that went wrong were more relevant:

- Biella is a small town but compared to Indian standards it is even smaller than a borough or a village, therefore offering few social opportunities for foreign visitors and considering the very low number of Indian immigrants and the almost zero number of Indian singles, the social community only comprised two: Amit and Jigar.

- Food was an issue as there were no oriental groceries and once the food flown from India finished, it was difficult to find proper replacements. The nearest Indian restaurant was 60 km away and logistically not easy to reach.
- Without a car, mobility is very difficult as the train station is not directly linked to main routes and the nearest highway is not easy to reach.

## CONCLUSION

Both the programmers still remember their Italian experience as a rewarding one, something that increased the quality of their resumé and gave them a special allure with colleagues. After some time they confessed to the Project Manager that during the interview they were not told about the Italian cultural aspects (i.e. food, language, socialization) and were expecting Italy to be like the stories they had heard about the United States (infrastructure, easy-to-live, Indian community, easy-to-find food). Although they were young and had a potentially open mindset towards different cultures, they both were planning a traditional Indian marriage and dreaming of a Bollywood-like love story where hero and heroine meet in a different state but get married and raise their children in their home country. Social aspects played a dramatic role and cultural diversity had its pros and cons. The software developed by Amit and Jigar has been upgraded to some extent, but the core modules are the same as the ones they coded. They still don't remember a word of Italian except for some greetings and typical food names but they are still remembered by the condominium neighbours who smelled their spices for several months after they left Biella.

### QUESTIONS FOR DISCUSSION

1. Using the case study examples, describe which cultural aspects will seriously affect your work if you live in a country with a different culture.
2. What will be the thing that will be missing from an easy lifestyle, especially in the details of everyday life?

## NOTE

1. Schwartz, S.H. (1992), 'Universals in the content and structure of values: Theoretical advances and empirical tests in 20 countries', *Advances in Experimental Social Psychology*, Vol. 25, pp. 1–65.

# References – Part IV

Bauman, Z. (2005). *Liquid life*. Cambridge: Polity.

Boden, S. (2001). Superbrides: Wedding consumer culture and the construction of bridal identity. *Sociological Research Online*, 6(1).

Cavusgil, S.T. and Zou, S. (1994). Marketing strategy–performance relationship: An investigation of the empirical link in export market ventures. *Journal of Marketing*, 58(1), 1–21.

Doctoroff, T. (2012). *What Chinese Want: Culture, Communism, and China's Modern Consumer*. New York: Palgrave Macmillan.

Douglas, S.P. and Craig, C.S. (1997). The changing dynamic of consumer behavior: Implications for cross-cultural research. *International Journal of Research in Marketing*, 14(4), 379–95.

Evans, J., Mavondo, F.T. and Bridson, K. (2008). Psychic distance: Antecedents, retail strategy implications, and performance outcomes. *Journal of International Marketing*, 16(2), 32–63.

Hamel, G. and Prahalad, C.K. (1985). Do you really have a global strategy?. *The International Executive*, 27(3), 13–14.

Hirsch, F. (2005 [1972]). *Social Limits to Growth*. Abingdon: Routledge.

Hofstede, G. (2011). Dimensionalizing cultures: The Hofstede model in context. *Online Readings in Psychology and Culture*, Unit 2. Accessed at http://scholarworks.gvsu.edu/orpc/vol2/iss1/8.

House, R.J., Hanges, P.J., Javidan, M., Dorfman, P.W. and Gupta, V. (eds) (2004). *Culture, Leadership, and Organizations: The GLOBE Study of 62 Societies*. Thousand Oaks, CA: Sage Publications.

Inglehart, R. and Welzel, C. (2009). How development leads to democracy. *Foreign Affairs*, 88(2), 33.

Jain, S.C. (1989). Standardization of international marketing strategy: Some research hypotheses. *Journal of Marketing*, 53(1), 70–79.

Katsikeas, C.S., Samiee, S. and Theodosiou, M. (2006). Strategy fit and performance consequences of international marketing standardization. *Strategic Management Journal*, 27(9), 867–90.

Lee, H.S. and Griffith, D.A. (2019). The balancing of country-based interaction orientation and marketing strategy implementation adaptation/standardization for profit growth in multinational corporations. *Journal of International Marketing*, 27(2), 22–37.

Levitt, T. (1983). The globalization of markets. *Harvard Business Review*, May–June, pp. 92–102.

Lim, L.K., Acito, F. and Rusetski, A. (2006). Development of archetypes of international marketing strategy. *Journal of International Business Studies*, 37(4), 499–524.

Lo, W.H. (2018). Marketing images of marriage rituals: A cross-cultural analysis of wedding magazine advertising. *Journal of International Consumer Marketing*, 30(2), 128–46.

Lukas, B.A., Tan, J.J. and Hult, J.T.M. (2001). Strategic fit in transitional economies: The case of China's electronics industry. *Journal of Management*, 27, 409–429.

Moon, T.W. and Park, S.I. (2011). The effect of cultural distance on international marketing strategy: A comparison of cultural distance and managerial perception measures. *Journal of Global Marketing*, 24(1), 18–40.

Nelson, M. and Deshpande, S. (2003). Love without borders: An examination of cross cultural wedding rituals. In C.C. Otnes and T.M. Lowrey (eds), *Contemporary Consumption Rituals: An Interdisciplinary Research Anthology*. Mahwah, NJ: Lawrence Erlbaum, pp. 125–48.

Pontiggia, A. and Vescovi, T. (2014). Medium size multinational firms internationalization strategies in China. In R. Taylor (ed.), *The Globalisation of Chinese Business: Implications for Multinational Investors*. London: Chandos, pp. 80–108.

Popkin, B.M. (2001). The nutrition transition and obesity in the developing world. *The Journal of Nutrition*, 131(3), 871S–873S.

Roth, K. (1992). International configuration and coordination archetypes for medium-sized firms in global industries. *Journal of International Business Studies*, 23(3), 533–49.

Schwartz, S. H. (1992). Universals in the content and structure of values: Theoretical advances and empirical tests in 20 countries. *Advances in Experimental Social Psychology*, 25, 1–65.

Shavitt, S., Lee, A.Y. and Torelli, C.J. (2009). *Cross-Cultural Issues in Consumer Behavior*. In M. Wänke (ed.), *Frontiers of Social Psychology. Social Psychology of Consumer Behavior*. Psychology Press, pp. 227–50.

Sousa, C.M. and Bradley, F. (2006). Cultural distance and psychic distance: Two peas in a pod?. *Journal of International Marketing*, *14*(1), 49–70.

Veblen, T. (2005). *Conspicuous Consumption*. London: Penguin.

Venkatraman, N. (1989). The concept of fit in strategy research: Toward verbal and statistical correspondence. *Academy of Management Review*, *14*(3), 423–44.

Wang, Y., Wang, L., Xue, H. and Qu, W. (2016). A review of the growth of the fast food industry in China and its potential impact on obesity. *International Journal of Environmental Research and Public Health*, *13*(11), 1112.

Wind, Y., Douglas, S.P. and Perlmutter, H.V. (1973). Guidelines for developing international marketing strategies. *Journal of Marketing*, *37*(2), 14–23.

Zou, S. and Cavusgil, S.T. (2002). The GMS: A broad conceptualization of global marketing strategy and its effect on firm performance. *Journal of Marketing*, *66*(4), 40–56.

# INDEX